EVENTS
THAT CHANGED
THE WORLD

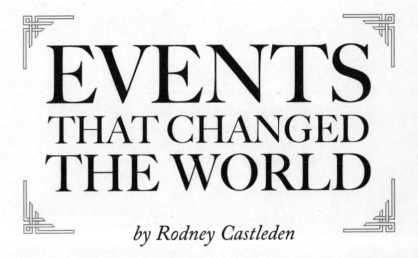

EVENTS
THAT CHANGED
THE WORLD

by Rodney Castleden

TIME WARNER BOOKS

First published in Great Britain in 2005
by Time Warner Books
Reprinted in 2007

ISBN 978-0-316-73158-4

Produced by Omnipress, Eastbourne

Printed in Great Britain

Time Warner Book Group UK
Brettenham House
Lancaster Place
London WC2E 7EN

www.twbg.co.uk

Photo credits:
Front cover – Alamy
Inside pages – Getty Images

CONTENTS

◎ ◎ ◎ ◎ ◎ ◎ ◎ ◎ ◎

I: THE ANCIENT WORLD

II: THE MEDIEVAL AND RENAISSANCE WORLD

III: THE ENLIGHTENED WORLD

IV: THE NINETEENTH CENTURY WORLD

V: THE MODERN WORLD

INTRODUCTION

⦿⦿⦿⦿⦿⦿⦿⦿⦿

IN A SENSE every single thing that happens changes the world in some way. Even small events change it in some small way, and a large number of small changes can change it a lot. Chaos theory famously argues that a butterfly flapping its wings on one side of the world can cause a hurricane on the other, by an unfathomably complex chain of reactions and interactions that amplify as they go on. The events that unfold around us are joined together by a fine mesh of causal connections. As Lenin said, everything is connected to everything else. All events are both causes and effects. The assassination of Julius Caesar was caused by apprehension about Caesar's ambition and the resentment and jealousy of lesser men; the murder led on, stepwise, to the reign of Augustus and a succession of Roman emperors.

Some events are small in scale and have no perceptible effect, like my neighbour falling over his fence. Some are small in scale yet have far-reaching effects, like the apple falling to the ground from a tree while Isaac Newton watched, or Lee Harvey Oswald, long before Dallas, taking a shot at a minor politician and missing his target. Some events are inevitably going to be small in scale and we don't see their eventual effects, even with the benefit of hindsight. So, disentangling the important from the unimportant is much harder than the reader might imagine, and perhaps ultimately, because of the interconnectedness of everything, there is really no such thing as an unimportant event.

President Kennedy knew that Texas was a dangerous place for him to visit. He could have decided to stay away, but he did not. He could have agreed to visit Dallas but refused the motorcade, but he did not. He could have agreed to the motorcade but only in a closed and bullet-proof car, but he did not. These and a multitude of other small-scale decisions led to the large-scale event of his assassination, but if the large-scale event changed the world, then so also did the chain of small-scale events that led up to it.

If it is so difficult to distinguish the important from the unimportant, the question inevitably arises: 'How were the events in this book selected?' Some historical events are very obvious candidates, like the Exodus or the Battle of Waterloo, and they present themselves as self-evidently world-changing. Some major events seem powerful and momentous at the time when they happen, though we can see, perhaps many years afterwards, that they have not changed anything. People were deeply affected by the death of Princess Diana but as far as I can see it did not change the world in any detectable way. Other events, conversely, were not seen as momentous at the time, yet they became so afterwards, like Abraham Lincoln's Gettysburg Address or the first aeroplane flight by the Wright brothers. And yet more difficulties lie in the path of the selection process.

Literally while I write this paragraph, the sad news of the British Labour politician Robin Cook's death is being announced. He was a major force in British politics, because of his selfless and fearless opposition to what he thought were wrongheaded policies. He sacrificed his place in the Blair Cabinet by speaking out against the Iraq war. He spoke for large numbers of British people who thought the foreign intervention unethical, and who did not want the invasion, still less the occupation, of Iraq to take place. He was one of the few leading politicians to go on telling Prime Minister Tony Blair that he was wrong. Cook's voice was the voice of Nestor in Agamemnon's ear, the very necessary voice of reason and conscience. What difference will Robin Cook's death make? Here we come to the nub of the problem. We shall never know, because we shall only know what happens without him; we cannot know what might have happened had he lived. The parallel universe in which Robin Cook survives his heart attack while climbing Ben Stack and lives on is inaccessible to us.

This problem recurs over and over again. In a similar way, we cannot know what might have happened if an earlier British Labour leader, John Smith, had lived to prevent Tony Blair from becoming Prime Minister, if Kennedy had not died in Dealey Plaza, if Pope John Paul

II *had* died in St Peter's Square. We have no way of knowing what would have happened if Einstein had, as he intended, studied geography, if Jesus had not been crucified, or if photography or the motor car had never been invented.

We can, in the end, only interpret the world as it is, not the world as it might have been.

There is a tendency for major world-changing events to be repetitive, even cyclical, in nature. Over and over again, political leaders have flexed their muscles and impressed their nations by taking them to war; the cry 'La patrie en danger!' - more recently translated as 'weapons of mass destruction!' - has always been a great way to rally your country behind you. On the other hand, history shows what a desperate remedy this can be, and often no remedy at all. It is surprising that political leaders have gone on making the perilous decision to go to war when it is clear from the lesson of history that wars and even individual battles are very uncertain as to outcome; resorting to declaring war has been shown to be so hazardous that, following the lesson of history, no sane political leader would undertake it.

One of the most famous battles in British history, the Battle of Bosworth in 1485, was one that could have been predicted to go one way but went the other; King Richard III looked likely to win, yet because of random and unforeseeable events during the course of the action, he lost. Not only was Richard defeated, he was killed, his ancient Plantagenet dynasty was erased, the Wars of the Roses came to an end and the usurping Tudors installed themselves on the English throne. It was a major turning-point in British history, and it was all decided on the unpredicted outcome of a single battle.

Ideas too can return cyclically. Monotheism, the belief in a single god, has been re-discovered, re-invented or re-asserted several times over at different times in different places: by Akhenaten, Moses, Jesus and Mohammed.

There is cyclicity in natural events too. On a short time scale, we see the twice-daily tides or the annual floods of rivers. On a longer time scale, we see larger scale and apparently random geological events. Destructive earthquakes recur in the same places, along the same known lines of weakness in the Earth's crust. Cities that experience a serious earthquake, such as Tokyo and San Francisco have experienced serious earthquakes earlier in the past. Volcanoes do not just erupt once, but repeatedly. Even the most violent eruptions, the so-called caldera (cauldron) eruptions that happen after many centuries of dormancy, have been shown by geologists to have erupted earlier in their history, and in the same violent way. The volcanic islands of Krakatoa and Santorini have both blown themselves to pieces with extreme violence at least twice. Once a repeating pattern is established for the past, we can be sure that the pattern will continue into the future. To some extent we can predict the world-changing events of the future, and we can see that some of the past events too could have been predicted. A major tsunami disaster in the Indian Ocean could have been foreseen, yet when it happened in 2004 we were unprepared for it. A similar tsunami disaster could occur in the future in the Atlantic Ocean, and we are totally unprepared for that too; we carry on building houses at sea level. Again, we are not making the best use of our knowledge of the world, its past and its patterns.

There are different types of world-changing events. The earthquakes and caldera eruptions are good examples of recurring natural disasters. There are other entirely and exclusively natural disasters too, such as the Black Sea flood.

Some events involve a step change. These are events that change the world so that it will never, and can never, be the same again. Examples of this type of event include the development of art, the invention of the wheel and the Industrial Revolution. Sometimes the step change is a change in perception. The rediscovery of Ptolemy's maps, which were significantly more accurate than existing maps, made more people think in cartographic terms than ever before; it is hard now to visualize a world without maps, but it would have been a very different world from the one we now inhabit. It would have been a world of journeys, voyages, routes and itineraries, a world of lines rather than a world of spaces.

I was very aware when preparing this book that there have been many more world-changing events than there have been world-changing people. This is partly because many of the world-changers were responsible for several world-changing events. Edison, for instance, was responsible for many inventions. Napoleon invaded many countries and waged many battles. So a relatively small number of activists can precipitate a large number of changes to the world. Because of the large number of events that seemed to clamour for inclusion in this book, I have covered many of them rather briefly – I thought it better to do that than leave them out.

After reviewing the more than 200 events that changed the world, I am left with an impression of human history as a turbulent, volatile, enormously complex web of interacting and interweaving human narratives. Some of the changes were predictable, some not. Some were natural, some man-made. The turbulent changeability of the world is largely the responsibility of a relatively small number of people. Marx had the idea that revolution was the huge mass of the proletariat throwing off the yoke of capitalist tyranny; in fact revolutions before and since Marx's time have again and again been the work of a small number of activists, often from the middle or even upper classes. Through most of human history, 99.9 percent of people have been getting on with the ordinary everyday activities of making a living, keeping a household and family together and trying to make sense of their lives through the medium of received ideas, beliefs and values; they have been largely a force for cultural stasis (standing still) or inertia. Meanwhile the remaining 0.1% of the population are the activists, disrupting those efforts to keep things as they are by changing them. Sometimes they have changed people's lives for the better, as with Wilberforce and the abolition of slavery, Lister and antiseptic surgery, Martin Luther King Jr and black civil rights, and sometimes for the worse, as with Osama bin Laden and the Al Qaeda attacks.

A hundred years ago history was seen, in a comforting and reassuring way, as a grand march of human progress. The Romans invaded Britain, and that was a good thing because it brought law and order and straight roads to a benighted land; Columbus discovered America, and that was a good thing because it opened up the New World to European colonization. But the Roman occupation disrupted and oppressed the indigenous cultures, and the European colonization of North America meant the oppression and eventual extermination of the indigenous peoples. Now, with the heightened awareness that comes from taking several viewpoints, the events of history look far more chaotic and morally random. We don't know how the human story is going to end, so we can have no way of knowing which events are leading towards that end and which are leading away from it. There was a time, in the recent past, when practically everyone believed that economic growth was a Good Thing; now, increasingly, we see that there must be limits to growth because it depends on an accelerating usage of natural resources, and many of those resources are finite and non-renewable. We look now for sustainability; in other words we evaluate cultures rather differently now from the way they were evaluated only fifty years ago. This book includes both positive and negative step changes, Good Things and Bad Things. The only criterion is whether the world was changed by them. Whether the world was changed for the better I leave you, the reader, to decide.

I
THE ANCIENT WORLD

THE TOBA ERUPTION
(75,000 BC)

ONE OF THE hardest things to do in compiling a book like this is to decide where and when to begin. It is inevitably hard to choose the 'first event' that changed the world, unless we go right back to the Creation, the origins of the Earth as a planet 4,700 million years ago. But to go back that far would turn this into a different sort of book – it would become in effect a geology book. Usually when we use the word 'world' we have in mind the planet as the dwelling place of the human race, so it makes sense to start the story later. 75,000 BC may still seem too early to begin, but there are good reasons for focusing on what happened at that time – a spectacular event that without a doubt changed the habitat out of all recognition, made the world a very different place to live in.

The 'Big Event' in 75,000 BC was a stupendous volcanic eruption, much bigger than any volcanic eruption that has taken place since that time. It happened near the northern tip of Sumatra, not far from the site of the seabed earthquake that caused the Boxing Day tsunami in the Indian Ocean in 2004, which is one of the reasons for starting here; several of the major events in this book will in some way or another reappear cyclically. The volcanic eruption was so violent that the cavernous lava chamber under the volcano was completely emptied of lava and the volcano collapsed into it, to form a huge circular collapse crater known as a caldera (cauldron). The crater that was formed, Toba, is still visible, and it covers almost the entire width of the island.

Large-scale events of this kind are an important part of the history of the Earth, each contributing something to the shaping of its surface. But the Toba eruption did something else. A huge volume of ash was thrown up into the upper atmosphere, the stratosphere, where, to judge from what happened in the much smaller Krakatoa eruption of 1883, it was caught up in a strong high-altitude wind, the Krakatoa easterly jet stream, and trailed right round the equator like a colossal smoke ring. From there, the ash was spread to higher latitudes until the Earth was completely wrapped in a thin veil of dust.

The dust veil stopped some of the sun's energy from reaching the Earth's surface, and the temperature dropped. After some medium-sized volcanic eruptions of modern times, such as the Pinatubo eruption of 1990 it has been possible to detect a measurable lowering of global temperatures by half a degree Celsius, for a year or two. The temperature record picked up in the sediments on the North Atlantic Ocean floor at 53 degrees North (the latitude of Nottingham) shows that the Toba eruption was much more catastrophic.

The temperature of the North Atlantic water fell from 14 °C to 6 °C in the space of a few decades. The air temperature above the North Atlantic, and therefore in Britain too, fell by 8 degrees – a huge drop. The effect was to trigger the onset of the Devensian cold stage, which some people refer to as 'the last ice age'. With a temperature drop of that severity, massive environmental changes must have followed, with snow and ice covering large areas in Canada and northern Europe.

This is one of the most extreme climate changes that we know about, and it shows how important the pattern of volcanic activity is in controlling global climate. One very large scale eruption can plunge us into an ice age; small-scale eruptions can cause small-scale decreases in temperature. The several medium-scale volcanic eruptions of the eighteenth and nineteenth centuries, such as Tambora and Krakatoa helped to keep global temperatures down. The lack of large – and medium-scale eruptions in the twentieth century has been a major factor in global warming. One big ash eruption could solve the current global warming problem.

THE EMERGENCE OF
HOMO SAPIENS
SAPIENS
(38,000 BC)

THERE HAVE BEEN people or at least manlike creatures on the Earth for more than three million years. The earliest ones, looking more like apes than people, are sometimes called hominids. More advanced types known as *Homo erectus* (upright man) were able to make tools out of stone as well as walk on their hind legs instead of on all fours. They were also able to make fire. There brains were, even so, very small and it is assumed that they were mentally quite limited.

The earliest real people, true human beings, appeared in Africa about two million years ago – *Homo habilis* (handy man). The Neanderthals, another species that was significantly closer to modern people, made their appearance around 200,000 years ago – *Homo sapiens* (wise man). They were well adapted to living in a cold climate, and that meant that they were far better equipped to living in a northern Europe that was subject to snow and ice cover in successive glaciations.

Then true modern people, called *Homo sapiens sapiens* (wise, wise man), appeared about 38,000 years ago. These people had brains that were as complex and versatile as ours. They had the ability to make themselves shelters and clothing. They were naturally able to make stone tools, just like the earlier species, but with increasing sophistication.

Above all, they made art. The thing that distinguishes modern people from earlier species is their interest in making two- and three-dimensional images. From 38,000 years ago onwards, that seems to be almost a defining characteristic of the human race. The images they painted in caves such as Lascaux in France show the animals they liked to hunt, so they may have been motivated by hunting magic. Drawing and painting the animals was

22

a way of conjuring them up, willing them to appear.

People hunted in groups, organizing chases in which large animals such as bison and mammoths were driven off cliffs or into ravines to kill them for their skins and meat. Some of the tusk, bone and antler from these kills was used to make carvings, which included engravings and figurines of reindeer, horses and bison. An ivory head of a woman carved in France 25,000 years ago may be the world's first portrait.

The sea level was low 38,000 years ago, and what are now shallow seas were then dry land. It was possible at such times for people to walk to Britain across the southern North Sea. We know from finds on the seabed out near the Dogger Bank that people hunted mammoths there. It was even possible to cross from Asia to North America by way of a land bridge across the Bering Straits. Shortly after this the first people arrived in Australia, also from Asia, and also by way of a land bridge, though they must have travelled part of the way by boat. Later, when the sea level rose, they would be cut off, as if by an incoming tide.

What happened to the human race 38,000 years ago was a quantum leap. Suddenly, as a result of an evolutionary jump forward, modern people had appeared.

GLOBAL WARMING
(10,000 BC)

AS THE LAST cold stage of the Ice Age came to an end in 10,000 BC, there was a rapid warming of the Earth's atmosphere that went on through many centuries. This warming had relatively little effect at the equator or the poles, but produced dramatic changes in every environment in middle latitudes. As the temperature increased, some plant and animal species were squeezed out while new species came in. Snow and ice gave way to tundra; tundra gave way to birch woodland; birch woodland gave way to pine forest; pine forest gave way to mixed woodland; mixed woodland gave way to deciduous forest.

At the same time, the sea level was rising, and had been since about 15,000 BC. The meltwater from the rapidly shrinking glaciers, snowfields and ice caps poured into the oceans and raised them by over 100m. The land bridges were gradually flooded and the sea encroached bit by bit on the lowlands and valleys. This had the effect of making people far more conscious of the coastline than they ever had been before and encouraged the development of a middle stone age way of life. People adopted semi-nomadic lives, following repeating routes through the landscape, often returning to a base camp on the coast or a riverside marsh.

The large-scale climate change that was under way in 10,000 BC was a major stimulus to human development, forcing people to change their way of life as the landscape itself changed, and even forcing them to get out of the way as the sea encroached. It was a time of rapid economic, social and cultural development. There had been global warming episodes like this before, at the close of each of the cold stages, and there had been people around to experience them too, but not *Homo sapiens sapiens*. The human race had reached a critical stage in its development where these great, wrenching environmental changes would stimulate a positive and creative response never seen before. Crises became challenges, and the human response would be so dramatic that it would make this interglacial (or warm stage) an interglacial like no other.

SETTLEMENT
AND PLANT
DOMESTICATION
(8000 BC)

AS THE LANDSCAPE changed around them, people became more aware of their environment. To protect themselves against these changes, people started selecting which plants and animals they would have living near them. Certain plants were chosen for domestication, such as wild grasses; selectively sown over several generations, these become wheat and barley. This transformation took place in the Near East. The ground was prepared by raking, digging with sticks or ploughing with simple wooden ploughs called ards, tipped with antler, bone or stone points; these earliest ploughs did not turn the soil, they only broke it up. Flint sickles were used for reaping.

Cattle, sheep and goats were also domesticated. With dogs it was different. Instead of people adopting dogs, dogs adopted people, scavenging their food scraps and in return allowing themselves to be used in hunting and in rounding up the sheep.

Once crops were planted, there was more of a focus on the particular places where the crops were. The crops needed to be tended and weeded, birds needed to be scared off, and in due course they needed to be harvested. Flocks of sheep and herds of cattle also made people less mobile. So with this change in food supply – with agriculture – came a change in lifestyle. People increasingly lived in one place, and this is how settled village life began. Within a very short period, people had changed from being old stone age hunters to being middle stone age hunters and fishers, and then changed again to being new stone age farmers: from being nomadic to being semi-nomadic to leading settled lives in villages.

Particular areas attracted settlement because they were good for food production, and during the next few centuries the Nile valley attracted many settlers. Later, around 5000 BC, the climate in Egypt changed and the landscape became drier; this was to stimulate all sorts of ingenious attempts to water the land artificially by irrigation.

The result of agriculture, which was a major revolution in living, was that food supply became more reliable, and the world's human population increased from about three million in 10,000 BC to five million in 5000 BC.

THE INVENTION OF
THE WHEEL
(6400 BC)

THE WHEEL, POPULARLY regarded as the greatest invention in prehistory, was devised in Mesopotamia by ancient Sumerians in 6400 BC. From this time onwards, clay models of carts or wagons with two or four wheels were made in the Middle East, and then a little later in eastern Europe. The earliest wheels were solid discs of wood, fitted onto wooden axles.

The wheeled carts were doubtless used initially for transporting agricultural produce. Later, when 'open' wheels with wooden rims and spokes were made, the lighter structures could be used for personal transport, including chariots, which changed the nature of warfare. With the advent of bronze for wheel-making, the potential increased enormously. A wooden wheel with a wooden bearing could only stand a limited strain. If, for example, a stone for Stonehenge had been loaded onto an all-wooden cart the wheels would certainly have disintegrated, however stoutly made. The wheel was available when Stonehenge was built, but it cannot have helped in the transporting of megaliths, except indirectly. Teams of oxen rather than people were probably used to drag the biggest megaliths, and it would have been necessary to use wheeled bogies or trolleys to separate the ropes and stop them from snagging the legs of the oxen. The megalith itself was probably lashed to a sledge. But, however the transporting of megaliths was achieved, the stones can never have been carried on wheeled wagons.

Once invented, some uses of the wheel would have been immediately obvious. Others followed later, such as using it to turn pottery on a potter's wheel. The history of the wheel went on through many transformations until the age of the train, the bicycle and the motor car.

THE BLACK SEA FLOOD
(5550 BC)

UNTIL 5550 BC, there was a land-locked lake at the centre of the Black Sea basin, rather like the Caspian Sea and Aral Sea further to the east. It was surrounded by an extensive plain with scattered settlers making a living by farming.

Then the sea broke in. As the glaciers melted, the global sea level had been steadily rising for several thousand years. Because the Mediterranean was connected to the open ocean by way of the Straits of Gibraltar, the level of water in the Mediterranean had been rising too. Eventually the Mediterranean overflowed into the Black Sea basin at Istanbul, causing a great flood. The sea water must have destroyed crops and flooded fields as it flowed in a great river of salt water, gradually enlarging the brackish lake to many times its original area until it became the Black Sea. Refugees from the expanding lake fanned outwards from it, many of them making for high ground in what is now Turkey.

Curiously, the Year of Creation as adopted in Constantinople (now Istanbul) in the seventh century AD was 5508 BC, within a few years of the date of the Black Sea Flood. This is probably just a coincidence.

Evidence for this early disaster has only recently come to light as a result of evidence trawled from the floor of the Black Sea. As sea level rose, all round the world, especially between 10,000 and 5,000 years ago, catastrophic floods like this happened in one place after another, causing whole communities to migrate to higher ground. The southern parts of the North Sea similarly had to be evacuated. Everywhere, people were on the move. The Bosporus, the broad channel of sea water that separates Istanbul from the rest of Turkey, was cut by the water from the Mediterranean as it flooded north-eastwards towards the centre of the Black Sea; now it is a major commercial waterway.

THE FIRST COPPER SMELTING
(5500 BC)

COPPER WAS SMELTED for the first time in Iran, around 5500 BC. The metal-workers used malachite as an ore, which is a naturally occurring copper carbonate. Smelting, which is simply roasting a metal ore until the metal melts and runs out, was a new technique that became a standard method for extracting not only copper but other metals from rocks.

Copper was found to be an accommodating metal that could be drawn, cast in moulds and hammered into shape. Later, experimental axes were made in copper, but the metal was too soft to hold a sharp and usable edge. Ötzi, the Iceman, owned a copper axe, but it may have been more of a status symbol than a useful tool. In an age when most tools were made of stone, a cast metal tool must have seemed a truly wonderful thing, even if it was not of much practical use, rather like a prestigious sports car that consumes a lot of petrol.

Eventually, an alloy of copper and tin – bronze – would prove to be a far more useful metal. Bronze was a stronger metal, one that would hold an edge. Then it became possible to make serviceable swords, knives, axes and other weapons and implements. The technique for making bronze was developed in the same region of south-west Asia. The invention of bronze was a major breakthrough in being the first metal that was hard enough to take an edge. Gold was even softer than copper and only useful for decorative work. Tin also was soft, but the experiment of combining tin and copper to make bronze, which was in effect an artificial metal, proved to be very successful.

It was not until 2500 BC that Middle Eastern metal workers developed a smelting technique that was suitable for iron. Temperatures of 1500 °C were needed to smelt iron – much higher than those needed for smelting copper. This was still very new technology, though, and it would not be until around 700 BC that iron smelting would become common. The swords that were made of iron were much more reliable than those made of bronze, and far less likely to snap in combat. The gradual development of metallurgy made way for the development of weapons technology.

THE BEGINNING OF
WARFARE IN
MESOPOTAMIA
(5000 BC)

IN THE MIDDLE East, the valleys of the Tigris and Euphrates became focuses for agriculture. Herds of domesticated cattle were becoming a common sight, but they needed water. The cultivation of crops necessitated artificial watering too and a high level of co-operation among villagers. The more sophisticated and extensive the systems of irrigation channels became, the more co-operation was needed between communities.

As population levels grew, so competition for resources grew. In some areas, where essential resources such as fertile soil or water for irrigation were in short supply, the competition flared up into fighting. In the Fertile Crescent (Nile valley, Palestine, Syria, Mesopotamia), villages were multiplying and the shortage of water for irrigation led to outbreaks of warfare.

It seems that the earliest large-scale fighting broke out in the Fertile Crescent. It was a cradle of civilization, but it was also a cradle of warfare. After 5000 BC, warfare became an increasingly common feature of human history. Some areas, especially those with low population densities, had far less fighting. In Britain during the period 5000–3000 BC, for instance, there are very few signs of warlike behaviour, partly because there was less competition for resources, though also because of the nature of society.

With the development of towns and cities, and the aristocratic elites that went with them, new motives for war emerged. Kings found it easier to rally their barons and subjects behind them when there was a common enemy to fight. All through history, kings both strong and weak have fallen back on the threat from abroad, whether real, imagined or invented, to maintain their own positions. So the emergence of city life and the institution of kingship in Mesopotamia made organized warfare likelier.

31

And we live with this phenomenon still. Political leaders today still take their countries to war for their own purposes rather than for their peoples' good. Was Baroness Thatcher's decision to fight a Falklands War taken entirely on the basis of tactical considerations in the South Atlantic – or was it at least partly to do with whipping up political support at home and ensuring a place in history?

THE BUILDING OF THE FIRST MEGALITHS
(4700 BC)

THE FIRST MEGALITHIC monuments were built just as agriculture was adopted as a lifestyle in Europe. The first true megaliths (giant stones) seem to have been raised in Brittany. The Dissignac passage graves and the Kercado chamber tomb were among the earliest of these monuments. At some sites, such as Barnenez, small chamber tombs were built and then, after a lapse of time, much larger mounds were raised over them, sometimes burying two or more of the earlier chambers and making a more impressive monument.

There were also isolated standing stones, and the largest of these was the Grand Menhir Brise (literally the 'great broken standing stone'). The Grand Menhir was a huge monolith weighing about 300 tonnes. It is estimated that it must have taken 3,000 people to pull it upright in 3880 BC, when it would have stood 20m high. It was an artificially dressed and smoothed hexagonal pillar of non-local granite that must have been transported at least 4km to the place where it was erected – a major feat in itself. The Grand Menhir now lies broken in four pieces and it looks as if it was deliberately pulled down during the megalithic period; other megalithic monuments in the area were also dismantled and in some cases the stones were re-used in new monuments. Some say the pillar slipped, fell and broke while it was being raised, which is possible; others say it fell as a result of an earthquake, which is also possible. But the fact that the fragments of the pillar point in different directions strongly implies deliberate destruction. The Grand Menhir originally stood at one end of a long barrow and was therefore really part of a tomb design; the associated tomb itself has been destroyed.

At Carnac there are multiple stone rows – rows and rows of standing stones, over a thousand of them in all. No-one has successfully explained their purpose, but they were probably connected with funeral ceremonies.

The Breton name of the place, Kermario, means 'The House of the Dead', which may contain an ancient folk-memory of the area's purpose.

In Brittany an entire, and to us rather mysterious and alien, culture grew up round these monuments, which became larger and more ambitious with time. They consumed an enormous amount of the stone age community's time and effort. The last great megalithic monument to be raised in Brittany was the Gavrinis passage grave, in around 3250 BC. At about the same time a huge burial mound, La Hougue Bie passage grave, was built in Jersey in the Channel Islands.

During the flurry of megalith building that focused on Brittany, megaliths were going up in other areas too. The Cueva del Romeral passage grave was built in Spain and some very fine stone temples were built on the island of Malta, at Mgarr and Ggantija in 3500 BC, at Mnajdra and Hagar Qim in 3400 BC and, the most spectacular of all, at Tarxien in 3300 BC.

Just as this Maltese sequence came to an end, around 3250 BC, the first megalithic monuments were raised in Britain, the earliest stone circles. The North and South Circles at Avebury were shortly after this. The famous stone circles at Stonehenge were a later creation still, although the earth circle was laid out at the same time as the Avebury stone circles, in about 3100 BC. It is possible that people in Britain were responding to an environmental disaster and were making desperate appeal to the gods to give them better weather. The Greenland ice cap tells us that there was a major volcanic eruption in 3200 BC (though no-one knows where in the world it took place), and narrow tree rings in ancient Irish bog oaks show that the climate cooled suddenly and significantly in the British Isles around 3150 BC. Here again we can see a connection between big volcanic eruptions and climate change, and this time a possible human response to environmental disaster as well.

That brings us to the fundamental question: what were the megalithic monuments for? They involved a colossal amount of labour, took a long time to build, and preoccupied a large proportion of the community. One obvious point is that megaliths are fixed in the landscape, and that implies that the people who built them had a focus on the places where the megaliths stood. It is no coincidence that megaliths – and other neolithic monuments like the long barrows that were made of earth – started to appear at the same time as agriculture. People were settling down to live in fixed and permanent farmsteads, and that must have given them a new view of landscape, especially particular tracts of landscape, as 'home'.

Some of the monuments were family tombs that were deliberately built so that they would be silhouetted on the skyline, when seen from the farmsteads where those families lived. They may have been intended as an ancestral claim to the territory they overlooked. If people were planting crops, they had a vested interest in claiming their fields and gardens where a harvest could be expected later. Claiming territory and defining boundaries became much more important once agriculture started.

Ploughing, sowing and reaping were key stages in the farming year, and some monuments were clearly intended to mark certain calendar dates. The orientation of Stonehenge on the midsummer sunrise is the most famous of these. But the monuments were doing more than marking the calendar: they were willing the succession of the seasons, and no doubt people thought that by carrying out the right ceremonies they were helping the gods to shift the sun and moon across the sky, and bring the next harvest round at the appointed time.

The megaliths also mark the beginning of public architecture. Already at this very early stage people were experimenting with designs that would impress others. They even used optical tricks to make their monuments look bigger than they really were. Some long barrows and chambered long cairns were built higher and wider at the end where the burials were placed, and where visitors arrived to take part in ceremonies; an observer looking from the forecourt in front of the 'business' end of a barrow would have got the impression, looking along the tapering mound, that it was much longer than it really was.

THE DEATH OF THE
ICEMAN
(3300 BC)

On 19 September 1991, Erika and Helmut Simon from Nuremberg discovered a body in the Alps. At first they and the rescue team who arrived shortly afterwards thought it was a mountaineer who had died there perhaps 10 or 20 years before. The body was brown, hairless, emaciated and half-buried in the ice of the Similaun Glacier. The warmer weather of the late twentieth century had thawed out part of the glacier, exposing this corpse. The odds and ends round the body suggested the remains of out-of-date equipment, so the authorities began to think in terms of a nineteenth century mountaineering accident, then something much older. The copper axe found close to the body suggested that it might date from the bronze age.

The radiocarbon date showed an even earlier date, 3300 BC. Bog bodies have occasionally been found, but they are only one or two thousand years old. There are Egyptian mummies that are much older, but nothing that old has been found in Europe. 'Ötzi', as he has been called, is the only well-preserved prehistoric European ever to have been discovered. The death and preservation by freezing of the Iceman have given us unexpectedly detailed information about the way people lived and died in the past.

Bits of the Iceman's clothing survived. His underclothing consisted of a loincloth and belt. He was also wearing suspenders that held up leather leggings, very similar to the leggings worn by North American Indians. A middle layer consisted of a tunic made of strips of animal skin carefully sewn together with twined animal sinews. Alternating strips of brown and black fur created a pattern of stripes. This tunic must have been quite a splendid sight when it was first made, but at the time of Ötzi's death it had been patched many times. The outer layer of clothing included leather shoes and a cloak about a metre long made of plaited grass, with seven or eight cross plaits holding the upper part together and a long fringe round the bottom. Ötzi also wore a beehive-shaped fur hat.

Ötzi was aged 35–40, 160cm tall, with wavy dark-brown hair. There were strange marks tattooed on his skin. They do not appear to be decorative. They may represent acupuncture points that were seen as appropriate to some medical problem he had. They may alternatively represent stages in his acquisition of adult status. In most societies there are rites of passage marking an individual's arrival at a new status – confirmations, bar mitzvahs, A levels, graduations, weddings – and it may be that the overall pattern of tattoos represents a complete CV of his status in his society. It seems unlikely that we shall ever be able to find out what that status was, as we have no way at all of decoding the marks, although the fact that he owned the earliest known copper axe in Europe suggests that he may have held some high status position. Or did he perhaps steal it?

The extreme thinness of the body was due to its drying-out after death. The forensic experts at first assumed that Ötzi had been caught in a sudden storm, taken shelter in a rocky hollow beside the glacier and died there of hypothermia. It was only ten years later, when a new set of X-rays was taken, that they realized they had overlooked something very significant. Embedded in the corpse's shoulder was a stone arrowhead. A fresh look at the corpse itself revealed that there was a fresh cut in the skin at that point. Ötzi had been shot. Further examination of the site and of his various belongings now suggested that Ötzi had not only been fatally wounded and chased up into the mountains, but his killers had visited or revisited his body, moved it and strewn his belongings about. There are lots of theories about Ötzi's murder. Was it an execution, a punishment for some crime committed in the village down in the valley? Or was Ötzi himself the victim of a crime, an undeserved attack by bandits?

The death of the Iceman was a personal disaster for him, but his accidental preservation through 5,000 years was an unexpected and unlikely bonus for us. It gives us a unique insight into the way people lived in the past. In some ways they were very like us, in others very different. And knowing about Ötzi somehow changes us a little. Our minds are extended by knowing more and more about the past; just as we learn an orientation to the world by listening to the experiences, beliefs and views of our parents and grandparents, we can adjust that orientation by referring to earlier generations. Through history and archaeology we can acquire some of the life experiences of those generations who have long gone before, and we are better equipped to evaluate our own situations.

THE BUILDING OF THE STEP PYRAMID AT SAQQARA
(2900 BC)

IT WAS IMHOTEP, physician and adviser to King Zoser, who designed the unique Step Pyramid at Saqqara, overlooking the city of Memphis. Not surprisingly, in time Imhotep came to be revered as a great guru. He is the earliest architect whose name we know.

Until Imhotep's time, royal burial monuments in Egypt were single-storey structures, big rectangular buildings called mastabas. These monuments were at first built with inward-sloping walls of brick encasing rubble interiors, and only later made of longer-lasting stone. The mastabas were built in imitation of the palaces of kings and nobles, houses for the dead imitating houses for the living. They said it was Imhotep who invented the use of stone for building.

Imhotep built his Step Pyramid in an enclosure that imitates the plan of King Zoser's palace in Memphis. It has blind doorways carved in solid stone, doorways that stand tantalizingly ajar; apparently open but giving mortals no hope of ever getting inside.

The Step Pyramid was a revolutionary design. It began as a limestone-faced square mastaba 8m high, covering a maze of underground royal burial chambers. Then Imhotep had the inspired idea of building another, slightly smaller, mastaba on top and then two further mastabas, each smaller than the last, stacked on top of that. At this point, he realized that he had created an imposing monument that could very easily be made even more imposing by increasing the area of the base and adding a further two storeys. The final version of the Step Pyramid had six tiers.

The new building was higher, more complex, more massive and far more impressive than anything that had previously been built in Egypt – or anywhere else. It was also very luxuriously fitted out with stone carvings and beautiful vessels of alabaster, porphyry and serpentine. Although many of the fittings have been plundered, a surprising number still lie in place at the site – and the pyramid itself still stands intact.

Later pyramids were built on an even grander scale, but the Step Pyramid had led the way. One of the pyramids, The Great Pyramid, would become one of the Wonders of the Ancient World. Imhotep achieved his remarkable design in one go, actually thinking it out during the course of building the Step Pyramid. By building something so original he gave his patron, King Zoser, the immortality he craved. In 3000 BC, kingship was itself in its infancy. With the new phenomenon of kingship came personality cults, and with those came the desire to make a visible impact on the landscape, the desire to be forever remembered. From the Step Pyramid on, spectacular buildings became a way of being remembered, from Trajan's Column to the Palace of Versailles.

THE INVENTION OF
CUNEIFORM SCRIPT
IN SUMER
(2500 BC)

IN 2500 BC, Britain was at the end of the new stone age, on the brink of the early bronze age, and people were still living in isolated farmsteads or villages. In Egypt and Mesopotamia, town life was well under way which included the craft specialisms that went with town life.

A major new development in Mesopotamia was cuneiform script. There was an earlier written script that consisted of thousands of picture-signs or pictograms, but this was clumsy. The new script was based on the older pictograms and was quicker to write.

With writing, other things became possible. It became possible to keep records of commodities that were being bought and sold, and one of the earliest uses of writing was for simple record-keeping of this kind. It was also possible to keep a record of agreements, for instance agreements between individual people regarding land holdings or political treaties between kings. It was also possible to write prayers, poetry, stories and histories. People would no longer have to commit information to memory and carry it in their heads. With writing, vast quantities of information could be stored and passed on to the next generation.

Writing made possible a great leap forward, because an ever-increasing volume of information and ideas could accumulate, year by year, generation by generation. Cultures were no longer limited by the amount of information that could be transmitted by oral tradition. Ever since it was invented, and right up to the present day, writing has been one of the principal ways in which civilization has developed.

THE INTRODUCTION
OF RICE INTO CHINA
(2300 BC)

RICE GREW NATURALLY in the Indus valley, where the food supply supported a civilization comparable to those in the Nile or Tigris-Euphrates valleys. In 2300 BC, rice was introduced into northern China, where it became the staple food for another civilization.

Rice was to become the food base for the population of most of South-East Asia for the next 4,000 years, supporting what would become massive population growth. Rice production therefore became critical to human well-being in the region. Rice was introduced from China to Japan in the first century AD. By 1950, the Asian rice crop had fallen below the level of the 1930s, while the population had increased by 10 percent; the result was a lower, poorer standard of living.

Rice was gradually introduced to one new region after another. The Moors introduced it from North Africa to Spain. Then the Spanish introduced it to Italy in 1468, planting it near the town of Pisa. But rice has never been consumed on the same scale in Europe as it has in South-East Asia. The average Asian eats over 135kg of rice a year compared with Westerners 2.7kg a year, showing how today rice still dominates the oriental diet.

THE BUILDING OF THE KNOSSOS LABYRINTH
(1900 BC)

ON A LOW hill a few kilometres south of Heraklioñ in Crete, the sprawling ruined walls of the Knossos Labyrinth cover an area about 150m across. Because of its disintegrated state, the original plan of the building is very hard to see, let alone understand, but it consisted of hundreds of chambers of different shapes and sizes connected by winding corridors, and grouped round a big rectangular courtyard. It looks and feels like a maze, and that is exactly how the ancient Greeks saw it too. They even used a stylized maze symbol on their coins, to represent the long-deserted Labyrinth that was still standing at the south-east corner of their city.

Homer left elusive clues about a royal court at Knossos, which Odysseus claimed to have visited, and which was the capital of bronze age Crete. There was a persistent tradition among the classical Greeks that there had been a great sea-empire stretching across the Aegean Sea and ruled from Knossos by a king called Minos. In the nineteenth century, as the lost site of Knossos gradually re-emerged from obscurity, it was inevitable that the first people to take an active interest in excavating it – Minos Kalokairinos, Heinrich Schliemann and Arthur Evans – should be predisposed to find evidence of the bronze age past as they had read it in classical literature. They expected the huge building that was gradually uncovered to be the palace of the bronze age kings of Knossos.

This line of thought was actually a false trail that misled not only them but also nearly everybody else since then about the true nature of the Labyrinth, as the building was called in antiquity. The people who designed and used the building kept records on clay tablets and the peculiar script they used (Linear B) referred to the city as ko-no-so (Knossos) and the building as da-pu-ri-to-jo (Labyrinthos, The Labyrinth). Amazingly, we can tell from these clay tablets that quite a lot of other places on Crete were also known in the bronze age, 3,000–4,000 years ago, by their 'modern' names. Amnisos, which was the bronze age port of Knossos, and Tylissos, a town a few kilometres to the west of Knossos, are today still known by their bronze age names.

When Sir Arthur Evans published the results of his excavations, he presented the building as the 'Palace of King Minos', just as Minos Kalokairinos had 50 years earlier. But the evidence in room after room of religious cult equipment and frescoes showing religious ceremonies proves that it was really a temple. The frescoes showing ceremonies performed in the temple clearly show that it was the priestesses who had the highest status there. One fresco, called the Grandstand Fresco, shows a huge crowd assembled to watch some great spectacle in the Central Court. A fresco discovered recently at one of the palace-temples on the mainland of Greece shows a central court surrounded by irregular blocks of buildings; in the central court itself the bull-leaping ceremony is going on. This dangerous acrobatic feat was evidently a religious ritual rather than a circus act. The bull represented Poseidon, one of the most important gods in the bronze age world, so the bull-leapers were in some sense dancing with Poseidon. The bull was evidently sacrificed at the end of the dance. This ancient ceremony still lingers on at the other end of the Mediterranean, in the Spanish bullfight.

The chambers round the Central Court were shrines and sanctuaries dedicated to many different gods and goddesses, some of whom are named on the clay tablets.

The Labyrinth was abandoned in 1380 BC and the Minoan civilization, which produced it, collapsed. From 1900 BC until 1380 BC, this great temple had stood at the centre of the Minoan capital. Then its upper mudbrick storeys gradually crumbled, until only a few walls stuck out above the rubble, some still carrying frescoes of the bull-leaping ceremony. The classical city of Knossos grew up to the north and west, and the crumbling ruins of the Labyrinth were left, perhaps as a forbidden place, untouched on its south-eastern edge. It half-stood, as a reminder of the mythic past, just as the Acropolis today half-stands as a reminder to modern Athenians of their ancient past. And then they wove legends round it, legends about Theseus and the Minotaur, about the tribute-children and the bull-leaping, about King Minos and Ariadne, and about Daedalus who designed the Knossos Labyrinth.

Knossos is a symbol, like the Acropolis, Stonehenge or the Pyramids, for an entire culture. It is unfortunate that most people misremember it as a palace when really it was a temple, but a lot of history is misremembering. Knossos is also the ancestor of all the labyrinths, from the simple 'swastika' maze on the classical coins of Knossos to elaborate modern hedge mazes like the one at Hampton Court. The labyrinth has always been, right from Minoan times, a symbol of life's journey, of the journey of self-discovery; it has a universal resonance.

THE THERA ERUPTION
(1520 BC)

SANTORINI IS A ring of islands, a kind of mountainous atoll, in the middle of the south Aegean Sea, immediately to the north of Crete. Within this ring of islands, Thera, Therasia and Aspronisi, is a huge oval bay 10km across. This was the focus of the unimaginably violent eruption that destroyed the bronze age civilization on Santorini. Where once hill country rose to volcanic peaks, the sea is now 400m deep. The steep walls of the caldera showing the layers of ash and lava of ancient volcanic eruptions give the bay a hostile coastline. Today Santorini's main town, Phira, perches precariously on the rim of the caldera, overlooking the bay from a great height.

Before the huge eruption that destroyed the ancient civilization on the island in 1520 BC, there were villages and at least one city on Santorini. The city was a harbour town on the south coast. It was probably called Therassos and the island was called Thera, just as it was in the classical period. The Minoan Cretans worshipped a goddess called Therassia, 'She-from-Therassos'. Now Therassos is called Akrotiri. A village had been standing there as early as 2500 BC, so the city was evolving over a period of 1,000 years. At the time of the eruption, a fully developed, civilized and prosperous Minoan way of life was in full swing. We know this because the ash that buried and destroyed Therassos as a living city buried and preserved much of it for us to see. Even more still lies buried under the ash.

The big eruption was preceded by a series of earthquakes and small eruptions of pumice, which fell on the stricken city like drifting snow. Repairs were done, so the island was not immediately evacuated. Then there was a lull of about five years before a series of major earthquakes and emissions of gas, steam and smoke started spurting from the mountain in the centre of the island. It was then that most of the people left the island. Only a few foolhardy people stayed behind. First the island was sprayed with a fountain of pumice that settled on the city like a layer of snow 2m deep. By then the eruption crater had grown large enough to let sea water seep into it and this caused some huge explosions which sent massive blocks of stone hurtling outwards like shells. The upper storeys of many houses were shot away by these bombs.

Eventually the lava chamber under the volcano was emptied. The island sagged into this yawning vault and networks of radial and ring fissures opened up. The volcano collapsed. Sea water poured into the searingly hot chamber, causing more violent eruptions and a series of tsunamis that raced outwards across the Aegean to Crete.

Not only was the Minoan civilization on Santorini completely wiped out by this catastrophic eruption, the civilization on the 'mainland' of Crete was seriously damaged too. The tsunamis wrecked the coastal settlements. I have seen the remains of waterfront houses at the harbour town of Amnisos on the north coast of Crete, with their huge wall stones sucked out of place by the tsunamis in 1520 BC. Many of the merchant ships that made the Minoans rich must have been sunk or smashed by the tsunamis. Then there was the ash falling from the huge ash plume that reached out from Santorini to cover eastern Crete. Only a thin layer of acidic ash was needed to put the fields out of production for a couple of years – enough to cripple the Minoan economy. It was not long before the Mycenaeans, the people of mainland Greece, exploited the Minoans' weakness, and reached out to snatch their trading empire from them.

The Minoan civilization did not come to an end immediately. It limped on for another century. But it was critically weakened, and the Mycenaean civilization, unaffected by the eruption, was able to develop and overtake it. At a stroke, the Santorini (or Thera) eruption of 1520 BC brought about the death of one civilization and the birth of another. By burying substantial parts of Therassos at Akrotiri, it also provided us with an incredibly detailed picture of the way of life in Minoan Santorini.

The frescoes have in many cases survived complete and in full colour, providing us with more information about Minoan religious beliefs than we have been able to reassemble at Knossos. In particular there is a remarkably poetic portrait of a beautiful goddess, who is probably the goddess of Therassos, Therassia. She sits on an elaborate stepped altar, where she is courted by her heraldic beasts, a monkey and a griffin, and offered a gift of crocuses by a girl. There is also an elaborate and complex series of images connected with rites of passage for adolescent boys and girls, which gives an idea of some of the ceremonies that would have taken place within the Knossos Labyrinth.

The area of the bronze age city that has so far been excavated is frustratingly small – about 20 buildings and a handful of streets – and the rate of excavation is frustratingly slow, but it has given us a wonderful opportunity to see what town life was like in the Minoan period. There has been nothing on the scale of the huge caldera eruption of Santorini anywhere in the world since 1520 BC. The awe-inspiring sequence of events and its consequences to human history should make us stop and consider the real nature of our relationship with the Earth. We and all our possessions and our entire culture can be wiped out in a single geological convulsion. The earth and its processes are far more powerful than we are. This is a painful lesson that we have to re-learn periodically.

AKHENATEN
INTRODUCES
MONOTHEISM
(1374 BC)

ABSOLUTE MONARCHS HAVE always had the ability to make radical and far-reaching changes, up to and including changing the religion of their nations. In sixteenth century England successive Tudor monarchs changed the national religion several times over. Henry VIII severed the connection between the English Church and Rome, supplanting the Pope and making himself Defender of the Faith; Edward VI established an English Protestant Church; Mary Tudor re-established Roman Catholicism and persecuted Protestants; Elizabeth I re-established the Church of England and persecuted selected Catholics.

When Amenhotep IV became pharaoh in 1374 BC, he decided to change the established religion of ancient Egypt. Up until that time Egyptian religion had consisted of the worship of many gods. Amenhotep decided there was only one god, and set up a cult for the worship of Aten, the sun-disc. He changed his own name, adopting the new name Akhenaten, which meant 'Aten is satisfied'. He even moved his capital from Thebes to a new city which he named Akhetaten, 'Horizon of Aten', which is now known by its modern name, Tell-el-Amarna. This new city was built on an unpromising strip of land on the Nile's east bank halfway between Thebes and Memphis, chosen because it was a virgin site dedicated to no other god. Then he set about filling his city with monuments that celebrated his new idea of 'living in truth'.

Other changes followed. Instead of the traditional stylized portraits which earlier pharaohs had commissioned, Akhenaten wanted realism. His sculpted portraits were apparently genuine and not at all flattering likenesses; he had a very distinctive long face with full lips, a pot belly and wide hips. There were also intimate and affectionate scenes of the pharaoh's domestic life with his queen Nefertiti and six daughters. The painted portrait sculpture of Nefertiti is a remarkably beautiful piece of artwork. For the first time we see a real family behaving naturally; we see Akhenaten bouncing his infant children on his knee and kissing his wife on the lips. It is not clear whether this change to realism was due to a respect for reality or to personal vanity.

Akhenaten's peculiar appearance has generated a lot of speculation among historians. Was he a mental defective, or a sufferer from Froelich's Syndrome (a disorder of the pituitary gland)? Was he a transvestite or even a hermaphrodite? It seems more likely that he was just an unusual individual, who looked unusual as well as having unusual ideas. His unusual ideas extended to the structure of society. The villas he caused to be built in his new capital city were designed without separate women's quarters, which strongly implies that men and women were living together domestically in much the same way that they do today – but in 1370 BC this was a real revolution in living, a move towards the equality of the sexes that was way ahead of other societies of the time.

Pharaohs often had the names or images of their predecessors defaced, but Akhenaten had the name of the god Amun removed from his temples. In making all these radical changes, the pharaoh inevitably aroused the hostility of the priests of gods who had been sidelined in this revolution, the priests of Amun in particular, and he alienated many others too.

The heretic pharaoh Akhenaten reigned for 17 years, during which time his new monotheistic religion became established. He died in 1358 BC and was succeeded by his 9 year old son-in-law Tutankhamun. Tutankhamun had accepted Akhenaten's monotheism but in time, though his reign was short, he returned to the old ways and the priests of Amun came back to the fore. He also moved the capital back from Akhetaten to the old centre of Thebes. Tutankhamun died under mysterious circumstances, perhaps in battle, but succeeding pharaohs maintained the traditional Egyptian religion, the worship of many gods. They also did everything they could to eradicate Akhenaten's name from the records.

Akhenaten did something remarkable. He pursued an idea of his own, one that must have dangerously alienated many of his courtiers, and pursued it with fanatical zeal. Although at the time Akhenaten's revolution seemed absurd as well as heretical, it was nevertheless a look ahead to a time when most religions would focus on one god. This is not to say that there is only one god, or any god at all, but rather that in terms of the historical process the experiment with monotheism was a significant invention. Moses in effect did the same thing, replacing the prevailing polytheistic religion with monotheism. The episode was also ground-breaking in another way, in giving us the first naturalistic images of ancient Egyptian people. Akhenaten also emerges as the first true individual in human history.

THE BATTLE OF
KADESH
(1280 BC)

THE BATTLE OF Kadesh was fought between two great empires, Hittite and Egyptian. In the run-up to the Trojan War, which took place about a generation after Kadesh, Muwatallis was the Great King, or over-king, of the Hittites. He ruled a huge sprawling empire that was sometimes called Hatti, covering most of what is now Turkey. Along the western coast there were problems with incursions by the Mycenaean Greeks, who attacked and ransacked several towns before finally attacking Troy in the north-west. The Hittite Great Kings frequently tried diplomacy in dealing with these incursions in the west, because there were larger-scale problems in the east, where there was a clash of interests with the Assyrians and Egyptians.

Muwattallis, a fat, good-natured man who led a life of action rather than contemplation, defeated Ramesses II at the Battle of Kadesh. Kadesh was an historic encounter because it visibly transformed the Hittite Empire and Egypt into rivals of equal status and strength.

Unfortunately, though there are extensive Hittite archives, very little written by Muwatallis, and nothing at all about the Battle of Kadesh, has been found. This may be because Muwatallis moved his capital from Hattusa, which has been both identified and excavated, to a place called Dattassa, and that site has yet to be found.

Muwatallis left little information about himself and his deeds. We have to turn to his enemy Ramesses to read a full account of what happened at Kadesh. Ramesses ordered that a full description of the origins and development of the conflict should be carved on the walls of the Ramesseum – and also at Karnak, Luxor, Abydos and Abu Simbel. The specific cause of the fighting was the defection to Egypt of the Hittite kingdom of Amurru, roughly corresponding to modern Lebanon. This small kingdom was important because it lay at the junction of three spheres of influence – Hittite, Assyrian and Egyptian. On the strength of this defection, Ramesses, who was an impulsive and energetic man in his early twenties, led an army out of Egypt in the hope of conquering the whole of Syria. Muwatallis was informed, and gathered an army to prevent Ramesses from achieving his goal.

A problem is that we hear of the Battle of Kadesh mainly from the Egyptian side, which is biased. An Egyptian poem empathized with the Pharaoh:

'When the earth became light, then did I join battle, armed for the fray like a lustful bull. . . I thrust my way into the tumult and fought as a falcon stoops ... I was like Ra at his appearance in the morning; my rays scorched the face of my foes ... Then did the Wretched One of Hatti send forth and revere the great name of His Majesty: You are a ruler, the likeness of Ra ... There is a dread of you in the land of Hatti, for you have broken the back of Hatti for ever.'

The 'Wretched One of Hatti' was King Muwatallis, but it is unlikely that he spoke in such terms to or about Ramesses because it was Ramesses who was defeated in the great battle. Some information comes from the Hittite archives, which reveal that the Hittites used clever subterfuge and skilled military strategy to trick and outwit Ramesses. Probably it was only nightfall that saved Ramesses from complete annihilation, and Ramesses escaped from the battlefield only because the Hittites did not chase after him.

This battle between the two empires took place in 1285 BC. Muwatallis lay in wait for Ramesses and his huge army, in effect setting up an elaborate trap. Ramesses took the bait – false information supplied by two Bedouin posing as Hittite deserters – and suddenly found his camp surrounded. A whole division of the Egyptian army was massacred.

Ramesses was an outstanding self-publicist, using his scribes and artists to create an image of him as a godlike figure. In the accounts of the Battle of Kadesh his scribes credited him with killing thousands of the enemy. In practice, Ramesses can have done little more than act as a battle standard, giving orders that were often unhelpful. Ramesses' leadership was the weakest link in the Egyptian military machine; his ideas of strategy – at Kadesh – were conspicuously naïve compared with those of Muwatallis. Ramesses lost the battle, and the territory round Kadesh that his predecessors had acquired, yet he succeeded in convincing his own and subsequent generations that he had won a great victory. It was a masterpiece of spin.

Ramesses' description of the battle is biased in favour of the Egyptians, but it is clear even from that that Muwatallis and his generals were master strategists unparalleled in history. Ramesses escaped to portray the event as a victory when he got home, but he was in reality defeated. Muwatallis had shown sufficient military might to draw a line in the sand; the Egyptians would never encroach any further to the north. But Kadesh was a landmark in another way too. It showed for the first time how 'spin' could turn an actual disaster into an historic triumph. Regardless of what happened in fact, Ramesses' official version of events was to have great impact in Egypt. The billboard version, showing Ramesses several times larger than life and causing havoc among the enemy, was what ordinary Egyptians absorbed during the years that followed – and which became history. Ramesses was the first great master of propaganda.

THE EXODUS
(ABOUT 1270 BC)

IN BRONZE AGE warfare it was standard practice to carry off large numbers of conquered people to use as slaves. A victorious army would pillage a conquered town, its palaces and temples and take home as much loot as it could carry. The conquered people were housed in shanty towns and used as cheap labour for major work projects. The Israelites had the misfortune to be taken into captivity in this way by the Egyptians. The Old Testament scriptures are imprecise regarding date, and although 'Pharaoh' is mentioned we cannot be sure which one. It may have been Ramesses, the same Egyptian king that fought at Kadesh.

Moses, who became the most important Old Testament Hebrew prophet and lawgiver, was born in Egypt during the time when the people of Israel were slave workers in Egypt. As a baby, Moses (Hebrew 'Mosheh') was saved from a general slaughter of male Jewish children, ordered by Pharaoh, by being concealed by his mother in a chest in bulrushes by the bank of the River Nile. He was found there and brought up by one of Pharaoh's daughters. When he grew up he killed an Egyptian who was bullying an Israelite, and had to take flight to avoid retribution.

As a young man he lived in Midian with the priest Jethro, marrying one of Jethro's daughters and becoming the father of Gershom and Eliezer. At the holy mount, Moses had a momentous encounter with God. Disclosing his name to Moses as 'Yahweh' (Jehovah), God told him to bring the people of Israel out of Egypt. The newly named god showed his displeasure at the Egyptians' behaviour by afflicting them with a series of plagues, culminating in the death of the first-born.

Moses had by this stage become the leader of the people of Israel. It was in about 1270 BC that he took a remarkable and risky initiative in leading them out of captivity, east into the Sinai peninsula, and from there into Kadesh and Moab. The Egyptians who pursued them, we are told, were drowned in the Red Sea. The departure from Egypt became known as the

Exodus, and it became one of the most significant migrations in history.

While on Mount Sinai, Moses had another encounter with Yahweh, who gave him the Ten Commandments, a very brief and simplified law code. In presenting the Israelites with this law code and mediating with Yahweh, Moses in effect became the founder of the Jewish religion.

After a long period of 'wandering', during which the Israelites were tested and proved by their new god, Moses led them towards the borders of what was seen as 'the promised land', the land of Israel that ever afterwards was claimed by them as God-given. This continuing belief lies behind many of the territorial struggles that have gone on in Israel/Palestine over the last half century.

At Mount Nebo, to the north-west of the Dead Sea, Moses died. It was left to his successor, Joshua, to lead the Israelites across the River Jordan into the Promised Land of Canaan. There is no doubt that Moses was the founder of Israelite nationhood. It was Moses who welded together the many tribes into one nation. The Exodus was a major rite of passage that made the tribes bond together. It was during this journey to the Promised Land that the Israelites' religion crystallized; they were introduced to their new god, Yahweh, thanks to Moses, who acted as the sole mediator between people and god. It was during the Exodus that Moses delivered the Ten Commandments. The Israelites' escape from Egypt, with all its implications for the development of Judaism and a creation myth for the Jewish nation, stands out as one of the great events in human history.

THE GREEK ATTACK
ON TROY
(1250 BC)

THE BRONZE AGE Greeks, or Mycenaeans, frequently raided the cities along the west coast of what is now Turkey and was then the Hittite Empire. They took female slaves as textile workers and male slaves to build fortifications.

Homer, writing in 750 BC, says the attack on Troy in 1250 BC was prompted by the theft of Helen, wife of King Menelaus of Lacedaemon, by Paris, who was one of the sons of King Priam of Troy. Agamemnon, the King of Mycenae, assembled a huge fleet with contingents from all over Greece, and sailed to Troy to take revenge. Troy commanded a harbour at the entrance to the Dardanelles, the route to the Black Sea. Probably the Greeks wanted to gain control over the trade route.

According to the Iliad, the war with Troy lasted ten years. Other ancient poems show that this included attacks on other coastal towns near Troy: Lyrnessos, Thebe, Pedasos and Thermi. The strategy was to isolate Troy, the wealthy capital of a kingdom called 'Wilusa'.

The Greeks set up camp in Besika Bay, 8km south-west of Troy, for fear of being trapped in the Bay of Troy by constant north winds. Several battles took place between the Mycenaean army and the confederate army of the Trojans and their allies; they were fought on foot and by chariot on the Plain of Troy between camp and city. Many warrior princes on both sides were killed, including Achilles and Hector.

The Mycenaeans brought in siege engines, covered trolleys with huge spears or prods mounted in front, to make holes in Troy's mudbrick ramparts – the origin of the 'Wooden Horse' story. The city fell to the Greeks, who killed many Trojans, including King Priam, and destroyed the ramparts.

Troy never dominated the region in the same way again, until it was rebuilt centuries later as a Homeric theme park in homage to the dead heroes. To the Romans it became an idealized, iconic city, until it was abandoned in AD 550 – though never forgotten in literature. Many Mycenaean leaders died, and some of their kingdoms fell into the hands of usurpers. They never recovered from their 'victory'; their strongholds fell to unknown attackers fifty years later, and the Mycenaean civilization fell apart shortly after that.

THE BUILDING OF THE
TEMPLE OF JERUSALEM
(950 BC)

IN 961 BC King David of Judah died and was succeeded by Solomon, David's son by his second wife Bathsheba. Solomon's long and distinguished reign lasted 40 years, which marks him out as an able, though not necessarily wise, ruler. Solomon established a long period of peace for his kingdom by negotiating alliances with Egypt to the south and with the Phoenician King Hiram of Tyre. In collaboration with Hiram of Tyre, the fleets of Judah sailed south into the Red Sea and traded produce at ports along the Arabian and African coasts. On King Solomon's initiative, gold mining began.

By creating a period of peace and prosperity, King Solomon was able to organize ambitious building projects. Solomon is perhaps best remembered for ordering the building of the Great Temple in Jerusalem. Jerusalem had once been a Jebusite stronghold, and it was captured by King David to house the sacred ark of Yahweh. David had intended to build a temple there, but was thwarted by the prophet Nathan. David died, leaving the huge task to Solomon. What Solomon built was a Great Temple to house the Judaeans' holiest relics, but also a new royal palace and a city wall, completely transforming the city. King David had built a palace in Jerusalem, but it was not grand enough for Solomon; Solomon spent thirteen years building his own palace (compared with seven building the Temple), where he then lived in incredible opulence. Solomon introduced taxation to finance these projects and forced labour from the Canaanites to get them built; he relied largely on Hiram to organize the projects, just as his father had. The kingdom was divided into 12 districts, which apparently did not correspond to the old 12 tribes, and they were called on in rotation to contribute cash and labour.

It is for this glorification of Jerusalem that Solomon is remembered, but it was only achieved by crippling his people with excessively heavy demands. The boast is made that the Israelites were not treated as slaves, but the unremitting exactions Solomon made of them must have reduced the poor to something very close to slavery. The ordinary people, who had no voice, must have been very unhappy, and it may well be that Solomon's big-spending policy led to the splitting of the kingdom under his successor.

The Labyrinth was built at Knossos in part to bring down from the peak sanctuaries both the spiritual power and the secular power associated with them. The nearest peak sanctuary to Knossos was the one perched on the summit of Mount Juktas, a few kilometres to the south; its remains can still be seen. There were political reasons for having the ceremonial gatherings in the towns, where they could be watched and controlled by the authorities, and where they could enhance the social fabric of urban life. In bronze age Palestine, too, the mountain tops were often a focus of early worship. In the Bible they are referred to as 'the high places'. What Solomon was doing, a few centuries after the Minoan priestesses, was the same thing – bringing the rituals and the cult objects down into the towns, where they could cement the spiritual, social and cultural lives of the people who lived there.

One of the earlier holy places that was superseded was Shiloh, a town 27 km north of Jerusalem. Once there was a sanctuary at Shiloh dedicated to the tribal cult. It was there that the Ark of the Covenant had its first home. This was the portable throne of the invisible god Yahweh, and it was housed in a tent-shrine called the Tabernacle. The hated Philistines later captured the Ark, and destroyed the cult centre at Shiloh.

The Jebusite town of Jerusalem, the Jerusalem taken over by King David, was a 450m long settlement running along the crest of a north-south ridge, the Ophel hill, overlooking the Kedron valley to the east and the Hinnom valley to the west. This town was enlarged by Solomon, who added about another 200m to the north, and then added the Great Temple site to the north of that, on higher ground still. The temple site was a huge rectangle, 300m from west to east and 500m from north to south, completely dominating the town of Jerusalem. When it was complete, the Ark of the Covenant was installed, no doubt with great ceremony, inside it. Modelled on older Canaanite temples, the Great Temple consisted of three rooms, one behind the other on an east-west axis. There was a vestibule or porch, a main hall and a Holy of Holies beyond that. The Holy of Holies housed the Ark of the Covenant guarded by two cherubim, winged mythic beasts made of gold. In the porch or in front of it were two free-standing basalt pillars, named Jachin and Boaz.

Solomon unquestionably made Jerusalem into a great city. By fitting it out with a palace and temple of legendary size and grandeur, he turned Jerusalem itself into a legend. He put the city on the map as a holy city for ever after. As far as medieval Europe was concerned, Jerusalem was the centre of the world, and a constant preoccupation and focus for the Crusaders. From that point of view, the building works were extremely successful. But as has often been the case throughout history, the extreme hardship endured by the ordinary people who had to work and pay for it has been forgotten. And – a sobering thought – not a stone of Solomon's Great Temple remains.

THE WRITING OF
THE *ILIAD*
850 BC

THE STORY OF the bronze age Greek attack on Troy was passed on from generation to generation by bards, who chanted it as a sequence of long epic poems that they had learned by heart. These recitations were probably performed as an evening's entertainment in an aristocratic household, and they were probably from the beginning divided up into evening-long slabs, each lasting perhaps two hours, the length of a modern feature film.

The events described in the poems happened in about 1250 BC. There was writing at that time, but it seems from the archaeological evidence that it was used mainly for recording transactions and listing inventories; as far as we can tell it was not used for literature, which was entirely oral.

Songs and poems were learned by heart, and the skill of committing to memory thousands of lines of poetry became highly developed. Some people have doubted that such feats of memory were ever possible, which is odd because the evidence is still with us that people can memorize huge quantities of poetry. There are still people in Ireland who have learned, just by listening, thousands of lines of epic poems, and can recite them just as they heard them decades earlier. In eastern Europe, there is a living tradition of performing epic poems learned in this way, often with pairs of performers taking it in turns to deliver sections of the story, presumably to reduce the strain on their voices, and to the accompaniment of music. There is a bronze age fresco at Pylos showing a bard with a lyre, and this is almost certainly how the poems that we now call Homer's were first performed.

Writing went out of fashion in what are called the dark ages, between 1200 and 850 BC, after the Mycenaean civilization collapsed. When writing was reinvented in around 850 BC, the poems were at last written down. The truth is that nobody knows who wrote them down, but the name of Homer is firmly attached to the *Iliad*, which tells part of the story

61

of the Trojan War, and the *Odyssey*, which describes Odysseus' journey back home to Ithaca. But a long sequence of poems referred to as the Epic Cycle includes the *Iliad* and the *Odyssey*, which have survived intact, and also several lost poems, the *Kypria, Aithiopis, Little Iliad, Ilioupersis, Nostoi* and *Telegoneia*, which survive only in summary.

Once the poems were written down, more people had access to them. There was an explosion of interest in the lost world of the heroes that the poems described, the Mycenaean world. Just a few years after the *Iliad* was written, the citizens of Mycenae decided to raise a special shrine dedicated to Agamemnon, as if the publication of the *Iliad* had reminded them of an heroic king of Mycenae about whom they had forgotten. From then on, the heroic tradition has been a vital part of Western civilization. The way the warrior-heroes behaved, in and out of battle, came to be seen as a role-model for the behaviour of later generations of warriors. Alexander the Great always slept with a copy of the *Iliad* under his pillow. Even as a boy he was fascinated by the idea of being an incarnation of Achilles, to the point where his tutor Aristotle actually called him Achilles. Alexander even acted out the *Iliad* in his career as a conqueror. Like Nestor and the other heroes, Alexander was to become a 'sacker of cities'.

Since the time when Troy was finally abandoned it has continued to exist in the world's imagination, and that was largely thanks to the writing of the *Iliad* in 850 BC. Troy is an immortal city with a human story immortalized by the poets and dramatists who wrote about it in antiquity. The ancient tale of Troy's downfall has been told and re-told, again and again – by Homer, Virgil, Chaucer, Shakespeare, Yeats, Berlioz and Tippett. Wagner considered writing his own version of the *Iliad* – an opera called *Achilleus* – but unfortunately the project got no further than the idea.

Buried within the *Iliad* are references to other poems, now totally lost, that told missing parts of the story. These cross-references to other poems in the cycle were probably left in deliberately to remind listeners of poems they had heard on other evenings; in this way the bard could extend the imaginative experience of his audience endlessly outwards. There was uncertainty in ancient times as to whether this story was history, legend or poetry, and that uncertainty persists to the present day. By the early nineteenth century, most scholars had come to the conclusion that it was poetry, pure fiction, and had no basis in fact at all.

Then, out of the blue, Heinrich Schliemann's excavations at Troy and

Mycenae seemed to provide archaeological proof that Homer was history after all. It was an intensely dramatic moment. Since then scholars have been engaged in fierce debate. But the debate for the past hundred years has revolved mainly around *how much* of the *Iliad* is based on historical events.

THE CAPTURE OF JERUSALEM BY NEBUCHADNEZZAR
(587 BC)

THE ISRAELITES HAD been taken into captivity by the Egyptian pharaoh, and freed from captivity in Egypt and led to the borders of the Promised Land by Moses. Several centuries later they were to be taken into captivity once again.

Nebuchadnezzar II was the last great king of the Chaldees. Although he was presented as an arch-villain by the Israelites, in the years around 600 BC he transformed Babylon into the most magnificent city the world had ever seen. The centrepiece of the city was hailed as one of the Wonders of the World, the Hanging Gardens of Babylon. The city was also equipped with over 50 temples, the greatest of which was the Tower of Babel, a soaring pyramid dedicated to the Babylonians' great god Marduk. The gate dedicated to the goddess Ishtar was covered with dazzlingly brilliant blue-glazed bricks and reliefs of griffins and bulls.

But the Israelites had very good reasons for hating Nebuchadnezzar. He took his army and invaded Judah. He laid siege to Jerusalem. After 16 months, in 587 BC, Jerusalem fell and the Israelites' holy city was sacked by the Babylonian army. The Great Temple of Solomon was wrecked and many Israelites were herded back to Babylon as captives. Nebuchadnezzar went on to the Mediterranean coast where he laid siege to the city of Tyre. After 13 years, Tyre fell to the Babylonian army in 573 BC. In 568 BC, Nebuchadnezzar invaded Egypt.

The Babylonian captivity of the Israelites lasted for 50 years, so probably very few of those taken captive ever returned to Judah. Nebuchadnezzar died in 562 BC after reigning for 43 years. He was succeeded by his son, Evil-Merodach; he released Jehoaichin, the King of Judah who had been kept imprisoned in Babylon for 36 years.

In 539 BC, a Persian army led by Cyrus the Great defeated the Babylonian army under King Nabonidus. Cyrus entered the city of Babylon, where he was greeted as a liberator by the Babylonians. Nabonidus, the last Babylonian king, was either killed or banished. Nabonidus's son Belshazzar made a final effort to drive Cyrus and his army from Babylon in 538 BC and failed.

Now undisputed master of Babylon, Cyrus the Great released the Israelites and allowed them to go back to Jerusalem, although it must have been the case that most of the Israelites were the children and grand-children of those taken captive, and were in effect travelling to a land they had never seen. Cyrus then set about destroying Babylon. On their arrival in Jerusalem, the Israelites began to rebuild their Great Temple to Yahweh.

The traumatic experience was remembered ever afterwards by the Jewish people as a test, another national rite of passage. They had been conquered, humiliated and abused by an all-powerful heathen king, but throughout their ordeal they kept steadfastly loyal to their god, Yahweh. Daniel, their prophet during the captivity, acted as their spokesman. During a banquet given by Prince Belshazzar, a mysterious hand wrote on a wall the words 'mene mene tekel upharsin'. Daniel explained that God had weighed the king in the balance and found him wanting. This was why he lost his kingdom to Cyrus. The god of the Israelites had prevailed. The whole terrible episode was a rite of passage for the Jewish people, one that they would remember as helping to shape their destiny as a persecuted nation. Like Ramesses, Nebuchadnezzar played a key role in creating the Israelites' sense of identity, and their historic sensitivity to oppression.

THE ENLIGHTENMENT
OF THE BUDDHA
(528 BC)

BUDDHISM WAS FOUNDED by Prince Gautama Siddhartha, who was born in about 563 BC. The prince was the son of a rajah who lived north of Benares. To begin with, he lived the conventional life of a prince, but when he was 29 he put court life behind him, abandoned his wife and all his possessions and began to lead the life of an ascetic. For six years he led an extremely austere existence, and at the end of this phase he achieved self-enlightenment.

He achieved enlightenment while sitting under a banyan tree near Bodh Gaya in Bihar. After this historic moment he became known as Buddha, 'the enlightened one'. He formed an order of monks and spent the next 40 years as a wandering teacher, gaining many followers. During his lifetime an order of nuns was also created. He died at the age of about 80 at Kusinagara in Oudh.

At one time it was thought that this biography of the Buddha was purely mythological, but now it seems likely that it was historically true. Monuments put up by Asoka after his conversion, some 200 years after Buddha's death, can still be seen.

Buddha probably did not invent a completely new religion, but was promoting a radical form of an existing Brahmin faith. The key ideas of Buddhism are that human existence is miserable, that non-existence or 'nirvana' is the ideal state, and that nirvana can be achieved by devotion to the rules of Buddhism. Death does not bring nirvana, because souls transmigrate after death. The unholy are condemned to transmigrate through many existences.

Buddhism became a very popular faith, spreading rapidly through India, especially after the conversion of King Asoka. By the third century BC it dominated the whole of the Indian subcontinent. Later it went into decline, especially during persecutions by Brahmanism in the seventh and eighth centuries AD and the ensuing invasion by Islam. Buddhism has nevertheless flourished by spreading to China, Sri Lanka, Burma, Thailand and Japan.

Buddhism became one of the great religions of the world. Because of the distinct beliefs involved, it had a major effect on the cultural development of south-east and eastern Asia. It is hard to imagine what the cultures of the East would have been like without Buddhism.

THE CONCEPT OF OVERPOPULATION
(500 BC)

IN 500 BC, the Chinese philosopher Han Fei Tzu wrote:

In ancient times, people were few but wealthy and without strife. People nowadays think that five sons are not too many. Each son has five sons too and before the grandfather dies there are already 25 descendants. Therefore people are more and wealth is less; they work hard and receive little. The life of a nation depends on having enough food, not upon the number of people.

This is the earliest known comment on birth rates and population growth, and the earliest statement of the concept of over-population.

They were ideas that would return again and again in antiquity. Aristotle emphasized the need for food production to keep pace with population growth. 'When there are too many farmers the excess will be of the best kind; when there are too many mechanics and labourers, it will be of the worst kind.' The concerns of the philosophers were justified. The population of the world grew steadily from three million in 10,000 BC to 250 million by the time of Christ.

In modern times, the person who did most to draw attention to the dangers of overpopulation was Thomas Malthus. In 1798, at the age of 32, he published his great work, *Essay on the Principle of Population*. In this landmark book, Malthus maintained that optimistic views regarding population are groundless, and that population has a tendency to increase faster than the means of maintaining it. Food production increases at an arithmetic rate; population increases at a geometric rate. In other words, human population will go on increasing until there is no food left, or until there is some other check, such as pestilence or war, and then collapse through famine.

Malthus concluded that the poor-law system at that time in England, with its indiscriminate doles given to large families, was actually destructive rather than helpful. Saying so seemed, and to many still seems, heartless and illiberal but it was an honest inference logically arrived at. It was not surprising that his book provoked a storm of controversy. Malthus offered readers the hope that the birth rate might be reduced by sexual abstinence and the use of birth control – and reducing the birth rate was the answer.

But was Malthus wrong? Writing at the end of the eighteenth century, he was unaware of the effects that improved transport in the form of steamships and railways would have. He was unaware that colonization of new regions would open up new areas to food production. As a result, the population collapse he predicted was long delayed. He may not have been wrong in the long term, of course – only wrong for the nineteenth and twentieth centuries.

Malthusian ideas also influenced important economists and ecologists during the 1960s and 1970s. Inspired by the simple Malthusian model, they argued that the human race was facing a 'population explosion' and subsequent starvation was inevitable. In fact, the Malthusian model works only for simpler organisms that depend on a narrow range of foods, the human race is much more flexible. Since the publication of *On Population*, people have developed new, high yield strains of wheat, rice and other key foods, so food supply is more elastic than it once was. The 'population explosion' scare campaigns of the 1960s and 1970s raised general awareness of population issues, and most nations now have more or less effective birth control programmes. Some countries were so effective in reducing population growth, that there are now not enough native young workers to support the rapidly aging population during their dotage.

For better or worse, the ideas of Malthus have continued to be extremely influential over the last 200 years.

THE GOLDEN RULE
(495 BC)

THE CHINESE PHILOSOPHER Confucius (K'ung Fu-tzu) lived from 551 BC until 479 BC. At 19 he became a government official in Lu. When he was 22 he set up a school for young men who wanted to be instructed in principles of right conduct and government; he was in effect training them for government service. He was promoted to ministerial rank, and initially had a very successful career as a civil servant, though later he fell victim to professional jealousy.

After Confucius died in 479 BC, his disciples wrote the *Analects*, a disjointed compilation of their master's sayings and doings. Most of the other writings attributed to Confucius were compiled later and were probably written by other people. The philosophy of 'Confucianism' is therefore only partly the work of Confucius himself. *The Doctrine of the Mean*, by his grandson, and *The Great Learning*, by his disciple Tsang Sin, probably give a good idea of his teachings.

The one book Confucius himself wrote, and referred to as his own book, *Spring and Autumn*, is full of inconsistencies between facts and conclusions, and scarcely seems like the work of a great mind. It has been commented that it would help the reputation of Confucius if it could be shown that he was after all *not* the author of *Spring and Autumn!*

The importance of Confucius lies in his central idea, which was to replace the old traditional religious observances with moral values as the basis for social and political order. In *The Way* (tao), Confucius emphasized the practical virtues of benevolence, reciprocity, respect and personal effort, which were to be developed pragmatically, according to circumstances. His Golden Rule is admirable in its simplicity and common sense:

'What you do not like when done to yourself do not do to others.'

Confucius was treated with great reverence by later generations of Chinese and Confucianism became the state religion of China – remaining so until recently. The sayings and ideas have done much to create the character of Chinese people. Many Chinese know the sayings by heart and they have seeped deep into the Chinese way of life. The main teaching of Confucius is the simplest, the one that lies at the foundation of all moral behaviour, and that is the Golden Rule; 'Do not do to others what you do not like done to yourself.' An individual or a society that accepts that is well on the way to becoming civilized.

THE BATTLE OF
MARATHON
(490 BC)

A PERSIAN ARMY 15,000 strong was sent by Darius against Greece. The Persians were met 25 miles north-east of Athens, between Mount Pentelikon and the Gulf of Marathon, by a Greek army. The Greek army consisted of 11,000 warriors, so they were outnumbered, but they were ably led by Miltiades and the Persian army was repulsed.

In the second century AD, a story was told of Pheidippides, a courier who ran 35km from the battlefield to Athens to tell the citizens of the great victory, and then fell dead from exhaustion. This may be true, but Herodotus told a similar story about a courier called *Philippides*, who ran from Athens to Sparta, a distance of about 260km, to call for help against the Persians. The similarity between the two stories, and even the names of the two couriers, suggests that one or both stories may be false. It was an occasion in Greek history which acquired mythic status, and dramatic embellishments were almost bound to be added.

The mythic quality of Pheidippides' run from Marathon to Athens led to celebratory re-runs over the same distance. The 'marathon' race of 40km (or 25 miles), which is still run today, is in effect a re-enactment of that Greek messenger's ordeal in 490 BC.

The Battle of Marathon was a victory for Athens – the city-state's first great military victory. It nevertheless heralded a long period of conflict with the Persian Empire to the east, including the Battles of Thermopylae, Salamis and Plataea. The struggle ended in victory for the Greeks under the command of Pausanias in 479 BC.

Just as the saga of the Israelites' periods of bondage in Egypt and Babylon became part of their national identity, so the traumatic struggle for survival against the invading Persians became part of the Athenians' sense of national identity.

THE BUILDING OF THE
PARTHENON
(438 BC)

PERICLES WAS THE greatest leader to emerge in ancient Athens. He held the office of general-in-command in the city-state from 443 until 429 BC, exerting power through force of personality; he was the most persuasive and influential speaker in the assembly. The rise of Pericles was associated with an expansion of Athenian power. His most ambitious project was the formation of a grand Hellenic confederation, which he proposed with the intention of putting an end to wars that were mutually destructive.

It was a time when Athenians were achieving incredible things. Aeschylus, Sophocles and Euripides were writing some of the greatest dramas ever to be written. Pheidias and his pupils and assistants were designing and creating some of the finest buildings and sculptures ever to be made. Pericles was in effect the patron of artists such as Pheidias, Callicrates and Ictinus. Under the rule of Pericles, Athens reached a peak of civilization that would never be surpassed – anywhere. It was Pericles who commissioned the Parthenon and many other buildings on the Acropolis.

It was natural that Pheidias, the best sculptor of his time, should be commissioned to create the most important statues for the city of Athens as part of a major rebuilding programme. Pericles also made Pheidias the superintendent for all public works, which meant that he controlled the architecture that would be a setting for his sculptures. He led a team of designers and craftsmen including architects, stone carvers and bronze-workers.

Pericles wanted to reshape the monuments on the Acropolis at Athens so that they made a more imposing and unified whole. Pheidias designed and created the Propylaea (the gateway buildings through which people were to enter the Acropolis). He also created the Parthenon, the huge and stately temple to Athena which still dominates Athens and which to many has come to symbolize not just ancient Greek but Western civilization as a whole. The layout appears informal, but it is governed by elaborate trigonometry, which makes the buildings more imposing.

Pheidias designed, but probably did not carve, the marble sculptures that fitted on the walls of the Parthenon. Pheidias was not known for marble statues; the works he was known for were made of bronze, gold and ivory. It is likely that the marble statuary on the Parthenon was the work of his pupils, very likely Alcamenes and Agoracritus.

Pheidias also designed and oversaw the construction of the phenomenal gigantic statue of Athena that stood inside the Parthenon. It was a hollow structure made of timber-framing, and its surface was sheathed in ivory and gold. The individual pieces of ivory were necessarily small, but they were individually crafted and tacked onto the wooden frame to create an illusion of vast expanses of pale skin. The statue, known as Athena Parthenos, the Virgin Athena, was dedicated in 438 BC. Although the statue itself was destroyed long ago, we know what it looked like because small-scale marble copies of it were made; two have been found in Athens. The statue showed the goddess Athena as the protectress of the city, wearing a helmet and carrying a shield and a huge spear. The concept was borrowed or recycled later on by the Romans for their goddess Fortuna, and by the British for their patron goddess Britannia. So Pheidias produced an enduring icon of a protecting goddess.

The Parthenon is an icon of Western civilization, and often seen as its starting-point. It also became a model for many later buildings, for instance in ancient Rome, Renaissance Europe and even modern North America, where the Lincoln Memorial (completed in 1922) owes much to the ancient temple, though the seated statue of Lincoln himself is modelled on Pheidias' statue of the enthroned Zeus at Olympia.

THE HIPPOCRATIC
OATH
(429 BC)

PLAGUE KILLED HALF the population of Athens in the year 429 BC. Some may have seen the plague as a punishment for sinful behaviour, but as the historian Thucydides later commented, it made no difference whether people worshipped the gods or not, they perished in the plague just the same. One of those who survived the plague was the physician Hippocrates.

Hippocrates was the first to say that diseases are not supernatural in origin and are not sent by the gods as a punishment. He was also the first to use medical terms that are in common usage today, including chronic, crisis, convalescence, paroxysm and relapse. He saw fever as the human body's struggle to cure itself. Hippocrates' approach to human illness was the beginning of scientific medicine.

Hippocrates devised the Hippocratic Oath. This included a series of undertakings:

I will use treatment to help the sick according to my ability and judgement, and will never use it to injure or wrong them. I will not give poison to anyone though asked to do so … Whatsoever in the course of practice I see or hear that ought never to be published abroad, I will not divulge, but consider such things to be holy secrets. Now if I keep this oath and break it not, may I enjoy honour, but if I transgress may the opposite befall me.

The Hippocratic Oath is still the foundation of ethical practice among doctors all round the world. It lies behind the objection that many doctors have to euthanasia and assisted suicide.

THE SPARTAN
CAPTURE OF ATHENS
(405 BC)

A GREAT POWER struggle developed between the city-states of Sparta and Athens. In 407 BC Lysander, the leader of the Spartans, refused to be tempted out of the port of Ephesus to do battle with Alcibiades, the Athenian commander. Alcibiades ran out of supplies and sailed north along the Anatolian coast to raid harbour towns for supplies. An Athenian squadron was left behind under the command of Antiochus, who against strict orders taunted Lysander. This time Lysander did respond, sailing out of Ephesus and defeating the Athenian squadron. This defeat, at Notium, gave Alcibiades' enemies in Athens the excuse they were hoping for to strip him of his command.

In 406 BC, Alcibiades fled to the north in disgrace, while he was replaced by a board of Athenian generals. The Spartans offered to make peace, but their offer was rejected. At this point Cyrus, the Persian leader, demanded that Lysander should take command of a fleet in the Hellespont.

In 405 BC, the Athenian fleet followed Lysander to the Hellespont, where it was destroyed while drawn up on a beach. Only ten Athenian ships escaped under the command of Conon. Lysander then took his fleet to Piraeus, the port of Athens, to blockade it, while the Spartan King Pausanias marched on Athens, laid siege to the city and set about starving it into submission. In the spring of 404 BC, Athens fell and the Athenian leader Cleophon was executed. In this dramatic way the First Peloponnesian War came to an end.

The Athenians were always to remember this as a humiliating and traumatic episode. Theramenes managed to secure terms from the Spartans that saved the city from destruction, but the Long Walls flanking the route from Athens to the harbour were torn down and the Athenian Empire was dismantled. It was the end of the great age of Athens, and a major rite of passage.

THE DEATH OF SOCRATES
(399 BC)

At THE AGE of 70, the Greek philosopher Socrates was condemned to death for flouting conventional ideas and for corrupting the youth of Athens with his heresies. Surrounded by a group of his pupils, he obediently drank hemlock and died. His best-known pupil, Plato, was very conspicuously not there, officially because he was ill though perhaps out of fear.

One major effect of Socrates' death was to make Plato very circumspect. As a result, some of Plato's writings have a curiously ambivalent quality. He claimed to be unwell at the time of Socrates' death, yet he wrote the definitive account of the execution, presumably after interviewing those who did have the courage to attend; it reads like an eyewitness account, even though it is not.

The ambivalence and equivocation reached a peak in his re-telling of the Atlantis story. During the narrative, Plato insists that the story is true, while the events described sound fanciful. In the end, he created an almost insoluble puzzle for later generations to try to solve. Atlantis might be true, or it might be completely fictitious. Was he being a novelist, a very clever story-teller, or was he passing on a piece of forgotten history? He said he was telling the truth. Many scholars have discussed what Plato meant by truth; he seems to have meant more than one thing by it. He also expounded views that he said were those of Socrates, but perhaps he was giving his own views and taking safe cover behind his dead teacher. If it came to a trial, a thought which must have hovered at the back of his mind all his life, he could always claim that he was only quoting somebody else. It was Socrates who had said all that.

Plato might have entered public life as a politician, but the double trauma of the defeat and humiliation of Athens in 404 BC and the death of Socrates five years later put him off politics for ever. Socrates had been 'the most upright man then living'. Philosophy was safer, but not totally safe. It may have been partly guilt at having let Socrates down at the last moment that made Plato commit so much time in presenting Socrates' ideas to the world. Socrates was a talker and a teacher, not a writer, so it was only through Plato that Socrates was able to reach later generations.

The execution of Socrates was a momentous event in itself – the judicial murder of a great philosopher. But it also showed that ideas, and especially ideas that are different from those of the political elite, are often regarded as dangerous. It was a similar episode to the Burning of the Books by the Qin emperor, or the ant-Communist witch hunt in the United States after the Second World War. Destroying ideas is destroying opposition.

THE BUILDING OF THE TOMB OF MAUSOLUS

(354 BC)

A GREAT TOMB was raised at Halikarnassos (modern Bodrum) on the south-west coast of Anatolia (modern Turkey) for King Mausolus. He was ruler of Caria from 377 to 353 BC. The building was so big and the sculptured decoration was so lavish that it stood out as something exceptional in the ancient world.

The site has been completely cleared by excavation and there is little to see except the reconstructed outline of the tomb chamber and a staircase down which the body of King Mausolus was taken. There is nothing left of the building itself, but it was described in antiquity and some surviving sculptures help to establish the scale. There was a rectangular stone base 34m across and 18m high. On top of this was a colonnade of 36 Ionic columns supporting a pyramid-shaped roof. The pyramid was a step pyramid, culminating in a platform for a four-horse chariot. The overall height of the monument was about 43m. Four famous Greek sculptors were commissioned, and each made the sculpted figures for one side of the building.

The tomb, ordered by the wife of Mausolus, Artemisia, was obviously intended to commemorate and glorify Mausolus himself. Lucian wrote an imaginary dialogue between Diogenes the philosopher and Mausolus in the underworld. In it, the dead Diogenes asked the spirit of Mausolus why he expected to be honoured more than everyone else. Mausolus answered, 'Because I have a gigantic monument such as no other person has.' Diogenes said he could not see any benefit, unless Mausolus wanted to prove he was a heavier burden than everyone else. Diogenes predicted that in the end Mausolus would be disappointed. Diogenes did not know if he, Diogenes, had a tomb at all, but the account of his life was in any event built on safer foundations than the tomb of Mausolus.

But it was probably in Artemisia's mind to do something more than just glorify her dead husband. The building was a fusion of Greek and non-Greek architecture and Mausolus and his wife hoped that a fusion of Greek and non-Greek civilizations would flow from a Carian empire with Halikarnossos as its capital. That did not happen.

The mausoleum stood more or less intact until the thirteenth century AD, when the upper part fell down in an earthquake. In the fifteenth century, the Knights Hospitallers decided to rebuild their castle at Bodrum and robbed the ruined Mausoleum of most of its squared stone.

The Tomb of Mausolus became famous as one of the handful of 'must-see' sights of the ancient world, the Seven Wonders of the World. It also gave its name – mausoleum – to a distinctive type of monument, an impressive building to house a tomb.

THE BATTLE OF
CHAERONEA
(338 BC)

PHILIP OF MACEDON was the ruler of a kingdom in the north of Greece, pursuing a policy of aggression against his neighbours. In 340 BC, Philip failed to take Byzantium after a siege. The Byzantine sentries saw the Macedonian warriors advancing by the light of the moon. The Byzantines then adopted the crescent moon symbol of their goddess Hecate as the symbol of Byzantium itself; it was the moon which had saved the city from Philip of Macedon. The kingdoms of Greece were struggling for their independence from Philip's ambition, but this struggle was lost when he defeated an army of Athenians and Thebans at the decisive Battle of Chaeronea in western Boeotia in central Greece. In this fateful battle, which established the supremacy of Macedonia over the rest of the Greek kingdoms, Alexander commanded a section of his father's cavalry. Though he was only 18, he already showed great skill as a warrior and leader. The battle was the making of Alexander, and he was entrusted with the task of acting as his father's ambassador to Athens. He was a youth carefully groomed for kingship.

When Alexander was 20, Philip of Macedon was assassinated at the wedding feast of his daughter. It is not known whether Alexander was involved in the conspiracy to kill his father, but the assassination looks like a well-orchestrated palace coup, and the timing suited Alexander perfectly. There is a suspicion that Olympias, Alexander's mother played a part in it.

While Alexander was away making war on a tribe in the north, the people of Thebes, to the south, heard a rumour that he was dead and revolted against Macedonian domination, inviting Athens to join them in a rebellion. Alexander stormed Thebes with his army and destroyed every building except the temples and the house of the poet Pindar. The incident shows several aspects of the nature of Alexander: the well-judged reverence for certain things, the poignant sentimentality, the grand gesture, the brutality, the wanton destructiveness.

The father had dreamed of conquering Persia; now the son wanted to outdo the father by achieving it. In 334 BC, Alexander crossed the Hellespont with an army 35,000 strong, to meet the Persian army on the banks of the Granicus River. The great adventure of the east had begun. But the Battle of Chaeronea was an important preamble to Alexander's empire-building, in that it established Macedon's precedence in Greece – and Alexander's ability as a military leader. It was at the Battle of Chaeronea that he proved himself.

THE BATTLE OF
ARBELA
(331 BC)

THE BATTLE OF Arbela (or Gaugamela) took place in northern Mesopotamia. Alexander had already won an earlier victory over Darius's Persian army at the Battle of Issus in 333 BC, but the Persian king had escaped from the battlefield.

After a seven-month siege, Alexander captured Tyre by building a causeway out to the island. He killed 8,000 citizens of Tyre, selling 30,000 more into slavery. This operation is considered Alexander's greatest military achievement. He went on to do the same to Gaza. After that came Egypt, where Alexander was welcomed as a deliverer; the Egyptians hated their harsh Persian rulers. On the Nile Delta, Alexander founded a new city, naming it after himself – Alexandria.

In 331 BC, Alexander turned back to deal with the Persian army. Darius had gathered an enormous host, including the Persian heavy cavalry and many chariots with scythelike blades protruding from the wheel-axles. The Persians cleared and smoothed a huge level plain at Arbela, east of the River Tigris, to make an arena where their chariots could be effectively deployed. In the Battle of Arbela (or Gaugamela) which followed, Alexander's army routed Darius's and the Persian army retreated. It was one of the most decisive battles in history. Alexander lost fewer than 500 men in this battle, while it is estimated that Darius lost up to 90,000 men. The Persian losses were crippling. The outcome of the battle was that Alexander became the undisputed master of the huge Persian Empire. Babylon surrendered, and Alexander took the Persian cities of Susa and Persepolis, yielding him vast treasures in gold and silver. The Achaemenid dynasty of Persian rulers, founded in 550 BC had come to an end. Now it was Alexander's empire – and he would have no dynasty, no real successor at all.

At Persepolis, Alexander committed some of his worst atrocities. All the inhabitants of the city were either killed or sold as slaves, and finally the great and beautiful city was burned to the ground. It was a terrible act of vandalism.

An almost inevitable outcome of the Persian defeat at Arbela was the death of Darius. In 330 BC, Darius III was murdered by his satrap Bessus. Ever-volatile, Alexander was moved to tears by this news. He, meanwhile, was free to do as he liked with his new-found empire. He disgraced himself by destroying the beautiful city of Persepolis, influenced perhaps by his saturation in Homer, with his heroic 'sackers of cities'. It took 5,000 camels and 20,000 mules to carry off the loot when Alexander sacked Persepolis.

The victory at Arbela and the conquest of Persia enabled Alexander to go on eastwards to conquer Samarkand in 329 BC and invade northern India in 327 BC. Without that victory, he would probably not be remembered as 'the Great'.

THE BUILDING OF THE PHAROS OF ALEXANDRIA

(285 BC)

THE ISLAND OF Pharos is a limestone outcrop that gave a solid foundation for building in the midst of an expanse of delta sand washed out by the Nile. Legend had Helen of Troy landing there but being bored because there was nothing to see.

In 332 BC, Alexander liberated Egypt from Persian rule. He was only there for a few months but made a lasting impact. On his arrival, the island was known only as the home of the sea-god Proteus. It stood a little offshore from the Western Mouth of the Nile Delta. On the coast was a small fishing village called Rhacotis. Like an early Laurence Llewellyn-Bowen, Alexander saw the potential of Rhacotis and ordered a make-over. A new city was to be founded there, the greatest though not the only one to bear his name. It was designed by Dinocrates of Rhodes following the very latest grid system of roads devised by Hippodamus of Miletus.

A mole was run from the island of Pharos south to the mainland, creating two harbours, one facing east and one facing west. This was a favoured arrangement in the ancient Mediterranean, where the square-rigged ships always had to sail before the wind. Then the Pharos lighthouse was begun. The work seems to have been ordered after Alexander's death by his boyhood friend and general, Ptolemy I, who acquired Egypt for himself. Ptolemy also acquired for himself the body of Alexander as it was being carried back for burial in the Macedonian royal burial ground at Vergina. Ptolemy snatched Alexander's body and took it to Alexandria where it was to be buried in a magnificent mausoleum near the Pharos. Alexander's tomb has never been discovered.

The Egyptian coastline is very flat and featureless, so a visible marker for the port of Alexandria was essential. Building work on the Pharos began in 297 BC, sponsored by Sostratus, a courtier who was possibly also the architect.

The lighthouse was a three-tiered white marble structure, 100m high altogether. The lowest (square) stage was 60m high, the second (octagonal) stage was 30m, the third (round) stage was 10m high. Mounted on top of that was a 5m tall statue of Zeus. The entrance was not at ground level, but reached by way of a ramp. At the top of the first stage there were statues of tritons, blowing trumpets to all points of the compass. The Pharos was an impressive building in its own right. At night it must have been awe-inspiring. The flames from a fire kept burning inside the tower were reflected out to sea by some huge polished bronze mirrors mounted at the top. Probably by day the sun would have been reflected in the mirrors, and most sailing happened by day in antiquity anyway. The Pharos became one of the Seven Wonders of the World.

The lighthouse was still standing to its full height in the early middle ages, but it was badly damaged by earthquakes in AD 956, 1303 and 1323. An Arab traveller who visited the island in 1166 described a visit to the lighthouse, giving its state in vivid detail.

The doorway is high up. A ramp 183m long used to lead up to it. The ramp rests on a series of 16 arches, each getting gradually higher until the doorway is reached ... Eventually we reached the first stage of the Pharos. There was no stairway but a ramp that gradually ascended around the cylindrical core of this huge building ... When we arrived at the top of the first stage we measured its height from the ground with a piece of string from which we hung a stone – it was 57.73m. The parapet was 1.83m high. In the middle of the platform of the first stage the building continued upwards, but now in the shape of an octagon with each face 18.3m long and 3.45m from the parapet. This stage was taller than its base line. Entering, we found a staircase with 18 steps and arrived at the middle of the upper floor. We measured again with the string and found that it was 27.45m above the first stage. In the centre of the platform on top of the second stage the building continued upward in cylindrical form with a diameter of 75m. From the foot of the wall to the parapet was 2.2m. We entered and climbed 31 steps. The height of the third stage was 7.32m. On the platform of the third stage is a mosque with four doors and a cupola.'

This description by people who were actually walking round it and taking measurements gives a very precise and compelling idea of what the Pharos was like in 1166. By 1326 it was no longer possible to enter the structure. Today the site of the Pharos is covered by the square fort of Kait Bey, which was built from stone recycled from the Pharos.

The Pharos was the first lighthouse in the world, and the definitive lighthouse much the same way the Parthenon was the most emblematic, the definitive Greek temple. The name of the Pharos of Alexandria would give its name to all lighthouses in the ancient Greek world.

THE BUILDING OF THE COLOSSUS OF RHODES
(282 BC)

THE ISLAND OF Rhodes, just off the south-west corner of Asia Minor, was at the crossroads of two important sea routes, one running between Miletus and Egypt, and the other running between Greece and Cyprus. In the ancient world it had enormous commercial value. For a long time it was divided into three territories, governed from the towns of Ialysos, Lindos and Kamiros. In 408 BC, the three city-states joined forces to build a federal capital at Rhodes; from then on the new port handled most of the island's commercial traffic in its five harbours.

Rhodes was hugely successful, quickly growing to become a city of 75,000 people. This also made it politically vulnerable, and when the Rhodians decided to join the Athenian island confederacy, Mausolus of Caria stopped them by setting up a garrison there. Rhodes sided with the Persians, but when it was clear that Alexander was the man of the hour it changed sides and so avoided disaster.

Rhodes endured a year-long siege by Demetrius in 305 BC. Demetrius was so impressed by the bravery of the Rhodians that he left them all his siege engines and ammunition when he withdrew. The Rhodians sold all this gear for a large sum, and used it to make an enormous bronze statue of their patron, Helios the Sun god. The sculptor they commissioned was Chares of Lindos. It took from 294 until 282 BC for Chares and his team to produce a bronze statue 33m tall.

The Colossus is mentioned many times by ancient writers, but they give little in the way of descriptive detail, even about its site. The figure was a naked standing figure of the Sun god, probably with its legs together and with one arm raised holding a torch aloft, rather like the Statue of Liberty in New York. The head was probably the same as shown on ancient coins:

a young man's head with long wavy hair and rays of light radiating like the spikes of a crown.

The story that the Colossus stood with its legs apart, straddling the entrance to the Mandraki harbour was current in the fourteenth century, but this can never have been true. The harbour entrance is 400m wide, and the statue would in any case have been unstable with its legs separated in this way. The Colossus is more likely to have stood on the site now occupied by Fort St Nicholas. This has a huge round base, which may represent the base for the Colossus, and the fort itself contains a lot of recycled stone, which could have come from the plinth for the statue.

The statue only remained standing for 50 years before it fell in an earthquake in 226 BC, breaking off at the knees. It was still a very impressive sight, with massive fingers that were in themselves larger than most statues. Where limbs had broken off, there were yawning holes where great masses of rock could be seen inside – Chares' attempt to weight the lower half of the statue and give it some stability. The broken statue remained where it fell for 900 years. Ptolemy III of Egypt offered to pay to have it re-erected, but the Rhodians declined the offer; they had been forbidden by an oracle to re-erect it. In AD 654, Arabs plundering Rhodes took away the fragments, which were last seen travelling slowly towards Syria on the backs of 900 camels.

The Colossus became one of the Seven Wonders of the World. Because of huge size and early destruction, it became a kind of legend. Other harbour towns of the ancient world copied the idea, raising statues and other monuments at their harbour entrances such as Ostia and Caesarea. The idea was even copied in modern times, in the Statue of Liberty designed by Auguste Bartholdi. Dedicated in 1886, this is 46m high, even taller than the Colossus of Rhodes. The Colossus was designed to express the spirit of a city, the ancient city of Rhodes. The Statue of Liberty came to express the spirit not just of a city, the city of New York, but the whole of the United States, welcoming the poor and the oppressed to the Land of the Free.

THE INVENTION OF
THE ARCHIMEDEAN
SCREW
(265 BC)

ARCHIMEDES, WHO WAS born in Syracuse in around 287 BC, moved in the upper circles of Syracusan society and was on very friendly terms with the king, Hieron. After travelling to Alexandria, Archimedes returned to Syracuse and devoted himself to the lifelong study of mathematics.

Archimedes has a central importance in the study of mathematics, but he is more famous for his inventions, on which he himself seems to have set no value at all. He regarded applied mathematics as a very inferior pursuit. It was probably while he was in Egypt that he invented the Archimedean screw that is still in use there for raising water to irrigate fields. It consists of a hollow cylinder, within which a spiral surface is rotated by a handle at the top. The lower end of the cylinder is placed in the water, and when the handle is turned the water is drawn up it, pouring out of the top.

In 212 BC, Archimedes was in Syracuse when it was besieged and attacked by a Roman force under Marcellus. Following the fall of Syracuse, there was a general massacre of citizens, in which Archimedes perished. When Cicero was posted to Sicily as a Roman administrator in 75 BC, he found the tomb of Archimedes overgrown with thorns and briers. Syracuse had forgotten the tomb of one of its greatest citizens.

The Archimedean screw was a most original and useful invention, one that has been in constant use since Archimedes' time for raising water from rivers and ditches up onto fields, or out of drainage ditches into embanked rivers. Like all good inventions, it is very easy to operate, efficient and adaptable. In the Netherlands, large steel Archimedean screws, electrically powered, are used today to raise water from drainage ditches. It is an invention of great versatility.

THE QIN EMPEROR'S BOOK BURNING

(212 BC)

THE QIN EMPEROR (259–210 BC) was the first emperor of China. It was the rulers of the state of Qin, on the north-west frontier, who unified the states of China into a single empire. The Qin emperor who ascended the throne in 246 BC styled himself Shi Huang Ti. He abolished the many small states and principalities, and set up a single state with 36 provinces. Over each province, the emperor set officials and administrators appointed directly by himself and responsible directly to him. It was a straightforward hierarchical system, and created at a single stroke.

Power was centralized, and to symbolize that centralization the Qin emperor built a new capital. He also introduced a uniform system of weights and measures, and a single currency, aiding commerce and unity. The infrastructure was improved by building roads and canals; food production was increased by digging irrigation and drainage channels. He also extended the empire by conquest, incorporating several new provinces. By the year 221 BC what is recognizable as China, which takes its name from this dynasty, had been created. To defend the new empire from the north and north-west, the most frequent direction of attack by barbarians, the emperor ordered the building of the Great Wall of China.

One of the most destructive and controversial actions of the Qin emperor was the suppression of free speech, which included the suppression of Confucianism, which he associated with the previous era. The attempt to wipe out all memory of the previous era was unpopular at the time – and has been condemned by subsequent generations of Chinese too. The scholars who remained loyal to Confucius were buried alive. The existing literature on philosophy and politics were collected and destroyed. This infamous 'Burning of the Books' happened in 212 BC. The only books to be exempt were on divination, pharmacy, medicine and agriculture. He ordered scholars not to discuss the past.

Shih Huang Ti died in 210 BC and was buried in a magnificent burial mound guarded by the famous Terracotta Army. Almost as soon as his strong arm was removed, China disintegrated again. The Qin emperor probably tried to achieve too much too quickly and with too much violence. How could he have expected to stop people discussing the past? It was in defiance of human nature. The recent rediscovery of the Terracotta Army ironically caused everyone to start discussing China's past all over again.

The Qin Emperor's book burning was only the first of many such gestures. In 1497, the Florentine prior-dictator Savonarola celebrated the annual carnival with a 'bonfire of the vanities' in the Piazza della Signoria. This included carnival masks, and books and pictures that Savonarola considered indecent. In Nazi Germany in the 1930s, books regarded as harmful were similarly burnt. It is a particularly vivid and extreme type of censorship, which invites the reaction, 'Why are you so afraid of other people's ideas? Are you afraid they might be right?'

CAESAR'S INVASION OF GAUL
(58 BC)

GAIUS JULIUS CAESAR was born in 102 BC to an old Roman patrician family. As a young man he progressed from one minor public position to another, just like any other young aristocrat. In 65 BC as curule aedile he spent lavishly on games and public buildings. He was elected pontifex maximus in 63 BC and praetor for 62 BC. In 61 BC he was governor of Hispania Ulterior and on his return was elected consul for 59 BC. He negotiated a reconciliation between Pompey and Crassus and then established the informal alliance called 'the First Triumvirate'.

At this stage in his life, Julius Caesar was building a conventional political career, collecting an impressive portfolio of offices and positions, establishing his position at the forefront of Roman public life.

Then, to give himself a clear political advantage over other Romans, he engineered his military career, spending nine years extending the Roman Empire to the west. He first defeated the Helvetii tribe at Bibracte in 58 BC, then went on to defeat the Belgic confederacy in north-west Gaul. By 56 BC, he was tackling tribes such as the Veneti in Brittany and Normandy and the Aquitani in south-west Gaul. Bit by bit he conquered Gaul for the Roman Empire. It was in itself an historic event.

Caesar's conquest of Gaul and his annexation of it for the Roman Empire also made possible the future conquest of Britain, and in 54 BC he forced a nominal surrender of south-east England. This prepared the way for the Claudian invasion a few decades later, and it must have impressed the Romans, who cannot seriously have expected the Empire to extend so far to the north. Along the way, he amassed great wealth and created a military establishment that few other Romans could rival.

Vercingetorix, the leader of the Arverni tribe, led a spirited final resistance to Roman domination; the Arverni were quickly joined by other tribes, especially the Bituriges. Caesar had believed that Gaul was conquered and had returned to Italy, but he reappeared in Gaul, slipping past Vercingetorix to join his legions. Vercingetorix knew that it was useless to take on Caesar and his experienced Roman legionaries in open battle, but could not expect to avoid it for ever. Caesar engaged the Gauls under Vercingetorix in battle near Dijon, beat him and then surrounded him and his warriors at the huge Gaulish fortress of Alesia in 52 BC. Caesar surrounded the fort with lines of earthworks, behind which his soldiers were able to circulate safely, rather like the trenches used in Flanders in the First World War. Another Gaulish chief, Vercassivellaunus, made a valiant attempt to relieve Vercingetorix, but was defeated after a desperate struggle. When Alesia finally fell, Vercingetorix surrendered to Julius Caesar. This major event marked the last gasp of Gaulish resistance, and the conclusion of the conquest of Gaul.

The success in Gaul was also the making of Julius Caesar's political career. He was able to return to Rome and go on, in 44 BC, to dictatorship for life.

THE ASSASSINATION OF
JULIUS CAESAR
(44 BC)

BY 45 BC, Julius Caesar was at the height of his success, the most powerful figure in the Roman world. A problem was that some people, both common people and courtiers, wanted to shower him with ever higher honours, while others were alarmed at the emergence of a personal dictatorship. It is unclear whether Caesar himself really wanted these honours. He certainly claimed that he didn't. When he was in the Senate, he made a point of behaving towards the others present as if they were all equals together, and he said that he should have honours taken away: he had too many already.

But the idea of making Julius Caesar king was put about, perhaps by enemies who wanted to see him fall. It was naturally assumed that men who had reached a certain level in the honours race would seek to climb to the next rung. This may be why so many republicans feared Julius Caesar. He could reach up to the next rung, so he certainly would.

Julius Caesar spent the last few months of his life planning a huge military campaign against Parthia. The idea was to avenge the defeat of Crassus. It may be that, to him, being away from Rome on campaign was actually preferable to staying in Rome and dealing with the possibly insoluble problem of his precise personal status. It may also be that a war against foreign enemies would unite Rome and make her forget all these petty quarrels.

Although he had said to the Senate that he had too many honours already, he went on accepting them, so as not to appear ungrateful. He was appointed 'perpetual dictator' and started wearing the red boots of the kings of Alba Longa. Antony publicly offered him a diadem, a white linen band, which was the Greek symbol of monarchy. Caesar refused the offered diadem, but it is not clear whether he was feigning modesty; he may have intended to accept it if offered it again.

The plot to assassinate Caesar seems to have been instigated by Cassius. Cassius was aggrieved because he felt he had been slighted by not being offered a command in the forthcoming war against Parthia. Cassius persuaded his brother-in-law Brutus to join the plot.

Brutus was fanatical and merciless. He had fought on Pompey's side at Pharsalia, like Cassius. Both had been pardoned by Casear. Julius Caesar had in effect been more than generous to both of them and they owed him a debt of gratitude. Perhaps that was one of the reasons why they hated him – the sense of obligation. Neither Brutus nor Cassius had any real reason to assassinate Julius Caesar, but Cassius's minor feeling of slight combined with Brutus's tendency to fanaticism was enough to do it. It became an obsession.

Caesar knew of the plot to assassinate him, but disregarded the warnings. He was attacked and stabbed to death at a senate meeting in the Theatrum Pompeium by a group of conspirators, most of whom had been pardoned by Caesar and had their careers advanced by him; the attack was a monstrous act of ingratitude.

The immediate aftermath of Caesar's death was a kind of paralyzed shock. The sheer pointlessness of the assassination was underlined by the assassins' failure to create an alternative government in the days and weeks that followed. Caesar had not nominated a political heir, but he had left a huge amount of money to one man. He had left three-quarters of his estate to the 18 year old Gaius Octavius, who was the son of his niece Atia. Octavian had been sent to Greece to serve with the Legions in the preparations for the war with Parthia. Now, of course, he returned at the head of Caesar's legions to claim his inheritance. With that huge fortune, and Julius Caesar's evident blessing behind him, he was bound to wield enormous power.

After a period of considerable chaos, the assassination of Julius Caesar led to the reign of Augustus and therefore, ironically, to a long line not of kings but of emperors.

THE CRUCIFIXION
(AD 33)

THE LIFE OF Jesus is extremely difficult to reconstruct, because the only documents available were written, with conversion in mind, by devoted disciples long after the events they describe. The information in the four canonical ('approved') gospels and the Acts of the Apostles covers a total of only 50 days in his life, and contains little in the way of personal detail. He was probably born in about 6 BC, the first-born son of Mary, the wife of Joseph, a carpenter.

As a boy, it is likely that Jesus followed his father's trade as a carpenter. At the age of 12 he was found, by his astonished mother, knowledgeably discussing serious religious issues with priests. When he was 18 he was baptized by his cousin John the Baptist, and this experience seems to have given him an intimation of his mission. Jesus spent 40 days in the wilderness, wrestling with all kinds of temptations. After this rite of passage, he gathered 12 disciples and organized two missionary journeys round Galilee, which culminated in a huge rally where it was said he miraculously fed 5,000 people.

It was while on his missionary journeys with his small group of disciples that Jesus revealed himself to his disciples as the Messiah, the promised saviour who would release the Jews, but also hinted at his impending suffering, death and resurrection. It is a great puzzle that Jesus never claimed to be the Messiah, never claimed to be the Son of God; these claims were made on his behalf. He allowed Peter to call him the Messiah, and he is alleged to have admitted it to the High Priest at his trial, though the account of the trial is suspect. He nevertheless made it clear that people needed to respond to him in an appropriate, special and reverential way if they were to be spiritually saved.

At his famous Last Supper with the disciples in Jerusalem, the Passover meal, Jesus hinted that he would be betrayed by one of them. Judas Iscariot, one of the disciples, immediately afterwards went to the authorities, and that betrayal led to the arrest of Jesus within a few hours in the Garden of Gethsemane.

Jesus was subjected to a hurried trial and condemned to death for blasphemy by a Jewish council. He was then taken before the Roman procurator for confirmation of the sentence. According to the gospels, Pilate could find no grounds for convicting Jesus of treason because he had not claimed to be the king of a territory, only the King of the Jews. The suspicion among scholars is that the narrative has been tampered with in order to vindicate the Romans and put the blame for Jesus's death squarely onto the Jews. It is likely that Pilate would have found Jesus guilty for causing a civil disturbance, and if the Sanhedrin had found him guilty of blasphemy the sentence should have been stoning.

Jesus was crucified on the Passover, the day when Jews by custom sacrificed the Passover lamb, hence the references in Christian mythology to the 'Lamb of God': Jesus was the sacrificial lamb. Pilate was surprised when he was told that Jesus was dead after hanging on the cross for only a few hours, but gave permission for the body to be taken down for burial. Joseph of Arimathea provided his own tomb.

Three days later the disciples had various indications that Jesus had 'risen from the dead'. A great deal of discussion over the centuries has failed to resolve the question of what really happened that first Easter Morning, but the gospel accounts invite us to believe that Jesus physically came back to life in the tomb, and walked out into the garden to greet Mary Magdalene, who had arrived to anoint his body. Some Christians believe that Jesus remained physically dead, but the disciples were overwhelmed by his spiritual presence. Another possibility is that Jesus was not actually dead but unconscious when taken down from the cross, and revived later, maybe even that the crucifixion was somehow stage-managed so that Jesus would survive the ordeal.

Whatever happened, followers who had scattered in dismay immediately after his shameful execution as a common criminal were reunited in Jerusalem a few weeks later. There were about 120 of them, and for some reason they were fired with a common conviction that Jesus was alive, had been seen by several people and would shortly return as the Messiah. They adopted an attitude that had been gradually evolving during Jesus's lifetime, an attitude of religious faith.

The disciples were so convinced that the spiritual presence of Jesus was still with them that they committed the rest of their lives, and risked martyrdom, to preach the Christian message. They did so with enthusiasm and success. Within a few centuries it became the official religion of the Roman Empire, and went on from there to become one of the major world religions. The Crucifixion as an image was not something that the early Christians dwelt on, possibly because in the Roman world it was as commonplace as a public hanging in eighteenth century England, and regarded as a humiliating and shameful end. It was only long after crucifixion as a routine method of execution had passed into history that the Crucifixion of Jesus began to acquire a mythic force.

The initial symbol of Christianity was not the Cross but the simplest drawing of a fish. There had been a superstition for hundreds of years that the name of God, Yahweh, should not be spoken. In the early days of Christianity a similar superstition grew up about the name of Christ; it could not be spoken. Instead he was referred to as Ichthys, the Fish, and the Fish became his symbol. Although it is not immediately obvious, the word Ichthys is a Greek acronym or rebus. The letters of the word are the initial letters of the phrase *Iesos Christos Theou Huios Soter*, which means 'Jesus Christ, Son of God, our Saviour'. In the early days it was dangerous to be a Christian, so secret codes like this were a safety measure rather than a game. It was also the case that early Christianity was saturated with fish symbolism – Jesus adopted fishermen from the Sea of Galilee and made them 'fishers of men'; he fed the 5000 with loaves and fishes, and so on. So the Fish seemed an apt symbol.

The Chi-Rho symbol was also used as a symbol for Christ. It was quite some time before the gallows on which Christ died became the pre-eminent symbol of the faith. Then it was to appear in various guises, as the Cross of St George, as the national flag of England, as the insignia of the Knights Templar, as the symbol of an international relief organization, the Red Cross, as the ground plan for churches and cathedrals.

It was not for hundreds of years that an image of the suffering Christ appeared, then that image came to dominate the entire medieval period. It was Christ's sufferings on the Cross that people focused on as the ultimate proof of his love for the human race, redeeming the whole human race of its sins, and it introduced a pervasive morbidity into the Christian religion. It greatly appealed to the sentimental Victorians, as is clear from the great Easter hymn, *There is a green hill far away*, which includes the lines, 'And we believe it was for us he hung and suffered there'.

THE DESTRUCTION OF ROME BY FIRE
(AD 64)

ON THE NIGHT of 18 July AD 64, a fire broke out in some wooden booths at one end of the Circus Maximus in Rome. The fire spread in one direction over the Palatine and Velia Hills as far as the low cliffs of the Esquiline. It spread in another direction through the Aventine and on to the banks of the River Tiber and the Servian Wall.

The fire was a catastrophe destroying almost two-thirds of the city of Rome. The fire spread easily and quickly because Rome was very over-crowded; the streets were narrow and the fire sped from the roof of one wooden tenement building to another through the Roman slums. Popular legend has it that the Emperor Nero fiddled while Rome burned. It seems he fretted rather than fiddled.

After the fire, Nero planned the rebuilding of Rome to a new master plan that gave the city straight, wide streets and broad squares. Officials would supervise the cleanliness of the new streets and squares. Nero himself has been accused of ordering the fire to be started, which seems very unlikely, and of exploiting the fire damage to rebuild Rome on a more lavish scale. In fact the wider streets made the movement of traffic round Rome – until then a major problem – a great deal easier. The new wider streets and the big squares also acted as firebreaks. The clearing of rubbish was also a measure to reduce the risk of fire.

The burning of Rome cleared the way for a more spacious plan. It also enabled the authorities to cast about for scapegoats. The Christians were accused of starting the fire. A feared subversive sect, it seemed possible that they had started the fire deliberately, and certainly the suspicion was a sufficient justification to launch a major purge of Christians in Rome. Christianity was gaining ground; it was at about this time that the Gospel of St Mark was written.

The persecution of Christians began. The climax of this persecution was the execution of St Paul himself, on 29 June AD 67. Paul came to occupy a position of importance in Christianity second only to Jesus himself – partly because of his missionary and theological work, and partly because of his martyrdom. The emperor Nero would not long outlive his victims. He was surrounded by plot after plot and he was sentenced to death by the Senate less than year after Paul's execution.

It was for a long time assumed that the accusation against the Christians was trumped up, but recent historians have proposed that the Christians may in fact have been responsible for starting the fire after all. The legend that Nero played music while watching Rome burn has had a life of its own. It is not true, but it is a powerful image, and one that has (perhaps unfairly) tarnished Nero's already poor reputation.

THE ERUPTION OF VESUVIUS
(AD 79)

THERE WERE 16 years of increasingly violent earthquakes that seriously damaged towns throughout Campania in southern Italy, and then Mount Vesuvius erupted. The impressive volcanic cone stands beside the Bay of Naples, with the modern city of Naples on its lower slopes. In the Roman period, the cities of Herculaneum and Pompeii were built on those same slopes.

The eruption began with a low growl on 20 August. There were intermittent rains of ash, but unfortunately the inhabitants of the two cities did not realize that this was a signal that something far worse was to follow. The most destructive episode in the eruption sequence came four days later with a huge explosion and the release of clouds of scalding gas and smoke that raced down the mountain sides, killing people instantly. Their bodies were in many cases buried in the ash and pumice that continued raining down on the cities.

One distinguished witness of the spectacular eruption sequence was the scholar Pliny, who watched it from a ship out in the Bay of Naples. But he was too curious, and stayed too long, taking refuge with a friend at the town of Stabiae, where he died of suffocation from the poisonous fumes given off by the volcano.

The AD 79 eruption of Vesuvius was a landmark event because it entombed the town of Pompeii, burying and conserving it under layers of ash. When archaeologists started to uncover the ancient city in 1748, it revealed in astonishing detail the everyday lives of people of every class and type of people. Buildings, frescoes, furniture, everyday objects and whole streets of shops were preserved. The discovery of Pompeii was also a great boost to the science of archaeology itself. Suddenly it was obvious to everybody that it was possible to gain access to the past by careful excavation – in the right places.

During the excavations archaeologists came across cavities in the ash, which they thought from their size and shape might be the moulds of human bodies. By pouring plaster into the cavities and removing the ash after the plaster had solidified, they saw that they were right. Part of the popular appeal of Pompeii over the last 200 years has been this poignant collection of human remains. A beautiful statue of a youth was discovered in 1925. It was standing in the porch of a house, which shows that the owners had brought it in from the garden to save it from being damaged by the ash falling out of the sky at the start of the eruption. The beautiful statue survived, but its owners almost certainly did not.

At one time it was thought that it was the 'unearthing' of the wonderful Laocoon sculpture in early sixteenth century Rome that was the beginning of modern archaeology, but recent scholarship suggests that the sculpture was a fake made by Michelangelo. In spite of being a very up-market forgery, it nevertheless had the effect of generating a huge interest in classical sculpture. The finding of Pompeii and its excavation, initially by Winckelman, was the real beginning of archaeology.

The Roman eruption of Vesuvius has also been of long-term interest to modern geologists, who now see the AD 79 eruption as just one in a cyclical pattern of eruptions. The last major eruption of Vesuvius was in the 1940s. The next eruption is long overdue. What vulcanologists fear is that because of the long delay the next eruption of Vesuvius will be a very violent one, of the same type as the one that destroyed Pompeii, and that it will in a similar way destroy the city of Naples. Many people died at Herculaneum and Pompeii, but Naples is a much bigger city with a much bigger population, and the fear is that a great natural disaster entailing huge loss of life is waiting to happen in Naples. Really, the lesson of history (and archaeology and geology) is that Naples should be rebuilt elsewhere, but it has always proved extremely difficult to move cities. Geographical inertia prevails. A similar plan to 'move Tokyo' to a safer location further to the west, for similar reasons, has led nowhere.

THE BATTLE OF THE MILVIAN BRIDGE (AD 312)

THE BATTLE OF the Milvian Bridge was fought 6.5km to the north of Rome on 28 October AD 312. The bridge, a Roman brick-built structure, is still there. In the battle at the bridge, the Emperor Constantine defeated the despot and rival emperor Maxentius. He killed Maxentius and by doing so became absolute master of the Western Roman Empire.

The battle was decisive in terms of Constantine's political career, but it was important in another way too. Constantine afterwards claimed that before the battle he saw a vision in the sky of a shining cross bearing the words *In hoc signo vinces* (By this sign you will conquer). Constantine interpreted this as meaning that he could win the battle in the name of Christ; the victory was conditional on his conversion to Christianity. After seeing this vision, and realizing what it meant, Constantine ordered his army to wear the Cross of Christ. The battle went in Constantine's favour, and the army of Maxentius was driven back towards the Milvian Bridge, back towards the Tiber and defeat. Maxentius himself was killed. Constantine needed no further proof of the power of the Christian God.

What Constantine actually saw in the sky we may never know. It could have been a weather phenomenon. Sometimes, and I have seen this myself, an arc of a halo round the sun may intersect a strip of cloud to make a luminous cross. It could have been a projection from Constantine's mind, a sign of the psychological turmoil and religious dilemma within him. It could have been a meteorite impact; it is thought that a large meteorite did fall to the Earth near Rome in the fourth century, and it could on impact have thrown up a mushroom-shaped cloud that from a distance of a few kilometres would have looked cross-shaped. But whatever it was, it had a decisive effect on the future of Christianity.

The following year, AD 313, Constantine and his co-emperor Licinius formally accepted Christianity. They also, by the Edict of Milan, returned property that had been taken from Christians. A few years later Constantine was to forbid work on the Sabbath, out of respect for Christian beliefs. Christianity suddenly became respectable. After nearly three centuries of being a persecuted minority, Christians now found themselves practising the religion of choice in the Roman Empire; it was the official religion. Constantine, as emperor, was able to order the rescue of sites that were of prime importance to Christianity. He ordered a search for Golgotha, the knoll outside the city wall of Jerusalem where Jesus was crucified. In Jerusalem itself, the tradition of the location had been secretly passed on through the Christian community, and the knoll was quickly found, as was the tomb of Jesus nearby. In AD 335, a church was built so that it covered and enshrined the two sites – the Church of the Holy Sepulchre.

The Battle of the Milvian Bridge was a watershed in Constantine's life, and he commemorated it by building a triumphal arch in Rome, the Arch of Constantine, in AD 315. And in the sign of the Cross, Constantine did indeed conquer – with spectacular success. He eliminated his co-emperor and ended up re-uniting the entire Roman Empire, ruling most of Europe and more; by AD 324 everything between lowland Scotland and the Euphrates fell under his rule alone. It was a high point for the Roman Empire. The battle was also a watershed for Christianity, making it for the first time the official religion not only of a country but of an entire continent. Christianity had arrived.

THE VANDALS SACK
ROME
(AD 455)

THE FALL OF the Roman Empire was not a sudden event, but a gradual decline marked by a series of downward steps. In the reign of the Emperor Valentinian III (AD 423–455) there were two of these downward steps: the conquest of Africa by the Vandals and the invasion of both Gaul and Italy by Attila the Hun. The force behind the invasions of the barbarians was simple land hunger, and they were ready to fight not just Rome but each other in order to gain land.

In AD 451 Attila invaded Gaul. This Hunnish invasion was rather different from the invasions of other groups like the Vandals and Visigoths. Attila was the ruler of a great empire straddling northern and central Europe, a kind of rival to the Roman Empire, and Attila confronted the Roman Empire on an equal footing. Attila was the leader not only of his own people, the Huns, but also of the German tribes along the Rhine and Danube valleys; they all regarded him as their king. Another complication arose because Attila was a pagan, and the Visigoths in Romanized Gaul were Christians, and they rallied to the aid of the Roman Empire to defend the faith. It was in this way, the division of the barbarians, that Attila was defeated in AD 451. He tried to invade Italy again, but got no further south than Lombardy, and in AD 453 he died.

The people of Rome must have been very relieved indeed when they heard that Attila the Hun was dead and that his Hun army had been driven out of Italy, but it was only a brief respite. Only two years later, there was a new onslaught from another horde of barbarians – in effect the third step down. After the murder of Valentinian in AD 455, the Emperor Maxentius ruled the Roman Empire for three months, during which time the Vandals invaded Italy and sacked Rome. Their pillaging was so thorough that their name became for ever after a by-word for wanton destruction.

In reality, Rome was finished from that moment. From the Vandal invasion on, it was the barbarians who made the decisions. In fact from AD 456 until AD 472 the real ruler of the Roman Empire was Ricimer, a kind of barbarian king-maker, and he put four emperors on the throne. After Ricimer, Orestes and then Odovacer fulfilled this king-maker role. It was Odovacer who gently and humanely deposed the last Roman emperor, a young man named Romulus Augustulus, and retired him, with a pension, to a villa in the country. The court at Constantinople was politely informed that there was no longer an Emperor of the West. It was all over.

The single key event in all of this was the Vandal invasion of Italy and their seizure of Rome in AD 455. That was the event that decisively brought the huge edifice of the Roman Empire crumbling down.

THE FIXING OF THE
CHRISTIAN CALENDAR
(AD 525)

IN ROME IN the sixth century, there lived a monk called Dionysius Exiguus, an impressive-sounding name that literally means 'Dennis the Small' or 'Little Dennis'. Dionysius Exiguus was a Roman scholar, theologian and mathematician. He originally came from Scythia, in the east, but he lived and worked in Rome and died there some time before AD 550. He is sometimes described as an abbot, but more usually as a monk. He had a great reputation as a theologian, was well versed in canon law and was an accomplished mathematician and astronomer. Among other scholarly activities, he translated many Greek works that have subsequently been lost, including ones about the lives of several saints.

If those were all the things that Dionysius did, we would not remember him at all. But he did one thing which changed the world in a very particular and all-pervading way. It was Dionysius who created the modern calendar, in use all round the world. He decided that Jesus was born on 25 December in year 743 of the Roman calendar, in other words 743 years after the founding of Rome. The first year of Jesus's life in the calendar of Dionysius was 'the first year of Our Lord', Anno Domini 1. Christian communities have been content to use this numbering system, and also the corresponding negative calendar, in numbered years Before Christ (BC). Non-Christian communities, Jewish communities in particular, have been less comfortable with the labels, preferring 'Christian Era' (CE) and 'Before Christian Era' (BCE) instead. But regardless of religious beliefs, the world seems to have accepted the numbering scheme, counting forwards and backwards from the time when Jesus was born. We all take it for granted, whatever we believe about Jesus.

Dionysius was almost certainly wrong about the year when Jesus was born. The Gospel accounts are not consistent with one another in terms of the historical detail they give. The Roman census that is used in the Gospel accounts to explain why Mary and Joseph were in Bethlehem rather than Nazareth happened a few years *after* AD 1. King Herod the Great who is mentioned as being alive at the time of Jesus's birth actually died in 4 BC, a few years *before* AD 1. So those two pseudo-historical elements in the story of the Nativity of Christ are incompatible.

The arrival of the magi from the East, guided by a star shortly after the birth of Jesus, has led people to look for an astronomical event that could connect up with this element in the story. It is possible to reconstruct the positions in the sky of the planets and the stars at any time in the past, and with the use of computers it is relatively easy to find those moments when there were perhaps two or three bright heavenly bodies close together in the same part of the night sky, giving the illusion of a very bright new star.

In the year 7 BC, the planets Saturn and Jupiter were very close together in the constellation of Pisces (The Fish). This conjunction gave the appearance a bright new star. Interestingly, Jewish astrologers at Sippar in Babylon had prophesied the arrival of a long-awaited Messiah at a time when Saturn and Jupiter met, and this in its turn would explain why magi, or astrologers from Babylon, were roaming about looking for the Messiah. And it would have been in 7 BC that they were searching.

Some astronomers have found a different solution to the puzzle. They looked at Korean and Chinese annals that describe an exploding star or supernova that blazed in the skies for 70 days in the spring of 5 BC. This too could have been interpreted as a sign by the astrologers in Babylon that something momentous was happening in the world, and sent them out to find it. Either way, the astronomical events would tie in with Jesus being born in 5, 6 or 7 BC.

If Jesus was really born in 7 BC, that is the year that should really have been Year 1 of the Christian Era. It means that the entire modern calendar is seven years out. The millennium was celebrated seven years too late, and any superstitious numerology attached to particular dates has no meaning whatever. The year when I am writing this is not 2005 but perhaps 2010, 2011 or 2012, or maybe 2748 in the Roman calendar. The date turns out to be no more than a man-made number – and a number resulting from Little Dennis's big mistake.

II
THE MEDIEVAL
&
RENAISSANCE
WORLD

THE JUSTINIAN
PLAGUE
(541)

IN 541, A wide-ranging epidemic of bubonic plague broke out; in fact it was on such a large scale that it would not be an exaggeration to describe it as a 'pandemic'. It spread, transported by rats in the holds of merchant ships, from Egypt to Palestine and from there to Constantinople. From Constantinople, which was the heart of a great trading empire, inevitably it spread in rat-infested cargoes carried in ships and carts, ever-outwards until it affected every part of the Byzantine and Roman world. At its peak, up to 10,000 people were dying every day in Constantinople.

At about this time, the Glastonbury monk and historian Gildas wrote a description of the political and cultural plight of south-western Britain in the aftermath of King Arthur's death; though he does not mention Arthur by name he does refer to his treacherous murder by a nephew. Evidently southern Britain was in a significantly weakened and divided state after Arthur's demise in 537, and this may have been one of the reasons why the Emperor Justinian saw it as a good moment to retake Britain.

Justinian had planned to invade Gaul and Britain, when he himself contracted the plague. He recovered from it after a few months, but was forced to abandon his planned invasion. So the plague saved both Gaul and Britain from being re-incorporated into the Roman Empire. Being left outside the Roman Empire meant that Britain would be progressively changed into an Anglo-Saxon kingdom; in a sense the thwarting of Justinian's invasion may have made England *England*.

This terrible pandemic, which is known as Justinian's Plague, brought agriculture in Europe to a standstill and caused a second disaster in the shape of widespread famine. Although the plague struck Italy in 541 and so saved Britain from invasion, Britain was not saved from the plague. It reached Britain in 547, just as King Ida succeeded to the throne of Bernicia, the northernmost Anglo-Saxon kingdom. The Justinian Plague killed many people in Britain. No-one was safe, not even the kings and princes. Maelgwn was the king of north-west Wales, and it was he who was probably responsible for ambushing and mortally wounding Arthur at Camlann, and who had subsequently become over-king of the Britons. But even Maelgwn fell victim to the plague. Kings and emperors were by no means immune.

The plague raged for the rest of the sixth century in Europe, the Near East and southern Asia. It was responsible for killing hundreds of thousands of people, depleting work forces, reducing food production and causing famine. It killed Maelgwn, the wicked king of Gwynedd who may have been responsible for Arthur's death. It saved Gaul and Britain from re-incorporation into the Roman Empire, which may have changed the direction of British history. It is possible that an external intervention by Justinian might have bolstered the native aristocracies and prevented the Anglo-Saxon 'take-over' of southern Britain. The result of that could have been a genetically more uniform population without the historical differentiation among England, Scotland and Wales that has become exploited and exaggerated for political ends. Perhaps today there would have been a more unified Britain, a genuinely United Kingdom.

ST AUGUSTINE'S LANDING IN KENT
(597)

GREGORY, WHO CAME to be known as Gregory the Great, was a powerful and autocratic pontiff, organizing and sending off missionaries to convert the pagan north – and sending them with very specific and detailed instructions and advice, copies of which have survived in the Vatican archives. It was in 597 that Gregory sent the monk Augustine with a company of 40 other monks to convert the inhabitants of south-east England to Christianity.

Augustine travelled overland to the Dover Straits and crossed the water, landing on the Isle of Thanet. He succeeded in converting the Jutish King of Kent, Ethelbert, which was the most economical way of converting the whole of Kent. Augustine founded an abbey at Canterbury, the ruins of which can still be seen, and some of the earliest churches in post-Roman Britain. In the following year, the first English school was founded, again in Canterbury. With Christianity came literacy, another landmark in the cultural development of Britain.

From this firm bridgehead, Augustine was able to reach out and convert other areas further west. He was also able to consolidate his position in Canterbury itself; Canterbury became the centre of a new archbishopric, and Augustine became the first Archbishop of Canterbury in 602. Rochester shortly afterwards became the seat of a bishop, and the first church in London was built, St Paul's Church. London too would have its bishop.

On 14 March 604, Gregory the Great died at the age of 64, having laid the foundations of a claim to absolute power for the pope, and also having established Christianity in south-east England.

There were some Christians in Britain already. Back in the fifth and sixth centuries, there were Christian missionaries working in Ireland,

Scotland, Wales and Cornwall. They and their followers formed what became known as the Celtic Church. Augustine, representing the Roman Church, was instructed to negotiate with priests of the Celtic Church and he met them at what is still the English end of an important crossing into Wales – Aust (St Augustine's Oak) at the eastern end of the Severn Road Bridge. In fact in 603, the year before his death, Augustine held two disastrous conferences with delegates from the Celtic Church. They were scarcely meetings of minds. Augustine was too rigid, too insistent that the Celtic priests must formally defer to him, and there was no union of the two churches. The question of assimilation was left for another generation of monks to resolve.

The episode is interesting in showing that Augustine travelled to the margins of the West Country during his mission. He did not just stay in the Canterbury area. In the Canterbury archives there is a story, often dismissed as a folk tale, of Augustine's visit to Cerne Abbas in Dorset and his attempt to convert the inhabitants there who were committed pagans. The earliest surviving version was written down in 1091 by a monk called Gotselin, a French monk who migrated from Normandy to Canterbury in 1053. As Augustine travelled to or from Aust, he may have visited Dorset to deal with worshippers of the famous pagan idol there, the chalk figure known as the Cerne Giant. Augustine was at first seen off in derision by the villagers. What he said as he departed from the village, '*Cerno Hel*', was translated by one Canterbury monk as 'I see God', but he may actually have been saying the ancient British name of the Cerne Giant, which was Helis, Helith, sometimes shortened to Hel. A thirteenth century version of the same story, possibly by a monk with more specific local knowledge, gives the name of the pagan god worshipped at Cerne as Helith.

Augustine went back, or more probably sent other monks back, to try again. We know Pope Gregory sent him and his companion Mellitus specific instructions, which were evidently replies to queries from the missionaries about what they should do about idols such as the Cerne Giant. 'Upon mature deliberation on the matter of the English, the temples of the idols in that nation ought not to be destroyed.' Gregory explained that destroying the pagan sanctuaries would only alienate the people. If they saw their temples respected they might be won round. Gregory advocated the piecemeal taking over of shrines and sanctuaries, the gradual conversion of the sites themselves into Christian sanctuaries. This explains how Augustine's followers came to set up an abbey directly between the Cerne Giant and the old sacred spring that became known as St Augustine's Well.

The missionary activity of Augustine and his followers therefore had a distinctive character. They set up churches and a recognizable ecclesiastical structure, with bishops and archbishops, and gradually converted pagan sanctuaries. Some of these are very obvious take-overs, such as the abbey at Cerne Abbas and the planting of churches in the midst of even more ancient ceremonial complexes at Rudston, Knowlton and Stanton Drew. But some are no longer obvious, as the pagan associations of places have been gradually forgotten – which is exactly what Pope Gregory and St Augustine intended.

Above all, Augustine's landing in Kent signalled the conversion of England, not just to Christianity, but to the Roman Church and to the dominance of the Pope. It also signalled the beginning of a severance with the past, the abandonment of the ancient religion and the ancient pre-Christian culture – and the beginning of forgetting.

MOHAMMED'S RETURN
TO MECCA
(629)

Mohammed claimed to be God's mouthpiece, but was extremely cautious in the way he asserted the claim. For three years his followers formed a secret society, and before that there was a period of preparation which involved a revelation on Mount Hirah near Mecca. The earliest revelations took the form of solemn utterances in the form of rhymes that were revealed only to his nearest relatives. He would speak in a trance and followers wrote down the utterances. The revelations would eventually make up the Koran.

This early work was done in private within the family but, by the time Mohammed made his first appearance as a public preacher in Mecca in 616, he was already had a united following. As he became more successful, some of his followers were persecuted and he found a refuge for them in Axum. The Abyssinian king took the side of the refugees, apparently thinking that they were persecuted Christians - completely mis-understanding who and what they were. They were nevertheless being supported and this diplomatic victory infuriated the Meccan leaders, who blockaded Mohammed in one-quarter of the city.

Mohammed was glad, for his own safety, to have an invitation to go to Yathrib (later named Medina) as dictator; the citizens at Yathrib suffered from feuding and wanted an outsider to act as arbitrator. Accordingly, he went into exile to Medina and the date, 16 July 622, is taken as the start of the Muslim era. The Meccan authorities were alarmed at the prospect of a hostile regime in control at Medina, which lay on an important caravan route, and plans were laid to have Mohammed killed. The Prophet, as he came to be known, took temporary refuge in a cave, delaying his arrival at Medina until 20 September (the Jewish Day of Atonement) in 622.

From this point on, Mohammed's power grew. He bound his followers to himself and then to one another by a range of ties, instituting brotherhoods. At first, Mohammed seems to have courted an alliance with the Jews, but found no possibility of compromise with them on religious questions. Islam began to evolve its distinct practices and customs, to distinguish it clearly from other sects. The spread of Islam was swift and proof of conversion was reduced to a simple test, the expression of belief in Allah and Mohammed.

He repelled an attempt by the Meccans to capture Medina. Mecca itself fell to Mohammed and his Islamic warriors in 629. It was an historic moment; the moment when the Meccans had to recognize him as chief and prophet. Remarkably, within the year, Mohammed had control over the whole of Arabia. Islam was now firmly established as a religion of regional importance, and its future as one of the world's major religions was assured.

THE DESTRUCTION OF THE LIBRARY AT ALEXANDRIA

(646)

AFTER THE DEATH of Alexander, Ptolemy Soter, the friend of Alexander who inherited Egypt, pressed ahead with the building of Alexander's new city, Alexandria. Ptolemy Soter, Ptolemy I, was a creative visionary. One vision was to bring all the people of Alexandria together, the unification of the Greek and Egyptian cultures. To achieve this, he created a new religious cult. He employed two men to create a new religious cult: Timotheus, an expert in Greek religious rites, and Manetho, an expert on the Egyptian mysteries. Between them they devised the cult of Serapis, at whose shrine both Greeks and Egyptians could worship. The building of the Temple of Serapis, the Serapeum, was a huge project in itself, and the resulting building was one of the most magnificent monuments in the ancient world. The creation of an artificial new religion and a splendid temple to go with it were in themselves achievements of the highest order.

Yet Ptolemy achieved something far greater than this in Alexandria – he founded the Museum and Library. The responsibility for designing and managing the Museum and Library was given to Demetrios of Phaleron, one of his close advisers. Ptolemy and Demetrios together worked together on the creation and expansion of the Library from 295 BC onwards.

Surprisingly little was written about the Alexandrian Library in antiquity. Since its destruction there has been a lot of speculation about what it may have contained – certainly an enormous reservoir of ancient literature on every subject under the sun – but while it was functioning it was not regarded as a great wonder. There were some books on the subject. Both Callimachus and Aristonicus wrote books entitled *On the Museum*,

119

but they were lost, perhaps when the Library was destroyed.

Demetrios was allocated large grants to buy as many books as he could find. If possible, he was to collect a copy of every book in the world. When he was asked how many books he had collected, he said, 'More than 200,000 and I am sending for the rest, so that a total of half a million may be reached.' Interestingly, Demetrios had put a figure on how many books there were in the world; whether he was right or not, the Library eventually reached his target. The Library was in two buildings. The Outer Library housed 42,800 sorted and catalogued rolls of papyrus. The Inner or Main Library housed 90,000 sorted rolls and 400,000 unsorted rolls. This made a total of around 530,000 rolls. Since some books were short, there might be two or three on a roll; other books were long and might occupy several rolls. Half a million books was probably about right. The source for the figures is a courtier called Callimachus, who did the cataloguing.

When Ptolemy Soter died in 283 BC, Demetrios was removed by Ptolemy II, and in his place Zenodotus of Ephesus became librarian. Later librarians included Eratosthenes of Cyrene (a great scholar in his own right), Apollonius of Alexandria, Aristophanes of Byzantium and Aristarchus of Samothrace. After Aristarchus, whose term of office ended in 131 BC, the names of the librarians are not known.

Julius Caesar famously visited Alexandria in 47 BC, where he would have seen the city in all its splendour and he would have been shown the sights, doubtless by Cleopatra herself. He would have seen the magnificent Serapeum, the Pharos and Alexander's mausoleum. Originally the hall of Egyptian marble housed a gold casket to contain the body of Alexander, but one of the Ptolemies had taken the gold casket; instead Alexander's perfectly preserved body was on display in a glass case, rather like the Iceman. And Caesar naturally visited the Library.

He was a bibliophile, and his mouth watered at this magnificent, unparalleled collection of books. Cleopatra allowed him to take away some of the greatest treasures from her Library. The librarians were shocked and horrified at having to give up so many books; wherever possible, they supplied inferior second copies in order to limit the impact on the collection, but they were powerless to resist Cleopatra's orders. The books were taken to warehouses on the waterfront, ready to be shipped back to Rome. A fire starting on one of the ships spread to the warehouses and the entire collection of 40,000 books was lost. Alexandria rose up in rebellion against Caesar and Cleopatra. In his reminiscences Caesar described the fire on his ships, but did not mention the books at all. Perhaps he was ashamed: he should have been.

There were huge losses, like the 40,000 books taken by Julius Caesar and then burnt, but there were also acquisitions. A later lover of Cleopatra, Mark Antony, gave her the Library of Pergamum in 41 BC.

The Library had a substantial budget for buying books, and the librarians and assistants at the Library were on regular wages. Hence the gibe of Timon of Phlius:

In the thriving land of Egypt,
There are many that are feeding,
Many scribblers on papyrus,
Ever ceaselessly contending,
In the bird-coop of the Muses.

The Alexandrian collection contained not only the whole body of Greek literature, but many translations into Greek of books originally written in other languages. Demetrios negotiated with the Jews to get copies of their books, which they were glad to supply, and he specifically asked the scholars in Jerusalem to translate them into Greek for him. A very valuable collection of Hebrew texts was duly deposited in Alexandria.

The collection was so huge that it was never fully sorted. There was even so a detailed catalogue, which was summarized in a document called the Pinakes. This represents all that survives of the first great library catalogue of Western civilization, and it ranks with the Gutenberg Bible as a landmark in literature. Books were catalogued according to category: epic poetry, drama, laws, philosophy, history, oratory, medicine, mathematics, natural science and miscellanea. The collection included a great many books of the ancient world that are familiar today, such as the *Iliad* and the *Odyssey*, but also many that have subsequently been lost, such as the other poems in the Epic Cycle, 50 plays by Aeschylus and scores of plays by Sophocles. Whether lost in the fire in the warehouse or in the final destruction several centuries later, those works have been lost beyond recall and their loss is a tragedy for the civilized world.

After Cleopatra's time there were occasional minor losses. Gradually the ancient world of the Ptolemies disintegrated. The Temple of Serapis was destroyed by Theophilus in AD 391. The Library itself lingered on until the seventh century. The Muslims captured Alexandria in 642. Amr ibn el-As killed the city's defenders, carried off the children as captives and then, in 646, destroyed the Library. Amr later explained that one book – the Koran – was enough. It took six months to destroy all the books. They were used to stoke the warming rooms at the 4000 bath houses of Alexandria.

THE BATTLE OF POITIERS

(732)

THE MOORS, WHO were Muslims from North Africa and the Middle East, established a strong grip over Spain in the early eighth century, conquering it in 711. They also launched pirate raids on the coasts of Europe, stealing food and taking slaves. The Moorish menace to Christian Europe, both on land and on sea, was huge, disruptive and potentially disastrous. Then in 720 a huge army of 90,000 Arab warriors crossed the Pyrenees and poured into Gaul (France).

Duke Eudo (or Odo), the Duke of Aquitaine, successfully stopped the Moors' progress for some years. But a new onslaught under a new leader, the intensely fanatical Yemenite Abd ar-Rahman, was too much for him, and he was finally defeated and the Moorish army surged northwards. The Moors captured and burnt the town of Bordeaux. They also destroyed the basilica of St Hilary in the town of Poitiers.

Then the Moorish army marched on the town of Tours, where they intended to seize the wealth of the famous church of St Martin. But Tours, the holy town of Gaul, was where they were stopped and where the Muslim advance into Western Europe was decisively halted.

The Frankish leader was the 44 year old Charles Martel, Charles the Hammer, and he was more than a match for the fanatical Moorish leader. Charles Martel was the son of Pippin II, and he had seized power in Austrasia and made himself 'mayor of the palace'. After that he seized power in Neustria as well, defeating the Neustrian mayor of the palace, Ragenfrid, in battle at Soissons in 719. Martel forced Burgundy to acknowledge his leadership. The general thrust of these seizures was to create a certain amount of unity in what is now France, and this proved to be extremely helpful in view of the huge Moorish threat from the south.

At the landmark Battle of Poitiers, which took place in October 732, just a hundred years after the death of Mohammed, Charles Martel inflicted a resounding defeat on the Moors. Martel's soldiers killed Abd ar-Rahman. After this rout, the surviving Moors limped back south to the Pyrenees. Charles Martel wanted to capitalize on this huge victory over the Moors, and followed them south. He was in the end unable to wrest Narbonne from Muslim control in 737, but he destroyed several fortresses – and set fire to the amphitheatre at Nimes.

The position of the Moors had been significantly undermined by the revolt of the Berbers, the people of Morocco, but Charles Martel's crushing defeat at the Battle of Tours brought what had been a growing menace from the Moors to a definite end. The Moors were out of Gaul.

Islam was penetrating into Europe from the East and it has been suggested that if the Moorish penetration from the south-west had ever been able to join forces with the Muslim penetration from the East, Europe would quickly have fallen to Islam. But as it was, the circuit was never completed and Christianity prevailed.

THE CROWNING OF PIPPIN THE SHORT BY ST BONIFACE

(751)

PIPPIN (or Pepin) THE SHORT was the son of Charles Martel. In 751, he was formally crowned King of the Franks at Soissons by the Archbishop of Mainz. This crowning ceremony may not sound historically important, but it was.

For one thing, the Archbishop of Mainz was no ordinary archbishop. He was St Boniface, born some 70 years earlier in Crediton in Devon and given the baptismal name of Winfrith. As Winfrith, he became a missionary on the European mainland, converting an astonishing 100,000 non-Christians in what is now central Germany and establishing a Christian domain that connected the Pope in Rome with the North Sea. Winfrith, who was awarded the name Boniface by the Pope, and often signed himself with both names, was well known to kings, princes and successive popes for his decided and definite views, and he became a great European statesman in his own right.

Winfrith-Bonface's involvement in this crowning ceremony was not accidental. He saw a unified church and a unified state – the two together – as the way forward, and in some ways he can be seen as one of the early advocates of a European Union. He wanted a strong church unified behind the Pope, and he wanted orthodoxy in teaching and ritual; it was very much due to Winfrith that church music was standardized and what we now know as Gregorian chant became the standard 'hymn book' in the early middle ages. That was Winfrith's idea, not the idea of any of the Pope Gregories.

Winfrith-Boniface would eventually be murdered, probably by robbers, at Dokkum in the Netherlands in 754. He would instantly be recognized as a saint, and have a plainchant composed and sung in his honour:

'*Exsultabo in Jerusalem, et gaudebo in populo meo*' (I will rejoice in Jerusalem, and be glad for my people).

The crowning of Pippin was a strange ceremony for its time. Coronations had not been the custom among the Franks. But Pippin and Winfrith together – and who knows which of them had the idea? – invented what would become one of the most potent and decisive signs of power in Europe for nearly one thousand years. The elaborate solemn ceremony that Winfrith performed conferred great status on Pippin. The crowning ceremony was repeated three years later, when it was reinforced at St Denis by Pope Stephen II. With that, the new Frankish dynasty was proclaimed holy and indisputable. Pippin was now hooked on coronations. They gave so much power!

Pippin III was to die in 768, when he was succeeded by his son, the 26 year old Charles, who would become known as Charlemagne, Charles the Great. The coronation, Charlemagne knew from his father's experience, had great potency. He had been 9 years old at the time of his father's crowning by St Boniface, an age when it would have made a great impression on him. On Christmas Day 800 Charlemagne was to have himself crowned in Rome as head of the Western Roman Empire. The Roman Empire did not really exist any more, except as an idea, but ideas had power too. Charlemagne and his successors were to become known as Holy Roman Emperors, in effect the spiritual successors of the ancient Roman Emperors. Winfrith therefore conferred status, dignity and a kind of mystique on Pippin and his son. The medieval mystery of monarchy was born.

THE DEATH OF HARUN AL-RASHID
(809)

THE FIFTH ABBASID caliph Harun al-Rashid (766–809), ruler of the Islamic Empire, came to the throne as caliph at the age of 22 on the death of his elder brother al-Hadi. He owed his succession to the influence of his tutor, Yahya ibn Khalid and his family, and he allowed his tutor's family to influence decision-making for a while. Then, in 803, Harun al-Rashid suddenly ordered the whole family to be arrested and imprisoned, and all their wealth confiscated. This is the kind of cruelty and capriciousness for which Harun has been long remembered.

The caliph was a great patron of the arts, and of poetry in particular. He was also a very enthusiastic fighter against the Byzantines, but was less interested in the actual details of government. He also weakened the empire by attempting to arrange its division among his three sons. He went on an expedition to quell a rising in Khurasan - one of many that plagued his reign - and died at Tus during this expedition.

Harun al-Rashid became the subject of endless colourful anecdotes, and he was to become an exotic, magical figure in Arabic legend. He is remembered world-wide now as the caliph in the *Arabian Nights* stories, published in English for the first time in 1888, a ten-volume edition translated by Sir Richard Burton. They were originally written in Arabic and existed in their modern form at least as early as 1450. The collection of stories is also known as *A Thousand and One Nights*. The stories are self-contained, free-standing tales, but unified by the figure of Scheherezade, the supposed story-teller. She postpones her execution by telling her husband a story night after night, but she ends her story each night with a cliff-hanger, so that her husband has to wait until the following night to find out what happened. Her life depends on the effectiveness of her story-telling.

Two of the most popular stories in the collection are *Ali Baba and the Forty Thieves* and *Sinbad the Sailor*. The stories, which have greatly enriched world literature, are a glossy and glorified presentation of the world of Harun al-Rashid. He has come to symbolize to Western readers the colour, barbaric magnificence and capriciousness of Eastern civilization.

ALFRED'S DEFEAT BY THE DANES
(878)

ETHELRED, KING OF Wessex, spent his final year struggling to defeat Danish invaders. The Danes had a strengthening hold on northern England and the Midlands (Mercia), and now they were trying to conquer the southern Anglo-Saxon kingdom of Wessex. Ethelred defeated the Danes in battle at Englefield in Berkshire in 870, was beaten by them in January 871 at Reading. He defeated the Danes just four days later at Ashdown, but was beaten again a few days afterwards at Basing. He had another victory over the Danes at Marton in March, but then died in April.

This was the embattled kingdom of Wessex that Ethelred's younger brother Alfred inherited at the age of 22. Luckily it was a fighting family, and Alfred had already had plenty of experience of fighting at his brother's side. The Danes were fighting to consolidate their position in Mercia, and Alfred was able to fend them off with money for a time.

In 877, the Danes seized Exeter in the West Country, while Danish leaders were deceitfully negotiating with Alfred. Alfred's response was to blockade Exeter. A Danish fleet sent to relieve the surrounded Danes was scattered by storm winds and therefore did not arrive and the Danes were forced to withdraw to Mercia.

In 878, came Alfred's low-point, his crisis as King of Wessex. He was relaxing in his palace at Chippenham, where he was celebrating Christmas, when the Danes surrounded him and made a surprise attack. Taken completely off-guard, many of Alfred's men were killed, and Alfred himself was lucky to get out alive. In the company of a small band of survivors, he managed to escape through woods and swamps, and took refuge on the Isle of Athelney, a small patch of dry rising ground in the Somerset Levels. It was well off the beaten track, very unobtrusive and surrounded by

129

uninhabited marshes, and for the time being Alfred was safe there.

At Athelney, in the January of 878, Alfred must have wondered whether he had reached the end of the road, and whether this was the end of Anglo-Saxon Wessex. Had the last Anglo-Saxon domino fallen, to make way for a new Viking empire? Instead of giving way to despair with such thoughts, Alfred planned a counter-offensive. Messengers darted about through the swamps and eventually, in May, the Athelney survivors were joined by troops from Somerset, Wiltshire and Hampshire to make an army.

The result of this re-grouping was that in the middle of May, Alfred managed to defeat the Danes in a great victory at the Battle of Edington in Wiltshire. The Danish king accepted defeat, and also accepted Christian baptism along with many of his chief officers.

During the months that followed, the Danes were cleared out of Wessex. Alfred was even able to push on into Mercia and restore much of that kingdom to Anglo-Saxon rule too. London remained in the hands of the Danes. From the low-point of early 878, Alfred gradually built up the strength of the Anglo-Saxon south, consolidating it by setting up a regular army and a fleet of ships. This turning-point would prove to be decisive in the history of England. Indeed, the saving of Wessex by Alfred the Great made England possible.

THE MAKING OF
ENGLAND
(925–973)

ALFRED SUCCEEDED IN fending off the Danish onslaught on Wessex, and establishing Wessex as the kernel of the Anglo-Saxon territory in Britain. It was the acorn that would grow into England. Alfred's successors took the process of growth further.

Athelstan, who reigned from 924 until 939, was the first born son of Edward the Elder. He succeeded to the throne of England on 17 July 924 and was crowned at Kingston-upon-Thames on 4 September 925. His reign was a landmark in English history because he became the first Saxon king to gain effective control over the whole of what is now England, with the exception of Cumbria. He also became nominal overlord of Cornwall, Wales and Scotland, so even at this early stage the emerging English monarchy claimed overlordship over the 'Celtic' West of Britain. This overlordship was not undisputed, though.

Athelstan's greatest victory was the battle of Brunanburh in 937. King Constantine of the Scots attacked Athelstan's army, which consisted of a full levy (or call-up) of troop from Wessex and Mercia, with a huge host of combined Scots, Picts and all the Vikings of the north and west. This was an unusual battle for its time, unusually large-scale in terms of the numbers of warriors involved, unusually long in that it lasted all day. It was a remarkable battle in that no less than five kings were killed. After this resounding victory for Athelstan, neither the Danes nor the Scots gave the English any further trouble during his reign.

King Athelstan was a great administrator. He assembled a team of clerks to deal with the details of administration and founded the English Civil Service.

In 959, the young King Edgar ascended the throne of England at the age of 15. His brother, the useless Edwy, had died in October 959 at the age of

131

only 19. Edwy's only claim to fame was his disgraceful behaviour. Dunstan's biographer described what happened. 'A certain woman pursued the king, wickedly enticing him to intimacy in order to ally herself and her daughter to him in marriage.' After his coronation, Edwy withdrew early from the celebration banquet to have sex with the two women. Dunstan and a kinsman went to fetch him. 'They found the crown carelessly thrown on the floor and he himself repeatedly wallowing between the two of them in evil fashion, as if in a vile sty.' Dunstan pulled him out. Edwy married the younger of the two women, Aelgifu, and Dunstan was exiled for interfering.

King Edwy's replacement, his brother Edgar, was a very different man. Edgar recalled Dunstan from his exile in Flanders and made him first Bishop of Worcester, then Bishop of London. In 961, Dunstan was made Archbishop of Canterbury. Although he succeeded to the English throne in 959 and was acknowledged as the English king, Edgar was not crowned immediately. In fact his coronation was delayed for a remarkable 14 years. By then Edgar had unified England, built a navy to consolidate his hold on the country, and received homage from the kings of Strathclyde and Scotland.

After his coronation at Bath in May 973, King Edgar was rowed on the River Dee by eight kings in a spectacular but characteristically peaceful display of his supremacy. The kings who rowed Edgar in this highly symbolic event were Malcolm of Strathclyde, Kenneth II of Scotland, Maccus of Man and five Welsh kings. From this defining moment on there was no question of the unity and integrity of England as a nation, nor of its supremacy over Wales and Scotland. In 973, the map of England was drawn.

THE INTRODUCTION OF ARABIC ARITHMETIC NOTATION TO THE WEST

(975)

WE TEND TO take our system of numerals for granted, and it is difficult to imagine a world where there were no numerals. Probably ever since *Homo sapiens sapiens* emerged people have counted at least to five on their fingers, and probably ever since language developed there have been words for those numbers. It is not by chance that a single-figure number is called a digit, from the Latin word for finger, *digitus*. But the marks for writing them down are not as obvious as one might think.

The earliest numerals we have any definite record of were simple tallies – straight vertical marks for each additional number up to nine, and then a different symbol to represent a batch of ten. This gives clear evidence that from very early on people were using both hands for counting. In Egyptian hieroglyphics in 3400 BC, a vertical stroke was used for 1 and an arch for 10. In the bronze age, Minoan script called Linear B, a vertical stroke was 1, a horizontal stroke represented 10, a circle was 100 and a circle with four rays was 1,000. This meant that quite large numbers could be recorded economically. Writing the number 1,357 did not entail drawing 1,357 vertical lines, which would have taken a long time to write and an equally long time to read; in the Linear B system it only took 16 symbols in all, and grouped with the thousands on the left and the units on the right – which was easy to read and easy to write. Linear B was a very good system for inventories, which is what the Minoans wanted it for.

Not all early counting systems used a base of ten, though. In Hindu culture, the number four was regarded as significant, so in the third century BC there was a special symbol for 4. In the Roman system a special symbol, V, was used to represent the halfway stage when counting to 10. The V symbolized the shape of a hand, the grouped fingers pointing one way, the thumb pointing the other. The X the Romans used for 10 represented two hands. As with the other systems, the Romans used vertical strokes for individual units. C represented 100, M represented 1000.

The Arabic numerals at first sight seem clumsier than the Roman, because more signs or symbols are involved: a completely different symbol for each unit from 1 to 9, but then the symbols repeat, however large the number. Instead of 1,357 taking 16 symbols it only needs 4. This much more economical system has become the system of choice.

In 975, Arabs introduce their method of arithmetic notation to the West. The system of numerals, the one which we all use now, came originally from India and was used by Arab mathematicians. The Arabic system of numbers (1, 2, 3, 4, 5, etc) proved to be much easier to manage than Roman numerals for mathematical calculations.

The zero was not mentioned in AD 650, but by 975 it had appeared, in its modern form, 0, and was possibly borrowed from the Sanskrit system. It was not for another two decades that the zero would come into its own; around the year 1000 the Indian mathematician Sridhara recognized the importance and usefulness of the zero. This development made all the difference in the world, turning the counting system into a flexible and powerful language, the decimal system, which spawned modern mathematics.

Once the Arabic system was introduced in Europe, mathematics took on a new lease of life. The Arabic system gave mathematics a coherent language with which it could argue and reason. Indeed, it is hard to imagine how the science of the twentieth and twenty-first centuries could have developed at all on the Roman system. Without Arabic numerals, there would have been no advanced mathematics, no theory of relativity, and probably no space programme either.

THE FOUNDING OF THE GREENLAND COLONY
(981—6)

IN 981, A Norse expedition led by Eric the Red, an Icelandic colonist, sighted the coast of Greenland and made landfall there. This gave Eric the idea of setting up a daughter colony. He returned to Iceland. Five years later, in 986, the preparations for this bold scheme were complete and a substantial fleet set sail for the west. Eric the Red took 25 ships with him loaded with 700 people as well as horses, cattle and provisions; it was a major colonial expedition.

The colonists set up the first Viking colony on the south-eastern coast of Greenland. The name 'Greenland' was not given ironically. The coastline was indeed covered with verdant pastures, and the newcomers can have had no idea that a colossal ice sheet lay behind the coastal mountain range. One of the Icelandic Norse adventurers, called Bjarni Herjolfsson, was blown off-course. Instead of landing on the coast of Greenland he sailed well to the south of the southern tip, Cape Farewell, and sighted the coast of Labrador. He described it as 'well-forested with low hills'. This was the first European sighting of North America – and it happened 500 years before Columbus.

It was inevitable that after hearing this tale others would be tempted across the treacherous, iceberg-strewn sea beyond Cape Farewell. In 995, Leif Ericsson, the son of Eric the Red, bought Bjarni Herjolfsson's ship in Greenland and set sail in it to try to rediscover the land that Bjarni saw. Leif Ericsson found it again, landed and spent the winter there before returning to Greenland in the spring. In 996, Leif's brother Thorvald sailed south-west from the Greenland colony to revisit the Labrador coast, which became known to the colonists as Vinland. Thorvald Ericsson intended to set up a colony in Vinland, but he got involved in a skirmish with the natives and was killed, shot with an arrow. Ericsson's crew decided

135

to overwinter in Labrador before returning to Greenland in the spring.

In the space of a few years, the Norse colonists settled in Iceland had made two very significant steps to the west, landing and founding colonies in both Greenland and Labrador. The settlements may have been only temporary, but they enlarged the European view of the world, extending it to the west. Experiences such as these made the Columbus voyages, which took place later and further to the south, an inevitability. It is Bjarni Herjolfsson and Leif Ericsson rather than Columbus who should be credited with the European discovery of the New World.

THE DANISH
TAKEOVER OF
ENGLAND
(1016)

ON 30 NOVEMBER 1016, Ethelred the Unready, Ethelred II, the King of England, died at the age of 48 after a long reign of 38 years.

Ethelred was succeeded by his son Edmund Ironside. Edmund should have succeeded to the English throne. He was the legitimate heir, and he was chosen by the people of London to succeed. Edmund had proved a more effective warrior than his father, but in 1015 he had failed to stop the Danish King Cnut's invasion of Wessex, largely because of the treachery of a Mercian prince. Edmund worked hard in the early months of 1016 to muster an army to hold Northumbria against Cnut's aggression. He was also undermined by divisions and infighting within the English camp.

The people of London and the witan members living there wanted him as king, but the witan majority at Southampton decided that Cnut should succeed. There had in fact been an earlier interlude of Danish rule, when Sven, the King of Denmark, had been king of England. Sven, known in England as Sweyn Forkbeard, had seized the Danish throne from his father in 987. Then he had seized the crown of Norway in 1000. Meanwhile he made frequent piratical raids on the English coast, bullying protection money out of the intimidated English from 994 onwards. The St Brice's Day massacre gave Sven an excuse to attack England in earnest; his sister Gunhild was one of those killed. In 1013, he succeeded in driving King Ethelred out of the country, making himself king of England in December 1013. He died just two months later, falling from his horse in Gainsborough. Then the reign of Ethelred resumed.

There had been a brief period of Danish rule, but it had been a clear

137

usurpation. Edmund marched on Wessex in an attempt to seize his birthright by force. He very nearly succeeded, winning three out of the four battles. Edmund was deserted by his brother-in-law Edric, who was angered by Edmund's marriage to the widow of a Danish earl. At this critical moment, Edric decided to rejoin Edmund, but the confusion led to the defeat of the English at the Battle of Ashingdon in Essex.

This battle, in which Cnut was the victor, decided the succession in Cnut's favour. In a meeting at Olney in Bedfordshire, Edmund and Cnut agreed on a way of resolving the stalemate: partition. Edmund Ironside was to rule in the south while Cnut would rule the north, but Edmund's death shortly afterwards on 30 November in 1016, at the age of 26, left the way clear for Cnut to rule over the whole of England. It was remarkably convenient for Cnut that Edmund died so young, and it is likely that Edmund met his end by foul play; Cnut probably had him murdered. Edmund's sons were taken out of the country for their own safety, and settled in Hungary, a measure which strongly suggests that some in high places must have suspected at the time that Edmund's death was not natural.

With this extraordinary sequence of events, the laborious work of Alfred and his dynasty went for nothing. England was quite suddenly not ruled any longer by an Anglo-Saxon or English king, but by a foreign interloper, a Dane. Cnut turned out to be a brilliant administrator. He divided England into four large earldoms, and gave one of them to Edric. Cnut in the course of time found that Edric was untrustworthy and had him executed. Cnut frequently resorted to judicial murder to get his way.

Cnut was also a remarkable empire-builder. He took not only the crown England and Denmark, but by 1028 the crown of Norway too, ending up as the ruler of a huge empire which held together just so long as he lived, which was until 1035. The power of the Anglo-Saxon aristocrats over England was severely shaken; they would regain it for a time, and then lose it finally and for ever in 1066.

THE NORMAN
TAKEOVER OF
ENGLAND
(1066)

EDWARD THE CONFESSOR, the last but one Saxon king of England, died childless in 1066. William of Normandy, a cousin of Edward's, claimed that the dead king had promised him the throne of England during a visit in 1051. He may have received such a promise - Edward was foolish enough to have given it, and he wanted to spite the Saxon Earl Godwin and his family, who were extremely powerful. Earl Godwin was the father of Harold, the heir apparent.

Harold was the second son of Godwin and Gytha, a Danish princess. He was destined to reign for only nine troubled months from his coronation in Westminster Abbey on 5 January 1066 until his violent death on the battlefield on 14 October, although in a sense he had ruled England for the previous 12 years. History remembers Harold through the distorting lens of hindsight, for losing one of the most significant battles in British history. He was nevertheless a great military leader, adding Hereford to his already huge personal estates and crushing rebellions in Wales by the year 1063. It was then that he acquired a Welsh wife, Aldgyth, the widow of Gryffydd ap Llewellyn, who replaced his mistress of legendary beauty, Edith Swan Neck. Harold had held England together during the reign of Edward the Confessor and could reasonably have expected, given his leading role in England, to have taken the crown on Edward's death. He had earned it. He had himself declared king, but there was confusion. There were three other rival claimants to the throne of England.

The first, the 16 year old Edgar the Atheling, he could afford to ignore because of his youth and inexperience. So Harold marched north to fend off an invasion by the second contender, Harold Hardrada of Norway. Harold of England killed both Harold Hardrada and his own brother Tostig at the Battle of Stamford Bridge on 25 September 1066. Then he marched south at the head of his exhausted and battle-scarred army to meet the invasion force of the third contender, William of Normandy, at Battle just north of Hastings on 14 October. Including Harold himself, there were four contenders for the English throne that year. It was one of the most chaotic moments in British history, and no-one at the time could have foreseen what the outcome would be. King Harold of England was a very strong and very experienced military and political leader and he was also in a position of great strength. On the face of it, Harold should have been able to maintain his position as king. But the outcome of warfare is very uncertain.

The pope approved William of Normandy's claim to the English throne, but it still did not amount to an entitlement. William assembled a fleet, crossed the Channel and landed his fleet on the shore of Pevensey Bay. He unloaded two timber forts, brought in kits, and raised one of them at Pevensey, inside the still-standing and still-complete walls of the Saxon Shore Fort built by the Romans, to protect his invasion fleet. William's invasion was extremely well planned. Then he marched inland, taking up his battle position in the fields north of Hastings.

At the Battle of Hastings, the English King Harold made a courageous last stand with his house-carls as they gathered round the English standard. The Normans broke through their shield wall and butchered Harold and most of his house-carls. Harold was cut down and hacked to pieces with swords, not shot in the eye. The last Saxon King of England was murdered. The 600-year-long domination of England by Anglo-Saxon kings had finally come to an end. The following day, Harold's mother, Gytha, sent a request to William offering him the weight of the dead King's body in gold if he would hand it over to her for burial. William shabbily refused, insisting on giving the King an anonymous, unmarked grave on the beach that he had tried to defend.

The English were severely shaken by the news of Harold's death. Two of Harold's sons landed in Devon during the 1068–69 rebellion against William, but no-one knows what became of them; it is not known whether Harold's line survived or was extinguished. There was a story that Harold himself had not died at the Battle of Hastings after all. He had survived and lived on for many years in monastic retreat in Chester. This story was widely believed at the time, and it is said that Harold was actually visited in Chester by Henry I. The Anglo-Saxon community could not bear to think that its great war-leader was dead, just as the Britons 500 years earlier had not wanted to believe that Arthur was dead. But – it is just possible. In the dark ages, it was customary for kings, especially if old, especially if defeated in battle, to go into total retirement, joining a religious community a long way from their sphere of secular power. And of course, in the case of King Harold, no body was ever produced to prove otherwise.

The victorious contender, Duke William, meanwhile marched on Dover, where he stayed for a week before setting off for London by way of Canterbury. In Southwark, on the southern edge of London, William met significant resistance. William set fire to the area, turned away to the south and marched through Surrey, Hampshire and Berkshire, ravaging the countryside as he went. By the end of the year, William and his army had scythed a great swathe of destruction right round London. He then approached London again, this time from the north, via Berkhamsted. Demoralized by the reports coming in of the devastation all round London, the Londoners knew they had to give in. On Christmas Day 1066 William was crowned king of England – king by usurpation – in Westminster Abbey by Aldred, Archbishop of York. The Abbey was almost completely deserted, emptied for security reasons.

On the strength of just the one battle, William claimed all of England, though the claim was not really supported by right or by military conquest. He had in truth only conquered those parts of England he had marched through. William saw that one way of avoiding further pitched battles was to allow the powerful lords of the north, such as Morcar, Earl of Northumbria, to hold their lands as a grant from him as their new lord. But most of the English landowners were robbed of their lands. William needed to reward the Norman knights and barons who had helped him to win Hastings, and giving them lands in England was the only way he could do that. Some of the leading supporters were granted huge estates.

On 1067, King William I led his army on a tour of England, confiscating land from English landowners and building wooden castles to keep the rebellious English under control. William had by now acquired a reputation for being harsh and merciless, and he felt secure enough to return to Normandy in the spring of 1067. While he was away, rebellions broke out in Kent, Herefordshire and the North, and in December William had to come back to put down the rebellions.

The English did not welcome William as a saviour or rescuer, nor did they quickly come round to the idea that his presence in England was acceptable, desirable or necessary. There was resistance to Norman rule in one county after another. William was simply not wanted. The only way he could hold onto this kingdom was by force, and he did not flinch from using it. The spate of castle-building was a clear indication that the populace would be kept in order by military force.

William also dismantled the English Church, dismissing all but two of the English bishops and replacing them with Normans. Lanfranc became the new Archbishop of Canterbury.

Then William launched his famous Domesday Survey of England. This was to assess people for tax and sort out exactly who owned the land. Today people look back on the Domesday Book as a valuable historical document, and are grateful to William the Conqueror for making it available to them, but at the time when it was compiled it was a culture shock, a phenomenon that was culturally alien to the way England was organized.

The motive for the Norman invasion of England was very clear to the English, for whose well-being William showed contempt. William is most remembered for conquering England and imposing a Norman elite on the English. The Norman invasion had the positive effect of introducing many new words to the English language and greatly increasing its versatility and flexibility as a language for literature. William thus inadvertently paved the way for English to become the second language of choice for the world as a whole. Duke William's conquest of England in this way indirectly changed the world by energizing English and creating a world language.

THE CLASH BETWEEN HENRY IV AND POPE GREGORY VII
(1076)

HENRY IV, THE eleventh century Holy Roman Emperor, was chosen as German king at Tribur in 1053. In 1055, he was appointed Duke of Bavaria, and when his father Henry III died in 1056, he inherited the kingdoms of Germany, Italy and Burgundy. Initially these lands were governed by his mother, until Henry came of age in 1065. In 1076, Henry IV called the Synod of Worms. He was pressed to do this by the German bishops, who then renounced their allegiance to Pope Gregory VII (whose real name was Hildebrand); they went even further, declaring him deposed.

There were allegations that Hildebrand's election as pope had not been conducted properly, that instead of the cardinals voting freely, they were compelled to follow public acclamation. Hildebrand brought a deep sense of mission to the office, and he worked towards enhancing the power of the papacy. The pope could be judged by no-one. One major step was his claim that he had the right to depose bishops and emperors. Naturally neither the bishops nor the Holy Roman Emperor approved of this claim. In accordance with the German bishops' wishes, and the wishes of the archbishops of Mainz and Trier, Henry IV demanded Gregory's abdication and he was supported in this demand by the bishops of northern Italy at Piacenza.

The message was taken to Rome by Roland of Parma, who was lucky not to have been lynched; his life was in fact saved by the direct intervention of the Pope. Pope Gregory's response to his dismissal was to assemble his own Lenten Synod in Rome, and to excommunicate and suspend all the German and north Italian priests who did not support him.

He also declared Henry IV deposed and excommunicated.

The result of this head-on confrontation between church and state was political chaos in the states concerned. At the Diet of Tribur in October, Henry IV was ordered to humble himself, submit to a trial and clear himself of the charges levelled against him before 22 February the next year, 1077.

In the middle of the winter of 1076–77, Henry IV made an extraordinary journey in secret across the Alps, with his wife Queen Bertha, in order to avoid the total humiliation of a public trial in Germany. On 21 January 1077, Henry IV arrived in front of the castle at Canossa, where Hildebrand was staying. Hildebrand kept him waiting, barefoot, outside the gates for three days as a formal penance. For this he was given absolution. Hildebrand grudgingly accepted Henry's promises and assurances, his solemn oaths of contrition. But Henry was not completely out of the wood. While he was doing all this – eating humble pie on the grandest scale – the German nobles elected an alternative monarch, an 'anti-king', in the shape of Rudolf of Swabia. The pope's representatives approved; it meant that Henry IV was marginalized and still in acute political difficulty. When Henry returned to Germany he was surprised to find that his throne had been usurped. Gregory VII was actually not to blame for this additional humiliation, but Henry understandably assumed that Gregory had somehow engineered it and sought to prevent the Pope from travelling to Germany. Henry struggled to regain his former position. He was supported by most of the German bishops and by the Lombards (north Italians), but still suffered military defeats at Mellrichstadt and Flarchheim in 1080.

In October 1080, Rudolf of Swabia, the rival king, was defeated and mortally wounded in battle, which brought the civil war in the German states to an end. Henry IV had gradually regained his political strength, and took the crown of Lombardy at Pavia. Once again deposed and excommunicated by Pope Gregory, Henry made two unsuccessful military attacks on Rome before taking the city in 1082. The Romans agreed that the quarrel between king and pope should be decided by a synod (church conference), though this was a failure. In March 1084, the pope was deposed by a synod of German and north Italian prelates, who installed a new pope, the Archbishop of Ravenna, to replace him as Clement III. Pope Clement in return obligingly crowned Henry emperor. After that, and a half-hearted revenge attack on one of Hildebrand's properties, Henry IV returned to Germany.

Quite apart from being a remarkable historic episode in itself, this clash between king and pope represented a conflict of interests, a conflict of powers and a conflict of mind-sets that would run right through the next millennium, creating crisis after crisis. It resurfaced in the power struggle between Henry II of England and his Archbishop of Canterbury, Thomas Becket. It repeated in the clash between Henry VIII of England and the Pope that resulted in the Dissolution of the English Monasteries.

THE INVENTION OF
THE MAGNETIC
COMPASS
(1086)

VARIOUS ACCOUNTS HAVE been given of the invention of the compass. At one time the Chinese were credited with inventing it as far back as 2634 BC. The emperor Hwang-ti was trying to attack an enemy enveloped in thick fog and built a 'chariot' for finding south, and this in turn enabled him to find his enemy. But this account is purely legendary, and in any case a 'south-finding chariot' is not at all the same thing as a magnetic compass.

It was much later, in AD 1086, that the magnetic compass was invented in China. The waterworks engineer Shen Kua was the man who was responsible for devising the compass. He wrote about his invention, explaining that it was possible for magicians and geomancers to find directions by rubbing an iron needle on a lodestone and allowing the magnetized needle to hang freely on a thread. The needle, he said, pointed south, which is a point of view; curiously, and no more objectively, in Europe compasses have always been regarded as pointing north. In reality they simply align with the Earth's magnetic field and therefore point both north and south.

The peculiar characteristics of lodestones and their ability to magnetize needles had been known about for a long time. The lodestone was actually mentioned in a Chinese dictionary dating from AD 121; 'a stone with which an attraction can be given to a needle.'

The invention soon found practical applications. By 1150 Chinese caravan masters were using Shen Kua's compass to find their way across the steppes and deserts of Central Asia, and ship's masters were using it to navigate in open water. The first mention of a magnetic compass on a Chinese ship was in 1297. The simple compass of Shen Kua meant that sailors knew in which direction they were sailing, even when they were out of sight of land. By a method called 'dead reckoning', they could calculate where they were in relation to the home port; this involved using the compass direction combined with the ship's speed and the number of hours sailing. The direction could be drawn as a line on a map. Then the distance travelled along that line could be marked to give the ship's exact position.

The Chinese navigators regularly sailed south to trade with the islanders of the East Indies, and occasionally sailed west into the Indian Ocean. At some point in the middle ages, the compass was passed on to the Arabs, and they in turn passed it on to Europeans. In a treatise on lodestones by Albertus Magnus, the north and south poles are referred to as Zoron and Aphron, which are names of Arabic origin, so it is probable that the earliest commentaries on the properties of lodestones and compasses were also of Arabic origin. It would be likely, given the Arabs' great reputation as mariners, that they acquired the compass early on.

The new technology seems to have spread across Eurasia very fast, as one would expect from its practical usefulness. As early as 1218, Cardinal Jacques de Vitry, a bishop in Palestine, spoke of the magnetic needle as 'most necessary for such as sail the sea.'

In 1498, Vasco da Gama was shown a map of the entire coast of India. The bearings were 'laid down after the manner of the Moors, with meridians and parallels (lines of latitude and longitude) very close together'. Da Gama was left in no doubt that this fine cartography was the work of Arabs and that a compass had been used to fix the cardinal directions – north, south, east and west.

A variant form of compass was used in the East Indies in the sixteenth century. Instead of a needle suspended from a thread, it was described as 'a sort of fish made out of hollow iron, which when thrown into the water, swims upon the surface, and points out the north and south with its head and tail.' A similar model using a needle mounted on a wooden float, so that it could move freely on the surface of water, was in use in Europe in the thirteenth century. The first detailed description of a medieval compass was written in 1269 by Peregrinus, who describes an improved floating compass with a circle marked out with 90 degrees in each quadrant, and fitted with movable sights for taking bearings.

In 1558, Dr John Dee, Elizabeth I's magician, mathematician and geographer, succeeded Robert Recorde as technical adviser to the Muscovy

Company. He devised an improved magnetic compass for navigation on the trade route between England and Russia. In the great age of exploration and discovery, no ship could be without the most accurate and up-to-date compass available.

The importance of the magnetic compass as an invention was recognized at once by those who used it. It is clear that it made the voyages of exploration and discovery more purposeful, because it became possible to locate any island or shoreline on a map with a fair degree of accuracy. Filling in the map of the world could begin. People would have travelled and explored without the compass, but equipped with the new technology a progressive, cumulative world map could be created fairly quickly and efficiently.

THE COMPLETION OF ANGKOR WAT

(1150)

THE HINDU TEMPLE of Angkor Wat was the biggest and most spectacular temple ever built in Asia. It marked the completion of the funerary complex of the Khmer King Suryavarman II, and formed the centrepiece of the Khmer capital. It was surrounded by a huge moat and is now one of the major tourist attractions of South-East Asia.

The rise of this South-East Asian civilization is shrouded in mystery, but it evidently owed much to trading and other cultural contacts with both China and India. By the sixth century AD, Chinese records are starting to refer to a territory or region called 'Zhenla', which seems to have been a region of chiefdoms in what is now Cambodia, with big defended settlements and temple architecture. In the ninth century, Zhenla was unified by King Jayavarman II to create the Khmer Empire. Shortly afterwards, King Yasovarmon I moved the capital of this new empire to Angkor. For about 400 years the city of Angkor dominated the Khmer Empire, which in turn dominated South-East Asia. It was a very important place. Finally, in the early fifteenth century, Angkor was sacked by Siamese (Thai) troops. After that most of the city was abandoned, but the temple of Angkor Wat itself was taken over by Buddhist monks and became an important centre of pilgrimage.

A constant factor in the development of temple architecture was the Khmer kings' desire to immortalize themselves. Undoubtedly the most successful Khmer king was Suryavarman II, who built the most famous temple complex of the city of Angkor Wat.

The layout of Angkor was determined by ideas drawn from Indian religion. The city was designed round a central pyramid that was built on Phnom Bakheng, which is the only natural hill in the area. This temple was associated with Mount Meru, the mountain at the centre of the universe according to ancient Indian beliefs. The temple of Angkor Wat is part temple, part mausoleum but, because of its shape and sheer size, it gives the awe-inspiring effect of being a man-made mountain. It is a landscape in itself. It rises in elaborately carved stone terraces with staircases towards a cluster of spectacular 'peaks', ancient skyscrapers loaded with sculptures. There is nothing anywhere else in the world quite like it.

After being abandoned and overtaken by the forest for generations, Angkor Wat was rediscovered in 1850 by a Catholic missionary, and from the 1860s onwards there have been many surveys and archaeological investigations. Perhaps the saddest episode has been the fairly recent destruction of Khmer monuments in the region. The area was taken over by the Khmer Rouge in the 1970s, and a 20-year period of deliberate and wilful vandalism followed. Many sculptures were removed to sell on the illegal antiquities market. Some of the buildings were used for target practice. Natural wear and tear has also taken its toll. A freak storm in 1989 uprooted more than a thousand trees at Angkor, and this damaged a number of the temples.

After the Cambodian Peace Settlement was signed in 1991, Angkor was hastily added to the UNESCO World Heritage List in an attempt to give the monument some rather belated care. Since then there has been a concerted effort to repair and maintain it. In spite of the damage and the long neglect, Angkor Wat remains a powerful iconic monument to the Asian civilizations of the past – a salutary and very necessary reminder in the midst of a poor region of the enormous wealth that has been lost.

THE MURDER OF
THOMAS BECKET
(1170)

THE RELATIONSHIP BETWEEN Henry II of England and Thomas Becket, his Archbishop of Canterbury, is one of the most famous personal quarrels in history. The story closely connects with that of the German King Henry IV and Pope Gregory VII, in being an intensely personal power struggle but also an institutional power struggle between church and state.

Thomas Becket (1118–70) was initially Henry II's chancellor. While he fulfilled this role conscientiously, he and the King remained on friendly terms. Thomas was the perfect courtier and the two men were the best of friends. They worked so well together that Henry thought he would make Thomas his Archbishop of Canterbury when Archbishop Theobald died in 1162. Thomas warned him not to do this, because he knew that what he saw as his duty as archbishop would bring him into conflict with the King, but it was to no avail. In his new role, Thomas worked equally zealously for the interests of the Church, which did indeed generate increasing conflict with the King. The conflict has sometimes been presented (for instance by the playwright Jean Anouilh) as one between Saxon and Norman, but Becket was no Saxon, even though born in London. Becket's mother came from Caen and his father, Gilbert, came from Rouen, so he was of Norman blood.

In 1159, an English army invaded Toulouse to assert the rights of Henry II's wife, Eleanor of Aquitaine. Louis VII of France was able to drive the English off. The English monk and scholar, John of Salisbury, wrote an extended and systematic treatment of political philosophy, Policratus, in which John denounced Henry II for exacting money from the Church to finance the invasion of Toulouse and (daringly) argued that it was justifiable to assassinate tyrants. John was clearly a churchman who saw Henry II as an extremely dangerous threat to the Church. Ironically, the

Toulouse campaign had been led by none other than the chancellor of England, Thomas Becket.

After his appointment as Archbishop of Canterbury in 1162, Becket and Henry began to diverge. By 1164 the quarrel was in full swing. At a conference at Clarendon, Henry II made a concerted attempt to remove the Church's involvement in the judicial system by redefining the areas where church and state should operate. Becket first accepted the proposals, but later rejected them, making his opposition to the King clear, but his change of mind exasperated many of his bishops, who found it increasingly difficult to support him. Later that year Becket was summoned to Northampton Castle, where he was in effect put on trial. Sensing that he faced imprisonment, mutilation and possibly judicial murder if he stayed, Becket fled in the night and made his way across to France. This was the start of a six-year, self-imposed exile, during which none of the political, ethical or personal issues was resolved and the mutual distrust grew. He spent two years in the Abbey of Pontigny, before moving on to the abbey of Sens.

In 1170, while Becket was out of the country, Henry II had himself crowned by Roger, Archbishop of York. This was a deliberate snub to Thomas Becket, because it was the prerogative of the Archbishop of Canterbury to crown monarchs. Becket did not accept or ignore Henry's insult; he persuaded the pope, Alexander III, to suspend Roger and the other bishops who had supported Henry.

Henry was trying to overhaul the administration of England, to make it not only more secular but to make it more equal. Clearly, if some people were tried by the church and some by the state, there were likely to be unfair judgements, and it was evident that the church was more lenient in its judgements. Henry II increased the power of the throne by replacing baronial sheriffs with men who were of lower social rank but with the appropriate administrative training. By doing this, Henry was not only giving people of lower social rank greater opportunities, but reducing the power of the barons and increasing his own power.

But the struggle to reduce the power of the Church in what Henry regarded as secular affairs rumbled on. The Pope put pressure on Henry to come to a reconciliation with Thomas. The quarrel was formally patched up in July 1170 and Thomas agreed to return to England from his voluntary exile in France. It was highly unsatisfactory for the Archbishop of Canterbury to be living overseas when there were huge estates to be administered.

Thomas returned to Canterbury in December 1170, with some apprehension. Although he was formally reconciled with the king, he was still well hated by many of Henry's barons. There was friction, which culminated in Becket excommunicating his enemies on Christmas Day. This provocative act was reported back to Henry, then in France. In an explosion of anger, the king accused those around him of being cowards for not removing 'this turbulent priest'. Four of Henry's knights saw this as a direct order to arrest Becket. They were all-too-familiar with the king's fits of rage and knew that he would later change his mind, so they slipped away in secret and rode as fast as they could to England.

On 29 December, the knights tried to arrest Becket in his palace at Canterbury, and when he refused to go with them they followed him into the cathedral, where he was going to take a service, and killed him in the north transept.

One immediate effect of the murder was to make Henry II travel to Ireland in response to a request for aid from the deposed King of Leinster, Dermot. But this was really a pretext. Henry's real reason for being in Ireland in 1171–72 was the fall-out from the murder of Becket. He wanted to be as far from the verbal and any other attacks there might be from the Pope for his part in Becket's murder. While in Ireland, Henry received homage from several Irish princes at Caskel Rock. The desire had always been there to extend the empire to include Ireland; the Becket murder helped the process on, and therefore played its part in what later became known as the Irish Question – the highly questionable involvement of England in the governance of Ireland.

Another effect of the murder was to weaken Henry II's political credibility. In 1174, he was forced to walk from Harbledown, just outside Canterbury, to Canterbury Cathedral, and submit to a flogging as a penance for causing Becket's death. Becket himself was already regarded as a saint, a saint by public acclamation well before his formal canonization, and quickly became the most important British saint of all. Canterbury Cathedral, the scene of his martyrdom, became a place of pilgrimage – indeed one of the two biggest pilgrimage centres in Europe, Santiago de Compostela being the other. Pilgrims brought wealth with them, and the pilgrimage business was much like modern mass tourism; it brought enormous wealth to Canterbury. The shrine of Becket became an Aladdin's cave of precious stones and gold. It stood in a specially designed extension at the east end of the cathedral, where there is now a large empty space. It may even be that it was specifically the phenomenal wealth of St Thomas's shrine that gave Henry VIII and his advisers the idea of dissolving the monasteries; here was enormous wealth waiting to be tapped. It must have been a great temptation.

Ironically, the martyrdom of Thomas Becket gave the Church renewed strength, making it unassailable for centuries; it had the opposite effect to the one Henry II wanted. The huge wealth generated in Canterbury by the cult of St Thomas may also have been one of the goads that drove Henry VIII towards an English Reformation.

THE YELLOW RIVER CHANGES COURSE

(1194)

THE HUANG HE, or Yellow river, one of the great rivers of China and its most northerly, flows eastwards across a great expanse of flat floodplain to reach the sea. The plain is really a huge shared delta made up of deposits laid down over a long period by the Yellow river, Huaihi and Chihli river. The Yellow river is a yellowish-brown colour because of the huge volume of loess (yellow earth) that it carries in suspension. The river flows through a variety of landscapes before it leaves the Tung Kwan Gorge to cross the huge expanse of the North China Plain. The river has throughout time regularly flooded the floor of its lower valley, spreading sheets of fertile loess across the fields and making them fertile. In 1194, during one of these floods, the Yellow river actually changed its course in the neighbourhood of Kaifeng, flowing south of the Shantung massif to flow into the Yellow Sea.

The Yellow river had changed course like this before, perhaps many times in prehistory, which is why the plain is so broad, and why there is so much land available for rice cultivation. There have been small-scale changes in the position of the river about every 100 years; the large-scale shifts in the lower course are less frequent. The reason is the sheer flatness of the plain. A very slight build-up of silt in one area can cause the water to flow away to another part of the plain. The deposition of sediment within the river channel itself can cause the river to overflow and shift to a lower area.

The Yellow river would change course again, in 1852 – back to the north of the Shantung uplands. These 'flips' from one course to another involve the river mouth in moving over 400km. They represent large-scale changes in the physical geography of the region. More than that – they wreak havoc with people's lives. The focus of flooding shifts, so that areas that were relatively safe from flooding because they were a long way from the river suddenly become much more endangered. Areas that were enriched with silt are no longer enriched and become less productive.

Fortunately the Yellow river has never been a great commercial highway. It is the effects of the flooding on crops and on the human population that have given it its bad reputation as '*China's Sorrow*' or '*The Ungovernable*' or '*The Scourge of the Sons of Han*'. When the Yellow river changed its course in 1194 it caused huge loss of life, as it did again in 1852.

MAGNA CARTA
(1215)

PRINCE JOHN, BORN at Christmas in 1167, was the youngest son of Henry II, the third son who should never have reached the throne of England. Because he was the youngest he was given no territories south of the Channel – hence his nickname, 'Lackland'. He was at a disadvantage even before he came to the throne. In 1177, at the age of 10, he was granted the lordship of Ireland and the homage of the Anglo-Irish barons. His father was conscious of the boy's lack of status compared with his brothers and tried in 1183 to transfer the duchy of Aquitaine from his elder son Richard, later Richard I, to John. This provoked a civil war in which Prince John showed a low level of competence. John joined his brother Richard and the French king in a great conspiracy against his father. When Henry II discovered his sons' treason he was heartbroken.

When Richard came to the throne, he was careful to confirm John's existing possessions and gave him the revenues of six English shires (counties). But Richard excluded him from the regency he appointed when he went off on his crusade, which was a major humiliation. John also discovered, after Richard had set off for the Holy Land, that he had named Duke Arthur of Brittany as his successor. John contrived to obstruct the regency in every way possible, and tried unsuccessfully to seize the throne during Richard's absence. When Richard returned, John was banished for a time, but the brothers were soon reconciled.

Prince John's career before he ascended the throne of England was profoundly unsatisfactory, and the stage was set for him to become an unsatisfactory king.

When Richard died in 1199, his brother John immediately usurped the English throne, but there was a problem in the French possessions. Many of the French noblemen refused to recognize the new King John of England as their king. They preferred to recognize Duke Arthur, who declared himself vassal of

Philip Augustus, the King of France. This was sufficient provocation for John to invade France in 1202.

Philip Augustus recognized Arthur's right to rule Brittany, Anjou, Maine and Poitou, so Arthur set about asserting his right in fact. He was doing so in Poitou when he was surprised at Mirabeau, where he was holding as a hostage King John's mother, Eleanor of Aquitaine.

Arthur was captured by King John's army and imprisoned at Corte. Early in the following year, 1203, he was transferred to Rouen under the charge of William de Braose. He vanished mysteriously in Rouen in April 1203. The mystery of Arthur's disappearance gave rise to many stories at the time. According to one contemporary account, the gaolers were ordered to murder him, but they could not bring themselves to harm him (this was the story William Shakespeare used in his play *King John*). When it was clear that the gaolers would not do the deed, King John himself murdered Arthur and had his body dumped in the River Seine. This scenario might sound too outrageously melodramatic to be true, and it is rare for monarchs to carry out their political murders in person, but there are reasons for believing that it is what happened. There were those in high places who had much to lose by telling the story, and yet that is the story they told.

The balance of the evidence points to King John as a usurper, since Arthur was next in line to the English throne, and it also points to King John as the murderer of Arthur in Rouen in April 1203.

The unproductive foreign campaigns alienated the barons and they resented the King's attempts to make them pay for the fruitless war. After lengthy negotiations, *Magna Carta Libertatum*, the Great Charter of Liberties, was signed at Runnymede, an island in the River Thames between Windsor and Staines, on 15 June 1215. Its significance lay in the formal limitation of the king's power. It was the first step in Europe towards ending the absolute power of the monarchy.

The power struggle between John Lackland and his barons had rumbled on for several years. The feudal barons of England met John with the intention of exacting major concessions from him. Now, we tend to look back on the event as a blow for democracy; the reduction in the absolute power of the king must mean an increase in the powers and rights of the ordinary people. In fact at the time it had much more to do with the barons wanting to conserve their own feudal privileges. Specifically what they required of John was an undertaking to maintain their rights as described in the accession charter of Henry I, 100 years earlier.

The Great Charter did nevertheless contain clauses that promised the maintenance of the nation's laws and ensured the protection of certain common rights – what we would call basic human rights. Central to its 63 clauses was the principle that everyone was entitled to equal treatment before the law. Clause 39 of Magna Carta for example states:

'No freeman shall be arrested and imprisoned, or dispossessed, or outlawed, or banished, or in any way molested; nor will we set forth against him, nor send against him, unless by the lawful judgement of his peers, and by the law of the land.'

This is a clear statement that everyone in England is entitled to the due process of law. It would be further clarified by the law of Habeas Corpus, which said that someone who has been arrested must be brought to trial; he or she cannot be detained in custody without trial.

Magna Carta enshrined the idea of trial by jury, which recent governments have begun to erode. It contains basic principles that have guided the development of English law over the centuries, and many worry when its principles are overridden. People are supposed to have equal access to the law, but in fact litigation has become so expensive that only the rich can take recourse to the process of law; the poor, or even the middle-incomed, have to put up with injustices.

King John's political position had been gravely weakened by his loss of territories in France. His position was the opposite of Henry V's; a successful foreign war and the extension of territory more or less guaranteed a stronger position at home. He had made the situation worse by his extremely unpopular attempt to impose taxes on those knights and lords who had failed to join his foreign expeditions. He was in a hopelessly weak bargaining position, and his barons insisted on his agreement to the charter.

King John's response to the imposition on him of the Great Charter was to appeal to Pope Innocent III, who issued a statement annulling the Great Charter. John brought in foreign mercenaries to fight the English barons, but the charter remained the foundation of English feudal justice for the rest of the middle ages, and on the justice system thereafter. The English justice system was then exported to the colonies, and has become a model for the systems in most Commonwealth countries, so the bedrock of Magna Carta underlies the legal systems of many countries around the world.

THE INTRODUCTION
OF ANAESTHETICS
(1236)

THE SEARCH FOR a drug that would alleviate pain went on throughout antiquity. A Dominican friar, Theodoric of Lucca, experimented with anaesthetics in 1236. Theodoric was a teacher at Bologna and also the son of a surgeon to the Crusaders. Theodoric recommended using sponges soaked in narcotics applied to the patient's nose. This induced a deep sleep during which surgery could be carried out with no pain.

Theodoric favoured using mandragora and opium, both known as opiates, for this pioneering anaesthetic. The idea of using anaesthetics came and went repeatedly through history. Some technologies and techniques were progressively built on, while others were devised, forgotten and re-invented later.

For hundreds of years after Theodoric's discovery, surgeons went on operating on conscious patients, who had to endure terrible pain. After Joseph Priestley discovered oxygen and nitrous oxide in 1772, there was continuing research into these and other chemical agents – and this research eventually led to the discovery of anaesthetics. Humphry Davy discovered that nitrous oxide could be used as an anaesthetic in 1800 and proposed that it should be used for that purpose by surgeons. Later, Michael Faraday inhaled ether and described its effect. It was not until 1842 that ether was used as an anaesthetic in surgery, by the American Crawford Long. In 1846, William Morton gave a public demonstration of the use of ether to induce unconsciousness, and therefore pain-free surgery. Ether was administered in the same way that Theodoric recommended – a drug-saturated sponge or cloth applied to the nose.

The use of anaesthetics for surgery has improved the quality of life of everyone who has had to undergo surgery. Pain-induced shock must have killed many people on the operating-table before anaesthetics were invented. Anaesthetics have also made it possible for surgeons to undertake more ambitious and time-consuming surgical procedures than before; medical conditions that might once have been considered inoperable became operable.

THE ARRIVAL OF GUNPOWDER IN EUROPE
(1249)

GUNPOWDER WAS INVENTED by the Chinese, who were using gunpowder several centuries BC. The Mongol forces used gunpowder-fuelled firearms to conquer much of Eastern Europe in 1237. The Mongol hordes led by Khan Ogadai, Batu Khan and General Subutai laid waste to Poland. In 1240, they conquered Kiev as they swept through southern and central Russia and the Ukraine. In 1241, the Mongols of the Golden Horde won the Battle of the Liegnitz in Silesia. There was no stopping them. They cut down the feudal nobles of eastern Europe, including the German Knights Templar. The death of Ogadai seems to have stunned the Mongols; they gave up their campaign of conquest and withdrew to Karakorum. They had invaded Poland, Hungary and much of Russia – yet they gave up these conquered lands when they lost their leader.

Such was the military superiority of the Mongols, with their firearms, that they might have gone on to conquer western Europe too. The accident of Ogadai's death put the process into reverse. They withdrew into central Asia and a very different history of Europe was allowed to unfold.

Up to this point gunpowder seems to have been unknown in Europe. Military weaponry was based on swords, halberds, axes and arrows. There were no European firearms. That was about to change, thanks to this brush with oriental culture.

The 35 year old Franciscan Roger Bacon made the earliest known European reference to gunpowder in a letter written in 1249. Bacon had discovered how to make gunpowder, which was 40 percent saltpetre, 30 percent carbon and 30 percent sulphur. He also discovered some of its properties, though he seems not to have known that it could be used as a propellent. Prior to Bacon's time, saltpetre, the main ingredient of gunpowder, was not available in refined form, and the earlier, unrefined type is not so good as a propellent.

Nevertheless, this transfer of knowledge from Asia to Europe was to revolutionize European warfare. From this point on, weaponry using gunpowder increasingly dominated warfare. From about 1250 on, gunpowder was used to shoot missiles from projectile weapons. Gunpowder eventually, by the sixteenth century, made castles obsolete, because it could relatively easily undermine walls of any thickness. Iron shot fired from cannons could break down the base of a wall and cause it to collapse.

The main and virtually the only use for gunpowder in Europe was for warfare – for 400 years. It was only in the seventeenth century that it was used for peaceful purposes, in the mining industry. In 1696, it was used to blast away rock in a road-widening project in Switzerland. More and more applications were found, until gunpowder was overtaken by dynamite and nitroglycerin, which became available at a competitive price in about 1870. Probably the biggest single project in which gunpowder was used was the destruction of Pot Rock, a navigation hazard in New York Harbour, in 1851–53.

THE BATTLE OF LEWES
(1264)

THE EARL OF Leicester, Simon de Montfort (1200–65), was brought up in France and arrived in England in 1230, when he joined the court of King Henry III. He managed to have the earldom of Leicester revived in his favour. Early on he showed a streak of unbending harshness when he cruelly expelled the Jews from Leicester. Later he was to show a similar taste for harshness when he was Governor of the Duchy of Gascony. He decided to take action against the local Gascon lords and took action that was regarded as excessive. There was an outcry against the Earl of Leicester's behaviour, and the king agreed to set up a formal enquiry into the earl's administration.

This was the turning-point in de Montfort's relationship with the King. Henry III's formal enquiry resulted in de Montfort's acquittal on charges of oppression, but Henry did not believe the account de Montfort had given of events. In 1252, de Montfort withdrew in disgust to France, where he was invited to become regent; the queen mother had died, leaving a vacancy, but de Montfort declined this honour. He thought it would be better to make his peace with Henry III. There was a partial reconciliation between them, but in the parliament of 1254 de Montfort led the opposition in resisting the King's demand for money.

By 1265, all parties involved were becoming angry and frustrated and the situation was overheating, though de Montfort was still nominally supporting the King. But at the so-called 'Mad Parliament' of Oxford in 1258 he headed the opposition. It is not clear what de Montfort had in mind, but he evidently hoped for a compromise, not liking the narrow self-interest of the barons any more than the extreme royalism coming from the other side. In 1261, de Montfort left England, despairing of a negotiated solution.

Two years later he returned at the request of the English barons, who were now convinced that Henry III was hostile to all reform. De Montfort raised a rebellion and for a while it looked as if the royalists would give way in the face of military force, but he made the mistake of agreeing to the King's request for arbitration by the King of France. At Amiens in January 1264 the French King decided that the King's constitutional proposals, or 'Provisions' as they were called, were invalid and unlawful.

That decided it. On the strength of this judgement of king upon king, de Montfort declared open war on Henry III. Even though he was supported militarily by only some of the towns and some of the younger barons, Simon de Montfort was a skilled enough general to defeat the King of England's army, which he did at the landmark Battle of Lewes on 14 May 1264.

De Montfort and Henry III both fought in person in this bloody battle. The King was ignominiously defeated – and captured – by de Montfort's troops. Two days after the battle de Montfort received the surrender of the King's son, the 25 year old prince, the Lord Edward, and he was forced to give up his earldom of Chester. As a result of this spectacular victory, Simon de Montfort became the unofficial king, protector or regent of England.

He set up the government by which his reputation as a key historical figure stands or falls. He set up a triumvirate consisting of himself, the young Earl of Gloucester and the Bishop of Chichester. This was a distinctly weak point in his new system of government, in that it was not a partnership of equals; it must have been obvious to everyone at the time, as it is now, that Simon de Montfort himself was going to make all the key decisions and the other two were there as window dressing, to disguise what could easily have degenerated into a dictatorship. The saving feature of his new system was the new importance that de Montfort gave to Parliament as an institution; there was to be thorough and complete parliamentary control over the executive, and that included the triumvirate. Even the earl himself was to be bound by what Parliament dictated. This was the great new idea that sprang out of the battle. This was the birth of the English Parliament as we know it today.

The reaction against de Montfort's Parliament came not from the people, but from the barons. Many of them resented and distrusted de Montfort's friends and allies. In particular the lords living in the Welsh Marches (borders) distrusted his alliance with Llewellyn of North Wales.

At Whitsun the following year, 1265, Prince Edward managed to escape from his captors. He succeeded in gaining support from the Lords of the Welsh Marches, rallying them and meeting de Montfort at Evesham. At this decisive battle on 4 August, de Montfort was defeated and killed. Prince Edward effectively ruled England during the remaining seven years of his father's reign.

Henry III died at Westminster in November 1272 after a reign that had lasted 56 years. Prince Edward was in Sicily on a crusade at the time and did not hear of his father's death for some weeks; he had unwittingly become King Edward I. The struggle for power with the barons led so ably by Simon de Montfort prepared Edward well for the hard task of being a king in medieval England. Edward was an aggressive, uncompromising warrior-king. At the first whiff of rebellion from the Welsh, Edward prepared to invade. Llewellyn II ap Gryffydd refused to pay homage to the English king, and the English king's response in 1277 was to take an army in, surround Llewellyn and starve him out.

But the major outcome of de Montfort's challenge to Henry III was the creation of a recognizable English Parliament, an institution which in time grew stronger and stronger. It acted as a check on successive monarchs, reining them in until, by the seventeenth century, it could throw out a monarch who was too uncompromising. Today it is a Parliament of democratically elected members that makes the decisions; the monarch acts mainly as a symbol of stability and continuity as successive Parliaments fall or are re-elected.

THE CHINESE
INVASION OF JAPAN
(1274)

THE EMPEROR OF Japan refused to receive dispatches from the Chinese calling on him to submit to the Emperor of China. The emperor of China, Kublai Khan, retaliated strenuously to this snub by sending an invasion fleet to conquer Japan. The Chinese invasion fleet consisted of 300 large vessels together with around 500 smaller ships. Loaded with around 8,000 Korean and 20,000 Mongol warriors, the ships made landfall in Hakata Bay on the island of Kyushu on 19 October.

The invading force used an armoury including iron cannons and iron cannonballs. They also used poisoned arrows, which was a violation of Japanese war protocol.

On 20 November a typhoon struck, sinking over 200 of the Mongol ships. Around 13,000 Mongol warriors were sleeping on board at the time and many of them drowned. After this disaster, the survivors withdrew to the Asian mainland. The invasion that was intended to humble the Emperor of Japan instead ended with the humiliation of the Emperor of China.

Kublai Khan was not so easily put off, though. In May 1281, he tried again. A second invasion was sent across to Japan. This time there were twice as many Mongol warriors, and they were reinforced two months later by a landing of 100,000 more troops from southern China. The Chinese emperor presumably thought the huge numbers would ensure success, but once again the Japanese were saved by natural events. Another typhoon arrived on 29 July, destroying most of the Chinese invasion fleet. This time over 2000 of the Mongol warriors were taken prisoner, and as many as 80 percent of the Mongol and Korean warriors were drowned.

After this second typhoon, the Japanese came to realize that natural disasters can be benign. They began to refer to the typhoons as 'divine winds'. China's great khan still saw himself as a conqueror. In 1284, he sent an invasion force of half a million warriors in another direction, this time south into Vietnam. The Chinese army quickly found itself in difficulties as a result of the guerrilla tactics used by the Vietnamese. Guerrillas organized by Tran Hung Dao destroyed virtually the entire invasion army. Another disaster for Kublai Khan.

The 'lesson of history' has become a platitude. Notoriously, people do not learn the lesson of history and that is why – another platitude – history repeats itself. The same mistakes are made over and over again. Kublai Khan just went on assembling huge invading armies that went on to be annihilated; it was an exercise in not learning from the past.

MARCO POLO'S VISIT TO CHINA
(1275)

Marco Polo was born into a family of Venetian merchants in 1254. He was born while his father and uncle were away on a commercial expedition to Bokhara and Cathay (China); the two brothers, Nicolo and Maffeo, had been engaged in ambitious long-distance trading of this kind for a long time. Their business dealings took them to Constantinople, then on to the Crimea and eventually to Bokhara in central Asia. It was there that they met some envoys from Kublai Khan, and travelled with them into Cathay.

Nicolo and Maffeo Polo were well-received there by the great emperor, Kublai Khan, who it seems had never seen Europeans before. He commissioned them to act as his ambassadors to the pope. He wanted them to ask the pope to send 100 Europeans who were learned in the arts and sciences. The Polos had every intention of carrying out this potentially epoch-making mission in 1269, but they found when they returned to the West and reached Acre that no new pope had been elected following the death of Clement IV the previous year. With an acute sense of failure they returned to Venice, resolving to go back to Cathay.

The Polo brothers set off again in 1271, this time taking with them the young Marco, who was then 17. They travelled through Mosul, Baghdad, Khorassan, the Pamirs, Kashgar, Yarkand, Khoton, Lob Nor, the Gobi Desert, Tangut and Shangtu, eventually arriving at the court of Kublai Khan in 1275. The places they passed through on the second half of their journey were almost totally unknown to Europeans, though they were familiar stopping-places for Asian traders. The Khan was once again very pleased to see them and specially interested in the young Marco Polo, who was soon sent off as an envoy to Yunnan, Burma, Karakorum, Cochin China and Southern India. Marco was taught the languages of the Khan's

169

subjects. For three years he served as governor of Yang Chow.

The Khan was very reluctant to let these useful Westerners leave his court, but they were apprehensive about what might happen to them in the wake of the old khan's death. For their own safety, they decided they wanted to leave Cathay before he died. Eventually an opportunity arose by chance. They were commissioned to escort a young noblewoman on a long sea voyage. After long delays in Sumatra and India, they managed to sail to Persia. The Polos finally returned to Venice in 1295, bringing with them the great wealth they had acquired along the way. But on arrival at their family mansion they were at first rejected and ridiculed as unrecognizable, as they were wearing worn and outlandish clothes; nobody believed they really were the Polos.

In 1298, Marco Polo commanded a galley at the Battle of Curzola, in which the Venetians were defeated by the Genoese. He was taken prisoner and kept in Genoa for a year. He had his notes, which he had originally written for the khan, sent across from Venice and another prisoner in Genoa, Rusticiano of Pisa, helped him to make a continuous prose record from them.

Map-makers tried to incorporate Marco Polo's geographical information into their maps. This was not done with any great accuracy, but at least hitherto empty areas of maps were now filled in. Marco Polo did not introduce the idea of block printing from China. Indeed he rather oddly did not mention the distinctive Chinese printing method at all. Discrepancies and omissions like this have led some modern commentators to dismiss Marco Polo's book as a traveller's tale in the worst sense of the phrase – a tall story with little truth in it. Indeed it is hard to understand why the great khan would have wanted to use as envoys foreigners with little or no understanding of the languages spoken in China. Perhaps the Polos exaggerated their importance in Cathay to make a good story better, but it cannot be seriously doubted that they travelled there.

The impact of their travels was profound. Europeans had to come to terms with the fact that there was a great civilization in eastern Asia that was in many ways more advanced than Western civilization. It encouraged a mental outreach that would bear fruit in the physical outreach of the Columbus voyages and other major European voyages of discovery.

THE EXECUTION OF JACQUES DE MOLAY
(1314)

JACQUES DE MOLAY was Grand Master of the French Knights Templar. This distinguished old gentleman was seized by order of the French king, charged with heresy and burnt to death. In order to understand this extraordinary and unexpected incident in 1314, we need to understand who the Knights Templar were.

The Knights Templar formed one of the three great medieval military orders of the early middle ages. It was founded in 1119 to protect the many Christian pilgrims who were flocking to Jerusalem and the other holy places in the wake of the First Crusade. The order of knights was a religious community and unlike other orders of chivalry it would not involve a quest for social rank. The King of Jerusalem, Baldwin II, gave them accommodation in his palace, next to the site of the Temple of Solomon, which is how they came by their name – the Knights Templar.

Through time, the organization of the order became more complex, formal and hierarchical. A detailed Rule of the Temple was created, which included lists of offences and the punishments that went with them. The order was headed by a 'Grand Master' and by 1150 it had Temples established in every Christian land and became richly endowed.

The Templars fought recklessly against Saladin and his army. Richard I of England was sympathetic to the Templars, consulting them on matters of military strategy. He even wore the livery of a Templar, apparently as a disguise, and sailed in a Templar galley when he left the Holy Land. Once Acre was recovered from Saladin it became the Templar headquarters. Their fortress, aptly called Castle Pilgrim, was built on a rocky headland.

It was from Castle Pilgrim in 1218 that the Fifth Crusade was launched – against Egypt. The Knights Templar fought heroically at the siege of

Damietta, where William de Chartres, the King of Jerusalem, was killed. The three great military orders, the Templars, the Hospitallers and the Teutonic Kinghts, were openly hostile to one another. Infighting led to the loss of Jerusalem in 1244.

The order remained on its pinnacle of wealth and power for one hundred years. The Paris Temple was the centre of the world's money market. It accumulated all sorts of privileges and immunities. As late as 1306, the French king Philip IV took refuge from a violent mob in the Paris Temple. But he also saw destroying the order as a way of replenishing his own empty coffers.

For decades rumours had circulated about strange midnight ceremonies conducted by the Templars. It was said that they worshipped a strange symbol or idol called Baphomet. Their ceremonies were secret, and must therefore be blasphemous; the Templars must be heretics, Satanists. The reality was probably that in a military order there were often military reasons for maintaining security – and secrecy had become a habit. In 1305, the so-called secrets of the order were betrayed to the Kings of Aragon and France by Esquiu de Floyran. Philip IV tried to goad the pope in taking action, but the pope was not interested. Philip instead activated the Inquisition, which was free to act without the pope. On 6 June 1306, the pope summoned the Grand Master Jacques de Molay from Cyprus to discuss the projected crusade. Philip ordered his seneschals to arrest all members of the order, and de Molay was arrested with 60 other members of the order in Paris in October 1307.

To obtain the incriminating evidence they needed, the king's officials were free to use torture. The Inquisition was ready to resort to torture too. Under this threat, the old Grand Master confessed in writing to denying Christ and spitting on the cross. In the wake of his admission, the pope demanded that other heads of state throughout Christendom must arrest all members of the order. In England, Sicily and Cyprus the arrests came in January 1308.

Complex legal wrangles followed, but in May 1310 over 60 French Templars were burnt to death. The 71 year old Jacques de Molay had avoided torture by volunteering his confession, but he found his courage at the last moment. In March 1314, he and Geoffrey de Charnay, the preceptor of Normandy, were led onto a scaffold in front of Notre Dame, where they were to confess yet again and receive their sentence of life imprisonment. Instead they withdrew their confessions and protested the innocence of the order. King Philip ordered them to be burnt. About to die, de Molay pronounced a formal curse on the king and the pope, and called on God to bring down justice on them. Both king and pope were to die painful deaths within the year.

The lasting legacy of this cruel episode was that it created a model for all the hideous witch hunts and heresy trials of the next 300 years. As for the Knights Templar and their grand master, they were almost certainly not guilty, though the belief that they practised unusual rituals still flourishes. It has been suggested that that the Templars really did revere a strange image, and that the image secretly honoured in Paris was the image of Christ preserved on the (folded) cloth later known as the Shroud of Turin. The image, 'brought in by the priest in a procession of priests with candles, was laid on the altar; it was a human head without any silver or gold, very pale and discoloured, with a grizzled beard like a Templar's'.

THE BLACK DEATH
(1348)

THE BLACK DEATH was a virulent outbreak of the plague that periodically swept across Eurasia, wiping out thousands of people. Like the Plague of Justinian, the Black Death was transmitted by rat-borne fleas. The rats travelled with cargoes in carts, wagons and the holds of ships, and so the disease spread easily along Europe's busy trade routes. Europe's commercial success was its undoing as far as the spread of disease was concerned. In 1347 the Black Death reached Cyprus. From there it travelled by sea to ports such as Livorno and from there to towns inland such as Pisa and Florence. The Black Death reached Florence in April, France in June and England in August.

The French doctor Guy de Chauliac stayed in the Auvergne in central France, even though most of the other doctors had fled. He wrote about the disease.

> 'The visitation came in two forms. The first lasted two months, manifesting itself as an intermittent fever accompanied by spitting of blood from which people died usually in three days. The second type manifested itself in high fever, abscesses and carbuncles, chiefly in the axillae and groin. People died from this in five days. So contagious was the disease especially that with blood spitting that no-one could approach or even see a patient without taking the disease. The father did not visit the son nor the son the father. Charity was dead and hope abandoned.'

There was absolutely no cure for the Black Death. De Chauliac's only remedy was blood-letting, which can have done his patients no good whatsoever, but only weakened them and hastened their death.

People habitually looked for scapegoats in times of crisis, and they picked on the Jews. It was said that Jews deliberately contaminated wells and 'anointed' houses with poison. The first persecution in the wake of the Black Death was at Chillon on the shore of Lake Geneva, and it was quickly followed by persecutions at Basel and Freiburg, where all the Jews that could be found were shut inside wooden buildings and burnt alive. At Strasbourg over 2,000 Jews were hanged on a scaffold raised at the Jewish burial ground.

Pope Clement VI issued two statements declaring that the Jews were innocent of spreading the Black Death, but it made no difference. The persecution continued. Thousands of Jews fled from Western Europe, heading for more tolerant countries in Eastern Europe such as Poland and Russia.

This violent outbreak of anti-semitism was one manifestation of the mass hysteria that the plague pandemic produced. Year after year, thousands of people died. By the time the pandemic was over, half the population of Europe was dead. In some areas, as many as two-thirds of the people died. Locally, it could be worse still. The population of Locarno on Lake Maggiore in Italy dropped from 4,800 to only 700. The Black Death was to wipe out the populations of some villages in England entirely. Others were reduced to a level where they could no longer continue. These plague villages were permanently abandoned. Their grassed-over street-plans can still be picked out on air photographs, and on the ground it is often possible to pick out rectangular bumps in fields marking the sites of individual houses and the hollows marking the streets.

There was also a serious shortage of workers after the Black Death. In 1377, it is estimated that there were two million people living in England; before the Black Death there had been five million. In England, a law was passed, the Statute of Labourers, which tried to compel workers to accept work if it was offered – but it also, unwisely, tried to fix wages at their 1346 levels. In 1360, English labourers who tried to negotiate higher wages were given prison sentences. The situation was sliding towards a peasants' revolt. The drop in population reduced pressure on food supplies and prices fell for lack of demand. Farming was suddenly far less profitable and many landlords turned their arable land over to animal pasture as a result. This led to an increase in sheep numbers and in wool production. Western Europe was thrown into an economic and social crisis.

The huge losses of people in both England and France caused the governments of the two countries to call a truce in the Hundred Years' War between the two countries in 1349. A Scottish army opportunistically invaded

England at this time, but the soldiers caught the plague and took it back to Scotland with them. By this stage the Black Death had swept eastwards across Europe, reaching Poland and Russia. There, people were already weakened by poverty and famine, and they quickly fell victim to the disease.

As the Black Death engulfed Europe, there were several repeat outbreaks. In 1371, for instance, there was a new outbreak of the plague in England, though not as ferocious as before. In 1374, the Venetian authorities put plague precautions in place; officials were appointed to inspect vessels wishing to enter ports and to prohibit the entry of any ships that were found to be infected with Black Death. The Black Death was a personal disaster for the individuals and families who caught the disease. It was also a disaster for many small settlements, which became non-viable and had to be abandoned after large numbers of villagers died. Some rural areas emptied. There were food and labour shortages. The Black Death, halving Europe's population, was a major demographic and economic disaster.

PEASANTS' REVOLT
(1381)

IN 1376, THE so-called 'Good Parliament' made efforts to improve the commercial lot of native Londoners by excluding foreigners from retailing there and banishing Lombard bankers. But it also enforced the 1351 Statute of Labourers. Then the Black Prince died and following his death his brother, John of Gaunt, packed Parliament with men who undid the work of the Good Parliament. In 1377, Edward III himself died, and his young son became king as Richard II. The government was then actually run by John of Gaunt, Duke of Lancaster.

The labouring class was angry at the wage restraint imposed by the Statute of Labourers, now renewed. Then they were provoked even more by the imposition of a poll tax; everyone, whether rich or poor, was to pay a fixed tax. The Poll Tax was extremely unpopular. Instead of sensing this and leaving well alone, the authorities stepped up the tax in 1381 and this proved to be the last straw; it produced the Peasants' Revolt. It was a heavy tax and a blatantly unfair one.

The Peasants' Revolt was led by Wat Tyler. It created chaos in southern England and the King's ministers were completely unequal to the situation. It had apparently never occurred to them, in their close-knit world of baronial alliances and rivalries that the people themselves might rise up against them. Farm workers and also craftsmen and other workers in the cities rebelled against the 1351 Statute of Labourers and the poll tax. Mobs gathered in Norfolk, Essex and Kent, ransacking palaces, castles and the houses of the rich. Rioters assembled in the eastern counties and converged on London, where they burnt a number of key buildings: the Temple, the Clerkenwell headquarters of the Knights Hospitallers, and the Savoy Palace, owned by John of Gaunt, widely suspected of having designs on the throne of England. Once in London, the great crowd of rioters were ably led by Wat Tyler. The mob broke into the Tower of London, where they succeeding in capturing the Archbishop of Canterbury Simon Sudbury. They dragged the unfortunate archbishop out of the Tower and onto Tower Hill, where many public executions were held, and hacked off his head. Elsewhere the Hanseatic traders were chased into their steelyard.

On 14 June 1381, at Mile End, the 14 year old King Richard II was presented with a list of demands by Wat Tyler. Richard II showed considerable ability in dealing with the situation. With the skill of a seasoned politician he made empty promises to abolish serfdom, the poll tax, restrictions on labour and trade and convinced Tyler that he was on the side of the people. He also agreed to abolish game laws, put an upper limit on land rents and road tolls – none of which he had any intention of doing.

At Smithfield the next day there was a further meeting between Tyler and the king. Tyler made fresh demands and the Mayor of London William Walworth stabbed Tyler, mortally wounding him. The crowd could have closed in on the king, but he handled the dangerous moment with incredible skill and aplomb, calling disarmingly to the crowd that they should take him for their leader.

The situation was similar in France, where there were similar economic and social problems, similar frustrations and grievances. In Languedoc, the peasants staged a rising against their tax collectors.

In 1382, in the wake of the Peasants' Revolt, Richard II re-established the situation as it was before the rebellion, reinstating serfdom. One effect that the revolt had was to make the King assert himself. One minister appointed for him by his council was the earl of Arundel; the young king disliked him and dismissed him in 1383. Richard II made his own appointees, and some of the choices he made were good. The episode led directly to his period of personal government, eventually to absolute power, and then he became extravagant and capricious.

The King's victory over his people was in any case Pyrrhic. He had lost the confidence and trust of the people, and the problems and grievances of the people remained unaddressed. They would not go away. Rebellion would break out again.

THE SACK OF DELHI
(1398)

TAMERLANE WAS GENGHIS Khan's great-great-grandson. As a young man he nursed the pipe dream of rebuilding his ancestor's empire, which had subsequently disintegrated into a large number of small principalities. It seemed unlikely that he would be able to fulfil this dream, as he was disabled. The locals nicknamed him Timur i Leng, Timur the Lame. Yet in spite of the limp, he is remembered as Tamerlane the Great, a ruthless and sadistic warmonger just like his great-great-grandfather. Tamerlane looked extraordinary. He was tall, with a huge head. He was also white-haired even from childhood. He was altogether a frightening figure, and he relied on fear above all to ensure the allegiance of his subjects.

He was 33 when he seized the Transoxian throne at Samarkand, acquiring the power base he needed for his scheme of conquest. He did not reward loyalty with loyalty. Governors who appealed to him often found they were betrayed once he had taken control of their kingdoms.

Timur made a great name for himself as a conqueror. He began his conquest of eastern Persia in 1381, which fell to him in 1385. He went on to take Iraq, Azerbaijan, Armenia, Mesopotamia and Georgia in 1394. Next he marched on Moscow, which he occupied for a year. Not content with these conquests, the 60 year old Timur decided to invade India. His pretext was that the sultans of Delhi were showing too much tolerance to their Hindu subjects, which is possibly the wickedest and flimsiest reason ever given for an invasion.

Timur led his armed hordes through the Himalayan passes into northern India. On 24 September, Timur crossed the River Indus, advancing at a rate of about 130km a day and leaving a trail of carnage. He was moving so quickly that he overtook refugees who were fleeing before him from various towns.

In December 1398, Tamerlane reached Delhi, where he took many prisoners. He killed 100,000 Hindu prisoners in a massacre there and then a few days later set about destroying the city, which he reduced to a mass of ruins. The army of Delhi was destroyed. Later in the month he moved on to Meerut, which he stormed in January 1399. After that he fought his way back through the foothills of the Himalayas to reach the Indus again on 19 March. In the space of just a few months, Tamerlane had completely devastated the kingdom of Delhi. The city of Delhi itself was a complete shambles; it took an entire century for it to be rebuilt – and to recover.

Timur returned to his capital with an immense quantity of spoil. Ninety The saga of the great conqueror with his huge army invading, killing and destroying was a story that was retold endlessly. Only a couple of years after the destruction of Delhi, Timur sacked Baghdad, a city that was still reeling from the atrocities inflicted by Halagu 100 years before, and set it on fire, killing 20,000 people. The reign of Tamerlane was a nightmare revisitation of an earlier era – just as he had hoped it would be. Quite apart from the loss of life and the sheer human suffering caused, the conqueror's pillaging kept kingdoms poor and halted social and economic development. Warfare and the gratuitous destruction it causes – the collateral damage – have been major factors in slowing down, and sometimes reversing, the march of progress.

THE ARRIVAL OF PTOLEMY'S *GEOGRAPHY IN ITALY*
(1405)

CLAUDIUS PTOLEMAEUS WAS born in a Greek colony in Egypt. Very little else is known about him, except that he was an astronomer and made his astronomical observations at Alexandria during the reigns of Hadrian and Antoninus Pius. Shortly after his lifetime it was said that he had lived in the Temple of Serapis at Canopus, near Alexandria.

Ptolemy's model for the motion of the heavenly bodies, known as the Ptolemaic system, assumes that the Earth is at the centre of the universe and that the heavenly bodies revolve round it. The Ptolemaic system was nevertheless to be challenged by Copernicus and Galileo.

Ptolemy's work as a geographer had further-reaching effects. A lot of Ptolemy's work was not original; he was largely a compiler and corrector of other people's work, but no less useful for that. Ptolemy's great work was the *Guide to Geography*. This, along with a lot of other classical learning, was forgotten or even lost in Europe, and only kept alive by Arabic scholars. It was the rediscovery by Europeans of those Arabic copies that fuelled the Renaissance. A copy of Ptolemy's book arrived in south-eastern Europe in the middle ages, where it was discovered, in a bookshop, and carried back to Italy in 1405. It was then that Ptolemy's book took on a new lease of life.

Before Ptolemy's time, the astronomer Hipparchus pointed out that the only way to construct a reliable and trustworthy map of the world was to use astronomical observations to fix the latitude and longitude of all the principal points on its surface. This was a good idea in principle, but the means of acquiring this sort of information were lacking. Then, just before Ptolemy's time, Marinus of Tyre started to collect determinations of latitude and longitude from itineraries. It is not clear how far Marinus got, but Ptolemy evidently used Marinus' work and started where he left off. Ptolemy divided up the equator into 360 parts, and these became our modern degrees. Ptolemy drew lines through these points, connecting them to the North and South Poles to make lines of longitude. He drew another set of lines parallel to the equator to mark the latitude. Then he located his known points on this grid.

Then Ptolemy made an odd mistake. Eratosthenes had correctly calculated the circumference of the Earth as 40,000km. Posidonius had wrongly reduced this to 29,000km, and Ptolemy unfortunately followed Posidonius instead of Eratosthenes. As a result, significant errors were built into his map from the start. Ptolemy was also working on relatively little data on longitude. All things considered, Ptolemy made an honest attempt at a world map, and Europe, Asia and Africa are recognizable. He also produced regional maps, and in effect invented the atlas. He established regional and world maps as a way of looking at the world – and that was a major step in changing people's perception.

The *Guide to Geography* included tables of places and their locations, showing an admirable scientific rigour of approach, one that would be a model to the Renaissance world. Ptolemy's maps, for all their faults, were better than most of the maps constructed in medieval Europe. The rediscovery of a copy of Ptolemy's maps, together with the statistical tables that had led to their construction, was a turning point in the European Renaissance.

It was in 1405 that a copy of Ptolemy's *Geography* was taken to Italy. 1405 was a turning-point in Eurasian history. It marked the death of Timur, which was good news for Asia, and the birth of modern geography in Europe, which marked the beginning of a period of outreach to the rest of the world; it was also the year when the very first major Chinese voyage of exploration was launched.

The errors in Ptolemy themselves had an effect on European history. Ptolemy extended eastern Asia a long way eastwards, shortening the distance between Europe and China by 50 degrees of latitude, and making a westward route from Europe to the Far East seem much more manageable. This in turn justified Columbus's belief that it was possible to reach China by crossing the Atlantic – which is what he was led to believe. Toscanelli sent Columbus a chart which showed Cipangu (Japan) as lying 7,600km to the west of the Canaries, which is under one-third of its true distance. Columbus needed to 'sell' his voyage to a sponsor, and this led him to use the most favourable figures, the shortest distances. He was deliberately choosing the largest credible extension of the Old World in order to make the estimated sailing time as short as possible. Ptolemy calculated the length of a degree of longitude as 80km, against the reality of 96.5km, but Columbus proposed an even short distance – 72.5km. The result of this mathematical jiggery-pokery was to pull Japan eastwards to the longitude of the Western Antilles and the coast of Cathay to the longitude of the west coast of Mexico. Columbus was using Ptolemy, along with other geographical sources, to window-dress his case for a voyage of discovery across the Atlantic.

The fact that Ptolemy included a set of maps made a huge difference to the impact that his work had on medieval Europe. The maps were clearly and self-evidently more accurate and more scientific than anything else that was then in existence. There were some inaccuracies, but most of them were fairly obvious. Ptolemy's world map showed an Indian Ocean that was landlocked. It was sealed off at 15 degrees South by a coastline that connected Africa to South-East Asia. On the other hand the Greek geographer Cosmas Indicopleustes, writing in the sixth century, and who had been to India, said that China, 'the country of silk', could be reached by a sea voyage; he even so recommended the land route to Cathay. What happened later, thanks to the development of Islam from the seventh century onwards, was the expansion of an Arab empire in the Middle East that made it increasingly difficult for Europeans to reach Cathay or India overland with any degree of safety. This too added energy to the quest for a sea route round Africa and across the Indian Ocean. There was some doubt in the fifteenth century about who was right, Cosmas or Ptolemy. The voyages of Dias and da Gama round the Cape of Good Hope and into the Indian Ocean showed that Ptolemy was wrong.

For many scholars and navigators looking at those maps must have been a revelation. Suddenly, much more was possible. The 'rediscovery' of Ptolemy by European scholars led directly on to the foundation of the Sagres school of navigation by Prince Henry the Navigator in 1421, to the first tentative explorations of the west coast of Africa by the Portuguese, and to the great voyages of discovery by Christopher Columbus, Bartolomeo Diaz and Vasco da Gama.

THE VOYAGES OF
ZHENG HE
(1405–33)

THE CHINESE MING emperor Yung Lo ordered the first major Chinese voyage of exploration in 1405. A fleet of 63 war-junks carrying an army of 28,000 men sailed under the command of the Muslim eunuch, Ma, who took the name Zheng He (or Cheng Ho). The war-junks in his fleet were gigantic vessels with five or six decks and weighing about 1,500 tonnes each. They were also equipped with magnetic compasses. There were support ships including horse-ships, carrying mounts for the expedition's soldiers. The ships carried enough grain, wine, livestock and other provisions for a year's sailing on the high seas. They carried cargoes of porcelain, silk, satin, gold and silver, to trade for lions, rhinos, myrrh and ambergris. The colossal fleet first sailed south from China to explore the islands of Indonesia.

In 1407, Zheng He returned to China with the Prince of Palembang (Sumatra) on board; Zheng He had defeated him in battle, put him in chains and taken him back to show him off to the Chinese emperor. The following year Zheng He was sent off on a second voyage. This time he took his invasion fleet westwards into the Indian Ocean, sailing as far as Ceylon (Sri Lanka). The Sinhalese attacked the Chinese, seeing the visit of the fleet as an invasion. They were easily overpowered by the Chinese. The Sinhalese royal family, including the King of Ceylon, were captured and taken back to China to show to the emperor.

In 1412, the great Chinese admiral Zheng He set off on a third expedition, this time sailing westwards right across the Indian Ocean. He reached the Straits of Hormuz, the entrance to the Persian Gulf. A fourth expedition in 1416 took the fleet right across the Indian Ocean again, to reach Aden. In 1421, a fifth voyage of the Star Raft, the great invasion fleet, was begun. The following year Zheng He reached Malindi on the East African coast (Kenya).

Ten years later there was a sixth voyage, led like all the others by Zheng He. This one visited the coast of East Africa and the Red Sea.

The purpose of the voyages was as much to display the might and prestige of China as to find out what lay in the world outside China. It was a travelling trade fair, a kind of floating Crystal Palace. The Chinese were interested in conquest, domination and trade. On the final voyage, during which Zheng He visited 20 countries, he exacted tribute from 11 of them, including the city of Mecca. What the Chinese wanted was the subservience of the outside world. They seem to have been unimpressed by the many varied cultures they encountered.

In 1433, Zheng He returned to China at the end of his seventh and last expedition, bringing with him tribute from 11 states to the Ming Emperor, who was presented with giraffes, zebras and other exotic curiosities from Africa. But the curiosity of the Chinese emperor seems by this stage to have been satisfied. There would be no more ambitious voyages, no more attempts to make contact with the outside world. Yang Lo had died and the new emperor forbade Zheng He to sail again. The voyages were always controversial in China. Powerful Confucian bureaucrats at court regarded them as trading adventures rather than adventures in diplomacy, and therefore frivolous and time-wasting. The new emperor was put under strong pressure by his civil servants to stop the voyages. When the new emperor also died, Zheng He was able to get permission for one final voyage - and that was the seventh. But the Chinese civil servants won the final victory. They successfully destroyed virtually every record of Zheng He's voyages, even the plans for his ships. It would be as if the voyages had never taken place, and China was able to turn its back on the outside world once more.

It is perhaps unfortunate that the fleet did not reach the Mediterranean. Would the Chinese have been impressed if they had seen Athens, Pisa, Florence or Rome? And if they had been impressed would they have been content merely to make diplomatic and commercial contact, or would Chinese conquest have followed? The voyages of Zheng He are something of an historical puzzle. If real and meaningful contact had been made between East and West in the early fifteenth century, it could have meant a very different direction for the cultural development in either China or Europe or both from the fifteenth century on. The very fact of stopping short was a significant historical event.

JOAN OF ARC URGES THE DAUPHIN TO CLAIM HIS CROWN

(1429)

IN 1429, A 17 year old French shepherd girl from Lorraine, Jeanne d'Arc, had visions of the Archangel Michael, Saint Catherine and Saint Margaret. These visions told her that the English must be thrown out of France – and that she would be responsible for their ejection. The voices had also told her to seek out the Dauphin, the heir to the French throne. Jeanne (or Joan as the English were to call her) persuaded an officer to fit her out with a soldier's armour and take her to Chinon to meet the Dauphin.

She succeeded in meeting the Dauphin and persuading him of her mission, which was to deliver Orleans from the English, who had the town under siege. She also succeeded in persuading the Dauphin that he was the legitimate heir of Charles VI, his father, in spite of the Treaty of Troyes which had disinherited him in 1420. She urged him to flout the Treaty, break it and claim the crown that was rightfully his.

Remarkably, the Dauphin was guided by Joan's visions, 'voices' or arguments, perhaps persuaded by her charisma, and provided her with a small army. She had her own standard made; it carried the fleur de lys and the words 'Jesus Maria'.

The English commander-in-chief, the Duke of Bedford, sent to London for reinforcements and strengthened his hold on Paris. He also visited Rouen to bind the Normans closer to the English cause. He assigned the regency of France to Philip of Burgundy, following the wishes of the Parisians.

Prompted by Joan of Arc's intervention, the Dauphin had himself crowned at Rheims on 17 July, taking the style King Charles VII of France. On 8 May 1429, in a full suit of armour, Joan led a French army to victory against the English, who were besieging Orleans. Thanks to her victory, the siege was lifted, and the French army were elated, and many of the soldiers came to see the struggle against the English oppressors as a holy crusade. Joan's voices from Heaven made a huge difference to morale.

Joan of Arc played a leading role in the attempt to retake Paris, in which she was wounded. She fought in a number of minor military engagements before she was finally captured by the Burgundians. On 23 May 1430, Joan of Arc entered Compiegne outside Paris and was taken prisoner along with her brothers. She was handed over to Jean de Luxembourg, and then sold to the English for 10,000 gold crowns. The English escorted her to Rouen, where they imprisoned her in a tower. Charles VII made no attempt to save her. The Duke of Bedford decided not to intervene either.

The following year, after months of inquisition, torture and degradation, Joan of Arc was handed over to Pierre Cauchon, the former Bishop of Beauvais, but the English threatened to re-arrest her unless the French authorities convicted her of 'treason against God'. Joan was then subjected to further questioning in secret, following the procedures of the Inquisition. She defended herself as best she could, stressing her purity and her devotion to France, but it was all to no avail; the English required a guilty verdict. Joan was duly condemned by the bishops after a show trial, but to life imprisonment, not to death. She resumed the wearing of men's clothing, which was expressly forbidden. This was seen as evidence that she was unrepentant and she was then condemned to death. She was burnt at the stake as a witch in the Old Market Square of Rouen on 30 May 1431. She could have been saved by an intervention from the French King, but his attitude seems to have been one of total complacency.

Joan's intervention prompted the coronation of Charles VII, for which he showed her no gratitude or loyalty. Later in 1431, with 'the witch' out of the way, the 10 year old Henry VI was crowned in Notre Dame in Paris. Later, Joan was to be seen as a national heroine by the French, a saint, though while she lived she was seen as a troublesome, ambiguous and problematic figure. Hindsight can be a distorting lens.

THE PORTUGUESE
REACH CAPE BOJADOR
(1433)

Prince Henry the Navigator initiated and co-ordinated a series of exploratory voyages, mapping the north-west coast of Africa. The Portuguese wanted to maintain their trading links with the East, but found it increasingly difficult to do this with a hostile Muslim bloc evolving in the Middle East. A sea route to the Far East, a sea route round Africa, would make that possible. Cosmas had many centuries before maintained that there was a sea route from the Indian Ocean eastwards to Cathay. It was just a question of finding a sea route to that, round Africa.

The initial voyages south were unpromising as the coastline trended towards the south-south-west, taking the mariners further and further away from India.

Eventually the coastline was mapped as far south as the Canary Islands and Cape Bojador another 325km further to the south-west. Voyage after voyage reached the Canaries, and a few reached the sandy headland of Cape Bojador, but none got beyond it. There was a psychological barrier to overcome. Some sailors were afraid of falling off the edge of the world if they went any further. Others were afraid the current sweeping along the coast, the Canaries Current, would prevent them from ever sailing home again. Others were afraid of the Sea of Darkness which they imagined lay beyond the headland. As the sailors went further and further south, nearer and near the equator, it became hotter and hotter, and the people they occasionally saw on the shoreline were coal-black, as if they had been charred by the extreme heat. Maybe they too would be roasted coal black if they ventured any further. There was plenty for the Portuguese sailors to be afraid of.

Prince Henry sent one of his squires, Eannes, to sail round Cape Bojador in 1432, but he had failed to do it, turning back out of fear at the

Canaries. Back at Sagres, the prince gently chided Eannes and sent him off again the next year on the same mission. This time Eannes reached and rounded Cape Bojador. The coastline he discovered was barren and uninhabited, which did not encourage further southward sailing, but there was at least no specific terror lurking beyond Cape Bojador.

Cape Bojador was a landmark in two senses. It marked a physical southern boundary of the Portuguese world until the early fifteenth century. It also marked a psychological barrier which the Portuguese navigators could not bring themselves to pass. The way south was now open.

Henry the Navigator followed this up immediately by sending another ship, commanded by Afonso Baldaya, to explore the coastline south of the cape. The southward creep gained momentum after Cape Verde was reached. After that the coast of Africa fell away to the east and there was great optimism that the West African coast, the coastline of what is now Ghana and Nigeria, was actually the southern coast of Africa. Could it be that there was now a clear run eastwards into the Indian Ocean? Unfortunately it turned out that the huge mass of central and southern Africa lay in the way.

In December 1488, Bartholomew Dias returned to tell the king of Portugal, John II, about his exciting discovery. He had not only found the southernmost tip of Africa, but rounded it. In his epic two-year voyage, Dias had sailed so far south (35 degrees South) that he has lost sight of the North Star, which had vanished below the horizon. He was blown south by a strong wind, out of sight of land, for 13 days. When at last he had been able to turn back he found that the coastline of Africa was trending eastwards. He had at last found the southern coast of Africa.

Dias spotted native herdsmen on the coast, and landed in order to meet them. They were unfortunately unable to understand each other, and the herders were so alarmed at the sight of the Portuguese caravels that they drove their livestock inland as fast as they could to get away from them. Dias told the king he had named the great southern cape with its table-like mountain the Cape of Storms, but the king wanted him to change that to the Cape of Good Hope, because of what it promised for the future. What it promised, of course, was the long-hoped-for sea route to India.

THE FALL OF CONSTANTINOPLE

(1453)

CONSTANTINOPLE WAS THE capital of the once-great Byzantine empire. The allies of the Byzantine empire had gradually fallen away; the garrison was equipped with obsolete weapons; the city itself had been in decline for some time and its days were numbered. Constantinople had been exploited by the Venetians and Genoese and betrayed by Slav and Byzantine princes. It was an isolated, friendless, vulnerable city: a sitting target for an attack by the Ottoman Empire. The Ottomans had for a long time nursed the dream of taking Constantinople

The army of Sultan Mohammed II spent February and March moving heavy artillery into position round Constantinople while, at the same time, several neighbouring towns on the Black Sea coast and the Sea of Marmara were overrun. On 6 April, the siege of Constantinople began, with the Sultan's great cannon pointing straight at the Gate of St Romanus, where the emperor and his Genoese soldiers had gathered. The Ottomans launched a ferocious attack.

The city's Byzantine defenders fought hard and long to prevent it from falling into the hands of the invaders, and the initial surprise attack was repulsed. The walls that were damaged by cannon fire were quickly rebuilt. At sea the Turks were similarly repulsed. Then the Sultan decided on a daring move. He ordered 72 ships to be dragged overland from the Bosporus to the Golden Horn. This penetrated the city's harbour defences. Captured Venetians were executed by the Ottomans in full view of the city; in retaliation, the defenders did the same with their Ottoman prisoners.

All the time the bombardment continued, and the doomed garrison was finally overwhelmed. On 29 May 1453, the storming of the city began. The Byzantine commander, Giovanni Giustiniani-Longo, left the action to

190

have his wounds tended. The emperor was killed in the thick of the battle. As Constantinople fell to the Ottoman invaders, people huddling in the church were dragged away into slavery, or killed on the spot, and the looting started.

The final flicker of the Roman Empire had finally gone out. The fall of Constantinople was much more than a spectacular historical event: it was the end of an era.

HENRY VI OF ENGLAND HAS FIRST BOUT OF INSANITY
(1453)

HENRY VI OF England came to the throne in 1422 at the tender age of nine, when his father, Henry V, died of dysentery while on campaign in France. Henry VI was a half-wit. His supporters and apologists have attempted to portray him as bookish, pious or devout; the reality seems to be that he was feeble-minded and unworldly. He used to point at women at court who he thought were showing rather too much cleavage and shout, 'Fie, madam! Fie!'

He had his first major bout of insanity in 1453. The insanity may have been hereditary. His maternal grandfather, Charles VI of France, was insane and he may have inherited the tendency from him. During this initial episode Henry was unable to function as king and a regent was appointed, Richard Duke of York. The king recovered at the end of the following year, dismissing his regent, the Duke of York, who also lost his place on the king's council. But the king's inadequacy to reign was plain for all to see, and a struggle to replace him was all but inevitable. Warring baronial families quickly fell into two camps, the Yorkists and the Lancastrians. The Wars of the Roses erupted in 1455. The House of York was headed by the recently demoted and snubbed Duke of York, who led his army into battle against the king's army at St Albans on 22 May 1455 – and won.

After the Battle of Northampton, on 10 July 1460, Henry VI was captured by the Yorkists. Richard Plantagenet, Duke of York, asserted his own claim to the throne and was assured by the lords that he would succeed on Henry's death. The matter was not resolved that simply though, because Richard was killed shortly afterwards at the Battle of Wakefield, where his army was defeated by an army raised by the king's loyal wife, Margaret of Anjou.

Southern England rallied behind Richard of York's son Edward. After further battles, in 1465 Edward and his Yorkist army succeeded in capturing Henry VI (again) and locking him up in the Tower of London. In 1470, Henry VI regained the throne briefly with the help of the Earl of Warwick.

Edward used artillery to defeat Warwick at the Battled of Stamford, and Warwick was obliged to withdraw to France. Edward defeated and killed Warwick at the Battle of Barnet in 1471, and won a decisive victory at the Battle of Tewkesbury on 6 May. Henry VI was murdered in the Tower a few days afterwards, almost certainly on Edward's orders, and possibly the murder was carried out by his brother, Richard of Gloucester. Surprisingly, this was one murder that Shakespeare did not lay at Richard's door, but it seems that he was at least present when Henry VI died.

The way was then clear for Edward to become king, and he was duly crowned as Edward IV. On his death, there was a problem, which Richard of Gloucester had kept quiet about, either out of loyalty or for his own safety, and that was the illegitimacy of Edward IV. He was, it seems, not the son of Richard Duke of York at all, but of a low-born English archer. That meant that his half-brother Richard, who was legitimate, was heir to the throne, but Edward IV's sons had no claim. The two young princes were set aside, possibly murdered in the Tower or spirited away to the Continent, and Richard became Richard III.

The saga of the Wars of the Roses only came to an end because of an unscrupulous usurper in the shape of Henry Tudor, who had a very weak claim to the English crown, and because of the random outcome of the Battle of Bosworth, which might have gone in Richard's favour but for the treachery of the Stanley family. Henry Tudor, as Henry VII, and his son Henry VIII were careful to eliminate the strongest potential Plantagenet claimants.

The turmoil and mayhem of the Wars of the Roses sprang mainly from the fact that Henry VI was totally unsuitable to be king. If he had been sane, strong and statesmanlike, the Wars of the Roses might have been avoided. Often the battles are thought of as picturesque pageants of armour glinting in the sun and banners fluttering in the wind to the accompaniment of trumpets and drums - an integral part of Merrie England - but the reality was wanton butchery and cruelty on all sides. In the Battle of Northampton, which was a particularly bloody battle, the River Nene literally ran red with blood as the battle ended. There was nothing merrie about it.

THE PUBLICATION OF THE GUTENBERG BIBLE

(1456)

JOHANNES GUTENBERG WAS born in Mainz in 1400. The family seems to have been expelled from Mainz and settled in Strasbourg. Gutenberg was in Strasbourg between 1430 and 1444, where probably he had begun work as a printer by 1439. By 1448 he was back in Mainz again, and by 1450 he was working in partnership with Johannes Fust, who financed Gutenberg's printing press with 800 guilders. This was not a happy partnership. It ended after five years, with Fust suing Gutenberg for the 800 guilders and receiving the printing equipment in lieu of payment. It is not known whether in amongst all the quarrelling they produced any books during this period, but Gutenberg must have devoted a lot of time to the preparation of the plates for his great project, the first printed Latin Bible.

Fust then carried on the business with the help of Peter Schoffer, his son-in-law, the two of them completing the famous 'Gutenberg Bible' that Gutenberg had begun. This historic and extremely ambitious feat was accomplished in August 1456. It involved the printing of 1,282 pages in two columns with gaps left for hand-painted illuminated initials. Meanwhile Gutenberg himself set up another press in Mainz with Konrad Humery. Archive evidence shows that Gutenberg went on struggling with debt repayments.

Gutenberg has been credited with the invention of printing, but it seems likely that printing already existed in a rudimentary form. Gutenberg nevertheless takes the credit for refining and using the new technology for a highly significant and ambitious project. Apart from anything else, the Bible is a very long book. Gutenberg remains the best claimant to the title 'inventor of printing', even though no books have survived bearing his name as their printer.

Until Johannes Gutenberg's time, bibles were hand-made, scarce and expensive. Producing them, whole pages at a time, on a press, made bibles cheaper and more accessible. Gutenberg's activity led to the democratization of Christianity, the reduction of the power of the priests who recited and interpreted the Bible for the rest of the community, and the consequent reduction of the power of the Church. The publication of the Gutenberg Bible led by a short route directly to the Reformation itself.

THE COLUMBUS VOYAGE TO THE NEW WORLD
(1492)

The events of Christopher Columbus's early life are uncertain. His son later recorded that he went to the University of Pavia, where he studied astronomy, geometry and cosmography; Columbus himself told a significantly different story – that he went to sea at the age of 14. There is a technical term used by psychiatrists for the tendency to make up stories about yourself – confabulation. There seems to have been some purpose to Columbus's confabulation; the overall picture that emerges is that he knew rather more about the geography of the world, and especially about what we now call the Western Hemisphere, than he made out at the time.

In 1474, after consulting the Florentine cosmographer Paolo Toscanelli, he arrived at the idea of reaching India by sailing west instead of east. The success of such a voyage depended on the now-widely-accepted idea that the earth was a sphere, and quite a small sphere. Thanks partly to an error of Ptolemy and partly to a bit of exaggeration of his own, Columbus underestimated the size of the earth and overestimated the size of Asia; the two miscalculations together put China where eastern North America actually lies, and the East Indies where the West Indies are. In fact Columbus got the latitudes of China and Japan wrong and he was looking for Japan in the West Indies and China in Mexico. But there was at least land that corresponded. Was all of this by chance, as we are led to believe, or was it arrived at by a process of reasoning back from reports of secret landfalls already reported from across the Atlantic? Certainly Columbus knew about reports of driftwood picked up 400 leagues west of Cape St Vincent, which implied that there was land not far off in that direction.

He needed a patron for his planned voyage west, and negotiated for seven years with Ferdinand and Isabella of Castile before they agreed to sponsor him.

It is not clear to what extent Columbus 'prepared' the discovery of the New World or had it prepared for him. The possible lying about his education suggests that there was concealment. Recent research strongly suggests that the existence of a landmass across the Atlantic was already known, and the Columbus voyage was a kind of 'show discovery'.

It was on 3 August 1492 that Columbus set sail on his historic voyage across the Atlantic, in command of the *Santa Maria*, accompanied by two even smaller ships, the *Pinta* and the *Nina*. He took 87 men with him. After reaching the Canaries, morale fell. The Pinta had already lost her rudder and they had put in at Tenerife to refit. There was talk of Portuguese caravels on the prowl with orders to intercept the voyage of discovery. The sailors saw a meteor fall into the sea, and the vast plains of seaweed known as the Sargasso Sea. It was a frightening experience.

Then on 11 October bits of driftwood were seen and a branch covered with berries; land could not be far away. Land was sighted the next day. Columbus called in San Salvador, and it was probably Watling Island in the Bahamas. Columbus put on his Sunday best clothes for the formal landing, and went ashore as if in a historical pageant, which in a way it was, bearing the royal banner of Spain. The Pinzon brothers carried banners of the Green Cross (Columbus's device). It was a tableau made for the painters of historical scenes, and designed to be just that. Columbus visited Cuba and Haiti, founding a small colony there before setting sail for home.

A second voyage with a larger squadron set sail in September 1493, reaching Dominica in the West Indies in November. This time Columbus was directed specifically to deal kindly with the inhabitants of any new lands and to try to convert them to Christianity. The third voyage in 1498, this time with six ships, led to the discovery, of the mainland of South America. Columbus had for a long time believed that a landmass existed there, and once again it must be suspected that earlier travellers, perhaps blown a long way off their intended courses, had reported the existence of such a continent. Columbus's voyages of discovery have an air of having been planned. It is almost as if he was following some sort of itinerary. A comparison between Columbus's voyages and Cook's is revealing in this respect; Cook's zig-zagging exploration of the South Pacific really does look like groping in the dark.

A final, fourth, voyage in 1502–04 explored the south coast of the Gulf of Mexico. Columbus was stranded for a whole year in Jamaica, where his crew behaved badly and he himself suffered badly from disease. The lawless behaviour alienated the natives, who had initially been friendly and hospitable, and they were often short of food. He finally set sail for Spain again in September 1504, arriving at San Lucar in November. He was too ill to go to court, so his son Diego went instead. After many years of hardship and ill treatment, Columbus died at Valladolid in Spain on 20 May 1506.

Opinion is still divided about Christopher Columbus. Some scholars still believe that Columbus was the first European navigator to cross the Atlantic, that he really was the first European to visit the New World. Others think Columbus knew the width of the Atlantic before he set sail because Portuguese ships had already crossed it unofficially, accidentally blown across by the trade winds. If so, the Columbus voyages were in effect a publicity stunt, a formal grand opening of the New World to Spanish and Portuguese colonization. His ill-concealed formal education in astronomy, cosmography and geometry certainly point to a level of navigational expertise that might be required to duplicate voyages that had already been undertaken, perhaps by Portuguese sailors. Either way, Columbus's voyages expanded the horizons of Europeans in an instant and opened the way to European colonization of North and South America.

In a very short time, the native Americans would come to regret the voyages of 'discovery' by the Europeans, which led to their humiliation and disinheritance, the destruction of the Aztec and Inca civilizations, and the wholesale destruction of the ancient ways of life of the first peoples of the New World. The ultimate consequence of the 1492 Columbus voyage was the European takeover of the continent of North America.

THE DA GAMA VOYAGE
(1497)

VASCO DA GAMA was born in 1469, the same year that Prince Henry the Navigator died and da Gama's voyages were the ultimate fulfilment of Prince Henry's programme of exploration and discovery. Prince Henry's main aim was to find a sea route round Africa, and da Gama was the first to find it and sail it. Da Gama was chosen by King Emanuel I of Portugal to find a sea route to India via the Cape of Good Hope, which was at that time thought to be the southernmost tip of Africa.

He set sail from Lisbon on 9 July 1497 with three ships and took four months just to reach St Helena Bay in southern Africa. The voyage round the Cape was a difficult one because of storms and mutinies, but he managed to reach Malindi on the east coast of Africa early in 1498. From this point on, da Gama's voyage was in known waters and therefore much easier. He was able to pick up a skilled pilot from Indian merchants at Malindi to help him navigate across the Indian Ocean to Calicut on the Malabar coast.

Muslim traders in Calicut were hostile as they sensed that significant new commercial competition had arrived – as indeed it had – and they stirred up the local Hindus against da Gama. Da Gama had to fight his way out of the harbour.

Vasco da Gama returned to Lisbon in triumph. The king was delighted with this totally successful enterprise and ennobled da Gama. The little chapel at Belem on the Tagus estuary where da Gama and his crew had prayed before setting off was demolished and a magnificent church was raised on the spot, commemorating the historic voyage.

Then came news that all 40 of the unfortunate Portuguese left behind in Calicut had been murdered. The king sought revenge, and fitted out a squadron of ten ships, again under da Gama's leadership, which sailed in 1502. Da Gama was now sailing under the title 'Admiral of India', showing

199

that the Portuguese were making a territorial claim. This expedition founded the colony of Mozambique, bombarded Calicut, and treated the inhabitants of Calicut with brutal savagery in retaliation for the murders.

Vasco da Gama returned to Lisbon the following year with his ships richly laden. Once again there were great celebrations in Lisbon and further honours and rewards were showered on him. Soon after his return, da Gama retired to his home in Evora, though he continued to advise Emanuel I on matters relating to India and maritime strategy until 1505.

The da Gama voyage is justly famous as the first European sea voyage to India, opening up a brand new trade route round Africa, a more reliable route to the Far East. It also opened, immediately, a new phase of European colonization. Da Gama himself founded Mozambique, the second European colony in southern Africa. The voyage marked the beginning of the controversial domination of India by Europeans, just as the Columbus voyage marked the beginning of the domination of the Americas by Europeans.

MONA LISA PAINTED
(1504)

Leonardo entered the studio of the painter Verocchio in 1470. His first great work, the mural of *The Last Supper* (about 1494), was technically unsatisfactory, a painting on damp plaster, which started deteriorating immediately, yet this ghost of a picture is still regarded as one of the world's masterpieces. The painting that has intrigued people with its secretive smile ever since it was painted in 1504 is the *Mona Lisa*. It was immediately recognized as a great work of art: Francis I of France bought it for 4,000 gold florins.

Leonardo was exceptional in many ways. He was a Renaissance painter who was influenced hardly at all by Greek or Roman models; he based his art on a searching observation of what he saw. In relying on his own senses he was one of the first 'modern men', a humanist free of conditioning by earlier ages. Leonardo filled his notebooks with drawings that show an astonishing range of scientific observations. He used looking and drawing as a medium for understanding.

Leonardo represents the fullest development of what has come to be known as 'the Renaissance man', accomplished in the arts and sciences, embodying all existing knowledge and striving to extend its boundaries. His life and work redefined for following generations what it means to be human.

It was in 1504 that Leonardo painted the *Mona Lisa*. For several years Leonardo had been making sketches of Lisa, the Neapolitan wife of the businessman Francesco (or Zanobi) del Giocondo. While Leonardo was painting the picture, Lisa left for Calabria on a long business trip with her husband, leaving the portrait unfinished. It is a haunting picture because of the sitter's enigmatic, questioning half-smile; it is a very ambiguous expression that has captivated many generations. The half-smile is one that Leonardo was particularly fond of in his sitters. Several of his paintings have it. Leonardo hired a musician to play for her during the sittings, in order to produce the expression he liked. Above all it is a frank and honest portrayal of a human being.

But the *Mona Lisa* is also a puzzle picture.

The lady sits, very composed and self-possessed, against the background of an elemental landscape of mountains, lakes and gorges. The setting may be an idealized view of the Tuscan hill country, but it is hard to see how this could be relevant to a sitter from Naples. The lady's almost superhuman composure is so strongly contrasted with the setting that the painting makes a statement about the relationship between man (or woman) and nature. The face is modelled on the face of a real woman, but she could almost be a classical goddess, and there is more than a hint of the Madonna about her. Was Leonardo telling us that this woman was so perfect that she could be a reincarnation of the Virgin Mary?

It is a picture that disturbs the mind with all sorts of questions, while at the same time appearing to be completely serene. It is also unusual in being a picture that has excited total critical approval. Endless lengthy critical rhapsodies have been written about this picture, which defines a human being, an artist and a particular moment in the history of art – a moment of discovery.

Leonardo's pre-eminent reputation as one of the greatest artists in one of the greatest periods in art history rests on a surprisingly small number of finished paintings. The many artists who have been influenced by him have resorted to the collections of his fine drawings in Milan, Paris, Florence, Vienna, London and Windsor. It is not just that the Mona Lisa is a great work of art by Leonardo; it is by its very nature a very rare work because Leonardo painted so little.

THE INVENTION OF
THE WATCH
(1511)

THE WATCH, THE small portable clock that we all now take totally for granted, was invented in 1511. It was described in the *Nuremberg Chronicles* by Johannes Cocleus.

From day to day more ingenious discoveries are made, for a young man called Petrus Hele makes things which astonish the most learned mathematicians, for he makes out of a small quantity of iron horologia devised with many wheels, and these horologia, in any position and without any weight, both indicate and strike for 40 hours, even when they are carried in the breast and in the purse.

These prototype watches had hour hands but no minute hands. Minute hands were not to appear on watches until 1670.

The invention of the watch meant that it was rather easier for people to be punctual for meetings, and this facilitated business of every kind. Maximum efficiency in the workplace, whether it is an office, a college or a factory, depends on synchronized activity, and that depends very often on everyone wearing a watch. In fact it is difficult to imagine how life would continue in urban Western society without watches.

THE CALL TO END
SLAVERY
(1514)

FOR THE GREATER part of human history there have been slaves. In medieval Europe, the greater part of the population, the peasantry, was systematically enslaved to the landed aristocracy. Most people had no rights and were completely at their masters' disposal. The ancient Greeks and Romans had slaves. Ancient Greece has been portrayed as a democracy, but it was only the privileged minority that belonged to it: the rest were slaves.

The slave trade – buying, transporting and selling people against their will – was also a part of the general picture. People were bought, sold and offered as sacrifices in the ancient Middle East. In the Roman Empire and the dark ages that followed, the slave trade was an important part of the economy. St Patrick was taken as a slave. It continued through the middle ages and later; John Knox was a galley slave for a time, until he was released in 1550. Slavery has been one of the ongoing evils of the human story. And it continues still. There are countries in Africa where slavery still goes on. It seems strange that Western leaders are prepared to invade countries in the Middle East to remove a dictator, yet stand back and remain silent about the continuing misery of tens of thousands of enslaved black Africans.

There has always been a voice in the wilderness calling for it to stop, sometimes a powerful voice. In 1513, there was a new pope, Giovanni de' Medici, a son of Lorenzo the Magnificent, who took the name Leo X. One of his first acts was to publish a bull (statement) about the evils of slavery. 'Not only the Chistian religion but Nature cries out against slavery and the slave trade.'

In spite of this clear command to stop, slavery and the slave trade continued and grew. In 1516, the first sugar exported from the New World to the Old was presented to King Carlos I of Spain by Hispaniola's inspector of gold mines. The Castilian Regent Jimenez forbade the importation of slaves into colonies of Spain, but Carlos, who was ruling from Flanders, continued to grant courtiers licences to import slaves into the colonies. In 1517, the Archduke Charles granted the merchants of Florence a monopoly in the African slave trade. The following year the Spanish colonists in Santo Domingo imported more slave labour from Africa to carry out the hard work of cutting cane in the colony's 28 sugar plantations. Importing slaves was made necessary as the island's native population decreased as a result of disease and maltreatment by the Spanish (Catholic) colonists.

The slave trade grew and grew, simply because it was the key to colossal wealth for those who ran it. By 1532, the Holy Roman Emperor Charles V was able to establish himself in Madrid in sumptuous style, paying for the improvements to his imperial palace with the taxes on Caribbean sugar. Both Spanish and Portuguese aristocrats had already grown rich on their colonial enterprises. They grew fat on the fruits of slavery. There was no incentive for them to stop.

There was a good deal of hypocrisy and dissembling over slavery. Francis Drake and John Hawkins have been developed into national heroes, but they were also pirates and slavers. In 1563, Hawkins sold a cargo of 105 slaves in Hispaniola. Queen Elizabeth tended to turn a blind eye if the profits were high. In a blatant piece of hypocrisy, she said, 'If any African were carried away without his free consent, it would be detestable and call down the vengeance of Heaven upon the undertaking.'

Transporting West African slaves to the New World created new and completely unanticipated problems for the white European colonists. With the slaves came a variety of new diseases, such as yellow fever, virulent forms of malaria and hookworm. In 1647, an epidemic of yellow fever swept through the West Indies.

Sometimes the slaves took the law into their own hands. In 1712, there was a slave revolt in New York; six white colonists were killed before the militia could restore order. Meanwhile a conscience regarding slavery was dawning elsewhere – and there were always those who thought it immoral. In Pennsylvania in 1712, the colonists decided that no more slaves should be imported. The lead was finally taken by a committed group of English reformers, led by William Wilberforce; but it was not until the nineteenth century that the tide turned against slavery.

THE REFORMATION
(1517)

IF THE REFORMATION, the reaction against the authority of the Catholic Church, had a specific beginning it was on 31 October 1517. On that day, Martin Luther drew up a list of 95 theses (assertions or beliefs) protesting against abuses, including the sale of indulgences, and nailed them onto the door of the church at Wittenberg. This formal protest marked the beginning of a long period of religious and civil unrest across central and northern Europe. Luther went on a mission to Rome in 1510–11, and was shocked by what he found there. Money was needed in Rome and selling indulgences was seen as an easy way of making money. An indulgence was in effect a paid forgiveness for sins.

When he returned to Germany his epoch-making career as a religious reformer began. Luther was very indignant at the shamelessness with which indulgences were sold, and could not contain his anger. Suddenly he emerged from an academic world into a world of decisive and committed action.

The practice of indulgence had grown out of the Church's system of penances. To punish sins, the Church had temporarily excluded people from the fellowship. To mitigate this punishment, the sinner might pay a sum of money to be readmitted. It was a practice that had become big business in the Catholic Church since 1300. The Wittenberg Dominican Johann Tetzel, who had been freely selling indulgences, published a set of counter-theses and burnt Luther's. Luther's students responded by burning Tetzel's.

In 1518, Luther was joined by Melancthon. At first Pope Leo X took little notice of Luther and the disturbance he was causing, thinking it was no more than a quarrel among monks, but in 1518 the summons to Rome came. Luther's university and the elector intervened and there were some negotiations. At Leipzig in the following year there was a memorable debate between Luther and Eck, the Pope's envoy to the Saxon court. The attempt to silence him made Luther even bolder. He went on to attack the papal system as a whole. Erasmus joined in. Eck went to Rome to raise the Curia against Luther. This resulted in a formal Bull of Condemnation, but it only made Luther more aggressive.

In 1520, Luther published his address to the Christian Nobles in Germany. A papal bull was issued containing 41 theses levelled against him; he publicly burned these in front of a crowd in Wittenberg. A frenzy of excitement was building up in Germany. Charles V convened his first diet (government) at Worms in 1521, and an order was issued for the destruction of Luther's books. Luther himself was ordered to appear at Worms. Finally he was arrested and confined, mainly for his own protection, in the Wartburg.

In 1529, Luther engaged in a conference on religious reforms with Zwingli and other Swiss theologians. Luther stood by his conviction regarding the consubstantiation: that Christ was actually present in the bread and wine of the Eucharist. When Luther and his followers protested about a ruling forbidding the teaching of Luther's ideas, the name 'Protestant' was given to them for the first time.

The drawing up in 1530 of the Augsburg Confession, at which Melancthon represented Luther, marks the climax of the German Reformation. Luther was unable to attend the meeting at Augsburg because he was now an outlaw. For Melancthon, Luther was a truly great figure on a level with the great prophets of the Bible, the prophets who drew their inspiration directly from God.

In 1534, Henry VIII broke with the Roman Church, because it has refused to annul his marriage to Catherine of Aragon and refused to acknowledge his marriage to Ann Boleyn. Henry established the Reformation at a stroke in England by the Act of Supremacy, which made the monarch the head of the Church of England. Dogma and doctrine remain for a time unchanged.

Luther put in motion a movement that would in a very short time create a sparer alternative to the Roman Catholic Church – Protestantism – which quickly came to dominate northern Europe. Unfortunately it led to a division of the Christian communities in Europe into two warring camps, and this in turn led to a great deal of persecution and abuse on both sides, which has continued to the present day. The breakthrough idea embedded in Protestantism is that priests and Popes are not needed to mediate between God and man; the mediation can be by way of the word of God in the Bible. With printed Bibles increasingly available in the reader's own vernacular language, people could find out what God wanted for themselves. It was a more democratic and a more empowering approach to Christianity. Protestantism was not just a religious revolution, it was a social and political revolution as well.

MAGELLAN'S CIRCUMNAVIGATION
(1519-21)

AFTER BEING SNUBBED by the King of Portugal, Ferdinand Magellan formally renounced his Portuguese nationality and offered his services as a navigator to the court of Spain. In particular he offered Charles V an ambitious scheme, in effect an extension of the Columbus scheme, to reach the Moluccas by the westerly route. Columbus had sailed west apparently under the impression that there was but one ocean between Europe and the Spice Islands; Magellan knew there were two. He would have to cross the Atlantic and the Pacific. What Magellan set out to do was therefore far more ambitious and daring than Columbus's Atlantic crossing just 20 years before.

He hoped to find a sea passage to the south of South America, even though none had been discovered. He is said to have declared that he was ready to sail as far as latitude 750 degrees South in search of the sea passage through to the Pacific. It was a terrific gamble.

Magellan had help from Faleiro, an astronomer, in planning his expedition, and from Christopher de Haro, a financial backer who had a grudge against the King of Portugal. On March 22 1518, Magellan and Faleiro, as joint captains general, signed an agreement with Charles V by which they would receive one-twentieth of the profits of the expedition. The government of any lands conquered would rest in their hands and those of their heirs.

Magellan set sail from Seville on 10 August 1519 with five ships and 270 men. Faleiro stayed behind; he had cast his horoscope and found that the expedition would be fatal to him. Statistically, he was probably right. Only one of the five ships, the *Vittoria*, was to return to Spain. While sailing south along the coast of Argentina Magellan dealt with a formidable mutiny and met the natives, whom he name 'Patagonians' (Big Feet). Magellan therefore inadvertently named the region of Patagonia. He found his way through the winding strait, which still bears his name, the Magellan Straits separating the mainland of South America from Tierra del Fuego. At that time it was assumed that Tierra del Fuego, the Land of Fire, was the northernmost tip of a huge southern continent, though it eventually proved to be an island. In November 1519, the tiny Spanish fleet entered Balboa's 'Great South Sea', which Magellan flatteringly named the Pacific Ocean.

By this time, one ship had been wrecked, one had turned and headed back to Spain. A third ship had later to be burnt and scuttled in the Pacific because so many men had died that only two ships could be properly manned. Then these two ships became separated. One was captured by the Portuguese.

The huge expanse of the Pacific came as a great shock and nearly killed everyone on the expedition. It took Magellan 98 days to cross it. In all that distance he only discovered two islands, both small, uninhabited and sterile. His crews had to do without fresh provisions, including fresh water, and the ravages of scurvy became terrible. They ended up eating sawdust, oxhides and rats. At last they made landfall in some inhabited islands, which Magellan unflatteringly named the Ladrones, after the thieving nature of the inhabitants. This was Guam.

Magellan himself was killed in a skirmish with natives in the Philippines. His ship nevertheless returned home to Spain, complete with a heavy cargo of cloves, taken by the last surviving Spanish captain, Juan del Cano. Del Cano reached Spain on 6 September 1522, the first man to sail right round the world in a single expedition. Of the 270 men who had started the voyage, only 18 made it back to Spain after this epic tour of the earth. Magellan did not make it back to Spain, but, falling at Mactan, he died at a point further west than the longitude of his earlier furthest point east in the Moluccas. In that sense, Magellan *did* go right round the world.

The Magellan circumnavigation of the world was a great human achievement, an epic undertaking. But it was also one of those defining moments in world history, when many things change in the wake of a single event. After Magellan, nothing was quite the same again. The circumnavigation proved what a lot of geographers had been arguing for some time, that the earth was a sphere, and it also demonstrated the true size of that sphere. From that point on there could be no doubting that the Earth was round, and not only that but about 40,000km round. It was incidental to the Magellan voyage that Patagonia, the Straits of Magellan and the Pacific Ocean were given their lasting names.

TYNDALE'S ENGLISH NEW TESTAMENT
(1526)

WILLIAM TYNDALE WAS one of the first people to dare to translate the New Testament into English. It was a landmark in the history of English-speaking people. What had been hidden in Latin for hundreds of years, and for most of the time confined in any case to monasteries, was suddenly available to everyone.

Christians in England were aware of the major events of the Christian year – Advent, Christmas, Lent, Easter, Whitsuntide – but few of them knew the actual words of Jesus, let alone the writings of St Paul. For their view of Christianity, they had remained totally dependent on what priests told them from the pulpit, and that was an interpretation of the Bible not the Bible itself. In 1526, when Tyndale's New Testament appeared, all that changed. Tyndale left England in fear of his life, visiting Luther in Wittenberg before getting his Bible published in Worms.

The Church was incandescent with rage when its authority was challenged. If people could read the Bible for themselves, they would not need priests to tell them what God required of them. In England his work was denounced by powerful enemies including Sir Thomas More. It was probably the sainted More who plotted his capture in Antwerp. More was incredibly outspoken about Tyndale, referring to him as, among other things, 'a bag of pus'.

The Church authorities did what they could to prevent the spreading of Tyndale's dangerous Testaments, even resorting to public burnings of copies. But all over England, groups of people met to read or hear the new Bible. It caused great excitement. For the first time people were reading the letters of St Paul. Some modern historians have expressed surprise that the English became so quickly and easily converted to Protestantism in the mid-sixteenth century, but the explanation is easy to see. From 1526 at least those who could read had direct access to the Bible, and this was the nub of the Protestant revolution.

The Tyndale Testament was a landmark in another way. In the 1520s, the English language was in an indeterminate state. It was made up of elements from Anglo-Saxon, Norman French and Latin. Some everyday documents were in English, but in the middle ages really important documents were in either Norman French or Latin. It seems to have been assumed that English was not an appropriate language to carry heavy freight. William Tyndale showed that this was not so. He devised an English style of great clarity and dignity, of great economy and power. There were earlier attempts at an English Bible, but the Lollard Bibles written 150 years earlier have not stood the test of time: they were heavily Latinized and are now virtually unintelligible.

Tyndale's Bible uses a simple and direct language that is still clear. 'Ask and it shall given you. Seek and ye shall find. Knock and it shall be opened unto you.' 'The spirit is willing but the flesh is weak.' Tyndale was a Gloucestershire man and that county was unusually rich in rustic proverbs; he caught the cadence of Gloucestershire proverbs in his Bible style.

The Tyndale Bible is a landmark in yet another way. Though poor William Tyndale himself was hunted down and done to death – condemned for heresy and strangled in October 1536 – his Bible lived on to be 'recycled' in the Authorized Version of the Bible commissioned by King James in 1611. A conference of leading English Christians at Hampton Court in 1604 came to the conclusion that a new and reliable translation of the Bible into English was essential. The King approved and work began. Fifty scholars worked on the project for the biblical seven years, and the new translation duly appeared in 1611, this time with a royal seal of approval; everyone could read it.

In the beginning was that word, and that word was with god: and god was that word. The same was in the beginning with god. All things were made by it, and without it no thing was made that was made. In it was life. And life was the light of men, and the light shineth in the darkness, and darkness comprehendeth it not.

This is a passage from the Tyndale Bible, not the Authorized Version, which closely copies it. It is very largely the Tyndale Bible that has formed the foundation of Christianity in the English-speaking world in the last 400 years.

THE FALL OF THE INCA EMPIRE
(1531)

FRANCISCO PIZARRO WAS a rootless man with few prospects in Spain, one of the many who decided to take their chances in the New World to see if they could make their fortune there. He became one of a dangerous, heedless band of emigrants to the Caribbean, the Spanish conquistadors.

In 1522, Pizarro formed a partnership with a priest called Hernando de Luque and a soldier called Diego de Almagro, with a view to organizing exploratory journeys to the south with conquest in mind. He went off exploring along the west coast of South America, feeling his way southwards, pushing on until he reached 9 degrees South of the Equator, all the time gathering detailed accounts of the nature of the Inca empire.

The governor of Panama showed no inclination to encourage Pizarro, so Pizarro decided to appeal to the King of Spain in person. He sailed back to Spain early in 1518 with this request in mind. Charles V was won over by what Pizarro told him. On 29 July 1529, at Toledo, Pizarro was given a formal official title deed to his new personal empire. He was to be governor and captain general of the 'province of New Castile', which was to extend along 200 leagues of the newly discovered coast of South America.

Pizarro sailed from San Lucar in January 1530, invading Peru with the intention of conquering the Inca empire. The Inca empire extended from Peru into northern Chile and it reached its zenith under its eleventh ruler, or Sapa Inca, Huayna Capac (1493–1525), On Huayna Capac's death in 1525, the Inca empire was divided in two between his sons Huascar and Atahualpa, which led to a debilitating civil war. Atahualpa succeeded in killing his brother Huascar, but then Pizarro captured the Inca capital, Cuzco, and imprisoned Atahualpa.

The Inca emperor tried to buy his freedom by filling a room with gold as a ransom. Pizarro had him strangled anyway. Pizarro then held the Inca empire for himself, but he did not enjoy his conquest for very long. After the Incas' final effort to get Cuzco back again in 1536–37 had been quashed by Diego de Almagro, a power struggle broke out between Almagro and Pizarro. They would not agree on the boundary separating their jurisdiction. There was a battle. Almagro was defeated and Pizarro had him executed, but Almagro's supporters in their turn conspired against Pizarro and assassinated him on 6 June 1541.

Pizarro conquered Peru for Spain, or rather for his own greed. He also murdered the Inca emperor, Atahualpa; he destroyed the Inca empire; he destroyed the Inca civilization. The fall of the Inca empire was one of the great destructive moments of history.

RENAISSANCE ARCHITECTURE

(1550)

THE RENAISSANCE WAS in part a rebirth or rediscovery of classical learning and literature. The rediscovery of Ptolemy was one element in this process. There was also a renewal of interest in classical art and architecture. The main rediscovery was the architecture of ancient Rome.

In the first half of the sixteenth century one of the leading architects was Donato Lazzari, usually known as Bramante. For S. Maria delle Grazie in Milan, Bramante added an eastern arm to a medieval church, with a great polygonal drum and apses; it was widely imitated. Bramante designed the Tempietto to mark the supposed site of St Peter's crucifixion; it is Bramante's interpretation of a circular Roman temple. The rotunda was something that was alien in the medieval pattern-book; now rediscovered, it was used again and again, with a vengeance.

Michelangelo, though primarily a sculptor, turned his hand to architecture late in life. Although he used classical elements, such as pilasters and cornices and pediments, the overall effect was really not anything like an imitation of ancient Rome. In some ways, Michelangelo leapfrogged the 'imitation' stage of the Renaissance and multiplied the classical detailing so that it became something else – Baroque – before its time. St Peter's Basilica in Rome defies classification. It could be seen as the apotheosis of the Roman basilica, which is what it was based on.

One of those leading the way in a more faithful reproduction of Roman architecture was Andrea di Pietro della Gondolo, who was known as Andrea Palladio. Most of Palladio's work is to be seen in Venice and Vicenza, and consists of churches, palaces and villas. He took some liberties with his classical models, for example in using two orders of column such as Doric and Ionic in one building. In the many palaces and villas he designed, he followed what he thought were authentic Roman features, but as domestic remains are very fragmentary he had to fall back on details from temples. In 1550, Palladio completed two neo-classical buildings, the Villa Rotonda and the Palazzo Chiericati at Vicenza.

Palladio's Villa Rotonda (or Villa Capra) was copied at least twice by English architects, by Lord Burlington at Chiswick House and by Colen Campbell at Mereworth Castle. These buildings have a central domed hall with four identical porticoes with entrance steps on each side.

In his churches, Palladio also used what he thought was the Roman temple pattern. He developed a type of facade which used two orders of different scales. This was a way of resolving the problem of relating the facade to two different roof heights in the nave and aisles. S. Giorgio Maggiore in Venice is perhaps his outstanding church design.

Another important influence in the Renaissance was Giorgio Vasari, who wrote slightingly and disparagingly of the medieval traditions in architecture, referring to medieval architecture as 'Gothic' – a name that has stuck. He suggested that this old style was originated by the Goths, 'those Germanic races untutored in the classics', and described Gothic churches as 'a heap of spires, pinnacles and grotesque decorations lacking in all the simple beauty of the classical orders.'

The influence of Palladio was long-lasting. In England, there was a movement in the early eighteenth century called Palladianism, which was based partly on the designs of Palladio and partly on those of Inigo Jones. It evolved as a distinctly 'English' style and dominated country house building in the period 1720–60. Its main architects were William Kent and Colen Campbell. The houses in this style were rather plain, severe and monumental on the outside. There was often a central block with portico, and colonnades on each flank leading to side pavilions. The buildings were often well-placed on rising ground, often with a vista and a lake, and the distinctly English park was laid out round it, often designed by Lancelot (Capability) Brown. Houses in this style include Holkham Hall and Houghton Hall, both in Norfolk.

This neo-classical style, which permeated the eighteenth century, would be resuscitated yet again in the neo-Georgian domestic architecture of the late twentieth century. The spirit of classical revival seems to go on and on, even if it no longer takes itself seriously.

THE MASSACRE OF THE HUGUENOTS
(1562)

FRANCOIS, THE CATHOLIC Duc de Guise, ordered a massacre of Huguenots on 1 March 1562. The Huguenots (French Protestants) came largely from the nobility and the new artisan class. There was friction, as in other countries, between the Protestants and the Catholics. Paris and north-eastern France remained mainly Catholic.

The enraged Huguenots retaliated by murdering priests and raping nuns. They were driven out of many French towns with a great deal of bloodshed, but succeeded in holding the towns of Rouen, Lyons and Orleans. Both sides in this futile struggle sensed that the king, the 13 year old Charles IX, had no real power; as in the reign of Henry VI of England, a power vacuum was being exploited by warring factions.

On 19 March 1563, Catherine de' Medici signed the Peace of Amboise, which was a command to end the year-long war between Catholics and Protestants in France. The edict followed by one month the murder of the Duc de Guise by a Huguenot assassin. This left Catherine in control of the Catholic forces. With the Peace of Amboise, she offered a measure of religious toleration to the Huguenots, but the peace was only short-lived.

In England, the persecution of the Huguenots had the effect of hardening Queen Elizabeth's face against the Catholics in her own country. She tolerated Dissenters, but viewed Catholics with increasing suspicion, a suspicion her advisers were later able to exploit regarding Mary Queen of Scots.

There was a demographic effect of these persecutions too. In 1564, the French Huguenot leader Gaspard de Coligny fitted out an expedition to colonize the New World. The fleet, commanded by Rene de Landonniere, sailed to northern Florida. Many Huguenots crossed the Channel to begin new lives in the safety of Protestant England.

In France, the religious war continued. In 1567, Catholic troops attacked a Huguenot army under the Prince of Conde at St Denis near Paris. The Catholic leader, the Constable of Montmorency, was killed. The following March Catherine de' Medici signed another 'Peace' treaty, but this too failed to stop the fighting, which erupted into a third religious war.

Then, in 1572, came the worst horror, the Massacre of St Bartholomew. On 23 and 24 August, 50,000 Huguenots were systematically slaughtered, in Paris and elsewhere in France. Urged on by the Queen Mother, Catholics disembowelled the young king's adviser, Gaspard Admiral de Coligny, and threw him, still living, out of the window. The loss of de Coligny and others in the massacre severely restricted the French economy, and brought French colonial expansion to a halt for decades. The religious wars generally, and the massacre in particular, were self-inflicted injuries from which France took a long time to recover. Pope Gregory XIII congratulated Catherine on her action. Queen Elizabeth made her displeasure known. The persecution of Protestants was part of the fall-out from the Reformation.

THE MURDER OF LORD DARNLEY
(1567)

MARY QUEEN OF Scots led a remarkably turbulent life. She was born in December 1542, and just a few days later her father King James V of Scotland died. The next year she was betrothed to the infant Prince Edward, the sickly son of Henry VIII of England, but Henry's too-obvious intention of joining the kingdoms of England and Scotland by this eventual marriage caused anger among the Scots. The Scots denounced the marriage treaty, and Henry VIII responded with an invasion of Scotland. All this before Mary was one year old.

Mary's marriages were to become a major problem. In 1548, when she was five, she was betrothed to the French Dauphin, Francis. She was sent to France, where she was brought up by her mother's relatives, the Guises. In 1558, the same year that her cousin became Queen Elizabeth of England, she was married to the Dauphin. Only two years later Francis II died, so in August 1561 Mary found herself sailing back to Scotland again. Shortly after that she encountered the only man who was ever able to stand up to her – John Knox. He spoke of his impression of her afterwards, of her 'proud mind, crafty wit and indurate heart against God and his truth.'

The Queen's second marriage had to be decided. Had she known how things would turn out she might have decided, like her English cousin, the Virgin Queen, that a celibate life was the only safe option. Elizabeth proposed Robert Dudley as her favoured candidate, but the idea did not appeal to either Dudley or Mary. Mary's cousin, Lord Darnley emerged as the hot favourite. Elizabeth decided she did not want Mary to marry Darnley, but by that time Mary had already secretly married Darnley at Stirling Castle, in the apartment of her secretary, David Rizzio. Assurances were given to Elizabeth that the marriage would not take place until the pope had approved the marriage of the two cousins; only then would they marry. In due course there was a public wedding in 1565. But the pattern of subterfuge, deviousness, deception and sheer bad behaviour was set.

The marriage roused the anger of Scottish Protestants, who raised an army. The Queen was defended by her own army. Darnley meanwhile wanted to raise his own status from mere king-consort to the crown matrimonial; he wanted to be king for real. Rizzio advised Mary to write a reasoned refusal, because it endangered her position. In giving this advice, Rizzio endangered himself. Darnley had him cruelly murdered in front of Mary. The killers of Rizzio fled to England, while Darnley's protestations of innocence were accepted.

There was a brief reconciliation, perhaps motivated by Mary's fear that Darnley might have her killed too, but Darnley continued to abuse Mary. A plot was hatched to kill him. There can be no doubt whatever that the Earl of Bothwell was a major player in this conspiracy. He certainly had many supporters, and everyone at the time thought that he had done it, but it is not absolutely certain whether Mary knew of the plot or encouraged it. Probably she was involved.

Darnley was ill. There were plans for him to take medicinal baths or to rejoin his father in Glasgow. Mary wanted him to go to Craigmillar Castle. But at the end of January 1567 Darnley was taken to a lonely and rather squalid house called Kirk o' Fields in Edinburgh. On 9 February Mary took her last leave of Darnley at Kirk o' Fields. The following night the whole city awoke to a huge explosion. Kirk o' Fields had been blown up. The next morning the body of Darnley was found strangled in the garden some distance from the house. The explosion had evidently been intended to kill Darnley, but he had survived it and escaped, only to be strangled by Bothwell's men in the garden outside.

It was widely assumed that Darnley's wife, Mary Queen of Scots, was involved in planning the murder and this marks the fatal moment in her career, the moment when she lost the support and sympathy of the Scots. From this moment it became inevitable that she would be deposed. Darnley's father demanded that the murderers should be brought to justice. Bothwell was accordingly put on trial but acquitted because there were no witnesses against him.

Mary was intercepted by James Hepburn, the Earl of Bothwell, on 24 April, at the head of 800 spearmen. He told her she was in great danger and must go with him. Whether this was a pre-arranged meeting or an abduction is very difficult to tell. Either way, the two were married in May. These developments made it look as if the two of them had plotted Darnley's murder. This prompted an open rebellion by the Scottish nobles who forced her to dismiss Bothwell and demanded her abdication in favour of her one year old son James VI. The infant king would be raised at Stirling Castle by the Earl and Countess of Mar.

The volatile and wayward ex-queen, now an acute embarrassment to the Scots, was confined at Lochleven, but in May 1568 she escaped, thanks to the help of a castle servant, Willie Douglas. After a skirmish at Langside, Mary had to travel for three days through the Southern Uplands, sleeping rough, with the idea of seeking sanctuary in England. Had she remained in Scotland, she would almost certainly have been executed there. It turned out that she risked execution by going to England too. The murder of Darnley was the great tuning-point in her life. By arriving in England, she became a thorn in the Queen of England's side. She was a constant problem to Elizabeth I, who could not allow her the freedom to muster support for an armed return to Scotland and could not allow her to plot to take the English throne instead. Mary Queen of Scots became a serious political problem for Elizabeth, and that problem did not go away when she had Mary executed.

OBSERVATION OF A CHANGING UNIVERSE
(1572)

IT WAS IN 1572 that the 26 year old Danish astronomer Tycho Brahe discovered a new star. This was not so much a newly discovered star that had been in the sky all along, but actually a new star. It appeared in the constellation of Cassiopeia. Brahe used instruments of his own design to build up a body of data on the positions of the Moon, stars and planets. He observed the sudden appearance of this new body, which will be called Tycho's Star. What Tycho actually saw was a nova.

A nova is a variable star, one that burns brighter for a short time. Usually this can happen only once in the lifetime of a star, though there are some that are known to have brightened more than once, such as Nova Coronea Borealis, which became brighter in 1866 and 1946. What Tycho saw was the very first nova to be seen, Nova Cassiopeia, and he rightly assumed the event was happening well outside the solar system, in the stellar universe. It was brighter than the planet Venus and could be seen even in the middle of the day. This puts it into the category of supernova.

A supernova was in fact observed several centuries earlier. The Chinese astronomers saw the explosion of the Crab Nebula in the constellation of Taurus in 1054. What astronomers today see in the Crab Nebula is the expanding, hazy, nebulous remnant of the star that exploded nearly one thousand years ago. The Chinese saw a supernova, a star exploding, in 1054, but did not make an inference from it. Tycho Brahe saw a supernova in 1572 and realised its significance to astronomical models at once. A star had 'appeared' that had not been visible before, so the universe had changed – and that in itself changed astronomy, and in time changed people's view of the universe they inhabit.

Tycho's discovery was a landmark in that it showed that the universe changes. It destroyed the Aristotelian (and therefore also the medieval) idea that no change can occur in the stars. If the stars could change, then the universe itself was not a fixed but an evolving entity. It was a significant step out of the middle ages, away from the flat Earth and towards the Big Bang.

SEBASTIANISM
(1578)

KING SEBASTIAN I of Portugal led a belated crusade against Islam in north-west Africa in defiance of warnings from both Philip II of Spain and Pope Gregory XIII. On 4 August, Sebastian and his army engaged in battle with a Muslim army at Al Kasr Al Kabir and were annihilated. Sebastian was killed in the battle, and so were the king of Fez and the Moorish pretender.

Sebastian was 24 and the hero of the Portuguese people. The battle was a national disaster. The Portuguese refused to believe that their king was dead. A cult, 'Sebastianism', developed. Its followers believed that the king was either away on a pilgrimage or waiting on an enchanted island for an appropriate moment to return. The hope that Sebastian was still alive led several successive impostors to appear, impersonating the dead king; they were all found out and executed. The last of these absurd pretenders was an Italian who could speak no Portuguese.

In 1580, a Spanish army defeated a Portuguese army in the Battle of Alcantara near Lisbon. After that, Philip II of Spain was proclaimed Philip I of Portugal, so Sebastian's place was filled.

The legend of the still-living king is a recurring one. The great British hero, King Arthur, similarly 'disappeared' after his final battle, the Battle of Camlann, and was mysteriously transported to the Isle of Avalon where he either died of his battle-wounds or was eventually healed. Some believed that Arthur lay sleeping in a cave somewhere, waiting for the moment when a national emergency would require his leadership again.

There were ancient beliefs in the west of Europe that associated the afterlife with an enchanted island, and the Isle of Avalon story may have its roots in these. The first century Roman writer Pomponius Mela described nine priestesses living on the Isle of Sein off the Brittany coast, which sounds rather like the mysterious veiled women who spirited the dying Arthur away in a barge to the Isle of Avalon. In AD 82, a Roman official named Demetrius visited Britain and noted one of the few myths of the British ever to be recorded in plain terms. His report was recorded by Plutarch and it told of an exiled god lying asleep in a cave on an island, a warm place in the general direction of the sunset. Probably both the cave and the island stories date back to pre-Arthurian beliefs about the afterlife.

Arthur and Sebastian are just two out of a great many charismatic leaders, many of them kings, who were believed to have somehow lived on after their 'official' deaths. The last Saxon king of England, Harold, officially died on the battlefield at Hastings. The Bayeux Tapestry is unambiguous about it: *Harold interfectus est* (Harold is killed). By the thirteenth century, an Icelandic story was told of Harold being found alive on the battlefield by two peasants who were looting corpses during the night after the battle. They took the still-living Harold home with them and discussed his future. He decided to retire to a hermitage at Canterbury rather than compromise the loyalty of his men who had now sworn fealty to William. Gerald of Wales, writing in 1191, affirmed that that the Saxons still clung to the belief that Harold had lived on after Hastings; as a hermit, deeply scarred and blinded in the left eye, he lived for a long time in a cell at Chester.

The Norwegian king Olaf Tryggvason was defeated in the sea-battle of Svold in 999. Wearing a scarlet cloak, he leapt from his ship, the *Long Serpent*, and drowned himself. The survival version of the story, that under the water he had swum beneath the enemy ships and been picked up and taken away by a friendly cutter, later going on pilgrimage to the Holy Land, was concocted immediately after his death: it was referred to by his friend Hallfredar the Troublesome, who did not believe a word of it. According to *The Longer Saga of Olaf Tryggvason*, Edward the Confessor, whose father King Ethelred had also been a friend of Olaf's, *did* believe the story and read it to his court every year on Easter Day. Eventually, Edward announced that news had come that Olaf had died, 36 years after his official death.

There are many other examples, most but not all of them kings; the Grand Duchess Anastasia, Richard II of England, Alexander I of Russia and Holger Danske, who is said to lie sleeping beneath Kronborg Castle until the hour of Denmark's greatest danger. Regardless of the mystification surrounding their deaths, all these people definitely existed as real flesh and blood. There is no question that they lived.

Sebastianism was just one manifestation of a recurring phenomenon – the charismatic leader who cannot be allowed to die. The refusal to accept the death of a leader may have significant after-effects. The mystery concerning the fate of the Princes in the Tower, 'Richard IV' and his younger brother, who may or may not have been murdered in 1483, opened the door for impersonation. Two high-profile pretenders, Perkin Warbeck and Lambert Simnel, appeared to make political ripples in the reign of Henry VII.

The belief in the sleeping but still-living Arthur seems to have pushed Henry II of England into staging the 'discovery' of Arthur's grave at Glastonbury in the twelfth century. By discovering the bones of King Arthur, he could lay to rest the simmering hope in the West of Britain that the Norman dynasty could be overthrown.

GALILEO AND THE PENDULUM
(1581)

GALILEO GALILEI WAS born in Pisa in 1564. He came of an impoverished noble Florentine family. Galileo was educated at the monastery of Vallombrosa near Florence. There he studied Latin and Greek, but found the science he was taught distasteful. He came to disagree with and despise the Aristotelian philosophy that prevailed in his day. He showed a practical aptitude for mechanical invention.

His father sent him to Pisa University in 1581 to study medicine. Just two years later Galileo inferred, first from casual and then from systematic observations of a swinging lamp in Pisa Cathedral, the properties of a pendulum. Whatever the range of the oscillations, however wide the swings, the time scale is the same. This phenomenon has come to be called isochronism. He then applied the same principle to the human pulse. Until this time he was kept completely ignorant of mathematics by his father, who uncannily sensed that Galileo would become preoccupied with it and that it would lead him to neglect medicine. Galileo by chance overheard a lesson in geometry, which caught his interest. He pleaded with his father to be allowed to study mathematics, and his father reluctantly agreed.

In 1585, Galileo was withdrawn from university before taking a degree, because his father could no longer afford to keep him there. Galileo returned to Florence, where he lectured to the Florentine Academy.

The observation and later proof of isochronism turned out to have a very useful application. Since it made no difference whether the pendulum swing was short or long, the time interval of the pendulum swings was a reliable constant. This was exploited in clocks. It is a phenomenon that is so familiar that we take it for granted, but it does regulate the mechanism of a clock extremely well, and therefore formed the basis of several generations of clock technology.

The earliest mechanical clocks were introduced into Europe in the thirteenth century. A clock was erected at Westminster in 1288 and another at Canterbury four years later. None of these early clocks was fitted with a pendulum. Instead, they had a crown-wheel escapement that was controlled by two slowly oscillating weighted arms; this device was known as a foliot. The time of swing of the two arms was very variable, so these early clocks were very poor time-keepers, often losing or gaining as much as an hour in a day.

The introduction of the pendulum was a very important stage in the development of the clock. Once Galileo had discovered its principle it was soon adopted into clock design. It consisted of a weight or bob mounted on the lower end of a vertical rod suspended from a flexible support. The time of the swing can be calculated very precisely by using a formula, but basically it is proportional to the length of the pendulum. Correcting the clock, if it is running slow or running fast, can be achieved by shortening the pendulum, or more usually by moving the weight up or down a little. The pendulum therefore made it possible to adjust clocks – and make them keep accurate time. By the time the age of the train and time-tables, this level of accuracy became all-important.

THE INTRODUCTION OF THE GREGORIAN CALENDAR

(1582)

A NEW CALENDAR was introduced by Pope Gregory in 1582. It replaced the old Julian calendar, dating from the time of Julius Caesar, which was becoming increasingly unsatisfactory. As time-keeping became more precise, thanks to improvements in clocks, there was increasing consciousness of accuracy in time-keeping generally.

The ancient Julian calendar, which was devised in 45 BC, had a serious error built into it, an error of one day in every 128 years. This in itself did not matter very much, but it meant that over a long period the spring equinox (the date when day and night are of equal length) had moved gradually further and further back through the calendar. By 1582, instead of being near the end of March the eqiuoinox was at the beginning. Clearly this regression could not be allowed to continue. What the new Gregorian calendar did was to restore the original date for the spring equinox, 21 March, and keep it there.

The new calendar was devised by Luigi Ghiraldi (known as Aloysius Lilius), an astronomer from Naples.

On 5 October 1582, all Catholic countries switched to the new calendar, and that day became 15 October. Because the reform was introduced by the pope, inevitably the Protestant countries refused to go along with it and kept to the old Julian calendar for another hundred or more years. By 1752, the gap between the two calendars had widened to 11 days, and the British government decided that the time had come for Britain and the British colonies to adopt the Gregorian calendar. By Parliamentary decree Thursday 14 September 1752 followed Wednesday 2 September. The change-over created widespread chaos. Bill collectors were confused, wage-earners feared they were losing 11 days' pay, and the uneducated and superstitious masses believed that the government had stolen 11 days of their lives. In London the cry went up, 'Give us back our 11 days!' There were riots to protest about the life-shortening calendar change.

The Russians kept to the Julian calendar right through to the Russian Revolution, only switching to the Gregorian calendar in 1918.

SHAKESPEARE'S PLAYS

(1590-1612)

IT WAS VERY soon after the beginning of his acting career that William Shakespeare started writing plays of his own. Shakespeare was remarkable in many ways, but perhaps the most remarkable is that he was immediately successful. There is no surviving sign of any 'apprentice work' that is substandard or unworthy of performance, which is really quite extraordinary. He wrote historical plays that were from the start finely written, immensely popular and commercially successful, the three parts of *Henry VI* (1592). The theatre impresario Philip Henslowe wrote in his diary that 'Harey the vi' played to packed houses at the Rose Theatre between March and June 1592.

The young Shakespeare's triumphant debut on the London stage was not universally applauded, and there must have been many who were jealous. In September 1592, a frustrated writer called Robert Greene wrote a pamphlet called *Greene's Groatsworth of Wit, Bought with a Million of Repentance*. This included a ranting attack on 'an upstart crow', a 'Shakescene'. It must have been very galling indeed for Greene to see Shakespeare make an immediate hit with his very first play – rather like the composers Igor Stravinsky and William Walton being extremely irritated by the success of Benjamin Britten.

His first seven years in the theatre included several other successes too. He completed two more history plays, *King John* and *Richard III*, a revenge tragedy, *Titus Andronicus*, and three comedies, *The Comedy of Errors, The Taming of the Shrew* and *The Two Gentlemen of Verona*. So, by 1592, William Shakespeare had attempted to write in each of the three most popular forms of drama of his day – and succeeded. Not only that, he had extended their range, and made his own highly original contribution to each genre. The play-goers in London must have been very aware that a dazzling new talent was at work, eclipsing even Christopher Marlowe, then generally thought to be the best playwright in England.

For two years starting in 1592, the London theatres were shut because of plague. While the theatres were shut, Shakespeare turned his hand to narrative poetry, writing the long narrative poems *Venus and Adonis* and *The Rape of Lucrece*. These poems, dedicated to the Earl of Southampton, were highly praised for their eloquent treatment of classical subjects. He wrote many sonnets too at this time when plays were banned, and these were in private circulation by 1598.

When the theatres re-opened in 1594, Shakespeare joined the acting company called The Lord Chamberlain's Men, and soon became its joint manager. The Lord Chamberlain's Men made a very clever choice in inviting Shakespeare in as a 'sharer'. Up to this point he had been freelance, and any company could perform his plays; now the Lord Chamberlain's Men had his exclusive services. Shakespeare had his financial security; the company had his plays.

There followed a torrent of great plays: a tragedy (*Romeo and Juliet*), three more histories and five more comedies.

When James I came to the throne in 1603, Shakespeare's company became The King's Men, and this change in status brought great benefits to the company. His later plays included tragedies such as *Hamlet* and *Macbeth*, plays that rank among the darkest plays ever written. Shakespeare crafted his later plays so that they could be performed with equal success on very different stages. His plays were still performed in open-air theatres such as The Globe, but now also indoors in the great halls of great houses, where artificial lighting and more elaborate stage effects were possible. Shakespeare was always an intensely practical man, well able to adjust to changing technical conditions - and changing fashion. Tragi-comedy was a form of drama now much in fashion, so Shakespeare supplied it. These 'last plays', as they are known, included *Pericles, Cymbeline, The Winter's Tale* and *The Tempest*.

Shakespeare was very prolific, writing 37 plays that have survived and several more that have not. *The Tempest* shows a thinly disguised Shakespeare taking his leave of the stage. He formally handed over the role of The King's Men's chief dramatist to John Fletcher and retired in 1612 to Stratford, where he died four years later, on 23 April 1616. In 1623, two of his friends in the King's Men, John Hemminge and Henry Condell, assembled all of the plays and published them in what is called the *First Folio*. It was not just a tribute to the greatest playwright of the age; it saved the plays from extinction. Without that publication, many of the surviving plays would have been lost.

Shakespeare was the outstanding playwright of the Renaissance, outshining all of his contemporaries and setting new standards for all subsequent dramatists. His plays range widely in subject and tone – challenging histories loaded with political agenda, atmospheric and romantic comedies and the darkest of tragedies. His work is astonishing for the richness and beauty of its language, showing the full potential of the English language for the expression of thought and feeling, building on the weight and majesty that William Tyndale had brought to it a few decades earlier. It also shows great insight into a wide range of human predicaments. Shakespeare's plays exemplify the questioning humanism of the Renaissance.

III
THE
ENLIGHTENED
WORLD

THE START OF THE ANTI-TOBACCO CAMPAIGN
(1604)

IT WAS IN 1492 that the first mention was made of smoking tobacco. Luis de Torres and Rodrigo de Jerez were sent ashore in the New World by Columbus; there they saw native North Americans who 'drank smoke'. Rodrigo de Jerez then tried smoking himself, picked up the habit, and was later imprisoned by the Spanish Inquisition for the 'devilish habit' that he had adopted. In 1518, Spanish colonists in Santo Domingo were taught how to smoke by a native chief; the colonists were given things that sound very like cigarettes or small clay pipes:

> *a little hollow tube, burning at one end without causing a flame, as do the incense sticks of Valencia. And they smelled a fragrant odour. The Indians made signs to the Spaniards not to allow the smoke to be lost.*

In 1604, James I published a piece expressing disapproval of tobacco. It was entitled *A Counterblaste to Tobacco* and published anonymously. In it, the King referred to two Indians who were brought to England from Virginia in 1584 specifically to demonstrate smoking. 'What honour or policy can move us to imitate the barbarous and beastly manners of the wilde, godlesse, and slavish Indian especially in so vile and stinking a custome?'

King James pointed out that tobacco was initially used as an antidote to the 'Pockes' (syphilis), but doctors now regarded smoking as a filthy habit that was harmful to health. From his own personal point of view, he regarded it as 'a custome loathsome to the eye, hatefull to the nose, harmefull to the braine, dangerous to the lungs and in the black stinking fume thereof, nearest resembling the horrible Stigian smoke of the pit that is bottomlesse.'

He made some very good points about the nastiness of smoking. 'It makes a kitchen of the inward parts of men, soiling and infecting them with an unctuous and oily kind of soot.' He regretted that 'the sweetness of man's breath, being a good gift of God, should be wilfully corrupted by this stinking smoke.'

King James's unusual public condemnation of tobacco smoking was far ahead of its time. The commercial interest in promoting smoking overcome his objections, in much the same way that Elizabeth I's humanitarian objections to the slave trade were overcome by the wealth that slaving generated.

By 1612, tobacco cultivation in Virginia had established itself as an economic activity that could provide a solid financial base for the colony. John Rolfe had obtained seed from the Caribbean islands and after a couple of years' coaching by the Indians he learnt how to grow and cure the leaves. On the back of tobacco production, Jamestown became a boom town, the Virginia Company became prosperous and James I himself was enriched by tobacco import duties. Because of this, his attitude towards tobacco softened.

Twelve years on, Pope Urban VIII was as hostile to snuff users as James I had been to smokers. The use of tobacco in Europe generally was on the increase and the pope did not like it. He threatened Catholics using snuff with excommunication.

But the tobacco industry grew and grew relentlessly, even in the twentieth century, when there was increasing scientific research evidence that smoking was extremely harmful. In 1966, a lawyer wrote to an American TV channel, pointing out that there were many commercials portraying smoking as 'socially acceptable and desirable, manly, and a necessary part of a rich full life.' He proposed that an equal amount of air time should be given to the presentation of contrasting views. Gradually, as the research evidence was published, showing that smoking caused a range of health problems including lung cancer and heart disease, the numbers of people smoking in the West gradually declined.

GALILEO'S OBSERVATIONS OF THE MOON AND JUPITER

(1610)

IN 1592, GALILEO became Professor of Mathematics at Padua, where his lectures attracted students from all over Europe. Rumours of the invention of a refracting telescope invented by the Dutch in 1608 reached northern Italy in the following year. Galileo investigated the principle of the newly invented instrument, started work on it at once and made significant improvements on its design shortly afterwards, for example raising the magnification to x32. Galileo's telescopes – and that is what people at the time were calling the new instrument – were much in demand, and he made hundreds of them with his own hands.

The new invention enabled to Galileo launch on a series of observations, which convinced him that the Copernican theory of the universe, with the sun at the centre, was right. It seems that Galileo knew from early on in his researches that Copernicus was right. He held back from publicly supporting Copernicus for a long time – not because he feared persecution, but because he feared ridicule. Within six months of designing his improved telescope, Galileo had already made some major discoveries about the nature of the solar system.

He looked at the Moon through his telescope and concluded from what he saw that the Moon's brightness was due to the reflection of sunlight from the Moon's surface. For the first time he could see for himself that the surface of the Moon was uneven. The facial features of the 'Man in the Moon' that people had been able to see with the naked eye for hundreds of thousands of years were explained by these unevennesses; they were in fact hills, craters, plains and mountain ranges. The Moon was covered with mountains and valleys. Galileo's discovery, which we now take for granted, caused a sensation in 1610 when he published it in his book *Siderius Nuncius*. It was literally another world, with all the possibilities and implications that that opened for the human race. A New World had been discovered across the Atlantic only 100 years ago, and now there were more new worlds to be seen out in space.

Galileo saw the Milky Way as a track of countless stars, though he did not manage to infer from it a disc-shaped galaxy – indeed, how could he? He saw spots on the Sun, and used their movement across the Sun's disc to infer that the Sun rotates. In January of that same year, 1610, he discovered by direct observation that Jupiter has four satellites. When the atmospheric conditions are favourable on the Earth, it is quite possible to do this; I have seen the moons of Jupiter through ordinary binoculars. Galileo named the satellites the Medicean stars, after the dedicatee of his book, Cosimo II de' Medici.

These amazing discoveries, made one after another with the aid of Galileo's magic cardboard tube, led in September 1610 to a summons to Florence, where he was warmly received by the Grand Duke of Tuscany; he was awarded a professorship for life, on a high salary. He was also appointed as philosopher and mathematician extraordinary to the Grand Duke.

Galileo used his improved telescope to great effect. He was a great observer; he looked carefully and was scrupulously honest about what he saw. Not only did he discover Jupiter's satellites: within two years of discovering them he had constructed fairly accurate tables of their periods of revolution. Not only was the Moon turning out to be a miniature planet like the Earth, a ball of rock with mountains and valleys etched on its surface, but other planets had Moons too. The discoveries were turning the universe into a more exciting place. Not only was the Earth not the centre of the universe; it was probably not even the most interesting part of it. It was a defining moment in human history, when our attention was pulled outward, and we were made much more conscious of all the remarkable possibilities that lie waiting for us 'out there'.

THE DEFENESTRATION
OF PRAGUE
(1618)

BY THE MIDDLE of the sixteenth century over two-thirds of the population of Bohemia was Protestant. The naturally conservative ruling classes remained mainly Catholic. As the Catholic backlash to the Reformation got under way (the Counter-Reformation), this Catholic aristocracy became more vigorous, determined and fanatical. The Catholic barons in Bohemia started to enforce Catholicism throughout their domains. The resulting religious conflict was partly a social conflict – a class war.

Rudolph II was not the man to pilot his empire through these dangerous waters. He was unstable, suspicious and had not been helped by a narrow upbringing in Spain. He arbitrarily tried to stamp out Protestantism in Hungary, and that provoked a fierce rebellion that had led to a climb-down in the Peace of Vienna in 1606. Rudolph then refused to ratify this treaty with the Protestants, prompting another rising.

Under Rudolph II, Prague had been the capital of the Habsburg domains. Matthias, the king's Catholic lieutenant in Hungary, moved the capital to Vienna, which aroused much suspicion and opposition. Protestant rebellion was simmering in the background, heated up by the situation in Germany, where conflict between Catholics and Protestants was intensifying.

The Catholic administration of Bohemia violated promises that had been made to the Protestants. The Bohemian Protestants were further embittered by Matthias's transfer of Bohemia's administration to ten governors, of whom seven were fanatical Catholics. When the Protestants' legitimate claims, presented formally in March 1618, were rejected, their frustration and anger boiled over. On 23 May 1618, two of the new governors were hurled out of a window in the Palace of Hradcany in

Prague. The two who were ejected were Jaroslav of Martinic and William of Slavata, the two most fervent Catholics on the Council. They survived their 15m fall into the castle moat with only slight injuries, but their 'defenestration' (ejection from a window) became a symbol of the struggle and a signal for a revolt.

A council of 30 directors was appointed by the diet (parliament). The Protestant leader, Count Heinrich Matthias von Thurn, was the one who ordered the defenestration, and who then took command of the rebel troops. Von Thurn led his Protestant army to attack Austria. In November 1619, he laid siege to Vienna, but he was forced to withdraw because of the coldness of the winter, the shortage of food and the action of the Catholic Elector of Bavaria's troops.

The Catholic aristocracy's reaction to this Protestant rebellion was extreme. Between 1620 and 1626, a selection of alleged revolutionary leaders was executed, their property was confiscated, the schools and the university were closed and the conduct of public instruction and censorship was handed over to the control of the Jesuits. The Protestant towns were made Catholic by the imposition of fines. The crackdown was so severe that an estimated 30,000 Protestant families emigrated and the country went into a decline for several decades, its national life stifled.

RALEIGH'S *HISTORY OF THE WORLD*
(1618)

TODAY WE TEND to associate Sir Walter Raleigh with the court of Queen Elizabeth I. He is for ever, in my mind's eye, the dashing overdressed courtier who laid his cloak over a puddle for the Queen to step across. He was, for a time at any rate, the Queen's glamorous favourite, a glittering peacock of a man in an historical tableau. But in the seventeenth century, in the decades immediately following his execution, he was a very different kind of icon, and an altogether more important figure in the general scheme of things.

Sir Walter Raleigh wrote his *History of the World* while he was in prison, in the Tower of London, from 1603 onwards. In the preparation of this ambitious undertaking, Raleigh had the support of Thomas Hariot, who acted as his principal assistant as well as one of his most loyal friends. It was and remains extraordinary that such a monumental work could have been written behind bars, but for the first four or five years in the Tower Raleigh wrote very little. The flurry of writing came in the later period, when he was anticipating and working towards his release.

Raleigh was allocated two rooms on the second floor of the Bloody Tower, with a view north over Tower Green and a view south to St Thomas's Tower, which in turn overlooked the river. His wife was allowed to live with him. He also had servants and a young schoolmaster, John Talbot, who acted as his secretary. It was a fairly comfortable existence, if cramped. He was allowed to walk around inside the Tower, and took his exercise along the walls of the fortress. In fact, the citizens of London used to go to the Tower at a set time of day especially to catch sight of the great man taking his constitutional round the walls. He was a celebrity, even in chains.

Raleigh started writing his *History* when he befriended Prince Henry, the promising Prince of Wales who unfortunately died after swimming in the filthy River Thames; his premature death made way for another of Raleigh's bad kings, Charles I. This intriguing friendship lasted the four years from 1608 to 1612, from the very time when the *History* was written. We must assume that in the book Sir Walter was speaking directly to the prince. Sir Walter took it upon himself to be the heir to the throne's tutor. What he produced was a stunning piece of work that has impressed generations of English people since it was written.

Raleigh started at the beginning and treated the kings of the ancient world as exhaustively and thoroughly as he could. The result was that although he produced a great tome he only got as far as 168 BC. It was even so a very popular work, going through at least ten editions after Raleigh's death, twice as many as either the works of Shakespeare or Spenser's *Faerie Queene*. The theme was that no king is above God's judgement, that however powerful a king may be, if he behaves unjustly or cruelly towards his subjects, he in turn will be punished by God. It was a neat and irrefutable argument for constitutional monarchy and for just kingship; kings have to behave as if they are answerable for what they do, because ultimately they are.

By today's standards it is perhaps not very rigorous as history, some of it veering into heavy sermonizing, but it is a very powerful presentation of a good idea. In order to put royal vanity in its place, he pointed out that for all the apparent power and splendour of some of the great kings of antiquity, little remains of their power today. It was an idea that the Romantic poets would revive – the colossal broken statue in the Egyptian desert with its inscription, 'Look on my works, ye mighty – and despair!' Raleigh wrote, 'And yet hath Babylon, Persia, Egypt, Syria, Macedonia, Carthage, Rome and the rest no fruit, flower, grass nor leaf springing on the face of the earth. No! Their very roots and ruins do hardly remain!' Conversely the nasty things kings do are never forgotten. He wrote that 'whatever the virtues and kindnesses of Alexander the Great, men were always to say of him, "But he killed Calisthenes."' Raleigh had at the back of his mind that he himself was in prison on suspicion of treason, and he was consciously or unconsciously warning the king that he would for ever be remembered for killing Raleigh, if he had him executed.

An interesting aspect of the book which makes it particularly vivid is

Raleigh's fascination with chronology. He was very intrigued by who was alive at the same time. He thought, from the evidence he had, that Prometheus and Atlas were around at the same time as Moses, and that the three men might therefore have known each other. He thought Jason and the Argonauts might have bumped into Gideon, who lived at the same time. The past, for Raleigh, was a very real place, a place of highly significant human interaction.

The *History of the World* avoided any overt criticism of James I, which would have been highly dangerous, given Raleigh's position as a suspected traitor. He listed in outline the misdeeds of some recent English monarchs, including Richard II, Henry IV, Henry VI, Edward IV, Richard III, Henry VII and Henry VIII – but cautiously stopping there. He could not accuse James I of being a bad king, and he would not have wanted to criticize Elizabeth. He wrote a lavish, over-the-top dedication to the still-living, still-dangerous King James I, doubtless heavy with irony – and nearly got away with it. When he was beheaded in 1618 it was for something else.

The book became a defiant reproach to absolute monarchy. It provided specific examples of bad kingship and was such a thorough-going tract for the abolition of monarchy that it became an emblematic work for the Parliamentarians 20–30 years after his death. Raleigh himself became a legendary figure in his own lifetime, but a different kind of legend to the generation that followed. Pym, Eliot, Milton and Cromwell saw Raleigh as their own forerunner, one of the great worthies of England who championed the principles for which they went to war with the king.

The men who idealized Raleigh in this way were revolutionaries, but they were also reactionaries who harked back to the golden years of Good Queen Bess, when monarch, parliament and people lived together in harmony. Their demons or villains were the Stuart kings, James and Charles. Raleigh's career fitted this mythology neatly; his star had risen under Gloriana, and fallen under James I.

It was a partial and distorted view. Raleigh did not really stand for principle or democracy; he was interested in personal power, privilege and wealth. Yet Cromwell loved the book and recommended it to his son. John Locke thought it the ideal reading for 'gentlemen desirous of improving their education.' Marvell, Prynne and Lilburne praised it. Milton was profoundly influenced by it. The historian Digory Wheare said it placed Raleigh in the same rank as Herodotus. Whatever and whoever Raleigh himself was, the book that outlived him became the backbone of anti-authoritarian thought in the run-up to the Civil War; in fact it can be seen as a catalyst to and an excuse for the Civil War. *The History of the World* was political dynamite, the equivalent of a seventeenth century *Das Kapital*. Just as Marx analyzed history to justify the proletarian revolution, Raleigh examined history to illustrate the workings of God through politics, in particular in punishing unjust rulers.

THE *MAYFLOWER* VOYAGE

(1620)

THE *MAYFLOWER*, A vessel of 180 tonnes out of Southampton, sailed across the Atlantic Ocean in 1620. She sailed with one hundred so-called 'Pilgrims' on board, plus another two who were born during the 66-day voyage. The Pilgrims were English dissenters, people who were in reality religious and social misfits. They had originated in Scrooby and Gainsborough, where they were separatists from the Church of England and set up Independent Churches. They were forced to emigrate to Amsterdam in 1608, and from there to Leyden in 1609. They decided, three years before the *Mayflower* voyage, to give up Europe altogether and began to organize this final migration to the New World. They obtained permission from the London Company to settle in North America. The London Company was established in 1606 under the Virginia Charter, under rules stipulating that new settlements were to be no closer than 160km from each other. Since 1606, several shiploads of settlers had set off to found colonies. The *Mayflower* settlers were just one more of these.

The Pilgrims have been portrayed as the victims of intolerance and oppression in the various places where they lived. It seems now that it was they who were intolerant of their surroundings. In American history, the Pilgrim Fathers have been set up as in some way the founders of North America, but they were by no means the first group of settlers to cross the Atlantic.

They sailed from Southampton in August 1620, calling at Plymouth in September, and made landfall in the New World near Cape Cod on 11 November. They founded their colony settlement at Plymouth, Massachusetts on 21 December. They were given help by some of the native North Americans, who have learned some English from earlier settlers. They generously share their tribal stores of maize with the colonists to help them get through the winter. But in spite of this help, half of the community dies during that winter, of hunger, scurvy and disease.

In 1621, another 35 English colonists arrived at Plymouth to boost the ailing colony. The colonists had difficulty in growing wheat and barley in fields that have not been properly cleared of rocks and tree stumps, but they were again helped by some native North Americans, notably the Wampanoag Indians who were kidnapped by the slaver Thomas Hunt in 1615. Tisquantum had, incredibly, made his way back to Cape Cod from Spain, presenting himself at the Plymouth settlement on 16 March. He spoke English and was able to teach the colonists how to catch eels, and how to plant maize and beans, and how to fertilize them, techniques that he possibly picked up from other colonists.

In 1625, the Plymouth colony for the first time had 'corn sufficient and some to spare.' The Governor of the colony, William Bradford, reported back to England that part of the success has been due to land being assigned to each family according to family size. The following year, the Plymouth colonists were in a position to buy out their London investors for £1,800.

There was nothing very special about the initial colonization. It just happened to be the one that survived. Of all the early European colony settlements in North America, this was the first to survive, if by the skin of its teeth, to become a permanent settlement. The granite boulder the first settler stepped onto when landing has been enshrined in a portico.

DESCARTES'
DISCOURSE
(1637)

IN 1637, RENE Descartes published his *Discourse* (*Discours de la Methode*). In this he established the principle that metaphysical demonstrations should be based on mathematical certainty, not on scholastic subtleties. Descartes argued that the proper way to reason is to doubt everything systematically until only the clear and simple ideas that are beyond doubt are left. Then you have arrived at the truth. This method of thinking became known as the 'Cartesian' method.

Descartes wanted to be able to doubt everything, but he vehemently affirmed his certainty in his own existence: I think, therefore I am. Whatever else the sceptic may doubt, he should not doubt his own existence. The saying entails believing that mind is more real than matter. This idea was not entirely new: St Augustine said something similar, but did not give it the emphasis that Descartes did. He also adopted as a general rule that all things that we conceive very clearly and very distinctly are true.

Descartes' view of the world was rigidly deterministic. Dead matter and living matter are equally governed by the laws of physics, so there is no need to follow Aristotle in thinking in terms of a soul, or some equivalent to a soul, to explain the growth of organisms. This got Descartes, a devout Catholic, into some difficulties. If all organisms, people included, were simply following predetermined laws of physics, how could free will exist? The Bible taught him that people did have free will, and that making the wrong choice resulted in the expulsion from Eden. In the end, Descartes was unable to resolve a fundamental problem in his philosophic system, because he had one foot in the scholasticism of the middle ages and one foot in contemporary science. If he had been able to leave his religion behind, he could have achieved philosophical consistency, and planted both feet in the modern world. Descartes' philosophy is all the more interesting because it stands on the division between two mindsets. It stands at a particular moment in human history, a particular threshold.

Descartes is generally regarded as the founder of modern philosophy. He was the first man of high philosophical capacity to be affected by the new physics and the new astronomy. He was bold in not accepting foundations that had been laid down by earlier philosophers; he tried to set out a complete philosophic edifice from scratch, something which had not really been attempted by anyone since Aristotle. He developed a simple, direct and clear literary style, one that could be understood by intelligent men of the world; he did not try for an obscure a jargon-ridden style that would impress without really communicating.

THE DEATH OF JOHN HARVARD

(1638)

THE ENGLISH CLERGYMAN John Harvard died on 14 September 1638, after spending only one year living in the Massachusetts Bay colony. He was 31 and died of tuberculosis. Like many other early settlers, he died young. What was unusual about John Harvard was his legacy. He was an educated man and a man of some means; he left his library and his estate of £800 to the college that had been founded at New Towne just two years earlier.

John Harvard was a Cambridge graduate, and because of this, New Towne was renamed Cambridge in his honour. In 1639, the Great and General Court of Massachusetts ordered that 'the college agreed upon formerly to be built at Cambridge shall be called Harvard College.'

Another colonist, Ann Radcliffe, contributed funds to the college, and by 1650, Harvard had established the four-year teaching programme that became standard for American colleges.

John Harvard's legacy was appreciable and appreciated by the community at the time of his death. After the passage of time, that legacy can be seen as the beginning of something of overwhelming importance in the cultural life not only of North America but of the West as a whole. He gave the name of his university in England to the colony settlement in North America; he gave his own name to one of the most distinguished universities in the world.

THE INVENTION OF
THE CALCULATING
MACHINE
(1642)

PASCAL AND HIS father collaborated in a variety of experiments that led to
the invention of the barometer, the hydraulic press and the syringe. The
idea of mathematical probability evolved out of a correspondence between
Blaise Pascal and Pierre de Fermat about the division of stakes in games
of chance.

In 1647, at the age of only 19, Pascal patented a calculating machine,
which he had built to help his father with his work, which involved
computing taxes at Rouen. The machine added and subtracted using
wheels numbered from 0 to 9. It had an ingenious ratchet mechanism to
carry the 1 of a number greater than 9. As in other areas of endeavour,
Pascal's calculating machine was a prototype that others later would come
along and develop further. His work can now be seen as a major stepping
stone to future developments.

In 1692, the German philosopher and mathematician Gottfried von
Leibniz devised a more advanced calculating machine. This could multiply
by repeated addition. It could also divide, as well as the basic adding and
subtracting that Pascal's machine could do. Leibniz used a stepped drum
to mechanize the calculation of trigonometric tables.

It is easy to see, with hindsight, how this in turn led on to the
development of Charles Babbage's 'analytical engine' in 1833. This was
a large-scale digital calculator. Babbage managed to get some money
(£17,000) from the British government, but he had to sink £20,000 of
his own money to develop the calculating machine. The government
pulled out of the project in 1842. Prime Minister Robert Peel joked,

'How about setting the machine to calculate when it will be of use?'

The steadily evolving calculating machine was the forerunner of the electronic computer of the twentieth century – and it started with Pascal's adding machine.

THE EXECUTION OF
CHARLES I
(1649)

CHARLES I SHOULD never have been king of England. He was the second son of James I and Anne of Denmark, and a backward child, so weak that he could hardly walk and was very slow in starting to talk. During his boyhood he grew a little stronger, and became quite a good horseman and walker, but the stammer stayed with him all his life.

Charles I's elder brother, Henry, Prince of Wales, was the Heir Apparent, the youth befriended by Sir Walter Raleigh, but Henry died after a swim in the polluted Thames and Charles became Prince of Wales in November 1616. Two years later there was a further misfortune when he fell under the malign influence of the Duke of Buckingham, one of his father's favourites, who dominated the king's royal councils. Charles would hear no criticism of his favourite. Parliament tried to impeach the incompetent Buckingham, so Charles intervened and dissolved it. 'Parliaments are altogether in my power for their calling, sitting and dissolution; therefore, as I find the fruits of them good or evil they are to continue, or not to be.'

Without Parliament as an instrument he found it difficult to raise money, so he tried a forced loan. From this point on the relationship between king and Parliament deteriorated, with the Parliament intellectually emancipated by the Renaissance and the king playing the part of a medieval absolute monarch. He was doomed. The assassination of the Duke of Buckingham in August 1628 removed one source of friction between king and Parliament, but the improvement in relations was only temporary.

A point of law seemed to work in Charles's favour. The notorious Ship Money which Charles levied to promote his foreign adventures was held

253

by English judges to be legal, because the king could levy money in the interests of national safety.

Increasingly, in the power struggle between king and Parliament, the army took the side of Parliament and a civil war became inevitable. Charles's visit to Scotland in 1641 in an attempt to raise a Scottish army to settle the English problem was yet another error in diplomacy. He dallied with the idea of promising the Irish leniency in return for their support. But he never considered the overall picture, the synergy of his monarchy. Nearly everything he did undermined his own position.

He was eventually defeated and kept under 'house arrest', but he refused to accept that he was defeated and began secret negotiations with the Scots, encouraging them to invade England and secure his restoration. His captors rightly construed this as a treasonable act and were left with little choice but to kill him. A treason trial was mounted and Charles put up a dignified if futile defence. There was a moment of particular ill-omen during his trial, when he accidentally beheaded his own walking stick. When the broken off knob rolled across the floor and no-one picked it up for him, he must have known that things were going badly against him. They were. On 30 January 1649 he too was beheaded in Whitehall.

It is the inescapable verdict of history that he was the most unsuitable person to become king at that time. It is significant that he rarely if ever read anything; a wider base of knowledge about the world around him might have helped him towards more sensible actions. With his ideas of absolutism and his dismissive view of Parliament he was certainly not the man for the times in which he lived. He was disarmingly clear about his position, saying that he 'did not believe the happiness of the people lay in sharing government, subject and sovereign being clean different.' His heedless military adventures cost an enormous number of lives, set families and communities against one another, caused brothers to kill brothers, and fathers to kill sons. The large-scale destruction of life and property and the dislocation of English society were entirely avoidable, and entirely due to the king's bad judgement. He was stubborn, yet he could not be trusted to honour his word and be resolute when it counted. He promised his faithful servant the Earl of Strafford that he would be safe, but when he thought his wife, the queen, might be in danger, he let that promise go and sacrificed Strafford. As Strafford said shortly before his own execution, 'Put not your trust in princes'. After the Earl of Strafford's death, the king repented his action and felt guilty about his own treachery for the rest of his life; at the end, he came to see his own execution as an expiation of his treachery.

Charles I's greatest crime was to be the single cause, by extreme provocation, of the English Civil War. As Sir Walter Raleigh observed when he was a prisoner in the Tower in 1603, several decades before these events, 'The greatest and most grievous calamity that can come to any state is civil war, a misery more lamentable than can be described.' Raleigh had in mind the terrible religious war he had himself witnessed in France when young, but what he said was just as true of the English Civil War, at that stage not even imagined.

Charles I did nothing to improve the lot of ordinary people in England during his reign, nothing to enhance the country's reputation abroad, nothing to strengthen England economically or socially, everything to destroy it. He ranks as one the most incompetent monarchs England has ever had. Under incompetent leaders there is mayhem, and miseries and injustices multiply.

What came next was a republic. Unfortunately, like the assassins of Julius Caesar, the Parliamentarians did not have a clear alternative to the monarchy they had destroyed. Cromwell had seen simply that there could be no way forward unless the king was out of the way, and imprisonment had not worked. Cromwell had become convinced that the king must die. Had the king been ready to accept the military defeat and simply abdicated, he might have been spared, but the king's persistent attempts to escape and arrange secret treaties with the Scots showed that he could not be trusted.

The Republic that Cromwell presided over from 1649 was a period of uneasy peace. Cromwell was not a modern democrat, by a very long way. He had little sympathy for the Levellers, an egalitarian movement that had contributed significantly to the Parliamentary cause during the Civil War. He moreover dismissed the Rump Parliament in 1653 and took dictatorial powers to himself. He became in effect a military dictator.

In 1657, a reconvened Parliament offered Cromwell the crown. This gave him a terrible dilemma. He had abolished the monarchy himself. He had even had the previous monarch beheaded. Would he now become 'King Oliver'? He took six weeks to think about it. He was evidently tempted, not least because the republican structures that had been tried were unsatisfactory. In the end he turned it down because senior officers in his army made it known that they would resign if he accepted. Instead he went for near-monarchy, accepting the title Lord Protector, having himself installed as such in Westminster Abbey (of all places), and sitting on the king's throne. He was as good as king, and there was even a succession, with his son Richard Cromwell, 'Tumbledown Dick', to follow.

When Cromwell died in 1658, possibly of poison, the succession proved inadequate; his nominee, his son Richard, had no stomach for the job. It was an already exhausted dynasty. Within two years the British establishment saw to it that the monarchy was restored, and Charles I's son Charles II was on the throne.

The experiment with an English Republic had been a failure, largely because there were too many interest groups with too many conflicting expectations. There was too little consensus. The goal of toppling a hopeless king had been an easy one to agree, but agreeing on how to run a republic from scratch was not possible at that time. It was perhaps too big a jump to make all at once. Looking at Cromwell's own behaviour and attitudes, it is clear that the political changes had accelerated way beyond the social transformation of England. But an important point had been made - that the English would not tolerate a bad king. The English would dispose of intolerable kings in the future; an important precedent had been set.

BOYLE'S *SCEPTICAL CHYMIST*
(1661)

THE YEAR 1660 was a major political landmark in England, Scotland and Wales, as it was the year the Commonwealth ended: the year of the Restoration of the monarchy. Charles II, the new king, was to be a great patron of the sciences, founding the Royal Society in 1662. One of the great scientists of the English Enlightenment and one of the founders of the Royal Society, Robert Boyle, published a work on atmospheric pressure in 1660. It was called *New Experiments Physical-Mechanical Touching the Spring of the Air and its Effects.*

Boyle's key work was published in 1661. It was called the *Sceptical Chymist.* Scepticism, asking probing questions and taking nothing for granted, was an important principle of the age, and it underlay the philosophy of Descartes. In the *Sceptical Chymist*, Boyle tossed aside Aristotle's theory that there are only four elements – earth, air, fire and water – and argued that instead there are many. Aristotle had proposed four elements. Other ancient scholars had proposed five or six such as spirit, salt, sulphur, water and earth, or water, oil, air and earth. Boyle defined elements as primitive and simple substances that are not made of any other bodies or of one another. He proposed an experimental theory of the elements. As a result, Boyle would become known as the father of modern chemistry.

In 1662, Boyle made an important advance in physics, proposing a law that the volume of a gas varies inversely to the pressure; in other words as the volume of a gas increases its pressure decreases. This important and fundamental principle became known as Boyle's Law.

Boyle's ground-breaking idea of elements would be developed and clarified by Lavoisier in 1789 and by others later. Lavoisier's approach was less descriptive than Boyle's and more analytical. Elements would be defined according to their chemical reactions. The discovery of current electricity by Volta in 1800 provided a way of separating the more active elements from compounds, and soon after that discovery Humphry Davy was able to produce the elements sodium and potassium by using electrolysis on their respective hydroxides. Once the periodic law had been formulated in 1869, the search for new elements was under way. More and more elements were discovered, and by the end of the nineteenth century the number of known elements had risen to 82. By the 1950s it had reached 98.

Boyle's *Sceptical Chymist* opened the door on an exciting treasure hunt for the material of which the universe is made. Before the *Sceptical Chymist* it was generally accepted that the world was composed of four, five or six basic ingredients – now we can see that there are 100, and maybe more. Some of the elements are rare, such as strontium and chromium, but others are very common indeed. Just five elements – oxygen, silicon, aluminium, iron, calcium – make up over 90 percent of the Earth's crust by weight. So maybe there was something in the old idea that there are five elements, after all.

PLAGUE IN EUROPE
(1663)

PLAGUE BROKE OUT in Europe again in 1663, striking hard at Holland. In Amsterdam, a city of 200,000, over 10,000 people died in 1663, and another 24,000 in the following year. The plague spread to Brussels and through much of Flanders. Because people travelled from country to country, they carried the plague with them. Evidently two Frenchmen visiting Flanders caught the plague and took it with them to London, where they died in Drury Lane.

The numbers dying of the plague were so great that dead-carts were wheeled along the street, collecting corpses from houses as they passed and dumping them in common graves or plague pits. The men who pulled the carts kept their pipes lit all the time in the mistaken belief that tobacco smoke was an antidote to plague.

The plague flared up in London, reaching a peak in 1665. It may have been introduced by French travellers, or by Dutch prisoners of war; or it may have arrived in bales of merchandise from Holland that had originally come from the Near East. London was a city of 460,000. People who were confined to their homes by plague marked their doors with a red cross, so that casual callers would keep away; food was handed in to them by constables. In this great emergency, two-thirds of the people fled from London to avoid catching the plague. Even so, nearly 70,000 Londoners died, and some of the evacuees took the plague with them to other towns. Several thousand people died in Norwich, Newcastle, Portsmouth and Southampton. Even remote rural villages were not safe. The villagers of Eyam in Derbyshire were persuaded by their vicar not to run away and spread the plague to other villages; they agreed to stay and as a result many of them died.

The Great Plague of 1665 was the last outbreak of plague to strike London, and the last outbreak to sweep through western Europe. Gradual improvements in living conditions and hygiene reduced the risk. The disease was still to strike elsewhere, though; 83,000 were to die in Prague in 1681.

NEWTON'S LAWS OF
GRAVITY
(1666)

IN 1666, ISAAC Newton withdrew to Lincolnshire on account of the plague outbreak in London. It was there that he made his first steps in understanding gravitation when, in his garden, he watched an apple fall from a tree. Newton 'began to think of gravity extending to the orb of the moon.' He wondered if the Moon was held in its orbit round the Earth by gravity, though he did not publish anything about it for 18 years. The idea, like many big ideas, needing mulling over.

He turned to the study of light and the construction of telescopes. After a range of experiments on sunlight refracted through a prism, he concluded that rays of light of different colour are refracted by different amounts. This discovery suggested to him that the indistinct, fuzzy, coloured-edged images seen through Galilean telescopes might be due to the different coloured rays of light having different focal lengths. This led on to the abandonment of the refracting telescope of Galileo and the invention of a new type of reflecting telescope.

At the Royal Society, Robert Hooke boasted to Edmond Halley and Christopher Wren that he had discovered all the laws of celestial motion. Halley admitted that he had not and Wren, in his own words 'to encourage enquiry', said he would give a prize of a book to the value of 40 shillings (£2) to the one who found the solution. Wren was unconvinced by Hooke's boast, but hoped that he might flush him out with the prospect of a prize, and make him publish it so that others better equipped than himself could evaluate it. Halley afterwards visited Cambridge and discussed the matter with Newton. Newton generously gave him a mathematical formula to explain the movements of heavenly bodies using his theory of gravitation, and Halley knew, as he wrote in a letter to Newton later, that he 'had brought the demonstration to perfection.' Halley excitedly reported back to fellow members of the Royal Society that Newton had shown him the draft of an important paper entitled *De Motu Corporum* (*On the Motion of Bodies*). It was in 1684, in *De Motu Corporum*, that he gave his first account of his theory of gravitation, and he expounded it more fully in his great work, *Philosophiae Naturalis Principia Mathematica*, in 1687, financed by Edmond Halley.

In *De Motu Corporum*, Newton had treated the planets and the sun as points in his equations, but by 1685 he had realized that it was inappropriate to treat the sun, which is huge, in the same way as the planets, which are small. He then came up with the crucial idea that the gravitational pull of a heavenly body must be proportional to its mass. This was immediately refined to allow for distance, because objects a long way away cannot have the same gravitational pull as those close by. He then arrived at one of the most momentous discoveries – that bodies attract one another with a force that is proportional to the product of the masses of the two and inversely proportional to the square of the distance between them. Like many great ideas, Newton's law of gravitation seems very obvious, even self-evident, once it is said. But until Newton no-one had even thought it, let alone said it. This was one of those moments that utterly change the world; after the first expression of Newton's law of gravitation, science and our general everyday perception of the universe were different.

His epic work, the *Principia Mathematica*, explained how the universe worked. Newton laid down a comprehensive scheme for the mechanics of the solar system that would be used for two hundred years and more, though it was to be added to in the twentieth century by Einstein. Newton's model for the solar system, with the principle of gravitation at its heart, was to be of great benefit to all subsequent astronomers and physicists – and even astronauts.

GREAT FIRE OF LONDON
(1666)

EARLY IN THE morning of Sunday 2 September 1666, a fire started in Pudding Lane near London Bridge. The shops, houses and warehouses in the old city were crowded together, many of them made of timber, and all with adjoining timber roofs. The fire spread quickly from house to house and roof to roof, so that very soon whole streets were on fire.

The Great Fire of London raged for four days and nights. By the end of it, 80 percent of the City of London had been destroyed together with another 255m sq of property outside the City walls. It is estimated that over 13,000 houses were destroyed. Many fine old buildings were destroyed in the conflagration, including the Custom House, the Royal Exchange, the Guildhall and 44 of the livery company halls. The greatest loss architecturally was the City's fine crop of ancient churches – 86 of them – and the great Gothic cathedral of St Paul's itself, which was London's greatest landmark.

Obviously the Great Fire was a traumatic event for Londoners. There were nevertheless major positive aspects to it. Some very cramped and unsanitary housing had been destroyed, and an opportunity was created to build more modern housing at a lower density. There was also an opportunity to lay out a completely new street plan. Instead of the maze of winding alleys that had evolved through a period of 1,500 years, it was now possible to design wider, straighter roads that would accommodate traffic better, and they could be made to link public squares or piazzas that would enhance the appearance of the capital. Broader roads would also act as fire-breaks and therefore make the city safer.

Early in 1667 Christopher Wren was given the task of rebuilding London. In January, four months after the fire, the ruins of the city were still smouldering. Commissioned by Charles II, Wren was asked initially to restore the medieval cathedral. The roofs had been burnt off and the building was gutted. Although restoration was possible, much of the stonework was damaged by the blaze, and Wren argued for demolition and replacement. The truth is that he wanted the chance to build his own cathedral. He also wanted to create a new street plan. It had after all just been done in Rome, where Bernini was putting the finishing touches to his spectacular St Peter's Square, 11 years in the making.

Wren's baroque design for St Paul's proved to be too revolutionary. Its plan was to be a Greek cross, that is to say a cross with arms of equal length. Wren was overruled in this by the Church authorities, who wanted a conventional full-length nave for processions. Interestingly, Michelangelo's initial design for St Peter's in Rome was also a Greek cross and also rejected by the Church authorities. Wren is said to have wept at the rejection of his plan. It was not surprising, as the Church commissioners did not just want a nave, they wanted a steeple as well; what they really wanted was their old cathedral back. Wren was determined to have his dome, and in order to get it he even put forward a design with a preposterous spire to make sure the dome was approved. A compromise design was eventually passed, with the connivance of the king. Building work began on 21 June 1675. The choir was opened 22 years later, but the last stone was not in position until 1710.

Wren's choice of stone for the new cathedral was also revolutionary. The Normans' first choice of building stone for churches and cathedrals was Caen stone from Normandy, a cream-coloured limestone. Later churches tended to use English stone that if possible looked something like it, or some locally quarried substitute. The Portland stone that Wren chose was a fine-grained pale grey limestone that had to be shipped from Dorset. He used Portland stones for St Paul's. He also used it for the many other London churches he designed. It became the favoured stone for all public buildings in London, including the British Museum.

Wren's style was also given an unusual dominance in London because of the Great Fire. Large areas were cleared for redevelopment, and he was responsible for all the major buildings, so his artistic personality was very strongly imprinted on the new London. Of Wren's many London churches, the most outstanding are St Bride in Fleet Street, St Mary-le-Bow, St Stephen Wallbrook, St Andrew-by-the-Wardrobe and St Magnus the Martyr at London Bridge.

Wren's plan for a new street layout was approved by both king and Parliament, but it fell foul of commercial city interests who refused to surrender their rights over certain areas. Allocating more space to roadways inevitably meant surrendering land for shops and warehouses, land out of which money might be made. Unfortunately, in this case, Charles II was not an absolute monarch and, following his father's unhappy end on the scaffold, he was not likely to try to impose his will. The result was that Londoners lost the chance to have beautiful open piazzas linked by broad vistas like those eventually achieved in Paris. They lost the chance to have riverside walks and broad boulevards. London was rebuilt round and among its maze of medieval alleys.

The same problem precisely emerged after the Blitz, when once again large areas of the City were demolished; vested property interests once again ensured that the post-war redevelopment and subsequent high-rise blocks were built on the same irregular and unsatisfactory medieval land plots.

PASCAL'S *PENSEES*
(1670)

THE FRENCH PHILOSOPHER-MATHEMATICIAN Blais Pascal died in 1662 at the age of 39. He left behind a collection of *Thoughts* (Pensees), which were in some ways a reflection of the same zeitgeist as the philosophy of Descartes. The spirit of scepticism prevailed. He wrote, 'If men knew what others say of them, there would be not four friends in the world.' Of religious zeal, he said, 'Men never do evil so completely as when they do it from religious conviction.'

Not all of the thoughts are totally negative.

Man is but a reed, the most feeble thing in nature, but he is a thinking reed. The entire universe need not arm itself to crush him. A vapour, a drop of water suffices to kill him. But if the universe were to crush him, man would still be more noble than that which killed him, because he knows that he dies, and the advantage which the universe has over him? – that the universe knows nothing of this.

The Enlightenment was taking the human race out of its comfort zone, out of its shelter, the comfort of religious faith, out into a possibly hostile, possibly entirely indifferent universe. It was a frightening transition. Pascal is on the brink of this loss of faith.

What a chimera, then, is man! What a novelty! What a monster, what a chaos, what a contradiction, what a prodigy! Judge of all things, feeble worm of the earth, repository of truth, a sink of uncertainty and error, the glory and the shame of the universe.

With thoughts as tormented as these on the tragedy of the human condition, Pascal was looking forward to the eighteenth and nineteenth centuries, to the *sturm und drang* of Romanticism.

THE DISCOVERY OF
NIAGARA FALLS
(1678)

IN 1678, THE missionary and explorer Louis Hennepin discovered the Niagara Falls. The 38 year old French Franciscan, who had been in Canada for only three years, was so staggered and moved by his discovery that he fell to his knees at the awe-inspiring sight. He said, 'The universe does not afford its parallel.' A couple of years later, the city of Minneapolis had its beginnings in St Anthony's Falls, which was given its name by Louis Hennepin, who had travelled with La Salle through the Great Lakes to the source of the Mississippi. The Mississippi itself had been discovered back in 1541, by Hernando de Soto, and the following year his men had navigated the Lower Mississippi from its confluence with the Arkansas river.

The Mississippi was part of the white American consciousness from fairly early on. Gradually, as the European colonists extended their territorial interests into the interior, they realized what extraordinary and unexpected natural wonders North America had to offer, and the sheer scale of the continent. At first they were looking for somewhere to live, for land that would support them, but the landscape gradually imprinted and impressed itself upon them. A bond between people and land developed that would eventually support a struggle for independence and a fierce patriotism.

THE FOUNDING OF
CALCUTTA
(1686)

THE ENGLISH EAST India Company began to impose its will by force in India after 80 years of trying in vain to negotiate diplomatic and commercial relationships with Indian rulers. Job Charnock, an English East India Company official, ran a factory and trading post at Hooghly on the Hooghly iver, the western distributary of the Ganges. The settlement was besieged, so in 1686 Charnock and his staff retreated about 40km down-river to a new location, a cluster of villages on the east bank of the Hooghly River and about 130km from the sea. One of the native villages was Kalikata, which gave its name to Calcutta.

By turning the new area into a trading station, and eventually a thorough-going river port, Charnock became the founder of the city of Calcutta. The founding of Calcutta formally dates from August 1690. Gradually the expansion of the villages caused them to merge into a single large settlement, all under East India Company control.

Charnock established the pattern of East India Company rule that would continue until 1858. The company's commercial interests were protected vigorously from a fort, Fort William, which was built with the permission of the local ruler in 1696. The natural geography of the site and the added defence provided by the fort made Calcutta one of the safest trading posts in India. Two years later the area as a whole was formally purchased from Prince Azim, the son of the Emperor Aurangzeb.

The city grew and grew in importance, becoming the major commercial centre for the region, and handling most of West Bengal's exports. Technically, Calcutta is the city on the east bank, but the huge settlement of Howrah on the west bank is in effect a suburb of Calcutta. In the days of the British Empire, Calcutta held a prime importance as the exporting port for the produce of West Bengal. Jute in particular was exported, the raw material for making sacks, which were essential for carrying all sorts of foodstuffs and other commodities – throughout the Empire. Calcutta prospered from its trade and became the second largest city in the British Empire, and it later held this status in the Commonwealth too.

The high status of Calcutta in the days of the British Empire was reflected in the numerous and lavish public buildings. It was called the city of palaces. One of the most impressive features of the city is the maidan (park) which covers 358km, a huge contrast to the intense overcrowding of the slums. The Victoria Memorial, opened in 1921, is thought of as the finest building in Calcutta. Next to it is the cathedral with a spire 63 m high; its graveyard contains the grave of Job Charnock, who died in 1693.

The 'imperial' history of Calcutta meant that every development was made in the interests of profit for the company, and the interests of the people of Calcutta were given scant consideration. The uncontrolled and unplanned growth of this huge city has led to a confused, congested and extremely inefficient layout. For a long time there was only one bridge over the Hooghly, and it was inevitably jammed with traffic for much of the time. Most of the people lived in squalor and dire poverty. It has proved very difficult to plan improvements for a city that is continuously expanding as the rural poor flood into it in the vain hope of making their fortune.

THE EDO EARTHQUAKE
AND FIRE
(1703)

ON 30 DECEMBER 1703, there was a major earthquake in Edo (the old name of Tokyo). The earthquake upset hearths and lamps, so fires spread through many parts of the city. Amid the falling buildings and the widespread fires that followed, 200,000 Japanese died. The movement along the plate margin that generated the earthquake generated other changes underground; four years later, Mount Fuji erupted – the last eruption of the volcano in modern times. But in spite of the virtual destruction of Edo, it was rebuilt and 20 years later it had reached a population of over one million.

The Edo earthquake of 1703 was one in a sequence of major earthquakes to strike the area. There was a disastrous earthquake (and fire) on 1 September 1923, known as the Great Kanto earthquake. It destroyed both Tokyo and Yokohama, which had for a long time functioned as the port of Tokyo. The earthquake killed 100,000, 752,000 people were injured, 83,000 houses were totally destroyed and 380,000 houses were damaged. A lot of the reconstruction that followed this great disaster was of a temporary nature, simply because of the scale of the operation, and a comprehensive new scheme for the city's layout was embarked upon. The new plan created a number of very wide roads at intervals to act as firebreaks, ribbons of open spaces to act as firebreaks and refuges for people, and apartment blocks built in such a way as to create fire walls across whole districts. These improvements went on until they were stopped by the outbreak of the Second World war.

Tokyo stands on a site that is prone to earthquakes. It stands at the junction of not two but three of the plates that make up the Earth's crust. The Japanese government is aware that it would be better if the capital were located elsewhere, and there is indeed a plan for a new capital on a safer site some distance away to the west. The problem is that, as with the rebuilding of London after the Great Fire, there are vested property interests that always favour the status quo. No-one who owns valuable land in the central business district of the capital of a rich country wants the city to be closed down, or for any key functions to be transferred to another location. This geographical inertia explains why Tokyo has remained where it is, ever since Tokugawa Ieyasu chose the site and made it his capital in 1590 – and why Naples remains where it is.

THE BATTLE OF
BLENHEIM
(1704)

BLENHEIM IS A village in Bavaria, on the north bank of the Danube. The battle fought there was the climax of the Duke of Marlborough's surprise march to the Danube. The armies of the French-Bavarian-Prussian lined up on the south-west side of the valley of the River Nebel, confronting Marlborough's and Prince Eugene's armies on the other side of the valley. The ground was rough and marshy, making it difficult for infantry to make any headway, but all right for cavalry.

On 13 August, at the Battle of Blenheim, the British army commanded by the Duke of Marlborough defeated the armies of the coalition. Marlborough was supported by Eugene, Prince of Savoy. While Prince Eugene was at Blenheim, his kingdom was overrun by French troops under the Duc de Vendome.

In this great battle, Marlborough himself led the cavalry charge that broke the enemy's resistance. He pursued his advantage, driving his enemies into the River Danube. Hundreds of soldiers were drowned. The forces of the coalition sustained 4,500 casualties and 7,500 wounded; the English sustained 670 casualties and 1,500 wounded. Marlborough and Prince Eugene took 11,000 coalition soldiers prisoner, including the French General Camille de Tallard and 24 battalions.

French survivors of this onslaught fell back to the River Rhine, then back again to the Moselle. The English victory was so decisive that the ten-year record of military triumph for France came to an abrupt halt. The French had been not only defeated but annihilated and humiliated. A shift in the balance of power had been achieved at a stroke.

The British Parliament erected a princely mansion for the Duke of Marlborough as a token of the nation's gratitude. The mansion was built at Woodstock near Oxford and named Blenheim Palace after his greatest victory. The battle was immediately recognized as an historic battle, a landmark in British military history that would be remembered with Hastings, Bosworth – and later Waterloo.

THE WRECK OF THE
ASSOCIATION
(1707)

In LONDON A Board of Longitude was set up in 1714. It offered a prize of £20,000 to anyone who could devise a method of determining a ship's longitude to within 48km after a six-week voyage. Given the value of money at the time, the prize was enormous, and it reflected the great importance to safe navigation of pinpointing a ship's position.

Determining latitude had been possible for a long time. The sun is high in the sky at low latitudes and low in the sky at high latitudes. By using a simple device called a sextant it was possible to measure the sun's altitude, the angle it makes with the horizon, at midday, and from this calculate the ship's latitude. Longitude was much more difficult, and knowing the latitude accurately, on its own, was not enough to fix the ship's position. Knowing both accurately would give the two co-ordinates needed to pinpoint where the ship was. After a number of major shipping disasters, caused by mariners not knowing exactly were they were, it became clear that making a device to determine longitude was essential.

The greatest of these marine disasters was the loss of a squadron under Admiral Sir Cloudesley Shovel in 1707. He had served under Sir George Rooke in the Mediterranean, where he had helped in the capture of Gibraltar and Barcelona. After an unsuccessful attack on the French port of Toulon, he was returning to England with his squadron when he miscalculated his position in relation to the Scilly Isles, and sailed his ships at full speed onto a reef. His own ship, the *Association*, went down so quickly that all 800 men on board were lost. She sank in just three minutes. Sir Cloudesly Shovel himself had the misfortune to be washed up on a beach still alive, only to have his throat cut by a woman who was looting the sailors' bodies.

In 1676, the Royal Observatory was set up at Greenwich near London. Its function was to study the position of the Moon among the fixed stars and establish a standard time that would help navigators to fix their longitude. The Greenwich Meridian, the line joining the North and South Poles passing through Greenwich in due course became the Prime Meridian, the zero line from which longitude would be measured, east or west. When the sun is overhead in the tropics on the Greenwich Meridian it is also seen as being at its highest point in the sky at Greenwich and at every other place along the meridian. In other words the sun time is the same, 12 noon, at every point on a particular line of longitude. Knowing the exact time could therefore tell you your longitude.

The man who achieved this was John Harrison, a Yorkshire carpenter. In 1728, he completed his design for a spring-driven time-keeper that would work at sea. In collaboration with George Graham, a clock-maker, he set about perfecting the design, which went through several versions before winning the board's prize in 1736.

The chronometer that John Harrison presented to the Board of Longitude was remarkably accurate – to within one tenth of a second per day. The principle was that Harrison's chronometer was to be set to the time at the Greenwich Meridian – and maintain it. During the voyage, the navigator could fix his position by determining local time, using the quadrant devised by John Hadley in 1731, and comparing the two times.

The chronometer was a complicated, heavy, delicate and expensive machine, but it succeeded in determining longitude. During subsequent years, chronometers were devised that were smaller and able to keep going through any kind of weather experienced aboard a sailing ship. Harrison's improved chronometer was given its first test in 1761. By this stage it was essentially a modern watch about 13cm in diameter fitted with a special pendulum made of two metals that expanded and contracted in opposition to maintain a uniform swing. The chronometer was mounted aboard *HMS Deptford* and taken on a voyage across the Atlantic to Jamaica; on the completion of that voyage it was declared to be a total success. From that point on, all mariners were able to fix the positions at sea with great accuracy, and a huge element of risk was removed from travel by sea. Finding longitude exactly also made it possible to improve the accuracy of maps, and this is why nineteenth century maps of the world were far more accurate than those of earlier times.

THE FIRST COPYRIGHT LAW (1710)

UNDER QUEEN ANNE, a British copyright law was established that would become the basis of all future copyright laws. It was followed in 1735 by a Copyright Act designed to protect artists and writers from piracy, such as the reproduction of their work in cheap rival editions. The gradual evolution of copyright law in Britain was imitated in other countries.

In America in 1897, Congress broadened copyright laws to give copyright owners exclusive rights to public performances of their works. The intention of the new law was good, but it was impractical and was widely flouted. In 1909, a United States Copyright Law was passed by Congress. It was designed to protect the interests of authors and composers and their publishers under terms that were to remain unchanged for almost 70 years. The law gave copyright owners the exclusive rights 'to print, reprint, publish, copy and vend the copyrighted work.' Small, minor, partial breaches of the law were treated as 'fair use', but this phrase became a major problem. If it was all right for someone to quote an excerpt of another author's work in their own, how long could that excerpt be? This was never (and has still not) been defined. In 1909, the US copyright law was extended to included gramophone recordings, giving works legal protection for a 28-year period.

The copyright protection afforded to writers in the West was not available in the eastern bloc countries. In the mid-twentieth century, it was common for books by Western writers to appear in pirated edition in communist states, and of course for no royalty payments to be made to the authors. In 1973, the Russians formally agreed to stop publishing pirate editions and to abide by the Universal Copyright Convention, which was trying to create world-wide protection for authors and composers.

The 1704 act was the first step towards ensuring that authors are justly paid for their work.

THE HARPOONING OF THE FIRST SPERM WHALE

(1712)

WHALING ON A small scale had been going on for centuries. It was only in 1596 that the first whale factory ship was built, designed by Francois Zaburu, a Basque whaling captain. He incorporated a brick-built furnace on his deck for extracting oil from the whales' blubber by boiling it down. This proved to be far more economical than taking whole whale carcases to the home port for processing. In 1626, Dutch whalers founded a whaling port called Smeerenberg in Spitzbergen. There they processed what the English called 'right whales' to distinguish them from all the others, which were 'wrong whales', because they unhelpfully sank when dead. The whales were hunted for their oil (used for lamps and machine lubrication) and whalebone (used for making 'stays' in women's corsets).

Christopher Hussey, the captain of a whaler from Nantucket in North America, harpooned a sperm whale from an open boat in 1712. This was the first time a sperm whale was killed by man.

The sperm whale, *Physeter catodon*, turned out to have an unusually high oil content compared with other types of whale – between 65 and 80 barrels. Virtually every part of the sperm whale had a use. Spermaceti from the whale were used to make millions of wax candles, the teeth were high-quality ivory, the skin was rich in glycerin. The sperm whale was also the only type of whale to produce ambergris, which was used as a fixative in perfume manufacture.

Following Hussey's landmark kill and the discovery that the sperm whale contained so much oil, more and more sperm whales were hunted down and killed for their oil. A new era in whaling began and ever-increasing fleets of whalers combed the world's oceans hunting for whales. By the middle of the eighteenth century, fleets of whalers were venturing, for the first time, into the Antarctic.

The great age of whaling reached a peak and a crisis in 1857. Too many whales were being killed and their numbers were in decline, so it was seen that the supply of whale oil too would decline. At the same time the population growth in Europe and the United States and the growth of literacy were greatly increasing the demand for domestic lighting – for evening reading. A gap between supply and demand was looming. An article in the Scientific American said 'The whale oils which hitherto have been much relied on in this country [USA] may in time almost entirely fail.' The crisis would spur on the development of the mineral oil industry, which would provide an alternative lamp fuel, and ultimately the development of electric lighting. The invention of the electric light bulb provided a more attractive alternative to oil lamps.

This did not save the whales. In the twentieth century, whaling continued on an industrial scale, especially by large commercial Asian whaling fleets, hunting whales for meat. It was this relentless, industrial-scale whaling that brought several species of whale close to extinction.

THE SOUTH SEA
BUBBLE
(1720)

THE SOUTH SEA Bubble was the nickname given to a series of financial projects originating in the South Sea Company. The company was formed in 1711 and granted a monopoly of British trade with South America and the islands of the Pacific. It proved highly successful, and in 1718, the king of England became its governor. Towards the end of 1719, the company put before the British government, then led by the Earl of Sunderland, a much more ambitious scheme.

The essence of the new scheme was that the South Sea Company would take over responsibility for the National Debt, which then stood at over £51 million, in return for further concessions. The company would also pay the government £3 million for the privilege. The company's aim was to get those holding state annuities (which is how most of the debt was held) to exchange them for South Sea Company stock. The complicated deal was accepted by the British government and about half the annuity-holders were persuaded to become shareholders.

The result of the deal was that the value of South Sea Company shares increased sharply, which encouraged the public in general to buy South Sea stock. Share prices soared from £128 each in January 1720 to an astonishing £1,050 by June. Then the company directors sold a huge amount of stock, but in August, the value started to drop and by November the share price was down to £135.

The South Sea Bubble had burst, causing widespread financial losses and also a loss of confidence among investors in distant overseas enterprises. Thousands were ruined, and many who were deeply in debt were driven to leave the country. When the company's books were examined in 1721, it was found that there were false entries. It was also found that government support had been bought by bribing ministers, some of whom made large sums of money out of the stock.

The main people who were implicated in this scam were John Aislabie, the Chancellor of the Exchequer, James Craggs, the Postmaster-General, and to a lesser degree the Earl of Sunderland. Craggs died in March 1721. Aislabie resigned, was found guilty of the 'most notorious, dangerous and infamous corruption', expelled from the House of Commons and imprisoned. By an Act of Parliament, the estates of the South Sea Company directors were confiscated and shared out among those who had suffered losses.

Sir Robert Walpole became Prime Minister and Chancellor of the Exchequer in April 1721, in the wake of the disaster. He reduced import and export duties in order to encourage trade, and averted financial disaster by amalgamating the South Sea Company stock with stock in the Bank of England and the East India Company.

The South Sea scheme was not the only such scheme. The French have major problems with John Law's so-called Mississippi Company, which failed to attract emigrants to North America with its fake promises of gold and diamonds in Louisiana. Law's grandiose scheme turned out to be a stock fraud much like the South Sea Company. New Orleans, the focus of the speculation, remained no more than a collection of squalid shacks on the banks of the Mississippi, its great days still lying far off in an unforeseeable future, and the collapse of this Mississippi bubble left many French investors financially ruined.

THE AGRICULTURAL REVOLUTION

(1730)

SIDE BY SIDE with the Industrial Revolution came a revolution in agriculture. When agriculture first began, selected grass seeds were sown so that gradually improved varieties with larger ears were produced; in this way wheat and barley were developed from grasses. In the same way livestock rearing used selection. The principle of selection and selective breeding was long established. It was only in the eighteenth century that they became scientific in approach, and then development became rapid. The first step in this new agricultural revolution was the invention of a seed drill by Jethro Tull in 1701. This simple device, which pioneered sowing in rows and facilitated weeding, was improved 80 years later by the addition of gears to ensure the even distribution of seed.

Charles Townshend resigned from the British government in May 1730, at the age of 56, to begin a new career as an agricultural improver. Townshend, who became known as 'Turnip' Townshend, observed the progress that the Dutch farmers were making by using scientific methods, and applied what he learnt on his own estates. He found that he could keep livestock through the winter by feeding them on turnips. By reserving a field or two for growing turnips as a fodder crop he eliminated the need to slaughter most of his flocks and herds each autumn. They animals could be kept alive through the winter and slaughtered as and when there was a demand. This development meant that for the first time in England fresh meat became available all the year round. It also reduced the need to use expensive spices to disguise the taste of rotting meat, improved the safety of food and allowed the cattle to grow bigger. By 1732, the average bullock sold at Smithfield cattle market in London weighed 250kg, compared with 170kg in 1710. There were many gains from just one change in practice.

Selective breeding by Leicestershire farmer Robert Bakewell led to the creation of a new breed of sheep, the Leicester, in 1755. Five years later Bakewell started experimenting with selective breeding of beef cattle, and by 1770 he had produced animals with deeper, wider bodies on shorter legs, animals that carried much more meat. He works on the simple idea that 'like produces like', each year only breeding from the most suitable stock.

Crop rotation was developed in a more scientific way, to ensure that each farm produced the maximum amount of food. This 'intensification' of agriculture led to a marked increase in food production in Britain and other European countries following similar paths. By 1770, England was producing a surplus of potatoes for the first time. The potato had until that time been grown exclusively as a subsistence crop; now there was a surplus that was available for sale in shops.

In 1772, Thomas Coke started a programme of selective animal husbandry that would result in the creation of Devon Cattle, Suffolk pigs and Southdown sheep. By 1780, the agrarian revolution was well under way, with higher quality seed in general use, more scientific crop rotation (pioneered by Jethro Tull in 1720), more efficiently designed tools and generally increased productivity. Thomas Jefferson wrote rather apologetically in his *Notes on Virginia* about the extensive nature of agriculture in North America at that time.

The indifferent state of agriculture among us does not proceed from a want of knowledge merely. It is from our having such quantities of land to waste as we please. In Europe the object is to make the most of their land, labour being abundant; here it is to make the most of our labour, land being abundant.

In other words, it was the pressure of a high population density that produced the revolution, the intensification of agriculture in Europe. But the need to produce more food throughout the world would eventually come, as population levels rose.

THE LISBON
EARTHQUAKE
(1755)

On 1 November, the city of Lisbon experienced the worst earthquake in Europe since an earlier one in the same place, the Lisbon earthquake of 1531. Like Tokyo, Lisbon was a city built in an unfortunate location, on low ground on an estuary close to a plate boundary. The earthquake was caused by a sideways shift along the boundary between the African and European plates; the earthquake's epicentre was not in fact in Lisbon but out on the seabed to the west of Gibraltar. Recent photography of the seabed in that area has revealed that a low vertical cliff was thrown up at the time of the 1755 earthquake, so it produced one enduring feature.

The shock-waves from this epicentre rippled outwards towards Lisbon on the Tagus estuary. The flimsy houses of the poor were shaken down and many were killed as their houses collapsed on them. Inside people's homes lamps, candles, lanterns and hearths were overturned and 1,000 fires broke out all over Lisbon, burning what was left of the city.

Then came the tsunami. Because the earthquake took place on the seabed, and the seabed on one side of the fault had risen sharply, shock waves travelled through the sea itself, producing a high wave that smashed through the burning remains of the lower town, drowning many who had survived the earthquake and fire. It was a triple disaster – earthquake, fire and tsunami. Within a few hours, 50,000 people had died. The All Souls Day catastrophe deeply shocked the whole of Europe, and caused many to question the existence of a benign God. In a very real sense, the Lisbon earthquake marked a shift in attitudes. It was a watershed separating the medieval confidence in the wisdom of God from a new and less comfortable world in which people had to look out for themselves.

The whole of the lower town was destroyed. The only buildings that remained were those that were built of stone, so the beautiful Tower of Belem built in 1520 and the St Jeronimos Monastery built to celebrate the da Gama voyage remained standing. The old town, the Alfama on higher ground, and more solidly built, was left more intact. The Castle of St George on its hill was undamaged. The cathedral built in 1150 had already been wrecked by an earthquake in 1344 and rebuilt in 1380; the 1755 earthquake wrecked it again.

One positive outcome was that a more spacious street plan could be created on the site of the ruined lower town. The chief minister of Portugal, Sebastião de Carvalho e Mello, was responsible for the rebuilding of Lisbon, and he managed to achieve what Wren had hoped to achieve for London after the Great Fire – he rebuilt to a more spacious and formal plan, with long straight streets, marble pavements, gardens, vistas and big set-piece squares. The western part of Lisbon therefore dates almost entirely from the period after the 1755 earthquake.

Shortly afterwards, Voltaire wrote his pessimistic poem about the Lisbon earthquake, *Customs and the Spirit of Nations*. The Lisbon earthquake was a great natural disaster in which earthquake, fire and tsunami followed one another in remorseless and pitiless succession. It was a demonstration that there was no presiding God looking after human welfare; the human race was incontrovertibly alone in the universe. It was in a sense the dawn of humanism, and certainly a landmark in the Enlightenment. Voltaire then wrote his masterpiece, *Candide,* a satirical short story ridiculing the philosophy of Leibniz. A world in which the All Souls Day disaster could happen was not the best of all possible worlds. Then, naturally, the first of Voltaire's anti-religious writings appeared. The Lisbon earthquake played its part in altering the way people thought about the world they lived in.

ROUSSEAU'S *SOCIAL CONTRACT* AND *EMILE*
(1762)

THE YEAR 1762 marked the publication of two major books, books which were to have enormous influence for many decades to come. Of the two, Rousseau's masterpiece, *Du Contrat Social* (*On the Social Contract*), had a remarkable effect on the development of French and American history. On the strength of this one work, Rousseau stands out as possibly the most important single figure in the eighteenth century. Eloquently written, powerfully argued, the *Social Contract* seemed to sum up the new spirit of the age, questioning the moral foundation of the existing social order, and preparing the way for both the French Revolution and the American Revolution.

The book opens with the ringing statement, 'Man is born free; and everywhere he is in chains.' Rousseau proposed a new social order in which each individual surrenders his rights to the collective 'general will', which is the only source of legitimate sovereignty and defines the common good. Rousseau's anti-monarchy text, complete with its slogan, 'Liberty, Equality, Fraternity', became the blueprint and the bible for the French Revolution 20 years later, and of other radical social movements. The *Social Contract* was written out of frustration with the injustices of the *ancien regime* in France, so it was understandably extreme in its recommendations. It was even so profoundly unfortunate that he advocated a totalitarian substitute for absolute monarchy. The 'general will' found its expression in such abominations as the Committee of Public Safety, and the rights of individuals were trampled underfoot. Rousseau must take his share of the blame for the appalling excesses of the Reign of Terror.

The publication of Rousseau's landmark book *Du Contrat Social* was accompanied by the publication of another book, also extremely influential, but in a very different area – *Emile*. *Emile* was a treatise on education, written as a kind of narrative fantasy describing the ideal education of a child. Rousseau's Emile is brought up apart from other children in an experimental way. The child is not forced; he learns at his own speed from the situations around him. It was a major landmark in educational thinking, a pioneer work which paved the way for several liberal experiments. Rousseau's *Emile* was a major influence on great educationists such as Pestalozzi and Froebel. It also paved the way for a long-continuing discussion about the desirability of a return to 'nature' and a debate about what exactly we mean by the word 'natural'. This can be seen continuing in the present environmental movement.

Rousseau's ideas were quickly adopted into the Romantic literature, with the English poet William Wordsworth advocating the moral power of landscape. Wordsworth attempted in *The Prelude* (1805) to persuade readers that he had been reared by the mountains and streams of the English Lake District, that he had been parented by the landscape.

Rousseau became a posthumous hero during the French Revolution, and in 1794 his remains were buried in the Pantheon – beside Voltaire's. The *Social Contract* and *Emile* to a great extent defined the spirit of the age. In his writings he was the spokesman for Romanticism in Europe generally, and his socio-political writings were blueprints for the revolutions that swept Europe and North America for the next few decades.

WATT'S STEAM ENGINE
(1765)

In 1759, James Watt began to think of steam power as a force that might be harnessed, to an extent far beyond its current restricted use to drive mine pumps. In 1763, in the course of his routine work as mathematical instrument maker for the University of Glasgow, he was sent a working model of the Newcomen steam engine to repair. He put the model engine back in order, and while he was doing so he noticed some significant defects in the machine's design. The old Newcomen engine was extremely inefficient, consuming enormous quantities of steam (and therefore coal) to do relatively little work. He also saw that fitting a separate condenser might be a way of improving it. Later he found additional ways of improving the engine's performance, including an air pump to remove the spent steam, a steam jacket for the cylinder to make sure the cylinder was as hot as the steam entering it and a double-action for the engine.

Watt's design improvements were relatively easily made in his mind, but making them and testing them cost him a lot of money and he put himself in debt in order to demonstrate the merits of his engine. He allowed Dr Roebuck, the founder of the Carron Ironworks, two-thirds of the profit from his invention in return for bearing the costs. An engine was then built at Kinneil near Linlithgow; in the course of constructing it, Watt saw further ways of improving the machine.

In 1768, Watt met Matthew Boulton, who owned the Soho Engineering Works. Boulton agreed to buy Roebuck's share of Watt's steam engine so that they could work together. In 1774, Watt set up in partnership with Boulton, and the improved steam engine went into production at the Soho Engineering Works, protected by a patent Watt had prudently taken out in 1769. The partnership was a very happy one; Watt saw to the engineering side and Boulton looked after the business. Between 1781 and 1785 he took out no fewer than six patents for further devices, including the centrifugal governor, a self-regulating device that ensured an even running speed in a rotating steam engine.

Watt's steam engine soon superseded Newcomen's as the engine of choice for mine and other pumps. For one thing, it used only one quarter of the fuel. But Watt's imagination ran on ahead. Why should this extremely efficient machine be used just to drain mines? Why not use it to drive carriages along roads or ships across the sea? In 1784, Watt described a steam locomotive in one of his patents, yet for some reason discouraged William Murdoch, his assistant, from experimenting with steam locomotion. What they had in mind was a steam carriage that would travel along ordinary roads. Watt had not thought of using rails, and when that was proposed by others in the last years of his life he would not consider it at all.

In 1817, his son, also called James Watt, fitted his father's steam engine to the first English steamship to leave port, the *Caledonia*. James Watt's outstanding contribution to the Industrial Revolution – and to life in the nineteenth and twentieth centuries – was the improved and more efficient steam engine, the engine that was to transform the nineteenth century world. Watt envisaged using his improved engine for locomotion. It was largely due to Watt's inventions and the imagination behind them that the steamship era began – and in spite of himself the great age of the railway.

THE BOSTON TEA
PARTY
(1773)

THE SPANISH WERE the first Europeans to begin serious colonization of North America, following the Columbus voyages. It was Dr John Dee, Elizabeth I's magician, who suggested that England might found colonies in North America, and the first English colonies were founded along the Eastern seaboard. The French aspired to colonies and penetrated up the St Lawrence and Mississippi, occupying a great swathe of North America to the west of the English. The Spanish occupied Florida to the south.

It was inevitable that a power struggle would break out, a scramble for America. There were repeated outbreaks of fighting between the French and the British colonists in the seventeenth and eighteenth centuries: King William's War (1689–97), Queen Anne's War (1702–13) and King George's War (1744–48). Fighting between the English and French broke out again in 1754, and back in Europe this became one of the issues in the Seven Years' War, which started in 1756.

In the Seven Years' War, the English colonists on the Eastern seaboard were under continual threat from French colonists. During this time, they and their territorial interests were protected by the British armed forces. Once the Seven Years' War came to an end in 1763, and the threat from the French had been removed as a result of British intervention, the English colonists felt that they no longer had the support of England to defend them. They began to hanker for independence.

The British government wanted to occupy and govern the old French territories. The occupying army cost a lot of money to maintain and the British government tried to levy higher taxes on the Americans. The colonial assemblies protested that it was unfair for the British to tax the Americans, as they had no say in the way the British government was run

LEFT: *The Fuller Building, known as the Flatiron Building, in New York City, was designed in 1902 by Daniel Burnham. Considered by some people to be New York City's first skyscraper, it is certainly remembered for its unique shape.*

ABOVE: *Illustration of lifeboats around the ocean liner* Titanic *as it goes down in the Atlantic Ocean. The extraordinary tragedy, which cost 1,523 lives, happened on the night of 14–15 April, 1912.*

ABOVE: *On 6 and 9 August 1945, the Japanese cities of Hiroshima and Nagasaki were destroyed by the first atomic bombs used in warfare. The mushroom-shaped cloud, shown here, billowed 6,000 foot in the air following the attack on Hiroshima.*

ABOVE: *Apollo 11 astronauts Mike Collins (left), Neil Armstrong (centre) and Edwin 'Buzz' Aldrin, in front of the Lunar Landing Module Simulator at the Kennedy Space Centre, USA, prior to their landing on the moon on 20 July 1969.*

BELOW: *American politicians (left to right) Senator Howard Baker of Tennessee, Senator Sam Irvin of North Carolina, Majority Council Sam Dash, Senator Herman E Talmadge of Georgia and Senator Daniel Inouye of Hawaii listening to the testimony of James McCord, one of the Watergate burglars, during the Watergate hearings.*

ABOVE: *1989 the Tienanmen Square uprising where students striving for democracy were brutally repressed by the Chinese government and some 1,000 were killed. This was one of the largest public demonstrations in the history of communist China and this picture shows two city buses blocking the main street to Tiananmen Square.*

ABOVE: *On Tuesday morning, 11 September 2001, the United States is attacked by terrorists in New York City and Washington, and the world changes forever. The picture above shows a hijacked passenger jet, American Airlines Flight 11 out of Boston, Massachusetts, crashing into the north tower of the World Trade Center, tearing a gaping hole in the building and setting it afire.*

ABOVE: *A man (left) walks past the damaged building on Phi Phi island in southern Thailand, 28 December 2004 following the devastating tsunami that crashed into the Thai coastline on the 26 December, killing at least 1,400 people. The confirmed death toll in Asia following the 26 December 9.0 magnitude earthquake off the coast of Indonesia's Sumatra island and resulting tsunami waves surpassed 40,000.*

ABOVE: *Long fêted as the crowning glory of the Acropolis and of Athens, the Parthenon is 2,500 years old and the largest Doric temple of Pentelic marble built by the ancient Greeks.*

BELOW: *Thomas Becket, English saint, martyr, knight, chancellor and Archbishop of Canterbury, is brutally murdered by four knights, Hugh de Merville, William de Tracy, Reginald Fitzurse and Richard le Breton, in Canterbury Cathedral at the request of King Henry II, 1170.*

ABOVE: *Joan of Arc (c.1412–1431), French saint and national heroine who led her troops to victory over the British during the Hundred Years War, carrying a sword and a flag on the battlefield.*

ABOVE: *Portuguese explorer and navigator Vasco Da Gama, famous for his completion of the first all water trade route between Europe and India, can be seen here being greeted by the Queen of Malindi.*

ABOVE: *The Mona Lisa was painted by Leonardo da Vinci between 1503 and 1506, and is widely recognized as the most famous painting in the history of art.*

ABOVE: *English mathematician and physicist Sir Isaac Newton (1642–1727) contemplates the force of gravity, as the famous story goes, on seeing an apple fall in his orchard, circa c.1665.*

ABOVE: *1666, Ludgate Hill and St Paul's burning during the Great Fire of London. The arched tower of St Mary le Bow is in the background. This illustration appeared in Wilkinson's* Londonia Illustrata.

ABOVE: *An illustration of Captain James Cook, the 18th century Pacific explorer who circumnavigated the globe and added new lands to the British Crown.*

'. . .I had ambition not only to go farther than any one had been before, but as far as it was possible for man to go . . .'
JAMES COOK, R.N.

ABOVE: *This drawing entitled Up Guards and at Them, is of the 1st Duke of Wellington (1769–1852) commanding his troops at the battle of Waterloo, 18 June, 1815.*

BELOW: *The illustration below depicts John Wilkes Booth preparing to assassinate president Abraham Lincoln in the balcony of Ford's Theatre, Washington DC on 15 April, 1865.*

TOP: *Orville Wright (right) (1871–1948) checking a Wright 'Flyer' biplane at Fort Myer, Virginia, in June 1909.*

ABOVE: *On 26 May, 1927, Henry Ford watched the fifteen millionth Model T Ford roll off the assembly line at his factory in Highland Park, Michigan. His 'universal car' was the industrial success story of its age.*

or in the decisions it took. It was 'taxation without representation'.

On 10 May 1773, a Tea Act was passed by the British Parliament. This reduced the import duty on tea coming into England to give some relief to the East India Company, which had seven years' worth of tea supplies warehoused on the Thames and was unable to afford the storage charges. The new Act permitted tea to be shipped at the full duty to the colonies in North America and to be sold directly to retailer, cutting out the colonial middlemen. This was offensive to the American colonists in two ways. It meant that they were being forced to buy tea at a higher price than the English; it also meant that their own businessmen were being discriminated against.

In December 1773, in a demonstration against the British approach to taxation, colonists disguised as native North Americans boarded British ships in Boston harbour. They threw the cargoes of tea overboard into the harbour. It was a vivid and clear demonstration that the American colonists were not prepared to be treated in this way. Unfortunately the obtuse British government did not read the Indian smoke signals correctly and made an absurd attempt at military repression.

The result was that the American War of Independence started with British troops attacking American soldiers at the Battle of Bunker Hill in 1775 and ended with the surrender of the British army at Yorktown in October 1781. Britain was forced into a formal recognition of the independence of the American colonies in 1783.

THE FIRST MILITARY
SUBMARINE
(1775)

THE ANCIENT ATHENIANS are said to have used divers to clear the entrance to the harbour during the siege of Syracuse. Alexander used divers to destroy any submarine defences the defenders of the city of Tyre might put in place there. These early attempts at underwater activity were undertaken in diving bells. But it was not until 1580 that there was any attempt to build a craft that could be moved about or navigated under water. In that year William Bourne, a British naval officer, designed a completely enclosed boat that could be submerged and rowed underwater. Bourne never actually built this craft, but a similar boat was built in 1605 by someone calling himself Magnus Pelagius. The first true working submarine was designed and built by a Dutch doctor, Cornelius van Drebel, who successfully navigated his craft in the Thames up to 4.5m below the surface.

By the early eighteenth century, more than a dozen different designs for submarines had been patented in England alone.

A 34 year old Yale graduate named David Bushnell designed and built the first military submarine in 1775. It was a one-man craft 2m long, pear-shaped and made of oak staves held together with pitch and iron hoops, just like a big wine barrel. It had ballast tanks that were operated by foot pumps, and a conning tower with windows level with the operator's head. The air was supplied through one hose and extracted through another, with automatic valves to close them during a dive.

The submarine, which was called the *Connecticut Turtle*, was propelled vertically and horizontally by hand-cranked propellers and steered with a flexible rudder.

Its military purpose was to approach enemy ships at anchor un-observed, plant explosives on their hulls, and then withdraw unobserved.

The submarine carried a powder magazine with a clock timer.

The *Connecticut Turtle* went into action for the first time on the night of 6 September in New York Harbour, in a scene that might have come from an Ealing comedy script. The *Turtle* had an auger mounted on it, so that it could bore a hole into the hull of the enemy vessel and plant its powder magazine. Unfortunately a crucial point was overlooked. Many of the British vessels had copper cladding over their hulls to protect them against worms. Several attempts at boring holes through the copper sheathing proved fruitless.

This first experiment with submarine warfare failed, but it was a first step nonetheless. In 1864, in the American Civil War, another small hand-propelled submarine, the *Hunley*, carried about six men into battle; the *Hunley* succeeded in sinking the *Housatonic*, a Federal corvette that was attempting to blockade the harbour at Charleston. The *Hunley* carried a torpedo suspended ahead of her as she rammed the corvette.

John Holland experimented with his first submarine as early as 1875, repeatedly changing his design, improving it gradually over a 20-year period. In 1895, the US Navy bought the first modern submarine, the *Plunger*, which had been developed by Holland. The *Plunger* used electric motors under water and internal combustion engines while on the surface; outstandingly, it used water ballast to make it submerge, and this turned out to be the most efficient way of making a submarine dive and surface. In 1897, another serious experiment was conducted. Simon Lake designed the *Argonaut*, and successfully tested it in open waters. In 1898, he successfully navigated it through November storms between Norfolk and New York. A few years later, Lake sold a submarine called the *Protector* to the Russians, who liked it and ordered several more from him.

In the twentieth century, the submarine took on a distinct role in warfare, pioneered by Germany and making a real impact on the nature of war in both world wars. The sinking of the *Lusitania* by a German submarine was partly responsible for bringing the United States into the First World War.

CAPTAIN COOK'S SOUTH PACIFIC VOYAGE

(1775)

COOK'S FIRST VOYAGE was such a resounding success that he was given command of a second voyage, taking the *Resolution* and *Adventure* to discover the gigantic but unseen southern continent that was for some reason thought to occupy the South Pacific.

Between 1772 and 1775, Cook took his ships in a zig-zag course through the South Pacific, reaching 71 degrees South and seeing ice but no continent. By sailing so far south, Cook put his ships seriously at risk from floating ice.

Cook headed for Easter Island, whose position he accurately established for the first time. Cook also visited the Marquesas and Tonga, again fixing their positions more accurately. He discovered several previously unknown islands, including New Caledonia. On the way home, he crossed the South Atlantic at a high latitude, showing that there was no large landmass there either. It was an incredible voyage of discovery, truly epic in scale; in this one voyage, Cook's ships travelled the equivalent of three times round the world.

Captain Cook's achievements were certainly under-acknowledged and under-rewarded during his lifetime. Cook's voyages produced an astonishing amount of information about the geography of the Pacific and Southern Oceans. He returned with detailed descriptions and accurately surveyed charts. His exploits were the talk of Europe, and everyone was intensely excited about the exotic new world that was suddenly opened up. Cook's discoveries showed conclusively that there was no large landmass in the Pacific Ocean, that the Pacific was virtually empty of land, apart from the hundreds of small islands. Any large 'Unknown Land' must lie in very high latitudes, beyond 71 degrees South. He prepared the way for the eventual discovery of a smaller Antarctica.

THE FIRST BALLOON FLIGHT
(1783)

THE MONTGOLFIER BROTHERS observed the way clouds were suspended in the air, and thought that if they could enclose vapour of the same nature as the cloud in a large light bag it might rise, carrying the bag into the air.

In 1782, the brothers constructed a small balloon which was lifted by igniting a cauldron full of paper underneath it. The smoke and warmed air inside the balloon decreased in density so that it became more buoyant than the surrounding air. They decided to make a larger version and demonstrate it in public. On 5 June 1783, in front of a large crowd of spectators, a huge linen globe 30m in circumference was inflated over a fire fuelled with chopped straw. When released, the balloon ascended rapidly to a great height, floated away in the breeze and then came down again 10 minutes later over 1.5km away. This event marked the invention of the balloon.

People everywhere were excited by the experiment at Annonay. Suddenly everybody wanted to be a balloonist. In Paris, Barthelemy Faujas de Saint-Fond set up a fund to repeat the Montgolfiers' experiment. The second balloon was built by two brothers by the name of Robert, and the work was supervised by a physicist, J. Charles. Initially the idea had been to use hot air like the Montgolfier brothers, but Charles wanted to try hydrogen. This balloon too was given a public audition, and it obligingly rose rapidly to a height of about 1,000m. Rain started to fall during the ascent, but the crowd stayed to see the spectacle and got drenched.

On 19 September 1783, Joseph Montgolfier repeated the Annonay experiment in Paris, in the presence of Louis XVI, Marie Antoinette and an immense crowd. The inflation took only 11 minutes, after which the balloon rose to about 500m, floated along in the wind, and came down in a wood about 3km away. Suspended below the balloon was a cage containing a sheep, a cock and a duck, which became the first air-borne travellers. The Montgolfier balloon was painted with ornaments in oil colours, and was very eye-catching, looking like a gigantic Christmas tree bauble. It was a marvellous piece of publicity.

The first person to ascend in a balloon was Jean Pilâtre de Rozier. In October 1783, he made several ascents in a captive balloon; it was held to the ground with ropes. He demonstrated that the balloon could rise with people suspended beneath it, and also carry fuel so that a fire could be kindled under the balloon while in flight. On 21 November 1783, Pilâtre de Rozier and the Marquis d'Arlandes travelled in a free balloon about 3km from the Bois de Boulogne. They were in the air for about 25 minutes and this was the first manned flight in a balloon.

The Montgolfier brothers were unable to develop the balloon technology any further before the outbreak of the French Revolution. Étienne fell foul of the authorities, and Joseph went back to the family paper factory. Whether the Montgolfiers would have developed their hot-air balloon technology any further if the Revolution had not intervened it is impossible to tell. They certainly succeeded in realizing one of man's oldest dreams – flying through the air – and their success encouraged others to go several steps further. Within just a few months from the initial experiment, the newly invented hot-air balloon technology had led to a manned flight. It opened up new possibilities that would lead on to hot-air ballooning as a 'rich' sport but to passenger airships too.

THE FALL OF THE BASTILLE

(1789)

IN THE LATE eighteenth century, France was in crisis socially and economically as well as politically. Ordinary people had a very low standard of living with few rights, while the clergy and the aristocrats lived in luxury. The contrast between rich and poor was enormous. There were food shortages, high prices and a government that had overspent its budget. There were widespread riots following rumours that the clergy and the aristocracy had plotted to collect all the nation's grain and sell it abroad.

The government could borrow money or raise taxes, but first Louis XVI's finance minister Jacques Necker decided that he had to order the recall of the States-General, an ancient assembly that had not met for 175 years. At the same time Necker ordered the requisitioning of all grain in order to ensure that it was distributed fairly to everyone regardless of rank or class. Necker was widely regarded as the saviour of France, the only man who could avert the nation's financial crisis. But because he had summoned the States-General and permitted the three estates to vote in common, he was also regarded by the court as the instigator of the Revolution.

On 17 June 1789, middle-class discontent turned the States-General into a National Assembly, which demanded reform. Its meeting was suspended three days later, so the members reconvened on a nearby tennis court where they swore an oath not to split up until they had given France a constitution. Perhaps surprisingly they elected an aristocrat, Count Honore de Mirabeau, to head the Assembly, and some members of the clergy and aristocracy joined the bourgeois 'third estate' in the Assembly.

The Assembly adopted a declaration of the Rights of Man. Man has: *natural and inalienable rights. These rights are liberty, property, personal security, and resistance to oppression ... No-one may be accused, imprisoned or*

held under arrest except in such cases and in such cases as prescribed by law …
Every man is presumed innocent until proved guilty … Free expression of
thought and opinion is one of the most precious rights of mankind: every
citizen may therefore speak, write, and publish freely.

Louis XVI blamed Necker for this rebellion and made the mistake of dismissing him on 11 July, gathering troops in a way that implied he intended to break up the Assembly. When the people of Paris heard about Necker's dismissal they took to the streets, rebelling against the king and his government. The situation rapidly escalated out of control at this point, and there were riots throughout France.

On 14 July 1789, as a direct result of Necker's dismissal and the anger that it provoked, a mob attacked the Batille, a massively built and imposing Parisian fortress and prison that symbolized the oppression of the 'old regime'. After an onslaught lasting two days, the mob managed to break in, unlock the cells and release the prisoners. There were only seven prisoners at the time, and one of them did not want to come out. It was an anticlimactic moment. The mob then went on to demolish the building. They destroyed the castle of oppression; next they would destroy the social and political system that created it. First the Bastille, then the king.

Louis XVI had chosen Versailles as a safe place outside Paris, but now a mob of Parisian women marched on Versailles, seized Louis XVI and his wife, Marie Antoinette, who was hated mainly for being Austrian, and took them back to Paris. Meanwhile the National Assembly recalled Jacques Necker and named General Lafayette commander of the new National Guard.

The French Revolution was under way, and the monarchy had already been supplanted. The old regime was over. Many aristocrats hastily made arrangements to leave France as the peasants rose up against their feudal masters. By September 1790, Necker realized the situation was beyond his control and retired to Geneva. In 1791, the Assembly formally created a new government, which wanted to purge France of the people who had ruined it. As many as 40,000 people were sentenced to death and beheaded on the guillotine, and perhaps as many 400,000 people perished altogether in the appalling chaos and cruelty of the Revolution. In 1793–94, the Reign of Terror spread through France and only ended when Robespierre, the Jacobin leader, was himself executed. There was relief that it was all over, and a general celebration, but France would never go back to the old-style absolutist monarchy with an over-privileged aristocracy and clergy.

IV
THE NINETEENTH CENTURY WORLD

NAPOLEON
PROCLAIMED EMPEROR
(1804)

IT WAS SUGGESTED to Napoleon, already an accomplished commander, that he should take command of the army of England and invade England, but he was possibly being set up. There were those who wanted to make him fail. But Napoleon saw that an invasion was futile while the British navy had command of the seas; even the narrow sleeve of the Channel was enough to make an invasion extremely risky.

He got himself out of this trap by cunningly proposing the invasion of Egypt instead, to sever Britain's trade route to India. This plan failed when Nelson destroyed the French fleet in 1798. Napoleon abruptly returned to France in 1799 and seized power in a characteristically bold way, marching into the government buildings with his bodyguards, dismissing the Council of 500 and appointing three consuls to run France, of which he would be one. It ought not to have worked – a coup as bare-faced as that – but it did. He just took power and everyone was too astonished to stop him.

Napoleon ruled France for 15 years, making himself emperor in 1804. The reasoning was that the consulate was too precarious. Since his enemies wanted to destroy him believing: 'he must be made king or emperor, so that heredity should reinforce his power by ensuring him of natural and unquestioned successors and by rendering useless crimes against his person, should remove the temptation to commit them.' In other words, as an hereditary monarch, he would have automatic successors and therefore there was no point in assassinating him. He made out that he wanted to be an emperor – because he was timid!

Lafayette and others opposed this move, and it was widely read at the time, by thinking people, that the coronation was a declaration of dictatorship, and certainly a step too far. Beethoven composed his Third

Symphony, the *Eroica*, as a tribute to Napoleon in 1804; it is virtually a portrait of Napoleon as the hero of Europe, full of charisma and nobility. The composer had completed it and written the dedication on the title page when the news came through that Napoleon had declared himself Emperor. Beethoven knew what that meant and in a state of acute disappointment erased the dedication.

Within France the Emperor Napoleon made many reforms, including an improved system of education, a re-organized government, a new legal code, a restoration of order. Modern France owes much to his reforming, centralizing changes.

The Emperor's aggressive military policy against the rest of Europe nevertheless had a very destructive effect. With his huge army of over two million, he caused enormous loss of life, untold misery. The continuing war with Britain, the fighting in central Europe, the Continental System (a trade blockade against Britain), the invasion of Spain in 1808 and the disastrous invasion of Russia in 1812 all weakened France and contributed to Napoleon's eventual downfall.

In France, not least because of the 'martyrdom' on St Helena, Napoleon is remembered still as a great hero, and he knew that he would be remembered in this idealized way; he said, 'What a romance my life has been.' The romance was the unification of Europe, and in this Napoleon followed in a long procession of political idealists who have chased the will o' the wisp of European union. His effect on Europe as a whole was nevertheless a long way from this romantic vision. His legacy to Europe was death and destruction on the grandest scale.

In the early days, people did not know quite who he was. Beethoven was not the only person to be deceived. In 1799, he could have been just part of a general picture that prefaced the reinstallation of the French monarchy. The royalist party in France certainly thought he was going to call on a legitimate claimant to the throne, rather in the style of General Monk – or indeed General Franco – but in this they were seriously mistaken. When the Comte de Provence, the pretender to the throne who eventually emerged as Louis XVIII, approached Napoleon for his support, Napoleon replied disdainfully. Napoleon had already decided – he wanted that throne for himself. The very fact that he made himself emperor indicated that his career was a programme of self-aggrandisement; he was on a straightforward power trip.

THE BATTLE OF TRAFALGAR

(1805)

ONE OF NELSON'S greatest victories, the Battle of the Nile, came in 1798 commanding *HMS Vanguard*, he inflicted a crushing defeat on the French fleet. It is often assumed that the British deliberately destroyed the French flagship, which blew up and sank during the battle, but it was accidental. The loss of the valuable flagship meant a huge loss in prize money to the British sailors; they were mortified. At the Battle of the Nile, Nelson was wounded on the forehead; he went below for a while to recover but was soon back on deck again. The victory of the Nile on 1 August 1798 was a landmark in his career, putting him in the front rank among the warriors of his time, and making him a national hero - which was indeed his main ambition.

Nelson was now raised to the peerage, becoming Lord Nelson of the Nile and voted a pension £2000 a year. The East India Company awarded him £10,000, and the King of Naples conferred on him the title Duke of Bronte. He characteristically wore all these honours at every opportunity. Nelson resigned his command after this triumph and returned to England with the Hamiltons; Emma was expecting a baby, undiplomatically named Horatia, and Nelson finally separated from his long-suffering wife.

In 1801, Nelson was promoted to Vice-admiral and appointed second in command on a new expedition to the Baltic, under Sir Hyde Parker. It is hard to see why someone with Nelson's proven ability should have been made subordinate to someone as ordinary as Hyde Parker. Parker himself seems to have been aware that he had a problem in giving orders to someone of Nelson's genius and, as is usual in such situations, became wary and suspicious of him. Nelson was good at handling people, though, and treated Parker with great tact. By the time they reached Copenhagen,

Nelson was able to make the decision to attack. But Parker was irresolute, and in the middle of the action stupidly tried to order Nelson to withdraw. Nelson took a massive risk, famously put his telescope to his blind eye, through which he genuinely could not see the signal flags that his officers were pointing out. He disobeyed orders, because doing so would have put his ships in increased danger, and continued to engage the enemy. He decisively won the Battle of Copenhagen.

When the Napoleonic War resumed in 1803, Nelson was commander of the Mediterranean fleet, but in March 1805 the French fleet that he was trying to keep bottled up there escaped into the Atlantic. Nelson searched the Mediterranean in vain. He had a hunch that Villeneuve, the French admiral, had taken his fleet to the West Indies for safety and sailed there in pursuit. When Villeneuve heard that Nelson had arrived, he ran away again, taking his fleet hastily back across the Atlantic towards Europe, once more hotly pursued by Nelson. The French fleet was bottled up at Cadiz by Collingwood, while Nelson returned to Merton for a break. Then he offered 'to give Monsieur Villeneuve a drubbing', an offer which the Admiralty accepted with alacrity, and Nelson left England for the last time.

He eventually caught up with the French fleet off Cape Trafalgar, on the coast of Portugal, in October 1805. The battle was one of those moments in history that becomes a kind of pageant, almost detached itself from reality, like the landing of Columbus in the New World, because it is too stagey and colourful and melodramatic to be true. But it happened.

Just before the battle started, Nelson ordered the famous signal to be run up: 'England confides that every man this day will do his duty.' 'Confides' was meant in the sense 'is confident'. Then at the last moment, with his left hand he scribbled a change. It became 'England expects', which is how we remember it today. Collingwood was rather irritated by the nannying command, as it implied that there had been the possibility that they might not do their duty. He felt patronized by it. But Nelson famously irritated people. He irritated Wellington the only time they met. Nelson did not know who Wellington was and showed off in a big way; Wellington thought him extremely vain and silly. Then something Wellington said made Nelson realize that Wellington was 'somebody', Nelson went off to check who he was exactly, and came back a changed man, full of sensible ideas about the future of the conflict in Europe.

Nelson directed the action at Trafalgar, which was planned with brilliance, daring and panache, from his flagship *HMS Victory* and it was a decisive British victory as well as a tactical masterpiece. It was also a very dangerous battle, the way Nelson planned it, and an appalling bloodbath. In Nelson's mind, the mayhem did not matter so long as the enemy were taken unawares, as they were, astonished by his bravery, as they were, and unable to retaliate. And so long as there was victory, victory at any cost. Unfortunately, Nelson insisted on being seen on the quarter-deck of the *Victory* dressed as always in full uniform, decorated with all his honours like a bird of paradise, and was easily identified from a great distance. He was a sitting duck. He was shot through the shoulder by a French sniper and mortally wounded. He languished in great pain for several hours in the cockpit, among the many other wounded and dying, receiving reports of the progress of the battle. He repeatedly muttered, 'Thank God I have done my duty', and died knowing that the battle was won. At the end he asked Hardy, one of the officers tending him, to kiss him.

An enormous crowd turned out to see Nelson's funeral; only 7,000 VIPs were allowed into St Paul's Cathedral, but among them, and it is extraordinary that he was there, was Nelson's opponent Villeneuve. The damage done to the French fleet by Nelson's great victories – the 'drubbing' he had promised Monsieur Villeneuve – ensured that the French could never contemplate an invasion of Britain. Although the Napoleonic Wars dragged on for another ten years after the Battle of Trafalgar, Britain was safe from any threat of a French invasion.

ROBERT OWEN ATTEMPTS SOCIAL REFORMS
(1809)

BY THE AGE of 19 Robert Owen was already the manager of a cotton mill employing 500 people. With his intelligence, energy and administrative ability, he made his mill the best of its kind in the country. In this factory, Owen used the first imports of American sea-island cotton ever to be used in Britain. He was the first cotton-spinner in England, and made big improvements to the quality of spun cotton. He became a partner in the Chorlton Twist Company in Manchester, and persuaded his partners to buy the New Lanark Mills and manufacturing village at New Lanark in Scotland.

It was at New Lanark that Owen set about creating a model community for the 2,000 people who worked in the mills, with better housing, better working conditions and better education. Among the inhabitants were 500 children brought in as cheap labour from the various poorhouses and charities of Glasgow and Edinburgh. There was little provision for the children's education; the housing conditions were appalling; the sanitation was poor; and there was a high rate of crime and vice associated with very low morale amongst the employees generally.

Robert Owen set about improving every aspect of these people's lives, training them to higher standards of order and cleanliness and improving their houses. He built an Institute for the Formation of Character and a school that incorporated the world's first day-nursery and playground. The school offered evening classes for those at work during the day. He also built a village store that offered goods at little more than cost price; this was the birth-place of the co-operative movement.

Although his social reforms were successful, they were expensive, and his partners complained about the effect they were having on profits. In 1813, Owen formed New Lanark into a new company with collaborators who included Jeremy Bentham and the Quaker William Allen. This time Owen forestalled criticism by guaranteeing his partners a 5 percent return for their capital; Owen was in return to have more freedom of action on the philanthropic side. In his book, *A New View of Society*, he expounded his ideas of educational philanthropy, arguing that character is formed by social environment. The great secret in the development of a person's character is to place him or her under the right influences from the earliest years; this was why he was prepared to invest so much care and attention in schooling and schools. From an early age he left all religious belief behind, becoming a thorough-going humanist and socialist and evolving his own creed. After New Lanark, Owen went on to create more co-operative 'Owenite' communities, including New Harmony in Indiana and Orbiston near Glasgow in 1825–28 and Ralahine in Ireland in 1831–33, but they were all failures.

In 1815, Owen launched a single-handed campaign to make factory-owners and managers adopt more humane practices. He drafted a bill directed at all textile factories, banning the employment of children under ten, banning night work for young people under 18, limiting working hours to ten hours a day for all under 18, and providing for inspection. There were many who sympathized with Owen's bill. It was introduced in Parliament, but Owen was disappointed by the way Parliament amended it to a point where it became unrecognizable. He was a man before his time, by a couple of decades; he was at the spearhead of nineteenth century social reform in Britain – a very necessary man.

In 1817, he put forward a report to the House of Commons committee on the Poor Law, outlining his socialist co-operative scheme. His detailed and comprehensive plans for dealing with poverty in the wake of the Napoleonic Wars were initially given a warm reception in the press and by many influential people. Owen could count the Duke of Kent, Queen Victoria's father, among his many friends and supporters. But then, at a large public meeting in London, Owen declared his avowed hostility to all organized forms of religion. This lost him at a stroke the support of the establishment. He himself thought the radicals, to whom he might have looked for support, were wrong-headed. Owen threw away his chance of getting large-scale government support for his idea of comprehensive reform through whole communities. Instead, he had to work for reform piecemeal, finding supporters who would help set up small communities here and there.

Owen declared in his *Report to the County of Lanark* that what was needed was not a reform but a transformation of the social order. This had a great appeal to the young and for the next ten years there was mounting pressure for Owen's doctrine to be accepted as the aspiration of the ordinary working class people of Britain. When Owen returned to England from New Harmony in 1829 he found himself hailed as a leader.

Robert Owen worked towards the empowerment of workers, emphasizing that labour is the source of all wealth. Various labouring groups formed craft-oriented unions such as the National Operative Builders Union. Owen himself organized the Grand National Consolidated Trades Union in 1833, and huge numbers of workers joined. But the employers and other members of the British establishment became alarmed and adopted counter-measures to stop the trade union movement becoming any stronger. It was to be another two generations before socialism again directly influenced trade unionism.

Owen's benevolent, practical and philanthropic ideas did not amount to a new philosophy, but their application to whole communities was entirely new. The New Lanark experiment was a model to those socialist activists who believe in social engineering. His work in the 1820s and 1830s to achieve social transformation through the trade union movement was heroic, though premature, and a model to later political activists. He prepared the way for the Rochdale Pioneers Co-operative Society founded in 1844, which in turn gave birth to the world-wide Consumers' Co-operative Movement. In a sense he prepared the way for socialist revolution.

NAPOLEON'S RETREAT FROM MOSCOW
(1812)

NAPOLEON EXTENDED HIS Empire as far as he could, reaching as far Bremen and Hamburg. Once he had reached the Baltic, he was getting very close to Russia, and consequently very close to conflict with Russia. He also knew that Russia would not consent to the endless extension of his Empire. Napoleon convinced himself that a great struggle with Russia was his destiny, and he assembled the greatest army the world had ever seen for what he saw as a kind of crusade against an alien Asiatic power.

In June 1812, Napoleon invaded Russia. His Great Army consisted of an incredible force of 600,000 men, an army of 20 nations, including troops from Austria, Holland, Germany, Italy, Poland, Prussia, Switzerland and France. But the army was not in good health and therefore lacked the strength that the numbers implied. Following the Battle of Ostrowo (July), as many as 80,000 of his soldiers went down with dysentery, enteric fever and typhus.

On 7 September, Napoleon's army encountered the Russian army on the Moskva river. The Russians had watched Napoleon's approach and kept their distance; it was their custom not to give battle if they could avoid it. The Battle of Borodino was a bloody victory for Napoleon. The Russian commander, Field-Marshal Kutusov, retreated to save his army from total annihilation. From the battlefield of Borodino, Napoleon was left to enter Moscow unopposed, but he found the city deserted and eerily silent. Napoleon was uneasy about this conquest and with good reason. Fires broke out all over Moscow, started by the Russians themselves; they would sooner see their capital destroyed than fall into Napoleon's hands. The fires raged for five days.

Demoralized, Napoleon left Moscow on 19 October and began the long retreat right back across Europe. But his retreat was not unopposed. The Russians followed and harried him as he marched. The retreating Great Army was attacked by Marshal Kutusov in November at Smolensk, where the Russians succeeded in defeating Marshal Ney and Marshal Davout.

The severity of the east European winter in the end defeated Napoleon. By the middle of December, his army was crippled by cold, hunger, salt deficiency and continual harrying by Russian irregulars and Cossack soldiers. The once-huge army had by the middle of December dwindled to only 100,000. Half a million men had died by the time Napoleon's beaten army crossed the Nieman river.

Napoleon had shown spectacularly that he was not invincible. This was defeat on a spectacular scale. The retreat from Moscow gave heart to Napoleon's enemies all over Europe. Wars of liberation broke out. In Breslau on 3 February, Friedrich Wilhelm III of Prussia issued an appeal for a volunteer corps; he wants students and other young men to rally behind the cause of freedom. On 28 February, the Treaty of Kalisch made Prussia and Russia allies against France. In March, a Swedish army took the field under the command of Crown Prince Bernadotte after Sweden and Britain signed a similar treaty. The downtrodden defeated states of Europe were taking great heart from Napoleon's humiliating defeat. They would give him some more. On 2 May, an Allied army of 85,000 attacked Napoleon on the Elbe, but his army was still greater, and in the Battle of Lutzen he managed to win, though only after suffering further heavy losses.

Napoleon won further battles, at Bautzen and Wurschen later in May, and forced the Allies back, but once again at great cost to his own army. He was gradually being worn down. In August, Austria declared war on France. Still Napoleon succeeded in winning battles, but the Battle of Dresden on 20–27 August 1813 was his last big victory. Ironically, Napoleon's battle cry had been the great battle cry of the Revolution – the liberation of nationalities. Now he was seeing it happen – nations liberating themselves from *his* dictatorship.

The Battle of Leipzig, which lasted four days, 16–19 October 1813, came to be called the Battle of the Nations. It ended in defeat and the loss of another 30,000 men for Napoleon, and he retreated. Now he was finished.

The military manoeuvres and the patterns of advances, retreats, victories and defeats are complicated in the extreme. But the overall picture is clear, that the retreat from Moscow signalled the beginning of the end of Napoleon's career. He rode back from Moscow – to Elba. If he had had any thought for the welfare of his soldiers, he would have abdicated there and then, but he was prepared to sacrifice any number of men for his own glory.

THE ERUPTION OF TAMBORA
(1815)

ON 5 APRIL 1815, the volcano Tambora on the island of Sumbawa in the East Indies erupted. This very violent eruption killed 20,000 people. The shock waves on the seabed produced tsunamis. The column of ash was sent high into the stratosphere, where high-level winds spread it all round the world, creating a dust veil encircling the Earth.

The local effects were obviously devastating, but there were also global effects. The veil of dust cut out significant amounts of the light and heat from the sun, so temperatures all round the world were reduced by a degree or two for the next few years.

In 1815, summer temperatures in North America and Europe were only slightly lower than usual. By the following year the dust had spread all round the world and the effects were more noticeable. The summer of 1816 was described at the time as 'the year with no summer'. It was cool, overcast, gloomy. The poets Byron and Shelley and their entourage were trapped indoors for much of the summer by the adverse weather – and consequently wrote rather more than they might have done. Mary Shelley, the poet Shelley's young wife, set to work to write *Frankenstein*. Published in 1818, it was an instant best-seller.

In the summer of 1816, from Canada to Virginia there were frosts every night from 6 to 9 June. Heavy snow fell on New York in June and July. Frost killed crops across the Midwest. Farmers would remember that year, without any affection, as 'Eighteen hundred and froze to death'.

THE BATTLE OF
WATERLOO
(1815)

ARTHUR WELLESLEY, ONE day to become the Duke of Wellington, was called to the Iberian Peninsula in 1809 after Moore's retreat at Corunna. Wellesley assumed chief command in the peninsula. At this crucial moment, Wellesley became one of the key warriors in the Napoleonic Wars.

He very nearly lost the Battle of Talavera in 1809 through a blunder, but retrieved the situation. For the victory at Talavera he was awarded a peerage. The Battle of Salamanca in 1812 was a more worthy victory. Gradually, Wellesley's determination succeeded in driving the French army out of Spain. He understood the physical geography of the peninsula well enough to know that Napoleon could not sustain a large army there, in hostile country, indefinitely. Most of Spain was too poor to feed an army. If Wellesley held on for long enough, with the support of the Spanish, he could outlast a French army of any size. And he was right. A formal admission of withdrawal from the Iberian Peninsula was extracted from the French at Toulouse in 1814.

Wellesley's conduct of the Peninsular War was hailed as a major success in England, and he was rewarded by being created Duke of Wellington.

Napoleon was thought to be utterly defeated and out of the way, but his escape from Elba after a few months threw Europe back onto a war footing again. Wellington rushed from the Congress of Vienna to take command of a hastily mustered rag-tag army to deal with Napoleon. Wellington referred to it as 'an infamous army'. He had a pleasantly rough way with his men, chaffing them affectionately. They in turn loved him.

Napoleon had somehow mustered a huge French army, which defeated Blucher and his German army at the Battle of Ligny. It looked as if Napoleon might after all be the overall victor. Wellington chose to make his stand at Waterloo, a battlefield he had reconnoitred beforehand and chosen with considerable care. Wellington came close to losing the Battle of Waterloo, which took place on 18 June 1815, but Blucher arrived just in time, after a heroic march with his German army, and the allied forces together routed Napoleon's army. The outcome was decisive. It was Napoleon's final defeat and the start of a long period of peace.

Waterloo led directly to Napoleon's final voyage, on the Bellerophon, to a lonely death on St Helena. It led to his transformation in the French imagination into a kind of saint. Waterloo led to a long period of peace in Europe. It also led to a remarkable second career for Wellington.

He was treated as a great English national hero, given a country house (Strathfield-saye) and a place in government as master-general of ordnance. Wellington's second career, his post-Waterloo career was less successful than his military career. In 1829, he assisted Robert Peel in his reorganization of the Metropolitan Police force. Wellington's policy was to avoid foreign entanglements, as Britain did not possess an army large enough to impose its will. It was a lesson learnt at Waterloo, where he had needed Blucher's help to win. When George Canning intervened to bind Britain, France and Russia to impose recognition of the autonomy of Greece on Turkey, he resigned.

In 1827, Canning died and the Ripon administration collapsed; the king, who was a great fan of Wellington's, called on the Duke to form a government and he became Prime Minister. His policies alienated Huskisson and the Liberals. He refused to intervene in the east after the Battle of Navarino, and this lost him the support of a large section of his party. He was unlucky in being a staunch conservative at a time when many cried out for reform. He opposed the unqualified enlargement of the franchise; he did not believe in votes for everyone, and this made him extremely unpopular. On the anniversary of Waterloo, a mob broke the windows of his London home, Apsley House, to show what the people thought of their national hero now.

In the political crisis of 1834, the king again called on Wellington to form a government; this time it was an intensely personal plea. Wellington was reluctant, but agreed on a compromise solution, proposing that Peel should head the new administration, and that he should serve under him as Foreign Secretary. Although not a popular politician, Wellington was a good man to have in high office because of his scrupulous honesty. From his earliest despatches on, everything Wellington said could be entirely trusted.

Waterloo perhaps unfortunately gave Wellington a political profile that he could not sustain. It certainly made him a national hero on a level with Nelson.

THE LIBERATION OF
NEW GRANADA
(1819)

SIMÓN BOLÍVAR VISITED Europe apparently to see friends. While he was there, in Rome, he told one old friend, his tutor, that he was pledging his life to freeing Venezuela from Spain. It was a remarkable pledge, and one that he more than fulfilled.

He travelled back to Venezuela by way of the United States, visiting many Americans in the eastern cities, reaching Caracas in 1806. The liberation movement in Venezuela was fuelled partly by the quarrel in Spain between Charles IV and his son Ferdinand VII, and the additional complication of Napoleon's imposition of one of his relations as king. Spaniards and colonists were divided into two camps. Bolívar and his friends were members of the Caracas junta, which after the crowning of Joseph Bonaparte as King of Spain favoured the restoration of Ferdinand. In April 1810, this junta forced the Captain-general, Vicente Emparan, to abdicate; then the junta formed the very first locally-created government in Spanish America. Bolívar was sent to England as diplomatic representative of the new Venezuelan government.

When he returned to Venezuela, Bolívar made a speech advocating a declaration of independence from Spain. Venezuela was accordingly declared independent in 1811, and the model of a federal republic, to be named Colombia, was decided on – though not by Bolívar. Bolívar travelled to New Granada (now Colombia) to raise an army. Fierce fighting followed in town after town, between the royalists and Bolívar's supporters. He was seriously outnumbered, but because he was mobile he was able to deal with the royalists group by group. In 1813, after fighting several pitched battles, he returned, entering Caracas as conqueror, and proclaimed himself dictator and Liberator of western Venezuela. The following year he was driven out, but made repeated attacks on Venezuela from the West Indies.

There were atrocities on both sides, and Bolívar himself committed some. In 1814, he cold-bloodedly executed 886 Spanish prisoners as a reprisal. Battle followed battle. At one point, in 1815, Bolívar was so disheartened by the lack of progress, and by delays and intrigues, that he resigned his command and set sail for Jamaica. From Jamaica, Bolívar wrote his famous 'Jamaica letter', in which he analyzed the causes of the failure of the enterprise and gave reasons for believing that it would eventually be successful.

An attempt was made to assassinate Bolívar in Jamaica. Further intrigues followed, and the support of the President of Haiti was enlisted before Bolívar returned to Venezuela.

After a new series of pitched battles and skirmishes in Venezuela, Bolívar at last made visible headway against the Spanish. Then he took the struggle over the Andes into Colombia. In Bogotá, he was given a rapturous welcome, and money and men were put at his disposal for the relief of Venezuela. In Bogotá in January 1820, Bolivár proclaimed the union of Greater Colombia. Meanwhile the Spanish Government opened negotiations for peace. Bolívar refused to agree to any peace unless it was based on the independence of Venezuela and the other colonies. The offer of an armistice was nevertheless a great encouragement to the freedom fighters. They fought on.

In 1821, Bolívar was chosen as president of a new state of Colombia, which was to consist of Colombia, New Granada and Venezuela. In 1822, Bolívar added Ecuador to this 'republic' that increasingly looked like an empire.

In 1824, came the decisive victory that for ever ended the domination of Spain in South America. It came on 9 December 1824 at Ayacucho in Peru. This battle was won by Bolívar's lieutenant Sucre, as Bolívar had already set off for Lima to organize the new civil government of Peru. Simón Bolívar drove the Spaniards out of Peru, and made himself dictator there for a while. Upper Peru was turned into a separate state, and named Bolívia in his honour. He was to be 'perpetual protector' of Bolívia, but the state's constitution gave many cause for concern and the Colombian troops were thrown out.

After he returned to Colombia in 1828, he assumed dictatorial powers there, which made the republicans apprehensive. The following year, Venezuela separated itself from Colombia.

Simón Bolívar liberated five South American states from Spanish colonial rule. This marked the beginning of Latin America's modern history, its independent, post-colonial phase. The negative side of the process of liberation was Bolívar's attempt to acquire dictatorial powers for himself – and the killing of large numbers of people. Venezuela, Colombia, Ecuador, Bolivia, Panama and Peru were independent. The idea of a federation of Spanish-speaking South American states was a fruitful one, and was a major part of South American politics for some time to come, though it never came to anything. It is reminiscent of something a British historian said recently about the European Union – that a united Europe is not part of the historical narrative of Europe. Individuals have tried to unify Europe – Napoleon tried to do it, Hitler tried to do it, ancient Rome tried to do it – but it is not something that is embedded in the hearts of the people of Europe. Its history has if anything resisted it. Perhaps it will prove to be the same for South America.

THE GREEK
DECLARATION OF
INDEPENDENCE
(1822)

IN THE WAKE of Napoleon's empire-building and the resulting nationalist campaigns for liberation from French rule, the Greeks too hankered for liberation from Turkish rule, which they had endured for several centuries. Change and freedom were in the air.

A Greek assembly at Epidaurus unilaterally proclaimed the independence of Greece from the Ottoman Empire on 13 January 1822. It was a declaration of intent. The Ottoman response was savage. An Ottoman fleet took the island of Chios two months later, and then massacred most of the inhabitants; the survivors were sold into slavery. Greek freedom fighters, virtually powerless to take effective action, were reduced to setting the Ottoman admiral's flagship on fire as a reprisal.

On 19 June, a small Greek fleet commanded by Admiral Konstantinos Kanaris destroyed the Ottoman fleet in the Aegean. But the following month an Ottoman army of 35,000 invaded Greece, overrunning central Greece. The newly formed separatist Greek government was forced to leave the mainland and take refuge in the islands. Greek guerrilla fighters on the mainland managed to inflict significant losses on the Turkish army of occupation. With its sparsely populated hill country, Greece was ideal country for guerrilla warfare.

On 19 April 1824, Lord Byron died at Missolonghi while helping the Greeks in their struggle for independence. In October that year, Greek forces at Mitylene almost annihilated an Ottoman army. The war continued the next year with the Ottoman army besieging Missolonghi again, under the leadership of Mustapha Mohammed Reshid Pasha, who invaded

Greece from the north. Egyptian Ottoman forces landed in the south.

The Ottoman grip on Greece seemed to be about to loosen when in 1826 the sultan's army, the Janissaries, revolted in Constantinople, but the people of Constantinople support the sultan Mahmud II and they joined in an attack on the barracks of the Janissaries; up to 10,000 Janissaries were massacred. It was a false dawn, and the Ottoman Empire now looked as invincible as ever. On 5 June 1827, Turkish Ottoman troops entered Athens and forced the defenders on the Acropolis to surrender. But a few months later Egyptian troops were brought by an Egyptian and Turkish fleet to Navarino Bay on the south-west coast of Greece, where they were destroyed by a combined Russian, British and French fleet in the Battle of Navarino. General opposition to the Ottoman Empire was growing and in 1828 Russia formally declared war on 'the sick man of Europe'. It was as if the great powers had succeeded in getting rid of Napoleon and now wanted to finish the job of tidying up Europe by getting rid of this much older nuisance, the line of decadent and tyrannical Ottoman sultans.

Greece finally gained her independence after 400 years of subjection to Ottoman rule and Russia brought the tottering Empire to the verge of collapse. The London Protocol of 22 March declared Greece an 'autonomous tributary state', but this odd status was clarified in the London Conference in November; Greece was to be completely independent. The Greek patriot Count Ioannes Kapodistrias became the new state's president.

THE DECIPHERMENT
OF THE ROSETTA
STONE
(1822)

THE FAMOUS ROSETTA Stone was found by a French soldier in 1799, during Napoleon's Egyptian expedition. What was interesting about this stone was that it carried texts in two different scripts, Egyptian and Greek. This opened up the exciting possibility that the Greek text could be used to expose the nature and structure of ancient Egyptian hieroglyphics, which until then had remained a complete mystery. The monuments were covered in carved texts, which obviously had a lot to tell about the nature of the civilization, and finding the key to deciphering these texts was a very exciting possibility.

It was generally assumed from the start that the two texts on the Rosetta Stone were really just the same text in two languages. Several early nineteenth century academics tried their hands at deciphering the hieroglyphic script, including the distinguished scholar Sylvestre de Sacy, who had to admit that he was defeated by the Rosetta Stone; he sent his paper copy of the inscription on to a Swedish archaeologist, David Akerblad. But Akerblad too was foxed. What he did not allow for was that in Egyptian writing the vowel sounds were often not written down, and his assumption that each sign represented a letter was mistaken.

Another scholar who tried to decipher hieroglyphic writing was Thomas Young. Young was a man who threw himself into all of his projects wholeheartedly. One assignment he gave himself was to learn to dance on a tightrope. He practised this with great determination and within a few weeks was able to perform in public, much to the consternation of his Quaker community. Young succeeded in 1818 in compiling a list of just over 200 words in hieroglyphics, one-quarter of which he had been able to translate. Then Young looked at the Rosetta Stone and concentrated on the cartouches that should have contained the name of the pharaoh, Ptolemy. A cartouche is a round-cornered box or bubble drawn round the name of someone important. He identified six signs inside the Ptolemy cartouche and gave each a letter or syllable: *p-t-ole-ma-i-os*. He was nearly right. In fact, he was so successful that is hard to understand why he stopped working on the hieroglyphs. Young had come to realize that the texts were mostly about the gods, the dead and the pharaohs, and he had been hoping for more substantial information about Egyptian history, chronology and astronomy. In other words, the actual subject matter of Egyptian hieroglyphic inscriptions did not interest him enough. He was also getting very little praise or encouragement for his work, so he quietly gave it up and watched his young rival, the French Egyptologist Champollion, solve the remaining problems.

It was on 23 December 1821 that Jean-François Champollion had the bright idea of listing all the hieroglyphic text signs on the stone next to the corresponding Greek text. He found there were far more hieroglyphs than Greek words, 1,419 compared with 486, which suggested that the hieroglyphic signs must stand for letters or syllables. He tackled the Ptolemy cartouche and translated the signs as *p-t-o-l-m-i-s*, which might have been pronounced Ptolemaios.

From his experimental translations of Greek demotic script into hieroglyphics, Champollion had already worked out what the name of Queen Cleopatra should be – and he was electrified to see the name in the inscription sent to him by Bankes as found on an obelisk found at Philae. It was exactly as he had constructed it: *c-l-e-o-p-a-t-r-a*. The collections of signs in cartouches were probably all going to be the names of kings or princes, so he combed all the inscriptions he could find and, sure enough, there were the names of Alexander, Tiberius, Germanicus, Trajan, Ramesses, Thutmosis and many more.

Champollion had spent 14 years on the project, reporting that the script on the stone contained both sound signs (phonograms) and sense signs (ideograms). These signs provided the clues necessary for deciphering all ancient Egyptian inscriptions.

In 1822, Champollion published his decipherment. It was a sensation in France. The Napoleonic expedition to Egypt in the 1790s had opened

Europe's eyes to the possibilities of this ancient civilization. It was a point of honour that the decipherment should be achieved by a Frenchman. After this breakthrough it became possible to read the papyri and stone inscriptions that would greatly expand knowledge of the civilization of ancient Greece. Champollion's health was nevertheless wrecked by diabetes and tuberculosis, and he knew he had too little time left to finish the work. He cried one day, 'My God, give me another two years, just two more years.' On another occasion, he reflected, 'Too soon. There is so much inside my head.' In March 1822, he died of a stroke; he was 42.

THE START OF OIL DRILLING AT BAKU

(1823)

THE 'ETERNAL FIRE' that burnt at natural gas fissures on the shore of the Caspian Sea were known about in the time of Alexander the Great, in the fourth century BC. But until the nineteenth century the eternal fire had never been harnessed or used.

The association between natural gas and mineral oil or petroleum was known about, and if natural gas was leaking out of the ground it was clear that there must be oil below. In 1823, drilling for oil started at the Caspian Sea port of Baku on the Aspheron Peninsula. The production of oil started in a small way, but gradually expanded during the nineteenth century. In 1873, Alfred Nobel and his brother Ludwig invested capital enabling a refinery to be built; this crucial investment was to turn Baku into the world's leading petroleum producer. The Baku oilfield was producing half of the world's petroleum by 1900.

The oil industry became significantly more important once fractional distillation had been invented. The Yale chemist Benjamin Stillman was the inventor of this new process. The effect was to 'crack' crude petroleum into a range of useful products, varying in density from bitumen, which could be used for road-making, to lubricating oils and light fuels that could power internal combustion engines or be burnt in lamps.

The new process was a massive boost to the petroleum extraction and refining industries. Petroleum production began in the United States at Titusville, Pennsylvania. An unemployed railway conductor named Edwin Drake was sent to Titusville by a New York banker. Using salt-well drilling gear, Drake's men drilled down into oil-bearing rocks, striking oil on 28 August 1859. Drake's 21m deep oil well was soon producing 1,500 litres of oil a day, and this marked the beginning of the very first commercial exploitation of petroleum in the United States. It inaugurated a new age in the history of North America, which turned out to be oil-rich; in a world that was to become increasingly oil-dependent in the twentieth century as coal resources ran down, this meant that the United States became extremely rich. The availability of mineral oil, which could be cracked to make kerosene (paraffin), also meant that a new age of kerosene lamps and stoves began, reducing the demand for whale oil.

The Baku oilfield continues to be the dynamo for the economy of the area, providing work in the drilling operation, the refineries and the associated chemical works.

The Baku oilfield played a crucial role in the Second World War. Hitler's drive to the east into Russia was in effect a thrust towards Baku. The German war effort was consuming huge quantities of oil and Germany had none of her own; annexing the resources of the Caspian Sea made perfect sense. Baku was producing over 24 million tonnes of oil a year in 1938. It was Baku that lured Hitler into engaging in war on a second front; it was a fatal strategic error. He over-extended the German war machine. He also exposed his army to the ferocity of the Russian defence. Because of his greed for Baku, Hitler endured the defeat of Stalingrad – and lost the war.

MALTHUS
ON POPULATION
(1826)

IN 1798, AT the age of 32, Thomas Malthus published, anonymously, his great work, *Essay on the Principle of Population*, following it in 1807 with a greatly enlarged edition. Malthus was constantly adjusting and amending his ideas, and brought out six editions of his essay, the last one appearing in 1826.

In this landmark book, Malthus maintained that the optimistic views of Rousseau and William Godwin regarding population were without foundation. He maintained that human population has a tendency to increase faster than the means of maintaining it. Food production increases at an arithmetic rate; population increases at a geometric rate. In other words, human population will go on increasing until there is no food left, or until there is some other check, such as pestilence or war, and then collapse through famine.

The book developed out of discussions with his father about the perfectibility of society. Daniel Malthus shared the optimistic views of Condorcet and Godwin, while his son Thomas took the pessimistic view that the achievement of a happy society will always be hindered by the problems caused by the tendency for population to grow faster than the means of supporting it. Daniel Malthus was very struck by his son's arguments and pressed him to put them into writing. When he read them, he pressed him to publish them. The first edition is really a long pamphlet, but a key feature is the high quality of Malthus's style of writing, which is both vivid and lucid.

Population growth was an issue that had been handled by others; what Malthus did was to express their views in a systematic form together with proofs from history. Nor was Malthus entirely pessimistic in his views. He argued that a population collapse could be averted by reducing the birth rate, but he was not convinced that the human race as a whole would be prepared to regulate itself in this way.

Malthusian ideas on population have had a huge influence on economics, geography, demography, biology and ecology. Charles Darwin happened to read *On Population* by chance. He saw that what Malthus was saying fitted his own ideas on evolution and used Malthus's theory to explain why evolution was necessary.

Writing at the end of the eighteenth century, Malthus was unaware of the effects that improved transport in the form of steamships and railways would have. He was unaware that colonization of new regions would open up new areas to food production. As a result, the population collapse he predicted was long delayed. He may not have been wrong in the long term, of course – only wrong for the nineteenth and twentieth centuries.

Malthusian ideas also lay behind the 'population explosion' scare-mongering that went on in the 1960s and 1970s, when many influential economists and ecologists argued that human population growth was running out of control – that starvation was just round the corner. The simple Malthusian model works for organisms that depend on a narrow range of foods, but the human race is more complicated. People have been able to develop new high-yield strains of wheat, rice and other key foods, so that the food supply is more elastic than once thought. The neo-Malthusian scare campaigns of the 1960s and 1970s nevertheless generated a great deal of interest in population control, and most countries now have more or less effective birth control programmes in place. Some countries have found that their attempts to reduce the birth rate were too effective and they now need immigrants in order to meet all their labour needs.

For better or worse, the ideas of Malthus have continued to be extremely influential over the last 200 years.

THE INVENTION OF
THE MECHANICAL
REAPER
(1831)

CYRUS HALL MCCORMICK was the son of Robert McCormick, a farmer in Rockbridge County, Virginia. Cyrus's father invented and patented several labour-saving agricultural implements and made several abortive attempts to design a mechanical reaper, but in 1831 he abandoned the project.

That same year, at the age of 22, Cyrus took up the challenge to see whether he could succeed where his father had failed. He studied the technical problems carefully and came up with a successful working design before the end of the year. The machine was built immediately and actually used to bring in the late harvest on their farm in 1831. Cyrus McCormick did not get round to seeking a patent for his reaper until 1834, by which time another reaper, designed by Obed Hussey, had been patented.

American agriculture had entered a phase of rapid expansion and there was fierce rivalry between the two men, Hussey and McCormick, to manufacture harvesters to meet the huge demand. Other companies were involved in this lucrative struggle too. McCormick moved to Chicago in 1847, and manufactured his harvesters there. In the end, the McCormick Harvesting Machine Company emerged as the leading manufacturer. The McCormick reaper, after a number of further improvements, had proved a complete success, not only technically but financially.

It was on the huge grain farms of the Prairies that the combine harvester was to make the biggest changes. With the new harvesters, huge fields of grain could be harvested at high speed, which meant that the best use could be made of spells of good weather. The new technology allowed food production to be stepped up enormously. Thanks to harvesters, the Prairies regularly produced huge grain surpluses, which the United States could export, and which were to become of profound political significance in the Cold War. The Soviet Union frequently suffered from crop failures and needed the American grain surplus, which gave the United States political supremacy. Mechanization also depended on the availability of cheap oil; as the American oil reserves run dry, it may be that the Prairies will one day need to return to man and horse power for farm production.

THE INVENTION OF
THE SEWING MACHINE
(1832)

THE MODERN SEWING machine was invented in 1832 by the New York inventor Walter Hunt. The new machine had a needle with an eye at its point that pushed a thread through cloth to interweave with a second thread carried by a shuttle. Hunt did not take out a patent on his invention. When he suggested to his 15 year old daughter Caroline that she should go into business making corsets with his new machine, she protested that it would put needy seamstresses out of work. Like so many inventions of the eighteenth and nineteenth centuries, the sewing machine brought both benefits and disadvantages – it saved human labour, but thereby created unemployment.

In 1843, the sewing machine was invented all over again by a 27 year old Boston machine shop apprentice called Elias Howe. His machine used two threads to make a stitch that interwove by means of a shuttle. Howe made his invention without any knowledge of Walter Hunt's machine, and patented his re-invention in 1846; there were widespread infringements of Howe's patent in subsequent years. In any case, tailors and clothing manufacturers were afraid to introduce it in case they antagonized their workers.

The Singer sewing machine, invented by the mechanic Isaac Singer in 1850, was destined to be the machine that took over the market. Singer watched some Boston mechanics trying to repair a primitive Howe sewing machine and could see ways of improving it. The Singer machine was patented in 1851. Isaac Singer went into partnership with his New York lawyer, Edward Clark, in order to mount the strongest defence against patent suits from Howe. Howe won his lawsuit, which did not prevent Singer from producing and selling his sewing machines, but ensured a royalty payment for Howe, who was to make a fortune, not from his own, but from Singer's machines. In 1858, Isaac Singer offered the earlier inventor of the sewing machine, Walter Hunt, 50,000 dollars in five annual payments to clear up any claims he may have on the machine design. Hunt died a few months later without collecting even the initial payment. Walter Hunt was one of those unlucky inventors who was unable to make money out of anything he invented – not just the sewing machine, but the breech-loading rifle and his Globe stove.

THE ABOLITION OF SLAVERY IN BRITAIN & ITS COLONIES
(1834)

THE ABOLITION OF slavery was achieved by the campaigning work of a number of people, but there can be no doubt that the leading light in the campaign to end the slave trade in Britain and its colonies – and therefore across a large area of the world – was William Wilberforce. The deaths of two relatives left Wilberforce with a large legacy, which gave him the freedom of action and the independence that most people do not have. In 1780, he became MP for Hull, and he soon became caught up in the fast-moving political set in London. He became a close friend of William Pitt the Younger, although he remained independent in his views and above party affiliation. In 1783, he went on holiday with Pitt to France, and on their return, Wilberforce's eloquence was a great help to Pitt in his fight against the majority of the House of Commons. In 1784, Wilberforce was returned as MP for both Hull and Yorkshire, and took his seat for Yorkshire.

In 1784–85, Wilberforce went on a tour of the continent with Dr Isaac Milner, who had been one of his masters at Hull Grammar School and would later become President of Queen's College Cambridge and Dean of Carlisle. During this tour, Wilberforce underwent a conversion to evangelical Christianity. This event caused a major change in his behaviour. In 1787, he founded an association for the reform of manners.

In 1788, with the support of Thomas Clarkson and the Quakers, Wilberforce began the historic 19-year-long struggle for the abolition of the slave trade. It had been just over 20 years since Jean Jacques Rousseau had drawn attention dramatically and ironically to the state of mankind: 'Man is born free, but everywhere he is in chains.' Wilberforce wanted to remove those chains. Pitt encouraged Wilberforce to give himself to this monumental project as one that was ideally suited to his character and talents. Thomas Clarkson took the campaign round the country, while William Wilberforce took every opportunity to raise the matter in the House of Commons. This long, slow, arduous campaign resulted in success in 1807, when the slave trade became illegal in Britain and throughout the British Empire. Then Wilberforce worked towards getting the slave trade abolished globally and the total abolition of slavery itself. This was obviously far more difficult to achieve – and he failed.

In 1823, Clarkson and Wilberforce became vice-presidents of the Anti-Slavery Society, which continued to campaign for total abolition. In 1825, failing health forced him to retire from parliament and public life generally. He moved to Highwood Hill near Mill Hill. The Emancipation Bill, which was the culmination of Wilberforce's life work, was passed in August 1833, a few weeks after his death on 29 July. From 1834 onwards, slavery was abolished throughout the British Empire. On Emancipation Day, 1 August, 1834, 750,000 slaves were freed – largely thanks to the work of William Wilberforce. It was an historic change for the freed slaves, but also a landmark in human development. One country after another would be shamed into abolishing slavery, Russia in 1861 and North America in 1863, but it should not be forgotten that there are countries in Africa where thousands of people are still kept in institutionalized slavery.

THE INVENTION OF
PHOTOGRAPHY
(1838)

PHOTOGRAPHY WAS INVENTED independently, at the same time, in England and France. From 1826 onwards Louis Daguerre developed and perfected his 'daguerrotype' process, working in collaboration with Joseph Niepce. Niepce had been trying since 1814 to make permanent pictures by the action of sunlight, and in 1826 he succeeded in making the first permanent photograph. In that year he heard that Daguerre was working on the same problem and proposed that they should start working together. The two inventors collaborated on what they called their 'heliographic pictures' from 1829 until Niepce's death in 1833. Daguerre went on experimenting alone, eventually discovering the photographic technique that bears his name – the daguerrotype.

Daguerre's process involved obtaining a photographic image on a copper plate coated with a layer of metallic silver that had been sensitized to light by iodine vapour. This revolutionary process produced some of the earliest, if not the earliest permanent photographs in the year 1838.

In 1839, the Englishman William Henry Fox Talbot Talbot announced that the previous year he had invented a photographic process, which he called 'photogenic drawing'. Curiously the two inventors had each invented photography, independently of each other and unaware of each other, in 1838. It is one of those recurring curiosities of history – a simultaneous invention. He devised his process for making photographs in the same year that Daguerre invented his. Talbot had produced his photographs in Wiltshire before Daguerre exhibited his pictures in Paris. As soon as Talbot heard about Daguerre's work, he communicated his own work to the Royal Society.

Fox Talbot's technique involved making prints on silver chloride paper. In 1841, he patented another technique, the calotype or Talbotype. This was the first process involving the creation of a photographic negative from which prints could be made. He also invented a third photographic technique, in 1851, the creation of instant photographs using illumination by an electric spark; this was in effect the invention of flash photography.

Fox Talbot's book, *Pencil of Nature*, was published in 1844. This was the first book to be illustrated with photographs.

The invention of photography had far-reaching effects. By the end of the nineteenth century, photography was regularly used for recording the appearance of places and people, and this released painters from the need to produce likenesses. Thanks to photography, we can see exactly what the elderly Duke of Wellington or Rossini looked like. The revolutionary art movements of the twentieth century, such as expressionism, futurism and cubism, were made possible by photography. Photography made the career of Picasso possible. Photography also showed what people, places and events were really like, and this had a dramatic effect on the transmission of news stories. It would eventually be possible to capture on photographs historic events such as the assassination of John F. Kennedy and the attack on the World Trade Centre. The immediacy of these images has had the effect of making people more engaged with world events than they ever were before.

THE TRAIL OF TEARS
(1838)

EUROPEAN SETTLERS FROM many different countries flocked to North America following the Declaration of Independence in 1776. Many of these people were poor and disadvantaged and hoped to be able to make a better life for themselves. The population of North America was four million in 1790; by 1830 it was 23 million and by 1850 it was 50 million. This huge increase was entirely due to the flood of European migrants crossing the Atlantic. Most of them passed through New York and to begin with most settled in the north-eastern states, close to their point of arrival.

As time passed, the immigrants moved south and west, crossing the Appalachian Mountains and reaching the Mississippi valley. Large areas wanted for European colonization were not, as portrayed by the white migrants, virgin wilderness but already occupied and utilized by native North Americans. The Cherokee Indians' traditional homelands were in North Carolina and Georgia, land wanted by the US government for white settlement. The Cherokees were offered 5.7 million dollars by the government to move out, but most of them refused. To most of the native North Americans the concept of owning land, let along buying or selling it, was completely alien. The landscape was your home, you mother and your father, your universe; you had a symbiotic relationship with it and were inseparable from it. Some of the chiefs spoke eloquently on the subject.

The government response was to send in troops to get them out by force. The Cherokees were driven west to settle on newly created reservations in the Prairies, which were dry with cold winters, a completely different environment from the woodland in which they had all grown up. The Creek, Seminole and Choctaw Indians were similarly forced to set off on the 'Trail of Tears' to the Prairies, a traumatizing journey on which many of them died. Their unhappiness at being separated from their homelands, with which they felt a special bond, is hard for us to imagine.

The US government bought the Prairies, a huge tract of land between the Mississippi valley and the Rocky Mountains, from the French in 1803. This transaction, which was called the Louisiana Purchase, doubled the size of the United States of America. Unfortunately this land too was occupied by native North Americans, but the government sold off a great deal of it, without regard for the native peoples, to farmers and ranchers. It was a breach of basic human rights that was repeated again and again.

The disruption of the native North American way of life continued throughout the nineteenth century. The dispossession and killing of so many native North Americans – and the destruction of their way of life – are seen by many as crimes against humanity.

THE INVENTION OF
THE BICYCLE
(1839)

THE BICYCLE WAS not an all-in-one-go invention. It evolved gradually, step by step. Throughout the nineteenth century there were experiments with two-wheeled vehicles powered by human legs, some more successful than others. One early variety was powered by the rider's feet scooting the ground past on each side; this was called the hobby-horse, and it was about as useful as a means of transport as the children's toy. The first true bicycle was invented by Kirkpatrick MacMillan, a 29 year old blacksmith in Dumfries. The frame and wheels of the modern bicycle had already been invented by Sauerbroun and Niepce as early as 1816. MacMillan added a pedal system and a brake, which in effect made it into a working machine, the recognizable predecessor of the modern bicycle.

The new bicycle weighed 26kg. It had iron wheels without tyres; the front wheel was 82cm in diameter and the back wheel 106cm. The bicycle made it possible for the first time for someone to travel under his or her own power faster than they could run, but the lack of tyres meant that the ride was rough and uncomfortable. Not for nothing were these early machines called 'bone-shakers'.

In 1861, the Parisian coach builder Pierre Michaux invented an improved version of the MacMillan bicycle, called the velocipede. This had its pedals directly mounted on its front wheel. Michaux built some prototype models and sold 142 of them in 1862. Further improvements were made in 1870 by the Coventry machinists James Starley and William Hillman. Their machine was lighter in weight and was also the first to have wire-spoked wheels, like most modern models; they called it the Ariel and put it on the market at a retail price of £8 – or £12 with a speed gear.

From here it was a short step to the appearance of the modern bicycle in 1885. This was rather like photography in being the invention of two people working independently on two sides of the English Channel. One of the inventors was the French engineer, G. Juzan. His bicycle had two wheels of equal size, with a chain-driven rear wheel; it used a stronger chain than the one used on the very first rear-drive 'Bicyclette' designed by Andre Guilmet in 1868. The Rover Company of Coventry introduced the safety bicycle designed by James Starley, also with wheels of equal size and solid rubber tyres and a chain-driven rear wheel. The French and English bicycles built in the 1880s converged on a design almost identical to the one drawn by Leonardo da Vinci in 1493. The new bicycle was much more suitable than the earlier versions for general use by the public and it quickly caught on as a very popular means of transport, enabling ordinary people to get to work easily and inexpensively, and it also made possible virtually free recreational travel.

GOODYEAR OBTAINS HIS VULCANIZATION PATENT
(1844)

CHARLES GOODYEAR, A 39 year old former Philadelphia hardware merchant, pioneered the effective use of rubber. In 1839, he acquired formal legal rights over a sulphur process for treating rubber. Goodyear discovered his new process, 'vulcanization', accidentally when he accidentally overheated a mixture of rubber, sulphur and white lead. The overheating changed the nature of the rubber, making it much harder and more durable.

Charles Goodyear sold the patent on his father's pitchfork, which was the first steel-tined pitchfork, in order to finance his experiments on raw rubber. A process for hardening rubber had already been invented in 1823, when Macintosh invented a method for making durable waterproof sheeting for making raincoats, or Macintoshes, as they became known. The usefulness of rubber as a substance has long been suspected, but it tendency to become sticky in hot weather and rigid in cold weather was a limitation on its practical use and commercial potential.

Goodyear obtained the basic rubber vulcanization process patent in 1843; this patent would ensure that Goodyear dominated the rubber industry. He licensed L. Candee Co. to make vulcanized rubber overshoes. Goodyear's vulcanization process was not the total answer, but it made possible the manufacture of good hard rubber that could be used for making tyres for bicycles – and eventually cars and lorries.

THE INVENTION OF
THE TELEGRAPH
(1844)

THE TELEGRAPH HAD a very long and slow evolution before it became a practical and useful invention. As early as 1747, the Englishman Sir William Watson demonstrated that an electric current could be transmitted through quite a long wire, using the Earth to complete the circuit. Eleven years later the suggestion was made by an anonymous correspondent to *Scots Magazine* that an electrical telegraph system could be devised; 'C. M.' – whoever he or she was – proposed using a separate insulated wire for each letter of the alphabet. At the receiving end of each wire a pith ball was to be suspended above a piece of paper marked with an alphabet letter. As a charge was sent along a particular wire, the ball would attract the paper beneath it, so that words could be spelt out. This ingenious suggestion, which sounds rather like a ouija board, was actually tried out by Georg Le Sage in Geneva in 1774. Several other similar systems were tried out during the next 20 years.

Once the electro-magnet was invented, a number of experiments with telegraph systems using electromagnetic needles were carried out, and by a large number of scientists. Lots of people were at work on the concept of an electric telegraph system. Then in 1832, Samuel F. B. Morse, an American artist, was travelling back to the United States from a trip to Europe on the packet ship Sully, when he fell into conversation with the other passengers about a recent publication by Michael Faraday about electro-magnetism. When Morse got home he made plans for a telegraph recording instrument and an outline scheme for a dot-and-dash code which could be transmitted according to the duration of the electrical impulses sent. Morse made an experimental model on a picture frame

In 1838, Morse gave a demonstration of his magnetic telegraph for

President Martin Van Buren and his cabinet and was granted a US patent for it. It was his assistant, Alfred Vail, who devised the 'Morse code' using a system of dots and dashes to represent the letters of the alphabet; this replaced an experimental earlier system that assigned numbers to letters. Vail later made the extremely useful discovery that the electric dots and dashes could be heard, and that with a little practice the receiving operator could interpret the patterns of sounds as dots and dashes. Enormous progress was suddenly being made.

Six years later, the US Congress made 30,000 dollars available to Morse to build an experimental telegraph line between Washington and Baltimore. Morse was helped in this ambitious project by Ezra Cornell and the businessman and banker Hiram Sibley; together they constructed the world's first long-distance telegraph line.

On 24 May 1844, Samuel Morse transmitted his first telegraph message from the US Supreme Court Room in the Capitol at Washington, DC, to his associate Alfred Vail at the Mount Clare railway station at Baltimore. His message was the enigmatic question, 'What hath God wrought?' To prove that the system worked, Vail sent the message back again.

With the help of Ezra Cornell and Hiram Sibley, Morse set up more telegraph lines. In 1848, a line was set up connecting New York and Chicago. Three years later Sibley organized the New York and Mississippi Valley Printing Telegraph Company. In 1856, Western Union was formed by Cornell and Sibley, Morse's financiers, as an amalgamation of small US telegraph companies; Sibley became its president. Western Union was enlarged, and in 1859 Morse agreed to the formation of the North American Telegraph Association, as a virtual monopoly. In 1866, Western Union absorbed two smaller companies, giving it control over 120,000km of telegraph wire across North America, and making it the first great US monopoly.

If it was possible to communicate by telegraph across continents, why should it not be possible to communicate across oceans too? The first submarine cable was laid on the seabed between England and France in 1850. The first transatlantic attempt in 1857, a much more ambitious undertaking in very deep water across unsuspected submarine mountain ranges and volcanoes, was a failure; the cable broke under 3,600m of water while it was being laid and could not be recovered. But, the following year, the Atlantic was successfully spanned between Newfoundland and Ireland, though the cable later parted in deep water. It was in 1866 that the first permanently successful transatlantic cable was laid. The rate of sending was slow at first; the first transatlantic cable could only take 15 letters per minute. It was also expensive; the charge was a minimum of 100 dollars per message. But improving technology allowed faster and faster rates of transmission. By 1950, it was possible to send 2,400 letters per minute.

Morse's telegraph revolutionized communication, making the rapid transmission of important political and business news right across North America possible for the first time, and then more or less instant communication right round the world. It was one of those technical advances that made the world a smaller and more connected place. It also revolutionized the business world: Western Union became a huge and powerful monopoly. It was becoming a world of powerful monopolies too, with the parallel rise of John D. Rockefeller's Standard Oil Company.

THE INVENTION OF
ANAESTHETICS
(1846)

ANAESTHETICS WERE INVENTED or discovered, and forgotten, and then reinvented or rediscovered several times through the course of history. One of the pioneers of anaesthetics in modern times was William Morton, a Boston dentist. Morton attended a lecture by Charles Jackson, in which Jackson mentioned that inhaling sulphuric ether could cause a loss of consciousness. Morton later tried it successfully on himself and his dog, then used it to extract a tooth from one of his patients. The patient leaked the news about the painless extraction to the press. Dr Henry Bigelow, a Boston surgeon, read about it in the newspaper and persuaded Morton to demonstrate his technique at the Massuchsetts General Hospital. There, John Warren used ether on 16 October 1846 to anaesthetize a patient during surgery for a superficial tumour.

Morton took out a patent the following month, but he was unable to enforce it. Oliver Wendell Holmes wrote to Morton about the technique, and proposes that the ether should be called an anaesthetic. It went into immediate use in operations on casualties of the Mexican War, opening a new era in surgery.

In 1847, the London physician John Snow introduced the use of ether in British surgery. It was the innovative Snow who in 1853 traced the source of a cholera epidemic in London to a particular pump, proving that it was a sewage-contaminated water supply that caused cholera.

Ether was not the end of the story. In 1884, cocaine was discovered to be an equally effective anaesthetic. Cocaine was derived from the leaves of the South American shrub *Erythroxylon coca*. The New York surgeon William Halsted injected a patient with cocaine for the first time, pioneering the new drug. Unfortunately, during the course of his experiments, Halsted became addicted to cocaine. After a couple of years he recovered, but after that he needed morphine in order to function. It was an early example of the bad side effects of drugs used to excess or inappropriately.

Effective anaesthetics made a huge difference to surgery. With patients unconscious, it was possible for surgeons to work more carefully, slowly and meticulously, and undertake altogether more ambitious surgery. By the 1890s, it was even possible for surgeons to contemplate open-heart surgery for the first time.

THE PUBLICATION OF MARX'S *COMMUNIST MANIFESTO*
(1847)

IN BRUSSELS, FOR the first time Karl Marx came into close contact with the socialist working-class movement. Together with Engels he set up a German workers' society, and then joined the League of the Just, which was an international secret society with branches in London, Paris, Brussels and towns in Switzerland. In 1848, Marx and Engels together wrote a handbook for the League of the Just, which now started calling itself the League of the Communists. The handbook was the famous *Communist Manifesto*, and this masterpiece of communist propaganda ended with rousing words that seemed to hold echoes of Rousseau's Social Contract, 'The workers have nothing to lose but their chains. They have a world to win. Workers of the world, unite!'

Because revolution was already in the air, revolution broke out in France and several other European states immediately after the *Communist Manifesto* was written. It was in February 1848, just a couple of months after the *Manifesto* was written, that revolution broke out in Paris. 'The crowing of the Gallic cock' proved to be the signal for revolution to spread through Germany, just exactly as Marx had prophesied.

Marx and Engels made a brief visit to France, and then went to Cologne in May 1848. There, Marx and his collaborators advocated non-payment of taxes and the organization of armed resistance. A state of siege was declared in Cologne, and Karl Marx was put on trial for high treason. He had after all advocated the overthrow of the state. He was found not guilty by a middle-class jury, and acquitted. He was nevertheless obliged to leave Prussian territory. He first went to Paris, but it was made clear to him by the authorities there that he was seen as a trouble-maker and he was not welcome there either; he took refuge with his family in London, where he lived for the rest of his life.

It was the *Communist Manifesto*, a major work outlining the history and the future of the working-class movement in modern society, that was the inspiration behind many communist movements in the twentieth century and which transformed the socio-political geography of the twentieth century world. Though he died before the twentieth century began, Karl Marx was a great unseen force in its history.

THE GREAT
EXHIBITION
(1851)

THE GREAT EXHIBITION, or more fully the Great Exhibition of the Works of Industry of all Nations, which opened in London on 1 May 1851, was the very first world trade fair. During the course of a few months it attracted over six million visitors to Britain, many of them from overseas. It was a far greater success than any of its organizers could have hoped.

The intention of the exhibition was to show off British industrial and commercial achievement and enhance trade. It was also a display of cultural richness. It was intended to pay tribute to the industrial advances that had given Britain unprecedented prosperity and economic mastery in the first half of the nineteenth century. Britain had been extremely fortunate in being the country where a great many of the inventions that drove the Industrial Revolution had been made. It was Britain where the steam engine had been invented. It was Britain where the mass production of steel using coke as a fuel had been pioneered. It was Britain where the railway had been invented.

The Great Exhibition was designed to flaunt British industrial supremacy. At the same time, exhibits were encouraged from other countries. The German steel manufacturer Krupp exhibited a colossal steel ingot, a single casting. The Americans displayed the Colt revolver, which alarmed British gun manufacturers who feared that American mass-production methods would take the market away from their own hand-made guns.

The exhibition was staged inside an enormous iron and glass building that looked like a huge greenhouse. This was the famous Crystal Palace, designed by Joseph Paxton, literally on the back of an envelope. It was 563m long, 124m wide and 20m high, with 30m long transepts, like a gigantic see-through cathedral. Within this huge birdcage 13,000 exhibits were on display. Paxton's design won in an open competition, from among 254 entries from all over the world. It was in fact an enormously magnified version of the Lily House at the Duke of Devonshire's mansion, Chatsworth House, where Paxton was head gardener. The building was prefabricated, in the modern style, and raised in just 17 weeks.

One of the most popular exhibits was the Machinery Court, where Jacqaurd's looms, De La Rue's envelope-making machine and McCormick's reaping machine were on show. Queen Victoria was very interested in the medal-making machine and the electric telegraph, using the device to send messages to Edinburgh and Manchester. Her husband, Prince Albert, had put an enormous amount of energy into the organization of the Great Exhibition, which incorporated many of his ideas. In fact, the success of the Great Exhibition confirmed that the Prince had enormous abilities, which his role as a Prince Consort were cramping.

The Great Exhibition did something more, which was to act as a major national focus; it fostered national pride on a level that nothing else in peace time had been able to achieve. It also spawned copy-cat exhibitions in other countries, such as the Paris Exposition of 1855, similarly celebrating French technological and economic progress. The idea of national exhibitions and big trade fairs caught on quickly.

THE INVENTION OF
THE SAFETY ELEVATOR
(1853)

ELISHA GRAVES OTIS was a master mechanic for a bedstead manufacturer. He was put in charge of the construction of his firm's new factory at Yonkers, a factory with several floors connected by a hoist. Elisha Otis knew of the mechanical dangers of runaway lifting platforms – existing models were dangerously unpredictable and could cause serious accidents. He designed a spring-operated safety device that would hold the platform in position if there was a failure in the tension of the rope. The device could position the lifting platform very precisely. This was invented and in use in 1853.

Otis patented his 'elevator' and exhibited it at a New York industrial fair in 1854. To begin with, interest was slight – he only sold three lifts – but then he had himself hoisted aloft and ordered the rope to be cut. The lift fell a short distance before safety ratchets engaged to halt his descent. Otis emerged from the lift cage saying, 'All safe, all safe, ladies and gentlemen,' removing his stovepipe hat and taking a bow. It was a risky piece of show business, but it worked. After the stunt, orders came in thick and fast for Otis lifts – for passengers as well as goods.

The first commercial passenger elevator was installed in 1857 in the 5-storey New York store of E. G. Haughwort, on the corner of Broome Street and Broadway. The elevator was completely enclosed, as is the case with most modern lifts.

In 1861, just before his death at the age of 50, Otis patented a new type of steam-powered lift. These high-powered lifts were installed in the multi-storey blocks that were built during the later nineteenth and twentieth centuries. Many of the great multi-storey buildings in New York dating back to the beginning of the last century still have their Otis lifts and original Otis engine rooms, still in full working order. The Otis lift made it possible to conceive of buildings of almost any height, as stairs were no longer essential. Elisha Otis's invention, a safe lift that would stop reliably at each floor, and at exactly the right level to within a few millimetres, made the skyscraper possible. The new lifts, in combination with the availability of cheap steel, made possible the skyline of Manhattan and other North American city centres. Thanks to the lift, we have the profile of the modern city.

THE INVENTION OF
THE BESSEMER
CONVERTER
(1856)

THE ENGLISH ENGINEER Henry Bessemer obtained a patent in 1856 for his steel converter. The traditional blast furnace produced pig iron, which contained quite a high percentage of carbon, and the carbon made the iron brittle. This brittle iron was suitable for making castings that required little strength, such as ships' anchors and fire-backs. To make steel, the carbon needed to be removed. It could be burnt off in the furnace, but making steel, especially in large quantities, was expensive.

Bessemer's revolutionary converter removed all the carbon from melted pig iron simply with a blast of air. The oxygen bubbled through the pig iron combined with the carbon and dissipated it by turning it into carbon dioxide.

The Bessemer process required iron ore that was fairly free of impurities such as phosphorus, but otherwise guaranteed an unlimited supply of steel. At a stroke, the Bessemer process enabled the mass production of steel. In the early nineteenth century, ships were being made of iron, which was a rather heavy metal in relation to its strength; but by the end of the nineteenth century nearly all ships were being made of steel. Steel made it possible to build hulls of thinner yet stronger sheets. The cheap mass production of steel made possible by the Bessemer converter also made possible the manufacture of larger and larger ships of steel. With the Bessemer converter, the modern supertankers became a possibility.

THE DISCOVERY OF
NEANDERTHAL MAN
(1856)

FOSSIL HUMAN REMAINS were found in the valley of the Dussel, a tributary of the Rhine, in the German Rhineland in 1856 by Johann Fuhrott. The valley, the Neanderthal, gave its name to the early human being reconstructed from the bones, which included the top of the skull, upper and lower arm bones, both thigh bones and fragments of the pelvis, shoulder blade and ribs. There were enough bones to make an approximate reconstruction, though it was unfortunate that the face was missing.

The skull was found in a cave in a layer of rock that was evidently many thousands of years old. It was given to Paul Broca to look at. He was a French surgeon who was also the world's leading authority on skull structure. Broca maintained that the skull did not belong to a modern man, but to an early form of man in some significant ways quite different from modern people.

The Berlin physician Rudolf Virchow disagreed with Broca, saying that the skull belonged to an ordinary savage with a congenital skull malformation or bone disease. But in time Broca was proved right, as further remains of the same type were discovered at other places, in Jersey, France, Belgium, Spain, Italy, Croatia, Russia and Palestine. They were found together with deliberately manufactured stone tools, especially of flint, which takes a sharp cutting edge.

The Neanderthal skull was big but low-browed, with a heavy brow-ridge. It had a receding chin. The thigh bones were thick and curved. The general impression was that this was an ape-man, a being half-way between apes and people. But the date of the bones was a surprise. They turned out to be fairly recent, and Neanderthal Man probably became extinct only 50,000 or 40,000 years ago, just as modern man, *Homo sapiens*

sapiens, appeared. It was surprising to find such a primitive human type so late in the evolutionary path.

In 1868, another discovery was made, this time in France. The French archaeologist Édouard Lartet was exploring a cave near Périgueux when he found four adult human skeletons and the skeleton of a foetus. These remains were eventually recognized as people of a previously unknown age, Cro-Magnon man, who lived in the Upper Palaeolithic period around 40,000 years ago. They were among the earliest modern people.

In 1890, a Dutch scientist called Eugène Dubois discovered the fossil remains of Java man while serving as a military surgeon in the Dutch East Indies. Java man is given the formal name *Pithecanthus erectus*. The rock layer where the human remains were discovered dated from 700,000 BC.

These discoveries were experienced as major jolts by archaeologists, biologists and anthropologists, as they implied a very complicated history for the human race, and certainly not a one-off biblical creation. For a time, scientists tried to construct a linear family tree, assuming that there was a direct ancestral line passing through all of these fossil men. But as more and more 'ancestors' were found, it became increasingly obvious that some of them, perhaps many of them, were not direct ancestors of modern people at all. The evidence pointed increasingly to Darwin's view of evolution being correct, that some strains of human being, notably Neanderthal Man, had actually died out because they were in some way less fit to survive.

THE PUBLICATION OF DARWIN'S *ORIGIN OF SPECIES*

(1859)

EMBARKING ON THE *Beagle* voyage was to be the greatest and most momentous decision of Charles Darwin's life. It was to be an epoch-making voyage, not only because of the huge volume of data which Darwin collected, but because of the freshness and originality with which he interpreted what he saw. Darwin's mind and the nineteenth century's collective mind were opened wide by that five-year voyage round the world of *HMS Beagle*. The Magellan circumnavigation in the sixteenth century fixed the size of the world and the arrangement of its continents and oceans. The Darwin circumnavigation in the nineteenth century opened up a whole range of new geological and biological insights into the nature of that world, and transformed our understanding of it.

The intellectual journey of the years 1831–36 left Darwin with a colossal bank of data that would occupy him for the rest of his life, and some ideas that he would find hard to digest. But by the end of the voyage, when he was still only 27, he already knew what the principal minefield, the origin of species, was and where the key evidence lay.

Darwin married and in 1842 settled at Downe House in Kent, living the life of a reclusive country gentleman. At Downe, he devoted himself to the one great problem that preoccupied him, the origin of species. He had the idea that 'laws of change' governed species and led to their extinction, something like the laws that control the growth, maturation and death of individual organisms. He also had the idea that one species must somehow give birth to other species or die out, much as an individual organism either reproduces or becomes defunct. Darwin stumbled on Thomas Malthus's essay *On Population*, which struck him as profoundly truthful. He became convinced that favourable variations in a species would help it to survive in the Malthusian 'struggle for existence' and unfavourable variations would lead to its destruction.

He mulled over his evidence for five years, then in 1844 wrote a 231-page paper for his own reference. This was the theory of natural selection; evolution by the survival of the fittest, or what came to be known as the Darwinian theory. But Darwin was a cautious man, and he probably understood the pain that would follow publication. He knew that people would say his findings were blasphemous and contradicted the Bible. He put off the evil day.

Then, in June 1858, Alfred Russel Wallace sent him a paper on the Malay archipelago which, to Darwin's surprise, contained a summary of the same idea as his own on natural selection. Wallace wanted Darwin's opinion on his paper and also wanted Darwin to forward his opinion to Sir Charles Lyell. Darwin wrote to Lyell, 'Your words have come true with a vengeance – that I should be forestalled.' Discussing the tricky situation with his friends, Darwin was persuaded that he and Wallace should submit a joint paper based on Wallace's paper and his own 1844 sketch. It was read at the Linnaean Society on 1 July 1858 at the same meeting as Wallace's paper. Neither Wallace nor Darwin was present.

Now that the cat was out of the bag, Darwin set to work to argue the case for natural selection more fully, again urged on by his friends. This turned into his great book, *On the Origin of Species by Means of Natural Selection, or the Preservation of Favoured Races in the Struggle for Life*, which was published on 24 November 1859.

The book was dynamite. It is hard now to imagine the furore that it caused. Many scientists were profoundly impressed by it. Some accepted its findings. Some violently rejected them. The Church was most hostile as the book seemed to fly in the face of the Biblical account of the creation of man and the animals. Darwin was ridiculed for suggesting by implication that people were descended from apes. The storm of controversy reached a climax in 1860, when at the British Association meeting in Oxford there was a noisy verbal duel between Thomas Huxley, who supported Darwin, and Bishop Samuel Wilberforce of Oxford ('Soapy Sam'), who opposed him.

Darwin was not the sole originator of the theory of evolution by natural selection – Wallace was thinking of it at the same time. Darwin was however the first thinker to argue the natural selection theory through in a way that was comprehensive enough for a large number of fellow scientists to find it acceptable, perhaps because of the long mulling-over period he gave to it. Darwin took the crude evolutionism of Erasmus Darwin and Lamarck and grafted on his own idea of natural selection; this raised evolution from a hypothesis to a theory that could be verified. Cultures and civilizations are by their nature conservative and resistant to large-scale change – that is how they defend themselves and preserve their identity. Darwin's great achievement lay in changing Western science, steering it away from religious fundamentalism and towards a new and frightening idea that the emergence of the human race might be a result of mere chance. He didn't say that – he was too cautious – but that was where his ideas would lead. Darwin changed the thought-world of the nineteenth century.

THE INVENTION OF THE GATLING GUN
(1861)

IN 1863, THE Gatling gun was invented by the American engineer Richard Jordan Gatling. This was the first machine gun, and it was capable of firing hundreds of rounds per minute. It first saw serious use in warfare in the American Civil War, starting in 1864.

In 1883, the 43 year old British engineer Hiram Stevens Maxim designed and built an improved version which was fully automatic. His Maxim-Vickers gun was adopted by the British army in 1889 and after that by every other major army. Maxim's gun was a significant improvement on the Gatling gun in that the energy from the recoil of each bullet fired was used to eject the spent cartridge, insert the next round and fire it.

In 1893, when the Matabele rebelled against Cecil Rhodes's British South Africa Company, Jameson was able to cut the rebels down with machine gun fire, suppress the revolt and force the Matabele's King Lobengula to give up his capital Bulawayo and go into exile. The new machine gun played a decisive role in the operation. It was used again at the Battle of Omdurman in 1898. This battle gave General Kitchener a decisive victory over the Khalifa of the Sudan. The British used Maxim-Vickers machine guns to kill 11,000 dervishes and wound 16,000 more, while sustaining only 48 casualties. When the Boer War broke out in 1899, as a matter of course the British troops were equipped with Maxim-Vickers machine guns. In a very short space of time the machine gun had become standard equipment in modern warfare.

The victory at the Battle of Omdurman was a vivid demonstration of the huge military superiority the machine gun could give; it could be the decisive factor in winning battles. It was also an horrific demonstration of the escalation of bloodshed that resulted from the industrialization of war.

The Industrial Revolution had produced many inventions that led either directly or indirectly to significant improvements in standards of living, to the mass production of useful materials and to the saving of human labour. But it was also producing machines for mass destruction. The invention of the machine gun was an indication of the direction in which technology was taking the human race, and in particular the rich countries of the West, able to afford the latest in weapons technology. It was preparing the way for the bloodbath of the twentieth century, when more people would die violently than ever before.

LINCOLN'S GETTYSBURG ADDRESS
(1863)

THE BATTLE OF Gettysburg in the American Civil War was fought on 1–3 July 1863. In the November of that year, a part of the battlefield was dedicated as a burial ground for those who died in the battle. The dedication ceremony was attended by a great throng of people, among them President Abraham Lincoln.

The main address was one lasting two hours, given by Edward Everett, the best-known orator of his day. Everett's speech was intended to be the main event that day. After it, Lincoln gave his own short speech, which he had started writing in Washington the previous day and finished on the morning of the ceremony. At the time, almost no notice was taken of Lincoln's short speech, which was consigned to the inner pages of the newspapers, while Everett's elaborate and long-winded peroration was widely praised. It was not until long after the event that the speech, as it stood on the printed page, rather than as it was uttered in November 1863, came to be recognized as one of the greatest speeches of all time.

Interestingly, Edward Everett knew on the day of the dedication ceremony that Lincoln's speech was a great speech. He wrote to Lincoln the very next day, 'I wish that I could flatter myself that I had come as near to the central idea of the occasion in two hours as you did in two minutes.'

Yes. Two minutes. The Lincoln speech is short enough to quote in full.

Fourscore and seven years ago our fathers brought forth on this continent a new nation conceived in liberty and dedicated to the proposition that all men are created equal. Now we are engaged in a great civil war testing whether that nation, or any nation so conceived and so dedicated, can long endure. We are met on a great battlefield of that war. We have come to dedicate a portion of that field as a final resting-place for those who here gave their lives that that nation might live. It is altogether fitting and proper that we should do this. But, in a larger sense, we cannot dedicate, we cannot consecrate, we cannot hallow this ground. The brave men, living and dead, who struggled here have consecrated it far above our poor power to add or detract. The world will little note nor long remember what we say here, but it can never forget what they did here. It is for us the living rather to be dedicated here to the unfinished work for which they who fought here have thus far so nobly advanced. It is rather for us to be here dedicated to the great task remaining before us – that from these honoured dead we take increased devotion to that cause for which they gave the last full measure of devotion – that we here highly resolve that these dead shall not have died in vain, that this nation under God shall have a new birth of freedom, and that government of the people, by the people, for the people, shall not perish from the Earth.

In this speech, Lincoln struck a note of nobility that rose above mere victory in battle or the winning of a war. It was more about building a nation, and building it upon the highest ethical ideals. It succeeded in seeing beyond the noise of battle to far greater issues, and as such it was a great inspiration to succeeding generations. It sowed the seeds of patriotism. Short though it may be, it is full of resonant ideas, such as 'this nation under God'. It even contains a characterization of the United States of America, as 'a new nation conceived in liberty and dedicated to the proposition that all men are created equal.' Above all, the speech contains one of the most vivid definitions of Western democracy that can be imagined; 'government of the people, by the people, for the people.' It also established the important - and possibly dangerous - idea that the United States was going to act as the world's policeman. The reality of American political and military intervention round the world in the interests of maintaining democracy has been more questionable.

In two minutes, Lincoln told his unimpressed listeners what they were there for that day, the nature of their country, the principles on which their nation was founded, and their nation's destiny - and all in rolling, majestic sentences that sounded as if they had come from the Bible. It was a wonderful literary achievement.

The Gettysburg Address was significant in another way too. It shows how the key event is often not noticed at the time. On the day of the address, Lincoln was scarcely noticed; it was the Everett address that was noticed. A photograph was taken of the crowd gathered for the occasion. It has only recently been pointed out that Abraham Lincoln's distinctive face can be made out – for one hundred years it was lost in the crowd. On the day, Lincoln was scarcely noticeable. His speech was scarcely noticed. It is only as time moves on and people have the opportunity to reflect, evaluate and consider what has happened that the really important things emerge. Of the things that are happening today, which will turn out to be important in one hundred years time?

THE GENEVA CONVENTION
(1864)

THE GENEVA CONVENTION was signed by representatives of 26 countries in 1864. The agreement pledged all the signatories to obey certain humanitarian rules in time of war. In particular, the normal human rights of prisoners of war, wounded and sick military personnel and civilians caught in war zones were to be respected. Those signing up to the Convention also agreed to respect the neutrality of the Red Cross.

The Geneva Convention was expanded in 1907 and again in 1929. In 1949, the Convention was revised again, this time to provide in the event of war for 'the free passage of all consignments of essential foodstuffs, clothing and tonics intended for children under 15, expectant mothers and maternity cases.' The Convention does not specifically outlaw sieges, blockades or operations involving the denial of resources, nor does it deal with conflicts that are partly international and partly internal, so it will not cover the events of the Vietnam War.

The principle of the Geneva Convention was extremely enlightened, but the reality of warfare in the twentieth century was far from humanitarian in character. In the Second World War, the basic human rights of prisoners of war were flagrantly and systematically ignored by the Japanese, and the Germans systematically destroyed civilian populations during the Holocaust. But at least the Geneva Convention made it easier to identify war crimes and war criminals. There was at least a benchmark for human behaviour in time of war, and the generally held view is that the world is a better place for having the Geneva Convention.

THE ASSASSINATION OF LINCOLN
(1865)

ON 3 APRIL, General Grant of the Federal Army captured Richmond, the capital of the South. Six days later, General Robert E. Lee for the Confederates surrendered to General Grant at Appomattox Courthouse, bringing the American Civil War to an end. President Lincoln's determination to free the slaves inflamed the passions of many racist extremists; many Southerners were bitter and frustrated at the Northern victory. One of them, John Wilkes Booth, decided to kill Lincoln.

During the 1850s, Booth joined the Know-Nothing Party, which was formed by 'nativists', people who wanted to preserve the country for native-born white citizens. The theme of white supremacy was a crucial element in Booth's psyche, and had a major role in his decision to kill Lincoln – the freer of black slaves. Booth day-dreamed about doing something remarkable. According to his sister Asia, he cried 'I must have fame! Fame!' He decided to be a famous actor like his father.

His early notices were not favourable and he was inevitably compared unfavourably with his much-admired father. Booth may have felt that he could never outshine his dazzling father and this may have driven him to try to make his mark in some other way.

Theatre companies often put on a different play each night, so after a performance Booth might have to stay up the rest of the night learning a new part, then go to the theatre for a morning rehearsal. This irregular lifestyle involved keeping unusual hours, and may have helped to make him less visible as a conspirator. He became more positively committed to the southern way of life and more entrenched in southern, white-supremacist political views.

In 1859, Booth appeared to make a fresh start altogether, enlisting as a soldier, but it was with the sole purpose of witnessing a political assassination, the hanging of the fiery abolitionist John Brown. Booth was part of the armed guard standing near the scaffold to prevent anyone from rescuing John Brown; then Booth was discharged. The episode shows Booth's fanatical support of the southern cause, his desire to be involved in historic events, his morbid interest in political assassination, and his unstable, maverick behaviour.

In November 1863, Booth acted in front of Abraham Lincoln. The Lincolns saw him in *The Marble Heart* at Ford's Theatre. With them in the box was a guest, Mary Clay. She reminisced that Wilkes Booth twice, when uttering disagreeable threats, came up close to Lincoln and pointed at him. When he came close a third time, Mary Clay said, 'Mr Lincoln, he looks as if he meant that for you.' Lincoln replied, 'Well, he does look pretty sharp at me, doesn't he?'

In October 1864, Booth started assembling a conspiracy to capture the president, take him to Richmond as a hostage and use him to compel the Federal government to return the Confederate prisoners of war who were held in Union prisons. The intention was to re-invigorate the Confederate army and enable it to win. It was a plot to kidnap, not to kill. The capture of the president was to take to place on 17 March, 1865. But after five months of detailed planning by Booth and the other conspirators, Lincoln changed his plans at the last minute. Instead of visiting the Campbell Hospital outside Washington to see a play, *Still Waters Run Deep*, he decided to attend a luncheon at the National Hotel, where he would speak to officers of the 140th Indiana Regiment and present a captured flag to the Governor of Indiana. Booth was thwarted.

Two weeks later, the Union siege of Richmond ended in Confederate defeat. One week after that, on 9 April 1865, General Lee was obliged to surrender. Booth was doubly frustrated; his conspiracy to kidnap Lincoln had failed and the Confederates had lost the war. On 11 April, Lincoln gave his last speech at the White House. Booth and two of his co-conspirators, Powell and Herold, were in the audience. Lincoln proposed conferring rights on certain black people, 'on the very intelligent and on those who serve our cause as soldiers'. Booth was now beside himself with rage. 'That is the last speech he will ever make.' Booth's fury made him think up a wild, last-throw attempt to get the better of Lincoln. Just four days later, he would murder him.

Booth visited Ford's Theatre one morning to pick up his mail and fell into conversation with the theatre manager, who mentioned that Lincoln would be attending that evening's performance of *Our American Cousin*. Booth decided that this was his opportunity to kill Lincoln. He spent some time walking round the theatre. He knew the play well, and knew that the biggest laugh would come at 10.15pm; that would be the moment to shoot. At noon he went to a stable and hired a horse before returning to the hotel.

At 6pm Booth rode to the theatre to rehearse the route he would use in the assassination, everything except the leap onto the stage. Then he returned to the hotel to rest, dine and change. At 8pm, Booth held a final meeting with the other conspirators. After that, Booth rode to Ford's Theatre.

At 10pm, Booth climbed the stairs to the dress circle, saw the white door of Lincoln's State Box. A footman sat next to it. Booth gave him his card and opened the door into the dark area at the back of the box, wedging it shut with the leg of a music stand he had left there earlier. Then Booth opened the inner door, approached the president from behind and shot him in the head at close range.

Major Rathbone, who was sitting in the box, thought Booth shouted 'Freedom!' immediately after the shot. Rathbone grappled briefly with Booth, but was stabbed in the arm. Booth jumped over the front of the box and onto the stage. One of his spurs caught in one of the decorative flags draped over the balustrade, and he landed awkwardly, breaking his left leg just above the ankle. He managed to run across the stage, out of the theatre to his waiting horse and rode away. Lincoln died a few hours later.

Lincoln was a fair, direct and forthright man, highly principled and ethical, abstemious, charitable and sympathetic. How charitable and sympathetic he was can be seen from his generosity in victory. When the Civil War was over, he asked his cabinet to consider a proposal to award 400 million dollars to rebuild the South. It was a generous proposal, so generous that his cabinet forced him to set it aside. He was familiar with the precepts of the Bible, though not a member of any church; he was driven by a simple idea of what was right. He was a powerful and eloquent speaker, as can still be seen in the texts of his Emancipation Proclamation of 1863 and the Gettysburg Address of 1863. He ranks as one of the greatest of American presidents because he preserved the unity of North America by winning the Civil War and preventing the Confederate states from breaking away – and because he abolished slavery in the United States.

His assassination seems with hindsight to have been a kind of punishment by the South for winning the Civil War, but in the longer term and in the larger scheme of things his death made little difference. The North's victory in the Civil War was not overturned, and slavery was not reintroduced. The discrimination against black people in the South continued, and was to continue for 100 years. Lincoln made a stand against it and others who followed would do the same, notably Martin Luther King Jr, but overturning the mindset of an entire people was too much for one man to achieve in one lifetime. But the assassination did turn Lincoln into a sainted martyr and a national hero with a guaranteed place in the United States history-pageant view of itself – rather like St Joan in France's history-pageant.

THE INVENTION OF DYNAMITE

(1866)

FOR A VERY long time, gunpowder was the only explosive available for industrial blasting in mines and quarries. The problem with gunpowder was that both making and storing it were hazardous; it was also not all that easy to detonate.

In 1866, the 33 year old Swedish engineer Alfred Nobel perfected his invention of dynamite, an explosive that was a great improvement on gunpowder in terms of reliability. It was a very important step forward. Ascanio Sobrero discovered the power of nitroglycerine in 1847, and what Nobel did was to find a way of harnessing that power. Nobel, who studied mechanical engineering in the United States, mixed nitroglycerine with absorbent earth, wood meal or charcoal. Adding the nitroglycerine to an inert solid material reduced its sensitivity to shock, so that it was far less likely to explode by accident while being handled. This created a safe blasting powder which replaced black powder. Dynamite was a great invention, aiding the mining and quarrying industry enormously. It would also be harnessed for military use in due course. In the United States this became known as straight dynamite.

In time, the use of pure nitroglycerine was discontinued because it tended to freeze at fairly high temperatures and did not store well in cold climates. Instead, nitrated mixtures of glycerine or sugars were used. The standard dynamite used in American mines is 40 percent nitroglycerine, 44 percent sodium nitrate, 15 percent wood pulp and 1 percent calcium carbonate.

In 1875, Nobel made another discovery, blasting gelatine. He found that 7 percent of collodion nitrocellulose dissolved in nitroglycerine converts the nitroglycerine in a stiff jelly that could be detonated with a blasting cap.

This jelly was not widely used as it is very sensitive to ignition by flame.

Man-made explosives are dangerous, but the main danger in the mining industry has always been the explosion of natural gases. Many disastrous explosions in coal mines, for instance, have been caused by explosions of fire damp (methane mixed with air) and of coal dust. In the mining and quarrying industry, Nobel's dynamite was nothing but beneficial. It was just unfortunate that dynamite could equally well be used for munitions.

THE INVENTION OF ANTISEPTIC SURGERY

(1867)

AT THE BEGINNING of his career, the British surgeon Joseph Lister made some important observations on the coagulation of blood and inflammation. When he started work at Glasgow, he busied himself with articles on amputation and anaesthetics for a textbook on surgery. His ideas on inflammation took a new direction when his attention was drawn, in 1865, to the work of Louis Pasteur. What Pasteur was discovering, Lister could see, had enormous implications for medicine. Pasteur had shown that putrefaction, like other fermentations, was caused by airborne microbes. Lister saw straight away that if wounds were infected by microbes from the air there must be some way of cutting the seat of the wound off from the air and preventing the putrefaction from setting in.

Lister decided to experiment with chemical agents and his first experiment was to apply undiluted carbolic acid to a wound. The acid formed a crust, with the blood, and the result was a success. Lister wrote up his result in the medical journal *The Lancet* in 1867: *On a New Method of Treating Compound Fracture, Abscess, etc.* Carbolic acid was unsuitable in many situations, and Lister worked to find a better alternative. He first settled on carbolic acid and shellac spread on calico, afterwards painted with a solution of gutta percha in benzene. Later he experimented more successfully with impregnated dressings of absorbent gauze.

His next step was to try to develop a germ-free environment for surgery, to reduce the danger of infecting wounds still further. This involved creating a very clean environment for antiseptic surgery by ensuring that the air in the operating theatre was free of microbes, and this he achieved by ensuring that the room was kept scrupulously clean.

All over western Europe, medics immediately realized the importance of the modern antiseptic approach to surgery. It was an obvious breakthrough. It was one of the greatest innovations of the nineteenth century, and one for which Lister will be for ever remembered. This one change ensured that from then on far more people would survive surgery than before, and this in turn raised life expectancy.

THE PUBLICATION OF
KARL MARX'S
DAS KAPITAL
(1867)

IN LONDON, KARL Marx and his family lived in poverty Soho, but he continued to develop his political thought, spending time in the British Museum Reading Room, where he began the research that led to his major works of political and economic theory. The most notable of these was *Das Kapital*, the first volume of which was published in 1867. Two further volumes were added in 1884 and 1894.

Das Kapital became one of the most influential works of the nineteenth century. In it, Marx developed his doctrines of the theory of surplus value, class conflict, the exploitation of the working class; he also predicted that capitalism would be superseded by socialism and that the state would give way to a classless communist society. The new political and economic order would only be achieved through a class struggle, the working class fighting for its rightful supremacy. There was a strong element here of Darwin's theory of evolution through natural selection – the survival of the fittest. The timing of *Das Kapital* is interesting in this respect, its publication coming a few years after Darwin's *Origin of Species*. The communist's role was to act as a midwife to this process, which was to be regarded as an inevitable historical evolution. Marx said, 'Philosophers have previously tried to explain the world; our task is to change it.' There is also in *Das Kapital* something akin to *The Ring*, written by Marx's almost exact contemporary Richard Wagner; in fact *The Ring* has been very successfully staged as a Marxist tract.

After constructing his historic time-bomb, in the shape of *Das Kapital*, Marx was ready to become politically active again. He was a leading figure in the International Working Men's Association from 1864 until the anarchist followers of Bakunin, a friend of Wagner, split away in 1872. The dissolution of the International at least allowed Marx time for his theoretical work. The final decade of Marx's life was a time of increasing ill-health and work on the second and third volumes of *Das Kapital* was repeatedly interrupted by illness.

Many of the predictions Marx made turned out to be false prophecies, and the practice of 'Marxism' as a political system has turned out to be extremely unpleasant, far from classless, and far from just. The Marxist view of capitalist society is a generalized vision of a huge undifferentiated class of labourers dominated and exploited by a capitalist class. The reality of German, French or British society in the nineteenth century was far more complicated than that, as Marx must have known from first-hand knowledge. But in spite of these major – and all too obvious – defects, Marx's grandiose and almost novelistic ideas exerted a hypnotic grip on one society after another in the twentieth century, and provided the dynamo for one revolutionary upheaval after another. And he was uncannily right about the 1848 revolution in France being necessary to trigger revolution in Germany. The secular adherents of Marxism outnumber the followers of most other religious or political creeds, and it has often been said that what Marx created was more than a political creed; it was a new world religion.

THE INVENTION OF
THE TYPEWRITER
(1868)

IN 1868, A patent was issued to Christopher Sholes, Carlos Glidden and Samuel Soule for their invention of a typewriter, a machine that was to revolutionize office work and also do much to undermine handwriting as a craft. The inventors' backers, the businessmen James Densmore and George Washington Yost, encouraged Sholes to lay his keyboard out in such a way that the most commonly used keys were widely separated on the keyboard. This was for purely mechanical reasons, so that there was the least likelihood of the metal arms bearing the type letters jamming. Sholes came up with the QWERTYUIOP layout that has been used ever since, and is still used on computer keyboards, where there is no possibility of mechanical jamming.

Densmore and Yost bought the patent off the inventors and negotiated with Remington Fire Arms Company to produce the new machine. Philo Remington was so confident that the typewriter would sell well that he acquired sole rights to the Sholes typewriter. The Remington typewriter, as it came to be called, went into production in 1874. Unfortunately the retail price of each machine was 125 dollars, which was more than a month's rent for most firms, and so only eight machines were produced. The Remington typewriter, which at this stage still did not have a shift key for capital letters, was displayed at the Philadelphia Centennial Exposition. In 1878, Remington brought out an improved model with a shift key system, which offered upper-case and lower-case letters on the same type key.

In 1895, the New York ribbon and carbon merchant John Underwood set up his Underwood Typewriter Company to develop and market a machine that had been invented a couple of years earlier by Franz and Herman Wagner. This 'Underwood' typewriter was a major advance on the

Remington because it enabled the typist to see what had been typed. It was not long before others joined the race to supply typewriters. In 1905, L. C. Smith & Brothers sold its first typewriter to the *New York Times* for the paper's news room. Smith was to be the biggest producer of typewriters for many years to come.

The Royal Typewriter Company was also founded in 1905 by Thomas Ryan, to exploit the machine designed by the inventors Edward Hess and Lewis Meyers. A major innovation on the Royal typewriter was the friction-free ball-bearing one-track rail that supported the weight of the carriage and enabled it to move freely backwards and forwards. It also had a new paper feed, and offered complete visibility of the words as they were typed.

Perhaps predictably the typewriter was slower to catch on in Europe than in the United States. It was in 1911 that the Olivetti Company was founded at Ivrea near Milan in Italy. Camillo Olivetti designed and built the first Italian typewriter. It was a daring venture, as few Italian firms had been prepared to countenance the use of steel-nibbed pens, and they were unlikely to be impressed by something as new-fangled as a typewriter. But Olivetti hit lucky. By the end of the year, he had landed an order for 100 machines from the Italian navy; by 1933, his factory would be producing 24,000 machines a year, and selling to as many as 22 foreign countries.

Very soon every office in the Western world had at least one typewriter. Many people had them in their own homes.

In 1933, a new era in typewriters began, when IBM entered the typewriter business, acquiring a firm that had been trying for ten years to perfect an electric office typewriter. The IBM Selectric typewriter designed by Eliot Noyes was introduced in 1961. This machine worked on a very different principle, a moving 'golf ball' cluster of type. Three years later this was linked to a magnetic tape recorder that permitted automated letters to be typed but with individual addresses. This led to an age of irritating, pseudo-personalized junk mail; not every innovation increases the sum of human happiness. By 1975, the IBM Selectric accounted for 75 percent of the electric typewriter market, though there were alternative models available, many of which were simply the old-style typewriters but with power-assisted keys; the keys had only to be touched – they did not have to be pressed any more. This made the work of professional typists much easier. From there it was a short step to the personal computer – and this operates, like the one in front of me now, from something that looks remarkably like the Sholes typewriter keyboard of 1868.

THE FIRST
REFRIGERATED
RAILCAR
(1868)

WILLIAM DAVIS FROM Detroit invented a refrigerated railcar in 1868. This had along its sides metal tanks which were filled from the top with crushed ice. The cooled car was then able to transport fish, fresh meat and fruit to distant destinations without any loss in quality. Davis took out his patent on this highly significant invention, but gained no financial benefit from it; he died in the same year. In 1869, Boston received its first shipment of fresh meat from Chicago by way of a refrigerated railcar. The new technique was resisted by the railroad companies, as they knew that transporting refrigerated meat would mean the loss of the lucrative transport of live animals to the east coast. The quality of the refrigerated meat was noticeably better, though, and it was clearly more humane to slaughter the livestock on the Prairies rather than transporting them very long distances; refrigeration quickly caught on.

At the same time in England a device was invented for keeping milk cool on trains. The milk was transported to cities such as London and Manchester in cold metal containers, and it was much safer than milk from cows kept in town sheds – the current alternative source of fresh milk. Earlier in the 1860s, the Dutch cows that had traditionally been kept in urban milk sheds (because they were considered the sturdiest) had turned out to be the most susceptible to disease. This had pushed British dairymen towards the greater use of milk trains; these took milk early in the morning, straight after the morning milking in the rural areas, into the towns for consumption there the same day.

By 1876, 16 brands of beer made by Anheuser and Co., including Budweiser beer, were being transported by refrigerated railcar.

As Western households, and especially American households, became wealthier, more and more of them had domestic refrigerators. In 1920, 10,000 refrigerators were sold; by 1925, that figure had risen to 75,000.

In 1937, the first frozen foods started arriving in British shops. Wisbech Produce Canners Ltd introduced frozen asparagus, peas and sliced green beans. S. W. Smedley of Wisbech had designed and built his own freezing process after studying the vegetable freezing process developed by Clarence Birdseye in the United States. But Smedley was a little ahead of his time, as in the run-up to the Second World War there were still only 3,000 British households with domestic refrigerators, compared with over two million in the United States. Now, of course, we all take refrigeration as a way of keeping food fresh entirely for granted; we all have refrigerators, we all have freezers – at least in the West.

THE COMPLETION OF
THE SUEZ CANAL
(1869)

IN 1869, THE transcontinental rail link was completed across the United States, the Union Pacific and Central Pacific Railroads joining up in Utah, and shortening the time it took to cross North America. In the same year, the Suez Canal was completed, connecting the Mediterranean and the Red Sea, and in effect making a short cut for ships sailing from Europe to the Indian Ocean, avoiding the long detour round Africa. The world became significantly smaller in 1869.

The Suez Canal, which was designed by the French engineer Ferdinand de Lesseps, was opened on 17 November 1869. It was 165km long, over 60m wide at its narrowest point and about 12m deep so that even the largest ships could pass through it. It crossed from the Mediterranean just east of the Nile Delta to the head of the Red Sea – at sea level and with desert on both sides. The effect of this major piece of engineering was to bring the ports of the Far East 8,000km closer to Europe.

In 1875, the Suez Canal came under British control, largely through the efforts of Prime Minister Disraeli, who obtained a loan from the merchant banking house of Rothschild to buy up over 176,000 shares in the Universal Suez Company from the Egyptian Khedive Ismail. Ismail was deeply in debt and Disraeli was able to exploit his desperate need for money. Disraeli's purchase of the canal was a brilliant political coup as far as the British were concerned, but it created consternation internationally and was to lay up major political problems for the future, when the colonial period was petering out. As it turned out the intention of the British was not to claim exclusive use of the Suez Canal, nor to make huge profits by levying dues on ships passing through; it was more to do with prestige, with painting the map red.

In 1888, a Suez Canal Convention was signed in Constantinople, declaring the canal to be free and open to merchant ships and warships alike in times of both war and peace. The canal was not to be blockaded, but the khedive had the right to take such measures as he thought were necessary to secure the defence of Egypt.

In April 1954, Colonel Nasser took over from General Naguib as Egypt's premier. The age of colonialism was over. Egypt had been colonized over and over again, ever since the time of Julius Caesar, and the Egyptians were determined to be free of foreign interference. Nationalism was in the air. A treaty signed in October agreed that British troops would be withdrawn within two years. In 1956, Nasser seized the Canal for Egypt on 26 July under a decree outlawing the Suez Canal Company. Britons in the Canal Zone were airlifted out in October. In November, the British Prime Minister Anthony Eden misguidedly ordered British troops in, to attempt to recover control of the Canal. They failed, but agreed to withdraw only when a UN force arrived, which it did on 15 November. In December, the UN fleet began the task of clearing the Suez Canal, which had been blocked with many scuttled ships by Nasser. The British ownership of the Suez Canal had ended up being an acute embarrassment; the Egyptians in the 1950s saw it as an affront to their nationhood to have this strip of 'British' territory running across one corner of their country. It was a matter of national pride. Gibraltar remains a similar problem.

The irony is that around the time when the Suez Canal was reopened for normal traffic, ship-owners were commissioning larger tankers to take oil round the Cape. The new age of the supertanker virtually rendered the canal obsolete.

THE PROCLAMATION OF A UNITED GERMAN EMPIRE
(1871)

ON 18 JANUARY 1871, a united German Empire was proclaimed in, of all places, the Hall of Mirrors at Versailles. This declaration inaugurated what became known as the Second Reich. The First Reich began in 955 and was brought to an end by Napoleon in 1806. It was a matter of German national pride to re-create the old empire. Prussia's Kaiser Wilhelm I became the new emperor and the first chancellor was Count von Bismarck, who had engineered the unification of four German kingdoms, Prussia, Bavaria, Saxony and Württemberg, thirteen duchies and five grand duchies.

This symbolic act came at the climax of the Franco-Prussian War. Paris surrendered to German troops in January 1871, Napoleon III was deposed in March and a peace treaty between France and Germany was signed in May. Germany had not only beaten but humiliated France, and at the climax of this adventure the unification of Germany had been declared, along with the aggrandisement of the Prussian king. The power and ambition of Germany were being declared in no uncertain terms; the Kaiser and Bismarck might as well have announced, like prize-fighters at a nineteenth century fair that they would take on all-comers – if necessary the whole of Europe.

It was a taste of things to come. The new, strong, boastful, arrogant Germany would swagger into the twentieth century under a new, unstable Kaiser who would lead Europe in the First World War.

THE CREATION OF THE FIRST NATIONAL PARK
(1872)

THE YELLOWSTONE NATIONAL Park was created in March 1872 by an Act of the US Congress. It set aside 5 million acres of wilderness on the fast-developing frontier in Wyoming. The explorer Nathaniel Langford was made the first national park's first superintendent. This was the world's first national park. The experiment was so successful that others were created in quick succession, not only in North America but across the border in Canada too.

Canada's national parks system had its beginnings in a much smaller reserve, just 26 km² set aside in the Canadian Rockies in 1885. It was an area where surveyors for the Canadian Pacific Railway discovered hot springs in 1883. A lake in the area was named Lake Louise in honour of one of Queen Victoria's daughters, whose husband had been Canada's governor-general until just two years before. This area in time became the Banff National Park. Over subsequent years other areas were similarly set aside for conservation: Waterton Lakes, Kootenay, Baner, Jasper, Yoho, Columbia Icefield, Glacier and Mount Revelstoke National Parks.

The guiding principle in the United States has been to preserve wilderness areas, spectacular landforms and also areas of historic or even prehistoric interest, especially those regarded as helping to shape the national destiny. An example of a spectacular landform is the Natural Bridges Park in Utah, a cluster of three natural bridges carved out of sandstone, the highest soaring over 60m above a streambed. One of the prehistoric national parks is Navajo Park in Arizona, which contains three of the largest and most intricate Indian cliff dwellings. Probably the best-known historic site is the Statue of Liberty. The areas are also meant to be enjoyed by visitors, though, and those visitors have to be accommodated appropriately in visitors' centres with car parking and picnic areas. There is frequently a clash of interests between recreation and conservation.

European countries followed North America's example, with England and Wales (though not Scotland) naming areas such as the Lake District, Peak District, North York Moors, Snowdonia, Pembrokeshire Coast and Dartmoor. In Africa, the national parks are mostly large game parks, such as the Serengeti, which are open for visitor safaris. Some are closed to visitors, as conservation is the only consideration such as the Djoudj and Niokolo Koba Parks in the Gambia. National parks vary enormously in size and purpose. The Abuko Reserve in the Gambia is a beautifully conserved piece of rain forest, complete with crocodiles, monkeys, lizards and snakes; this beautiful miniature national park it is open to visitors to walk round.

The creation of the Yellowstone National Park started a global trend towards conservation. As more countries become aware of the need to conserve a threatened environment, more parks have been created, and it is interesting to note that even a small and very poor country like the Gambia has as many as seven. As these protected areas are extended and multiplied, there is hope for endangered landscapes, and endangered species. Even the poorer countries of the world have begun to create parks, seeing the commercial advantage of parks for tourism; national parks are not just areas that cannot be developed – they have the ability to be commercially valuable commodities in themselves, major assets in an increasingly lucrative tourist industry.

THE CREATION OF DDT
(1873)

THE FULL NAME of DDT is dichloridiphenyl-trichlorethane, which for most of us is instantly forgettable; everyone uses the short form. DDT was for a time hailed as the wonder chemical that was going to solve the world's problems. It was prepared for the first time in 1873 by Othmar Zeidler. Zeidler was a German chemistry student at Strasbourg. He created the new chemical by reacting chloral hydrate and chlorobenzene in the presence of sulphuric acid. Chloral hydrate was the notorious 'Mickey Finn', the knock-out drops used by the underworld. Zeidler described his experiment to produce the chemical with the impossible name in a chemistry journal the following year, but he had no idea what his newly discovered (or invented) substance might do.

It was not for a long time that any use was found for Zeidler's DDT. In 1939, it was introduced in Switzerland and applied almost immediately with great success against the Colorado beetle, a major pest infesting the potato crops. The Swiss chemist Paul Muller of the chemical firm Geigy developed DDT as a low-cost hydrocarbon pesticide. In 1943, DDT was introduced into North America to fight insect pests that destroy crops. In the post-war era, DDT was seen as the answer to many of the problems of food production in the poorer countries of the world. Spraying with DDT would rid crops and soils of all pests and crop yields would rise; there would be no food shortages, no poverty.

By the 1970s, there was a reaction to this view. DDT seemed to be a very persistent chemical. Once sprayed onto the landscape it tended to stay there. Some scientists started to portray it as a dangerous chemical pollutant, a chemical that could do harm rather than good. The use of DDT practically ceased. Now there is new generation of scientists who say that maybe DDT was a useful chemical after all.

The DDT issue represents an ongoing dilemma – we need to manage the land in order to make it produce the amount of food we want, but is there an optimal yield beyond which we should not try to push the land? Have we been too greedy? The problem is usually that natural ecosystems have been interfered with and unbalanced without anyone really knowing what the end of the chain reaction will be. On the whole it seems unwise to interfere with natural processes and alter them unless we know what the result will be.

THE INVENTION OF THE TELEPHONE
(1876)

SCOTTISH BY BIRTH, American by choice, Alexander Graham Bell opened a training school in Boston for teachers of the deaf and also gave lectures on the mechanics of speech. He became Professor of Vocal Physiology at Boston in 1873, devoting himself to the teaching of deaf mutes and promoting his father's system of 'visible speech'. In this system, Bell's father devised an alphabet system of his own in which the alphabet 'letters' were graphic diagrams of the positions of the organs of speech needed to make the sounds. The elder Mr Bell was a respected authority on physiological phonetics.

Bell experimented with various acoustical devices, finally building a primitive telephone. He sent the first successful telephone transmission on 5 June 1875. He patented this major invention in March the following year. He had to defend his patent against Elisha Gray, and formed the Bell Telephone Company in 1877. Bell's telephone consisted of two identical microphones and receivers, each made of a solenoid mounted next to a metal membrane. Vibration set up in the transmitting membrane induced a current in the solenoid that travelled down the wire, causing the membrane in the receiver to vibrate in the same way. It was on 10 March 1877 that Alexander Graham Bell gave his historic demonstration of the newly invented telephone. The first phone call was to his assistant: 'Mr Watson, come here. I want you.' Just a few weeks later, on 3 April, Bell made his first long-distance telephone call, from New York to Boston, again to his assistant, Thomas Watson.

The same year, the Bell Telephone Company was formed, by Bell in conjunction with Gardiner Hubbard, with Bell holding a 30 percent interest in the patent and his assistant Thomas Watson a 10 percent interest; 30 percent went to Thomas Sanders, who had provided Bell with the 100,000 dollars' worth of backing he needed to carry out his experiments. The first telephone switchboard was installed in May 1877 at the Boston office of Edwin Holmes, the proprietor of Holmes Burglar Alarm Service.

In 1880, Bell set up the Volta Laboratory, invented the photophone, which was an instrument for transmitting sound by vibrations in a beam of light.

In 1879, Leroy Firman invented the multiple switchboard. This was to make the telephone a commercial success. It enabled the number of callers to be increased, and the number of American subscribers went up from 50,000 in 1880 to 25,000 in 1890. Businessmen in New York found the new telephone invaluable for making deals. At this stage the telephone service was available from eight o'clock in the morning until six o'clock in the evening. The business users, led by the Fulton Fish Market, pressed the Bell Telephone Company to open at 5 am and keep the service going until later in the evening.

Bell's telephone was one of the inventions that transformed the twentieth century. It made communications and decision-making quicker and easier, and was, along with the motor car, responsible for a major acceleration in the pace of life. It has also been possible for politicians, even heads of state, to discuss matters with one another, from country to country, even from continent to continent. Whether that has done anything to improve international relations is an open question.

The telephone has also been the medium for the fax machine, for electronic mail and for the Internet. It was a remarkable invention, that has spawned further inventions and found one new application after another.

THE OPENING OF THE FIRST BIRTH CONTROL CLINIC
(1878)

IN 1878, THE first birth control clinic in the world was opened in Holland. Aletta Jacobs, a 29 year old campaigner for the emancipation of women, became the first woman doctor to practice in Holland, and it was she who opened the clinic. This was a landmark event. In the years running up to this event, there had been court cases in Britain in which people had been charged with disseminating information about birth control. Now, suddenly, here was a birth control clinic at which such information was freely available. It was the turning point. From then on, average family size in the richer countries began to fall. It had been relatively common in the mid-nineteenth century for families to consist of ten or more children. This was partly because of a high infant mortality rate – people had more children because they expected some of them to die – but also partly because of ignorance or taboos regarding contraception.

In 1914, the American feminist Margaret Higgins Sanger published her book *The Woman Rebel*, in which she used the phrase 'birth control' for the first time. Margaret Sanger was threatened with federal prosecution for publishing and circulating a leaflet on contraception called *Family Limitation*. To avoid arrest she left the United States for England.

Marie Stopes, who was based in England, was another campaigner for women's emancipation. She started her own crusade to spread information about contraception. Her 1916 book, *Married Love*, caused a sensation and brought her widespread disapproval. The book was banned in the United States. In 1918, she married the aircraft manufacturer Humphrey Roe, with whose help she opened the very first birth control clinic in Britain, in North London. In all, Marie Stopes wrote 70 books on themes related to birth control, parenting and sexual matters generally.

Marie Stopes's crusade paved the way for more birth control clinics, which are now a routine facility in every town and city. She also established a healthier climate in which sexual issues could be discussed openly and freely, and sexual problems could be resolved.

Side by side with these early attempts to spread information, there were technical advances in contraceptives. In the United States, the manufacture of condoms was pioneered by a disabled 18 year old German-American called Julius Schmid. He had been making caps for perfume bottles out of lambs' intestines, and switched to using the same raw material for making condoms. In 1920, Youngs Rubber Company was founded by the American entrepreneur Merle Youngs to make Trojan condoms; these became strong competitors to Julius Schmid's brands, Shiek and Ramses. Trojan condoms were to become the biggest-selling brand of condom in the United States, available in most drugstores. And that availability was an important factor in the use of contraceptives. Nowadays it is routine for contraceptives to be not only available but visible on the chemists' counters, and even available from slot-machines in pubs. It has become very easy to get hold of contraceptives.

It was a combination of information, education, technology and availability that led to the steady increase of contraception in Western countries during the twentieth century. This increase in use in turn led to steadily falling birth rates and also to a stabilization in population totals; it was also associated with steadily improving standards of living. As the birth rate fell, so the growth rate in the population as a whole fell. The same programme of education and availability has gone on in the poorer countries, but with a time-lag of several decades, but zero growth rate has now been achieved in some regions of the Third World, such as the state of Kerala in southern India.

THE DESTRUCTION OF
THE ZULU NATION
(1879)

THE ZULU ARE a tribe of the Nguni group of the Bantu people. It is not certain when the Bantu entered southern Africa. The white South African version of events, as taught in South African schools in the old apartheid days, had it that they arrived there *after* the Dutch colonists; this of course was argued in order to improve the Afrikaans claim on the territory. If the Bantu arrived later, they had less right to be there. However, it seems that the Zulu were in southern Africa before the end of the seventeenth century. Shipwrecked Europeans landing on the Natal coast in 1756 saw them, describing them as very proud, careful in the preparation of their food, very clean in their personal hygiene and very protective of their women.

In 1800, the Zulu still had no special prominence, and there seem to have been only about 2,000 of them. One of their chiefs was Dingiswayo. He began to convert the horned crescent formation used for hunting into a military formation, and to set up a military organization consisting of regiments (called impis). Then Shaka came to Dingiswayo's kraal (settlement enclosure), as a refugee from another kraal. Dingiswayo was impressed with Shaka, who invented the short stabbing spear, the assegai, and named him as the heir to the Zulu throne.

Shaka set about creating a proper royal kraal, impounding a herd of white cattle, importing cooks and expert brewers. He used scouts and spies to increase his control over the Zulus. In 1821, Shaka began the systematic conquest of the Natal, inflating his army as he extended his territory. This was how he created a Zulu nation.

Shaka has been described as Africa's Attila, yet he was succeeded by a king who was even more cruel and bloodthirsty, Dingaan. When the British

385

took Natal from the Boers, a new Zulu king was in power, Cetshwayo, who was described as able, cold, selfish, proud, cruel and untruthful.

The Zulu nation, which was founded by Shaka in 1816, was brought to an end by the British in 1879. Lord Chelmsford invaded with a force of 5,000 British soldiers and 8,000 natives; he was attempting to conquer a Zulu army of over 40,000. He divided his army into three columns, which were to converge on Ulundi, the royal kraal.

British soldiers using breech-loading rifles killed 8,000 Zulu warriors and wounded 16,000 more. The British suffered about 1,000 losses in action, 230 wounded and around 1,400 were invalided home as a result of disease. The British also killed about 900 Xhosa people from Natal. The British troops were commanded by General Thesiger (Lord Chelmsford) and the Zulus were led by Cetshwayo.

On 22 January 1879, the central column had camped without any particular thought for defence at Isandhlwana. It was attacked by 10,000 Zulus, overwhelmed and almost every man was killed. A party that had been sent out to reconnoitre returned to find the camp completely deserted, so they retreated to Rorke's Drift. There was a small garrison of 80 able-bodied men; 40 more were in the hospital and therefore non-combatant. The garrison was led by Lieutenants Chard and Bromhead.

The Zulu War finally ended after a remarkable stand by the British at Rorke's Drift, where 140 British soldiers managed to hold off 4,000 Zulu warriors. It emerged much later that the Zulus could have made a final attack and wiped out the surviving British defenders but that a Zulu superstition compelled them to return home; they had been away from their wives too long. In Britain, the action at Rorke's Drift was seen as an heroic victory for white over black and 11 Victoria Crosses were awarded, which was (and still is) a record for any single action.

The other two columns remained intact, and they converged as planned on Ulundi. One incident caused international ripples. Prince Louis, the 23 year old French Prince Imperial, was killed on 2 June by a Zulu spear. English-hating French people claimed that the heir to the French throne – he would or might have become Napoleon IV – was killed with Queen Victoria's connivance. That seems very unlikely. Lord Chelmsford won a brilliant victory at Ulundi, just three days before Sir Garnet Wolsey arrived to replace him. The capture of Ulundi broke the military organization of the Zulus, and the king became a fugitive.

On 20 August Zulu King Cetswayo was captured by the British, made to wear ill-fitting European clothes and exiled to Cape Town. Zululand was divided into 13 separate kingdoms, and the territory was eventually to be absorbed by the province of Natal.

This 'hammering' of a native kingdom was typical of the behaviour of the European colonial powers in the Third World. There was large-scale destruction of human life, of native economies and of indigenous cultures. The destruction of the Zulu nation was an act of the same kind as the Trail of Tears in North America.

THE INVENTION OF THE INCANDESCENT LIGHT BULB

(1879)

IN OCTOBER 1879, after a great struggle involving 40,000 dollars' worth of mostly failed experiments, Thomas Edison invented the incandescent electric light bulb. This consisted of a loop of carbonized cotton thread glowing in a vacuum inside a glass bulb for over 40 hours. Edison spent much of the next ten years of his life refining and improving the light bulb and devising a system of generating and distributing electric lighting. He experimented with a three-wire system, an underground mains system, dynamos and motors.

The invention of the electric light bulb relieved the West of its dependence on whale oil and then on paraffin (or kerosene) from mineral oil for lighting. If lighting was powered by electricity, then that in turn could be generated in a number of ways, by power stations powered by coal, oil, gas, peat or water. Electric lighting made evening or night work possible, which has had some negative effects on people's working conditions. In the days when there was only candlelight after sunset, most office and industrial work had to cease; the sun in effect guaranteed workers some time off. Once high-quality artificial lighting was available, first gas, then electric, employers were able to lengthen the working day to suit themselves – and they did. Thanks to electric lighting there are now all-night petrol stations and all-night supermarkets, which is not so good for those who have to man them.

In 1891, Edison patented what was in effect a movie camera, which he called a 'kinetoscopic camera'. This took moving pictures on a band of film; these were then viewed on a peepshow, then later projected onto a screen.

Edison thus pioneered cinema. The projection onto a screen required the steady strong light of his incandescent light bulb, so this development depended on the light bulb. Edison invented the first talking motion pictures, and therefore created the great new art form of the twentieth century. The moving picture camera also made it possible to film historic events such as the Battle of Jutland. For the first time it was possible for people to see them, rather than just reading about them in newspapers, and this made warfare more immediate - and more repellent. The invention of the electric light bulb transformed twentieth century life by making cinema possible.

THE COMPLETION OF COLOGNE CATHEDRAL
(1880)

IN 1880, COLOGNE Cathedral was finally finished after 634 years of construction. It was the biggest medieval cathedral to be built in northern Europe. Located 20m above the Rhine near the Hohenzollern Bridge in the oldest part of Cologne, the 'new' cathedral had twin spires that soared 160m into the air, making it the tallest building in the world. Unfortunately, this was the beginning of the age of the skyscraper, and the cathedral was only to hold its record-breaking position for nine short years.

Cologne Cathedral is like Regensburg Cathedral in having a facade dominated by twin towers. The surrounding landscape is very subdued, so the two towers are a distinctive landmark for many miles in all directions.

Cologne had probably the longest building history of any great medieval cathedral. It stands on the site of a church that was begun in the ninth century by Hildebold and finished under Willibert. The structure was ruined by the Normans, then rebuilt, then destroyed by fire in 1258. The present cathedral was begun in 1248 by Archbishop Conrad to a plan designed by Gerhard von Rile. It was the eastern arm, the choir, that was built first, as almost a replica of the equivalent part of Amiens Cathedral. When Conrad died, the impetus went out of the building work, and from then on the cathedral was only advanced very slowly.

Both the interior and exterior are very imposing in scale and detail. It is like St Peter's in Rome, huge in scale and also rich in detail, though very different in style. The transepts are impressive structures in their own right, with lavish detail piled over their triple doors. At the eastern end there is an ambulatory with seven semicircular chapels opening radially from it.

Of what we see today, only the choir is medieval in construction. The western half, the nave and the west front, was completed in the nineteenth century, to the original design. Close up it is easy to see the difference, though, as the modern stonework has a more mechanical finish. The west front with its vast crocketed steeples is harder in treatment. It is 142m long and 83m wide. The nave is 46m high. The overall design is French in inspiration, yet less elegant than French cathedrals. It is considered to be the finest example of decorated Gothic in the whole of Germany.

This late completion of Cologne Cathedral marks the very end of a long tradition of Gothic architecture. In the art world at the same time, there was a brief renaissance of the medieval in the Pre-Raphaelite school in England, but it was a last gasp. In the world of painting and architecture, new cultural and social forces were at work that would sweep all that away, as Sir Edward Burne-Jones, himself one of the leading Pre-Raphaelite painters, observed at the time. Frank Lloyd Wright and Picasso were waiting just round the corner.

THE DISCOVERY OF
THE TB BACILLUS
(1882)

IN 1882, ROBERT Koch discovered the tuberculosis bacillus. He established for the first time that the disease was communicable: one person could catch it from another. His findings along with those of other bacteriologists confirmed that certain diseases such as beriberi and TB were caused by bacteria rather than by dietary deficiencies. Several decades later, the psychologist Carl Jung was still proposing that tuberculosis was a psychological condition, not a disease, but he was entirely wrong; he was himself suffering from a nineteenth century delusion.

Tuberculosis was one of the great killer diseases in eighteenth and nineteenth century Europe. Huge numbers of people died of it. The Bronte sisters died of it. The poet John Keats and his brother died of it. Perhaps the most surprising thing about the disease is that, even though it passed through entire families, nobody seems to have realized that it was infectious. John Keats started displaying the symptoms of the disease after nursing his dying brother Tom, and the Bronte sisters died one after the other, living at close quarters in their father's small rectory at Haworth. It seems to be a case of fixed mental attitudes, as with smoking. Even though there is now a huge body of medical evidence to show that smoking is extremely harmful, large numbers of people continue smoking, believing that they are safe.

The new knowledge that people could catch tuberculosis from one another led to the establishment of isolation hospitals called sanatoria for those with TB. Many of these were built in Alpine resorts such as Davos in Switzeralnd, in the belief that the clean pure mountain air was good for patients – though it probably made no difference whatever.

In 1900, the average life expectancy in North America was still as low as 47, partly because of the number of deaths from TB. Far more people were dying of TB than of influenza, pneumonia or heart disease. But the new knowledge, that TB could be caught from family members, was being applied and the death rate dropped. By 1920, in fact, the death rate from TB had halved in North America. Living conditions played a part, and as living conditions improved through the twentieth century, the incidence of the disease fell. As people lived in roomier, better built houses that were warm and dry, and as people ate healthier diets, their resistance to diseases such as TB increased.

The introduction of the drug streptomycin made a decisive improvement. It then became possible to cure people suffering from TB with a course of injections; it took many months, but they were cured. By 1970, it looked as if TB was really consigned to history as far as the richer countries of the West were concerned, but shifts in the patterns of migration have changed things. Migrants from poor countries often carry TB with them. Refugees from the Yugoslavian conflict, from eastern Europe generally and from other trouble spots elsewhere in the world have arrived in Britain, bringing with them the increasing risk of spreading TB. So, from a low point around 1970, TB has begun to increase again in Britain.

THE INVENTION OF
SYNTHETIC FIBRE
(1883)

AN ARTIFICIAL SILK was developed in 1883 by the French chemist Hilaire Bernigaud, who was also the Comte de Chardonnet. The artificial silk, or rayon, was made from nitrocellulose. In 1892, two English chemist Charles Cross and Edward Bevan patented a new method for making viscose rayon which was safer than the Chardonnet technique of 1883. The Cross and Bevan method was to dissolve cellulose in a mixture of carbon disulphide and sodium xanthate. They then squirted the viscous solution through tiny holes to produce fibres that could be spun and woven.

Rayon was patented by the American chemist Arthur Little in 1902, who used a different process again to make the artificial fibre. Commercial production of rayon began in England in July 1905, at a factory on the outskirts of Coventry run by the 29 year old Samuel Courtauld. Courtauld had bought the English rights to the rayon patent for £25,000. French and German companies also bought rayon production rights and they started production in competition with Courtauld. By 1910, Courtauld was founding American Viscose Company in Pennsylvania. The following year, his American branch started production, making rayon from spruce wood pulp, and it was the first successful American rayon producer; it would dominate US rayon production for many years.

Work on improving artificial fibres went on behind the scenes until 1935, when nylon was developed. Wallace Carrothers produced a synthetic polymide which he called 'Polymer 66'. Its potential was quickly seen; it appeared to be superior in many ways to other fibres, and for many uses it came to replace silk, rayon and jute. Drawing the filaments out to a certain length aligned the polymer chains and pulled them out to their full extent; this made the filaments strong, resilient and hard-wearing, whilst also giving them many of the characteristics of silk and wool. The new fibre was quickly used to make stockings. Nylon stockings were found to be harder-wearing than silk stockings, yet looked very similar; they were very popular.

Shortly after nylon came fibreglass, another artificial fibre; this could be spun into yarn and woven into fabric or used as insulating material. It found a special used in strong lightweight mouldings, and was to find a widespread use in making hulls for small boats.

The textile and clothing industry was revolutionized by the introduction of artificial fibres. Clothes made of them were popular with busy working people because they were drip-dry and non-iron. The vogue for nylon shirts, socks and blouses wore off when people realized some of the negative properties of synthetics; they often failed to 'breathe' in the way that natural fibres did. This gave way to a further development, which was the careful blending of artificial fibres such as polyester with natural fibres such as cotton and wool, in order to get the best properties of both.

THE ERUPTION OF KRAKATOA

(1883)

THE ISLAND OF Krakatoa lay on the equator in the Sunda Strait between Java and Sumatra. Where the original island had stood, there was now deep water surrounded by a broken ring of smaller islands marking the outer flanks of the original volcanic mountain. Krakatoa had destroyed itself once before. At the centre of the little group of islands was an island with a large volcano rising to 800m; it had built up from the floor of the ancient caldera. It erupted in 1680; earthquakes were reported from the area and lots of pumice was ejected, but the evidence of this significant activity was quickly covered over by dense vegetation.

From 1877 onwards, there was a long series of minor earthquakes. This started to escalate in early 1883, and in May there were eruptions of ash and pumice. Then Krakatoa erupted very violently in a series of explosions on 26–28 August 1883. The most violent of these were the four on the morning of 27 August. It was the greatest volcanic eruption since the bronze age eruption of Santorini. The Santorini eruption was five times more violent than the Krakatoa eruption, but even so the Krakatoa explosion was heard nearly 4,800km away four hours later at Rodriguez. It was heard in Bangkok, the Philippines, Sri Lanka and Western and South Australia. There is no other event that is known to have been heard over such a large area, though it can be assumed that the Santorini eruption was heard at least as far away.

An atmospheric shock wave, called an oscillation, rippled outwards from Krakatoa, travelling to the point on the opposite side of the world from Krakatoa. There it was reflected back again to its point of origin, Krakatoa, where it 'bounced' back again, and so on. The shock wave was observed at some places to pass no less than seven times.

Huge amounts of ash were ejected. At Batavia, 160km away, the sky was darkened by the ash. Lamps had to be lit at midday, because it was so dark. The darkness reached as far as Bandung, which was 240km away. Krakatoa threw up a tall column of ash that went right up into the stratosphere, 55km up, where it was picked up by the fast-moving east-west jet stream known, from this point on, as the Krakatoa Easterlies. The dust travelled westwards at over 110km per hour. It soon encircled the Earth along the equator and was gradually spread polewards by other high level winds. The dust affected the entire inhabited world, and it was observed from the North Cape in Scandinavia to Cape Town in South Africa. The pattern was the same as with Tambora earlier in the century. Some of the dust started raining down ten days later up to 4,800km away, but much of it remained in the upper atmosphere for a couple of years. The dust in the atmosphere had the effect of reddening the sunrise and sunset for a year afterwards – as far away as England. Artists noticed it and made a point of painting the unusual phenomenon.

There was a marked cooling of the Earth, which showed up in temperature readings at many weather stations. The temperatures for 1885–95 were noticeably lower, though it is difficult to be sure whether this was due to the eruption or to the coincidental lack of sunspots during that period.

The violent eruption emptied the lava chamber under the island. It was a huge hollow vault. Unsupported, its roof collapsed. Cold sea water rushed repeatedly into the hot chamber, turned instantly to steam and causing the four violent explosive blasts. Because these blasts were on the seabed, huge tsunamis were generated, rippling out from the hole where Krakatoa had stood. The coastal villages on neighbouring islands were engulfed by the tsunamis. 163 villages were wiped out, drowning more than 36,000 people. Floating pumice was carried hundreds of kilometres away. The tsunami is known to have reached Cape Horn and was detected even in the English Channel.

After the eruption and the area could be revisited, it was clear what had happened. The whole of Krakatoa that had been built within the original crater ring had been blown out. The original caldera had been re-created. Where the volcanic peak had stood, the sea was now over 300m deep. The surrounding islands and their forests had been buried by ash and rock thrown out from the centre.

After the big eruption of 1883, Krakatoa was quiet, but from 1927 the area became volcanically active again for a few years and a new cone has built up in the middle of the caldera, Anak Krakatoa (Child of Krakatoa).

The eruption of Krakatoa was a major event in the history of the Earth. It changed the shape of the Earth's surface radically. It killed an enormous number of people. More than that, it demonstrated that there is a cyclicity to many such events. Krakatoa had erupted in much the same way in remote antiquity. And one day it will do it again. These are things we need to know about the planet on which we live.

THE INVENTION OF GASLIGHT USING MANTLES
(1885)

IN 1885, GASLIGHT was given a significant new lease of life. For several decades before that date, piped gas had been used to illuminate factories and even some private houses, but this lighting was in the form of flares, burning rather like the white flame from a Bunsen burner. A disadvantage with this light was its inconstancy; it wavered and flickered and was therefore not much better to read by than candlelight. But in 1885, an major improvement was made. The 27 year old Carl von Welsbach devised and patented a gas mantle. This was a bag of woven cotton mesh impregnated with thorium and cerium oxides that was fitted over the gas flame. The effect was to make a steady white incandescent glow, which was much better for reading or any kind of work.

Interestingly, this improvement came along close to the moment when Edison invented the incandescent electric bulb. The electric bulb might have superseded gas lighting very quickly, but for the invention of the gas mantle, which extended the era of gas lighting by many decades.

IDENTIFICATION BY FINGERPRINTS
(1885)

IN 1885, THE 63 year old British scientist Francis Galton invented a system for identifying people from their fingerprints. Galton had earlier founded the 'science' of eugenics with a book called *Hereditary Genius*. With this new idea, however, he had come up with something really useful – that no two people have the same fingerprints.

Galton's idea was not new. The knowledge that everyone has different fingerprints was available in antiquity; the impression of an eastern monarch's thumb was his signature. The permanent character of the fingerprint was first put forward scientifically by J. E. Purkinje, a professor of physiology, who read a paper about it in Breslau in 1823. He identified nine basic patterns and suggested a system of classification. Nobody took any notice of Professor Purkinje.

Francis Galton worked on the very specific idea that a person's fingerprints might be used to trace his or her criminal activities. From there it was a short step to the idea of taking the fingerprints of people suspected of committing crimes, by inking their fingertips and dabbing them on a piece of paper, and then comparing them with the fingerprints found at the scene of a crime. It was found that a light dusting of white powder could make fingerprints visible on a great variety of smooth surfaces, from glass window panes to metal door handles and polished wooden furniture.

To be sure of the match, Galton recommended taking the prints of all ten fingers. They could be arranged on an identification card in a set order, left hand on the left, right on the right. It was the Bengal police who adopted the system first, under the administration of E. R. Henry, who afterwards became Chief Commissioner of the Metropolitan Police.

One advantage of fingerprints was that they did not change during life.

Once the police had someone's fingerprints they could be used at any time after that for identification. The patterns lend themselves to easy classification, into arches, loops, whorls and composites. Each of these types has subclasses.

The idea quickly caught on and became the standard means of identifying the presence of people at crime scenes for much of the twentieth century. The identification division of the American FBI was set up in 1924, and at that time the several previously separate collections of fingerprints were put together to make a single database. By 1952, the FBI had amassed a collection of over 125 million fingerprint cards – not all of them relating to criminals. The fingerprint technique was only superseded by DNA in recent years, and in the course of a century, identifying people by fingerprints must have solved hundreds of thousands of crimes world-wide.

THE INVENTION OF
ESPERANTO
(1887)

IN 1887, THE 28 year old Polish philologist Lazarus Zamenhof invented a new language. He called it Esperanto and he hoped that it would help to achieve world peace. The principle of Esperanto was to extract ideas and roots of words from a range of languages and compile a new one that would not be tainted by association with any particular country, culture or events.

The idea was a good one. Some years ago, there was some suggestion that the cause of European unity would be helped by having not just a common currency but a common language; the French vetoed this idea – because they knew that the common language would be English. One idea was that the common currency unit should be called the ECU, standing for European Currency Unit. I liked that proposal because, as it happened, there was at one time a French currency unit called an ecu. It was a word with a history, a background. But the Germans vetoed the idea – just because it would seem to be favouring the French. And this is how we ended up with a sterile, cultureless and bureaucratic word such as 'Euro', which is actually quite difficult to say in some languages and sounds unpleasant in all of them.

Esperanto was not the only universal language to have been devised. In 1880, J. M. Schleyer published *Volapuk*, which was popular for a decade and then was heard of no more. There was Zamenhof's Esperanto in 1887. Then in 1907 Louis Couturat and Louis de Beaufront published an edited version of Esperanto that became known as Ido. An international committee set up in France in 1907 to choose the best language for international use came to the conclusion that Esperanto edited in the direction of Ido would be best. The supporters of pure Esperanto rejected this proposal. Already, ironically, loyalties and patriotisms were developing. Between 1907 and 1950 no fewer than 50 schemes for a new language were proposed, most of them wanting a reformed Esperanto or an edited version of Ido. For a time the Esperantists thought they were gaining ground. Their language was the only constructed language that had a world-wide group of living speakers – there are thought to be one million of them.

Esperanto should have been a huge success in the world of the European Union, but it has not been. One problem with it was that it operated on rather complicated rules and was therefore difficult to learn. Another was that there was no literature written in Esperanto.

Esperanto was one of those ideas that should have been big, but was not. When Esperanto was failing, it looked as if French was going to be the language, not only of Europe but the common world language. That was why everyone in my generation was made to learn French at school. Now it looks as if English is fast becoming the world language; it is certainly the second language of an enormous number of people. Now there can be no hope for Esperanto.

THE INVENTION OF
PNEUMATIC TYRES
(1888)

JOHN BOYD DUNLOP was a veterinary surgeon from Edinburgh but working in Belfast. In 1887, Dunlop fitted his little boy's tricycle with inflated rubber hoses instead of solid rubber tyres. Apparently unknown to Dunlop, the principle had already been patented in 1845 by Robert Thomson. Dunlop nevertheless took the idea and turned it into a practical reality. Dunlop himself took out a patent in December 1888. In 1889, Dunlop formed a business to manufacture inflatable tyres on a commercial scale. This business, which was called the Pneumatic Tyre and Booth Cycle Agency, was run in partnership with William Harvey Du Cros. Dunlop sold the pneumatic tyre patent to Du Cros for a moderate sum and took 1,500 shares in the company. Difficulties arose because it then emerged that the idea for the tyre had already been patented 40 years earlier, but the company managed to hold its position because it held patents on various accessory processes.

He produced practical pneumatic tyres for bicycles, later producing them for cars as well. Dunlop did not make a vast fortune out of his pneumatic tyres, as he took no part in the great development that followed the sale of the company to E. T. Hooley in 1896. By then the business was worth £5 million.

The effect of Dunlop's innovation was to make riding bicycles far more comfortable, and so to make long-distance cycling more practicable. Whether Dunlop can be credited with inventing the pneumatic tyre or not, he certainly made regular cycle journeys to work possible, as well as cycling for leisure. Dunlop tyres made cycling into the major recreational activity it has become today. Similarly, it is impossible to imagine the modern motor car without pneumatic tyres. Solid rubber tyres on a car would inevitably have meant short journeys at low speeds. Dunlop's invention – if that is what it was – made long-distance driving at speed possible. Dunlop made his contribution to 'the great car economies' of the West.

THE INVENTION OF THE GESTETNER TYPEWRITER STENCIL
(1888)

IN 1888, DAVID Gestetner, a Hungarian immigrant living in London, invented the first typewriter stencil. It was seven years earlier that Edison invented the first stencil duplicating machine. But Gestetner's machine was a significant improvement; it worked on the principle of a waxed sheet fixed to a cranked rotating drum. Handwriting, a drawing or a map could be drawn on the sheet with a metal stylus and the areas where the stylus scraped the wax off allowed ink through onto the sheets of paper as they were fed through the copier. In this way, it was possible to write a list of instruction for employees, run them off on the copier and give them to the employees.

The fact that these stencils could be typed opened up the possibility of copying whole documents, and each turn of the crank handle produced another copy. It was very easy – and cheap – to produce hundreds of copies from one stencil.

This innovation made mass communication in the factory, the office, the school and the university significantly easier. It also made it easier for teachers and lecturers to produce their own teaching materials, encouraging creativity rather than slavish dependence on textbooks. It also helped to generate more administrative documents and increased the amount of paperwork that everyone would have to deal with in the twentieth century. The Gestetner was one of those great, but underestimated and undervalued, inventions that changed the texture of modern culture. It has to a great extent been superseded by spirit duplicators, which allowed the use of several colours, and the photocopier. But it is still used – and it is cheap.

THE INVENTION OF STEEL-FRAMED BUILDINGS
(1888)

THE TACOMA BUILDING in Chicago was built using a new technology, a load-bearing steel skeleton. The technique was pioneered in the Home Insurance building designed by LeBaron Jenney in 1885, but the Tacoma building was the first building to be built in this way throughout. William Holabird was the Chicago-based architect of the Tacoma building, and his firm of Holabird & Roche was to be the major developer of Jenney's idea into modern office buildings in Chicago. Holabird was in effect responsible for transforming the Chicago skyline, adding the Caxton building in 1890, the Pontiac building in 1891, the Marquette building in 1894 and the Tribune building in 1901. He went on after that to design and build many more Chicago office blocks and hotels.

The steel-framed method was the first serious advance in building construction technique since the invention of the medieval Early English arch and the flying buttress. The steel-framed construction method, which depended on cheap steel being available, changed the shape and style of buildings enormously. They became distinctly box-shaped, and as the architects became more confident with the technique, they became taller and taller. This was the beginning of the age of the skyscraper.

THE INTRODUCTION OF OLD AGE PENSIONS

(1891)

TRADITIONALLY, THE OLD have either died in poverty because they can no longer work or they are supported by their children. In many parts of the world this is still the case, but in the richer countries of the West there are pensions.

The very first old age pension plan in the world was introduced in Germany in June 1891. Bismarck brought in the Old Age Insurance Act, which compelled people over the age of 16 to contribute part of their income if they were in full-time employment and if they earned over 2,000 marks a year. Employers were obliged to contribute equal sums. These contributions would entitle every worker to a pension, once he or she reached the age of 70, so long as they had paid pension contributions for at least 30 years. It was an imaginative and far-sighted scheme.

The German old age pension idea was not adopted at once by the British Parliament, though in 1908 the British did introduce something at a lower level and on a nineteenth century 'dole' principle. The British pension was to be non-contributory, payable only to 'needy' people over 70, and amount to five pence a week. Meagre though this pension was, it put the British government into difficulties. To pay for the new social security measures, new tax measures were needed, and David Lloyd George's budget imposed a supertax on incomes exceeding £5,000 a year.

Other countries followed suit with their own plans for providing old age pensions. The existence of pensions changes the texture of life, removing anxiety about income. There is no need for the elderly to starve or freeze to death. There is no need, either, to depend on children for support. In the poorer countries of the world, one of the reasons why people have large families is to ensure that there will be offspring to take care of them when they can no longer work; the many children are the pension. So, indirectly and long-term, setting up an old age pension scheme has an effect on family size. Introducing old age pensions in Germany and Britain was one factor in reducing family size during the twentieth century.

HENRY FORD'S CAR

(1893)

In April 1893, the Detroit mechanic Henry Ford road-tested his first motor car. He was an employee at the Edison Illuminating Company at the time. Ford had been working on his 'gasoline buggy' for just a few months. Three years later, Ford caused a stir by driving his tiller-steered Quadricycle through the streets of Detroit early in the morning. He was already showing a flair for innovation and publicity.

In 1899, Ford joined the new Detroit Automobile Company as its chief engineer. This promising beginning turned out to be a false dawn. In 1901, the Detroit Automobile Company went bankrupt after selling only five cars in two years. Ford was then hired as experimental engineer by the businessmen who bought the firm's assets. When a car designed by Ford won a high-profile race, some of the old Detroit Automobile stockholders rallied round to form the Henry Ford Company, giving Ford himself one-sixth of the stock in the new company. Again, it was a false dawn; he had dropped out within two years.

In 1903, the Ford Motor Company was founded with 28,000 dollars raised by a dozen stockholders including John and Horace Dodge. Henry Ford was given 225 shares for his car design and the 17 patents on its mechanism, and then production began in a converted wagon factory on Mack Avenue, Detroit. Out of this came Ford's first commercial vehicle, the Model A Ford. This was a two-cylinder, 8-horsepower, chain-driven engine. It weighed half a tonne, was about 2.5m, and it cost just 750 dollars.

Henry Ford's big success came with the Model T Ford in 1908. This car, which was a neat-looking convertible, would soon outsell all its competitors. Nicknamed the 'flivver', it cost only 850 dollars, so that most middle-income people could afford to buy one. It had a wooden body on a steel frame. Customers could order a Model T Ford in 'any colour you want, so long as it's black'.

Ford's genius was in designing something that worked, was reliable, and above all affordable. He knew his market. There were lots of Americans who wanted cars. Already in 1908 car production in the United States was up at 63,500 a year. What the Ford car did was to put millions of people on the road. What the Ford car did was to mobilize the twentieth century, transforming people's lives in a thousand ways. It became easier to travel to work, easier to go on holiday, easier to keep in touch with friends and relations, easier to live out of town.

LENIN'S JOURNEY TO GENEVA
(1895)

In May 1887, Vladimir Ilich's eldest brother, Alexander, a student, was hanged for taking part in a plot to assassinate the Tsar, Alexander III. This traumatic event had the effect of electrifying him, making him become extremely radical; it was his brother's execution that turned Ilich into a revolutionary. Later in that same year he was arrested and expelled from Kazan University, and from Kazan itself, for taking part in student protests.

This did not stop him from continuing his studies at various places on the Volga and by 1892 he had a licence to practise law. But the earlier events took over now, and he decided to devote more of his time to politics. He involved himself in revolutionary propaganda efforts. He also studied Marxism, mainly in St Petersburg, and became an authority on it.

In April 1895, Vladimir Ilich, then 25 years old, went on a journey to Geneva. It is not clear what he hoped to achieve by this, but he seems to have seen himself as part of some international revolution; whether he hoped to inspire other Europeans – or be inspired by them is not clear. In Geneva he met Georgi Plakhanov, and then went on to Zurich, Berlin and Paris. He returned to Russia apparently hell-bent on getting into trouble with the authorities; it is almost as if he wanted to die for a great cause, like his older brother. At any rate he returned to Russia with illegal political literature in a false-bottomed trunk, and set about organizing strikes, printing anti-government leaflets and manifestoes. He had somehow been conditioned, or conditioned himself, to get into serious trouble. He was by this stage a profoundly disturbed character.

On 7 December 1895, predictably, he was arrested as a subversive and held for a year in prison, after which he was sent to Siberia. While there, in 1898 he married Nadezhda Krupskaya, a socialist activist. In April 1899, he published a book, *The Development of Capitalism in Russia*. The next year his exile came to an end and he settled for a time in Pskov, not far from St Petersburg, from which he was still banned. He used his freedom to travel in Europe, leaving Russia on 29 July 1900 for more than five years. He resumed his earlier pattern, of networking in Europe, though it is still unclear what he hoped to achieve by this. He travelled to Switzerland, Germany, London, Paris, then back to Switzerland, at the same time publishing tracts about the revolutionary movement. He also founded a newspaper, which he called *Iskra* (the *Spark*), which was published abroad but circulated in Russia.

At the end of 1901, Vladimir Ilich Ulyanov assumed the pseudonym, or nom de guerre, of Lenin.

From 1903 he became the leader of the Bolshevik faction after a split with the Mensheviks that was in part precipitated by his pamphlet *What is to be Done?* The revolution of 1905 fell short of Lenin's expectations. He arrived in St Petersburg in November and stayed for a while, but lived for the next two years in Finland, visiting Stockholm and London. In 1906, he was elected to the Presidium of the RSDLP. As his profile increased, so also did the danger of arrest, so in 1907 he moved to Finland again for safety.

When the March 1917 Revolution broke out, Lenin was in Switzerland, unable to get back to Russia without crossing enemy territory. The Germans provided the facility of a sealed train, in which he and other Russian socialists might travel across Germany. On 16 April, Lenin arrived in St Petersburg, now Petrograd (and one day to be named Leningrad in his honour), to take a leading role in the Bolshevik movement. The Tsar, Nicholas II, had been deposed. A Bolshevik rising in July failed, and Lenin had to withdraw to Finland once more. In October, he returned to Russia to lead an armed coup, this time successfully, against the Provisional Government led by Kerensky.

Lenin was elected Chairman of the Council of People's Commissars by the Russian Soviet Congress in November 1917. Lenin played a leading role in instigating the Russian Revolution, and must carry the major responsibility for the blood shed and the crimes against humanity committed during that revolution and for all the ills that followed – including the long, cruel, destructive reign of Stalin.

DISCOVERY OF X-RAYS
(1895)

THE GERMAN PHYSICIST Wilhelm Roentgen discovered X-rays or roentgen rays. He had been Professor of Physics at the Physical Institute at Wurzburg since 1888. On 8 November 1895, he noticed a phenomenon while working with the cathode-ray ultra-vacuum tube that had recently been invented by the English physicist William Crookes. When a current was passed through the tube, a nearby piece of paper painted with barium platinocyamide appeared to fluoresce brightly. This phenomenon took place even when Roentgen covered the tube with black cardboard. What Roentgen had discovered was an effect caused by an invisible ray.

He found that he could use the invisible rays to 'see through' objects. Perhaps his most significant discovery was that he could use X-rays to take photographs of the interiors of people's bodies. He took an X-ray photograph of the hand of one of his colleagues. The bone structure showed exceptionally clearly. The rays could pass through skin and flesh very easily, denser tissue less easily and bone not at all, so it was possible to look inside someone's body. This was an historic image, often reproduced to illustrate this landmark in diagnostic medicine. It was a major breakthrough in medicine and, by providing doctors with a brand-new and wholly unexpected tool, it changed the quality of medical care throughout the twentieth century.

Roentgen announced his discovery to his colleagues in Wurzburg on 28 December. He was awarded the first Nobel Prize for Physics in 1901.

In 1903, the German surgeon Georg Perthes made the first observations that X-rays could inhibit cancerous growths. So here, already, was another major use for Roentgen's magic rays. They could not only diagnose – they could cure.

THE INVENTION OF WIRELESS
(1895)

GUGLIELMO MARCONI ATTENDED the Technical Institute of Livorno, where he studied physics under Vincenzo Rosa.

He became fascinated with the electromagnetic waves discovered by Heinrich Hertz, experimenting from 1894 onwards with a way of converting them into electricity. He carried out these experiments on his father's estate at Pintecchio, just outside Bologna. He used fairly crude apparatus: an induction coil with a spark discharger and a simple filings coherer at the receiver. In September 1895, Marconi started transmitting over short distances, successfully sending a message to his brother who was out of sight beyond a hill. Then he knew he was on to something.

After that he tried ways of extending the range of transmission. He found that using a vertical aerial increased the distance of transmission to over 1.5km; with reflectors fitted round the aerial to concentrate the signal into a beam, he could increase the distance still further.

Marconi was convinced that he had stumbled on something of great importance, but he received little encouragement in Italy. He was advised by his mother's relatives to take his invention to England, where its value would be appreciated, and this proved to be the case. In February 1896, Marconi arrived in London, where he met William Preece, engineer-in-chief to the Post Office, and Preece gave him every encouragement and all the help he could. Marconi filed his first patent for wireless telegraphy in London in 1896. Marconi gave several demonstrations of his wireless telegraph system, trying out kites and balloons to give his aerials greater height in order to increase the transmission distance. He succeeded in this way in sending radio signals about 6km on Salisbury Plain and twice that distance across the Bristol Channel. The demonstrations and Preece's lectures on the technology attracted a lot of public interest, both in England and abroad.

By this stage even the Italians were interested. Marconi was able to erect a wireless station at La Spezia, and a communication link was established with warships up to 19km away. A further major step was taken when in 1898 he set up a land station on the South Foreland in Kent, to communicate with Wimereux in France, about 50km away; he used this to transmit radio signals right across the English Channel. With finance from his cousin, Jameson Davis, Marconi was able to set up the Marconi Wireless Telegraph Company in 1900. The great advance of Marconi's invention was that it allowed practical communication between places without using any connecting wires – hence the name 'wireless'.

Marconi's greatest breakthrough was yet to come. Many physicists thought that the curvature of the Earth would put a natural limit on the distance radio waves could be transmitted. Probably 160km would be the limit. In December 1901, Marconi proved the experts wrong; he managed to send signals in Morse code right across the Atlantic. The signal was transmitted from Poldhu in Cornwall and received at St Johns in Newfoundland. This achievement was sensational news. Many improvements and refinements remained to be made during the next 50 years, but the principle of international and even intercontinental radio transmission was established.

On the US liner *Philadelphia* in 1902, Marconi received radio messages from distances up to 1,125km by day, and three times as far by night. Marconi had discovered that conditions for reflecting radio waves on the upper layers of the atmosphere were more favourable at night. By 1918, Marconi was able to send radio signals from England to Australia.

For this epoch-making invention, Marconi was awarded the Nobel Prize for physics, with Karl Braun. Later, in 1924, Marconi was commissioned to developed a short-wave radio network for the British government, so that London could communicate instantly with any country in the British Empire. Marconi's wireless made world-wide communication possible; it was first used merely for messages, but later it was used for entertainment, and eventually it spawned television. Marconi inadvertently launched the age of mass entertainment.

The instant communication it allowed was invaluable for police work too – and almost straight away. In 1910, Dr Crippen was famously arrested while trying to escape across the Atlantic after murdering his wife – thanks to a wireless message sent by the captain of the *SS Montrose*, when he suspected he had the murderer aboard his ship. Chief Inspector Walter Dew pursued the *Montrose* across the Atlantic on the *Laurentic*, ambushing the *Montrose* in the Gulf of St Lawrence. The outside world followed the sensational chase in successive newspaper editions. The arrest of Crippen was a world news story, and this in turn was very good news for Marconi's business. From then on, most large ships were equipped with wireless. Thanks to Crippen, the Titanic was fitted with wireless and at least those who took to the boats in 1912 were rescued by the *Carpathia*, which was summoned by the *Titanic's* wireless operator. After the *Titanic* disaster, there was some criticism of the way Marconi sought to exploit the sinking in order to advertise his company.

THE INVENTION OF
MOTION PICTURES
(1895)

IN 1891, THOMAS Edison patented what was in effect a movie camera, which he called a 'kinetoscopic camera'. This took moving pictures on a band of film; these were then viewed on a peepshow, then later projected onto a screen, which required the electric light bulb, which Edison also invented. Edison thus pioneered cinema.

Others also contributed to the development of cinema. The first theatre showing of motion pictures took place on 22 March 1895 at 44 Rue de Rennes in Paris. Members of the Society for the Encouragement of National Industry were treated to a film of workers leaving the Lumiere factory at Lyons for their lunch hour. This was the first public display of the cinematograph developed by its inventors, Louis and Auguste Lumiere. It was a great improvement technically on the kinematograph peepshow which Edison introduced the previous year. The peepshow could in any case only be viewed by one person at a time, whereas the cinematograph could be seen as a shared experience by a whole crowd – it was to be a shared experience much like the 'legitimate' theatre. The Lumiere brothers used 16 frames per second for their films, and that was to become the standard for films for decades.

The first commercial presentation of a cinematograph film on screen took place on 20 May 1895 in New York. An audience in a converted store watched a four-minute film of a boxing match.

As everybody knows, the early films were silent. But the means were available to supply them with sound. Edison had independently invented the gramophone in 1877, and this enabled him to record sound and then play it back. Ten years later, Edison invented an improved model, a motor-driven machine using wax cylinders. It made no difference whether the sound was music or speaking voices, his machine could record both. In fact on one of his wax cylinder recordings it is possible to hear, among the crackles, the barking voice of Brahms introducing himself – 'Dr Johannes Brahms' – and then playing the piano. The two separate inventions, recording moving images and recording living sound, were eventually to be put together to make a powerful new medium.

It was Thomas Edison who invented the first talking motion pictures, and therefore created the great new art form of the twentieth century. With the moving picture camera, it was now possible to film great historic events like the Battle of the Somme. For the first time it was possible for people to see them, rather than just reading about them in newspapers and this made warfare and other news events more immediate.

THE DISCOVERY OF
ATOMIC STRUCTURE
(1897)

THE ATOM WAS believed by the ancient Greeks to be indivisible. In 1897, the English physicist Joseph Thomson discovered that the atom has a nucleus that was orbited by one or more electrons, like a miniature solar system. Thomson modified the ideas of John Dalton, showing that the structure of each element was characterized not just by a different atomic weight but also by an atomic number. He further showed that this number was the number of electrons orbiting the nuclei of that element's atoms.

In 1911, Ernest Rutherford of the University of Manchester proposed a nuclear model of the atom in which the nucleus was positively charged and the electrons surrounding it were negatively charged.

In 1926, the Austrian physicist Erwin Schrödinger made a major contribution to quantum theory by advancing a radical theory that the electron, like light, should have a double nature – it should behave as a particle and as a wave. In the Schrödinger model, the electrons 'wash' round the nucleus of the atom.

The twentieth century saw a revolution in thinking about the nature of the atom, the nature of matter, the nature of time and the nature of the universe. The upheaval had many roots, but one of them was J. J. Thomson's model of the atom.

THE DISCOVERY THAT MALARIA IS CAUSED BY MOSQUITOES
(1897)

THE BRITISH DOCTOR Ronald Ross discovered that the parasite that causes malaria was carried by the Anopheles mosquito. Ross had been investigating the possibility that mosquitoes might spread malaria, as it had been suggested by Carlos Finlay in 1881 that mosquitoes might be to blame for yellow fever.

Ross's breakthrough discovery was to have far-reaching effects. Mosquitoes bred in swamps and other wetlands, so the way to reduce the number of mosquitoes was to drain the swamps. During the next few decades, huge areas of wetland were drained to deprive the mosquitoes of breeding grounds. Although this was effective in cutting down the number of mosquitoes, it also deprived a great many other organisms of their natural habitat. There is now a feeling among ecologists and geographers that the world is now rather deprived of wetlands; tropical swamps have been drained to get rid of the mosquitoes, temperate floodplains have been drained to create grazing land or – worse – settlements, and saltmarshes have in many areas been reclaimed for grazing.

There was also a much more systematic use of window screens and door screens in the tropics, to keep mosquitoes out of houses, and more conscientious use of mosquito nets over beds.

A further effect was the widespread use of insecticides – DDT especially – in order to eliminate the mosquitoes.

THE INTRODUCTION OF HEROIN AS A MEDICINE
(1898)

HEROIN WAS INTRODUCED under the brand name 'Heroin' – as a cough suppressant. The German pharmaceutical company Farben fabriken vorm Friedrich Bayer und Co created the new drug as an extract from opium.

In the nineteenth century, it was relatively common for people to take opium, indeed to become addicted to opium. There seems to have been little awareness of the dangers of addiction to opium or its derivatives. It comes as quite a shock to discover that a drug as powerful and dangerous and destructive as heroin could be sold as a cough mixture.

Heroin addiction has caused untold misery to addicts and their friends and families through the twentieth century. In the United States, trafficking in marijuana and heroin has become a major problem. Taking marijuana, the less dangerous of the two drugs, has often been represented as 'the slippery slope'; it is argued that taking the one may lead to taking the other. In the United States in 1969, the federal government set up Operation Intercept to try to restrict the flow of marijuana from Mexico into North America. The result of this (in one way) highly successful project was to raise the street price of marijuana so high that it was as expensive as heroin. The schoolchildren – whom the police had been trying to protect from smoking marijuana – simply switched to buying heroin instead. More recently it has been argued that smoking marijuana should be legalized because it is much safer than heroin. The debate continues and the problem continues too. One thing is certain: that the world would have been better off had heroin never been manufactured in the first place.

V
THE MODERN WORLD

THE FLATIRON
BUILDING, NEW YORK
(1902)

IN SOME WAYS the transformation of New York from a nineteenth century city into a twentieth century metropolis can be seen as starting with the raising of a single building.

The Fuller Building, as it is formally and more properly known, is the one that broke the new ground. It was completed in New York in 1902 and it was designed by the Chicago architect Daniel Burnham to stand to the south-west of Madison Square. Most American city centres were laid out on a uniform grid pattern, so the building plots were normally rectangular. The high-rise steel-frame buildings that rose from them in the course of the twentieth century were therefore cuboid in shape, quite literally 'blocks' as Americans describe them. Here and there a diagonal road passed through the grid plan, creating some odd triangular building plots. The unusual triangular floor plan of the Fuller Building gave rise to its nickname – the Flatiron Building.

Daniel Burnham was an architect who came from Chicago where, as we have seen, steel-frame buildings were going up one after another and transforming the urban skyline; it was perfectly natural that when commissioned to design this building for New York Daniel Burnham should adopt the same construction technique. The Chicago style was spreading.

So it came about that New York got its first medium-rise, steel-frame building. At a height of 20 storeys, it no longer seems a very impressive building, but in 1902 it seemed to soar above the other buildings. Its exceptional height made it a major focus of attention among New Yorkers. It was fitted with an Otis elevator and people flocked from great distances to see the strange-looking new building and also to go up in the Otis elevator to see the panoramic view of the city of New York from the top floor.

THE ERUPTION OF MOUNT PELEE

(1902)

MARTINIQUE IS AN island in the Lesser Antilles island arc in the Caribbean. It is about 65km long, with a lumpy backbone made of a line of volcanoes; the island arc as whole is nothing more nor less than a chain of volcanoes. The flanks of the clusters of Martinique's volcanic peaks are deeply eroded by ravines clothed in forest.

Martinique is a dangerous island. It is occasionally hit by hurricanes. As early as 1767, 1,600 colonists died in a hurricane, and there were also hurricanes in 1839, 1891, 1903 and 1928. The island is prone to earthquakes. But the worst natural disaster to strike Martinique was undoubtedly the eruption of Mont Pelee, the north-westernmost of the line of volcanic peaks, at the beginning of the twentieth century.

On 8 May 1902, Mont Pelee erupted with great violence, ejecting rock, lava and scalding clouds of gas and sending them rolling down the mountain side at high speed into the capital and commercial centre, the town of St Pierre. The eruption killed up to 50,000 people, mainly in the capital. All the ships in the harbour were destroyed in the eruption except one, the *Roddam*.

The high volcanic peak, soaring 1,350m above St Pierre, had in fact given the inhabitants a series of signals that a major eruption was about to happen, such as the heavy ashfall on 25 April and the large-scale eruptions of 2 and 3 May, in which extensive sugar plantations were wiped out and 150 people were killed. The people of St Pierre, which lay on the bay 8km to the south of the volcanic vent, nevertheless carried on with their normal everyday routines. They were preoccupied: there was an imminent election, which was far more important, and they ignored the clear warnings from the volcano. A few days later there was news that there had been a big eruption of the Soufriere volcano on the island of St Vincent. This removed any fears that the inhabitants of St Pierre may had had; they assumed the Soufriere eruption had relieved the subterranean pressure building beneath Martinique and that Mont Pelee would simmer down.

It did not. The final calamity on Martinique came without any further warning. There was an explosive eruption and an avalanche of lava and searing gas swept down the southern slope of Mont Pelee, engulfing the town of St Pierre, killing all the inhabitants instantly and burning nearly all the ships in the harbour.

There were further eruptions on 20 May and 30 August, which devastated more of the island. Overall about one-tenth of the land surface of Martinique was destroyed.

The Mont Pelee eruption was one of a series of natural disasters that has functioned as a cautionary tale to the human race. One message that the event has for us is that we court disaster by building towns or cities on the flanks of volcanoes. The fact that the volcanoes may not have erupted for hundreds of years gives no guarantee of safety. Another message is that there is a characteristic eruption sequence and, with the right local knowledge – because different volcanoes have different personalities – it is possible to predict that a major eruption is about to happen. A third message is rather a depressing one, that the human race does not learn from such events, or at any rate is very reluctant to modify its behaviour.

THE WRIGHT
BROTHERS' FLIGHT
(1903)

ORVILLE AND HIS brother Wilbur Wright started out in life working in the bicycle repair business, and they both became interested in the problems of flying when they read of the experiments of Otto Lilienthal in Germany. Lilienthal's experiments came to an abrupt end when his glider crashed in 1896 and he was killed; he had lost control of the balance of the glider and the Wright brothers believed that his attempt to maintain equilibrium just by shifting his body weight about was inadequate.

They developed the theory that the air pressure exerted on different parts of the machine could be altered by making the wings adjustable, and that this would maintain equilibrium. This system, now known as aileron control, is used today on all modern aircraft. The Wright brothers took out a patent on it. They carried out workshop experiments, using a wind tunnel, to test the aileron principle.

Starting in 1902, the brothers developed a full-sized power-driven heavier-than-air machine. The machine weighed only 340kg and was powered by a four-cylinder, petrol-fuelled motorcycle engine of 12 horsepower; the engine block was cast aluminium, which gave it a high strength-to-weight ratio. It was piloted by Orville Wright on its first successful flight on 17 December 1903, near Kill Devil Hill at Kitty Hawk in North Carolina; on that momentous day the first aeroplane made four sustained free flights, the longest lasting 59 seconds at an altitude of about 4.5m and at a speed of about 50km. Several newspaper men were at the scene, but for some reason it was not considered very newsworthy; only three newspapers reported it. It was rather like the Gettysburg Address, a momentous event that was not recognized as such at the time.

The machine on which the Wright brothers made their epoch-making first flight was for 20 years a major exhibit at the Science Museum in South Kensington. On 17 December 1948, the 45th anniversary of the Kitty Hawk flight, the pioneer plane was finally taken back to North America and installed as an exhibit at the Smithsonian Institute in Washington D. C.

Others in France and Germany were working on flight at the same time. The German aviation pioneer Karl Jatho, claimed that he had made a flight on 5 August, more than four months before the Wright brothers' flight. Jatho flew a petrol-fuelled biplane he had built in 1899 and went on to set up an aircraft factory at Hanover in 1913. This looks like another case of coincidental simultaneous invention.

The experiments at Kitty Hawk continued. In 1905, Orville and Wilbur Wright learned how to prevent the tail-spin that had made short turns a problem. After that their flights became longer and more ambitious and in September that year Wilbur piloted the plane in a circle over a distance of more than 38km.

The brothers worked on an improved aeroplane which in 1908 stayed in the air for 1 hour 15 minutes. Further tests in 1909 satisfied the US government that this was a practical and reliable aircraft and led to the machine's general acceptance. In 1908 and 1909, the Wright brothers flew their plane at numerous demonstrations in Europe. Flights at Le Mans, Pau and Rome attracted huge crowds to see them – crowds that included the kings of England, Spain and Italy.

The Wright brothers' test flight showed that their joint efforts had succeeded in creating what is generally agreed to be the first successful aeroplane. It showed that powered flight was possible, and within ten years there were planes that could be used for reconnaissance in a war zone, and even as fighting platforms. The German air ace Baron Manfred von Richthofen led the 'flying circus' that brought down hundreds of Allied warplanes in the First World War. The Red Baron was himself brought down in April 1918.

By 1910, aviators were taking planes much higher in the sky; the French airman Louis Paullan took his plane to over 1,200m over Los Angeles. Louis Paullan also won *The Daily Mail* prize of £10,000 in an air race from London to Manchester.

In 1919, the first flying boat was built, a plane that could take off from water and land on water. This was the NC-4, designed by Jerome

Hunsaker, and it was used to make the first transatlantic flight, leaving Newfoundland on 16 May 1919 and arriving at Lisbon on 27 May. It was flown by a five-man crew led by Albert Read. The first non-stop transatlantic flight was achieved by John Alcock and Arthur Whitten-Brown, flying a Vickers Vimy bomber across from Newfoundland to Ireland in 16 hours on 14 June 1919. Alcock and Brown won the £10,000 prize offered by the *Daily Mail* for this feat, even though the flight ended in an undignified crash landing in an Irish bog.

In the 1920s, aviation developed very fast, with longer and longer flights achieved and larger planes built that could carry passengers. By 1924, the first flight round the world had been achieved; two World Cruisers made of plywood, spruce and linen canvas arrived in California after 15 flying days.

Aviation shortened distances between places, made it easier for people to travel from country to country, from continent to continent. The development of bigger and bigger passenger planes eventually brought relatively cheap air travel within the reach of millions of people.

EINSTEIN'S THEORY OF RELATIVITY

(1905)

ALBERT EINSTEIN, PROBABLY the greatest scientist of the twentieth century, went to Zurich University where he studied mathematics and took his PhD. Einstein considered taking up geography as a career, but decided the subject was too difficult; it is interesting to speculate what might have happened, in both geography and physics, if Einstein had followed this alternative path. We shall never know.

While studying for his doctorate, Einstein worked in the Swiss patent office. It was while working there, in 1905, that he published his first, restricted, theory of relativity.

This theory of relativity was prompted by the difficulties encountered by two other physicists, Michelson and Morley, when they had tried to measure the absolute value of the Earth's movement through space. Their negative result, which they put down to a property of light, prompted Einstein to put forward the idea that if the speed of light was to be taken as a constant, as measured by all observers, anywhere and moving in any direction, then that would require a modification of Newtonian mechanics. Einstein also proved mathematically that nothing could move faster than the speed of light, that objects must become shorter and shorter as they approach that speed, and that clocks would slow down and stop as they approached the speed of light.

Some of these propositions had been put forward before, but they had been proposed as absurdities. Einstein was putting them forward as actual properties of the universe. At the time, there were no means of testing his theory, and only a few German mathematicians accepted what he was saying.

The 1905 ideas bore fruit later. Ten years afterwards, Einstein put forward his epoch-making general theory of relativity. In this, he added the idea that gravitation might affect measurements through space and time. He also suggested that observations already made might be used to prove this, such as the observed irregularity in the orbit of Mercury, and the slight shift in positions of stars when they were observed close to the sun. The differences in position were very slight, but enough to suggest that gravitation might bend light. Measurements of high-speed electrons were showing changes in mass that agreed with Einstein's formulae.

Because of the real-world evidence Einstein was able to offer, his theory was given much more serious attention from scientists everywhere. One important implication was that the two forms of universal energy readily available for measurement, mass and the energy locked up in matter, were in a sense equivalent. The energy locked up in matter, E, was equal to its mass, m, multiplied by the square of the velocity of radiation, c . This formula, $E = mc^2$, became one of the most famous equations of all time.

Marie and Pierre Curie had already realized that vast amounts of energy were locked up in matter, but it did not occur to them that that energy was accessible, that it could be got at and used. Einstein was a key reaction in a long intellectual chain reaction that resulted in the releasing and harnessing of nuclear energy. It remained for Rutherford to verify Einstein's formula experimentally; for James Chadwick to discover the neutron; for Enrico Fermi to transmute half the elements in the atomic table; for Otto Hahn and others to recognize that a certain uranium isotope might be split; and for Enrico Fermi to design the first nuclear reactor.

Einstein changed science, not just by proposing his theory of relativity, but by showing that there were other ways of looking at the universe besides Isaac Newton's. He also changed the way many outside science saw the world and the universe beyond it. Instead of functioning like a large and elaborate clock, as in Newton's model, the universe is full of exciting and wonderful possibilities – many of them beyond our wildest imaginings.

THE SAN FRANCISCO
EARTHQUAKE
(1906)

THANKS TO CONTINENTAL drift, North America is moving steadily westwards away from Europe. The western edge of North America has been shoved onto an adjacent plate which is moving northwards. This is shearing off a narrow strip of North America that includes the coast of central and southern California; the long narrow peninsula of Lower California has already been ripped away from the continent. The great crack or tear fault that marks the boundary is known as the San Andreas Fault. The land on the west side of this fault jumps a few centimetres to the north from time to time, generating earthquakes. West coast cities such as San Francisco and Los Angeles are therefore very unfortunately located, on or close to a fault line that is likely to cause earthquakes.

The San Francisco earthquake happened at 5.13 am on 18 April 1906. It was the worst earthquake ever to hit an American city. Many brick-built buildings were shaken down completely, many in the huge initial quake, some in the many smaller aftershocks. Gas mains were fractured and fires broke out all over the city. Fire-fighting was difficult because the water mains were broken in the first shock. The fires that raged for three days after the earthquake destroyed two-thirds of the city, in particular causing havoc in the central business district and destroying large areas of housing. An estimated 28,000 buildings were destroyed. In the disaster, about 2,500 people were killed, 250,000 were made homeless. Thousands fled from the city, filling all the available ferries and trains in their panic to get out. The damage to property is estimated to have amounted to 400 million dollars.

San Francisco had had fires before. In fact the city had been swept by as many as six earlier disastrous fires, one in 1849, three in 1850 and two in 1851. None of these compared in severity with the fire following the 1906 earthquake. The authorities tried to save the city by clearing firebreaks ahead of the fire, using dynamite to demolish buildings and open spaces. The effect of this was the deliberate destruction of many expensive buildings, but it was felt necessary to sacrifice them in order to save other areas. Martial law was declared in an attempt to maintain order, and the army was brought in to help the police. Several looters were shot down in the streets.

After the initial pandemonium, San Francisco very quickly recovered from this crippling disaster. Aid flooded in from all over North America, Europe and Asia. Although many people had to sleep rough in the parks and streets for weeks afterwards, the city gradually returned to normal. One year after the earthquake, San Francisco was looking very like a normal American city. The main difference was that there were a lot of very new buildings, mostly built along more modern lines, and using more expensive construction techniques. There was an awareness that the new Chicago steel-frame buildings were more likely to survive an earthquake than the brick buildings, which had just been shaken to heaps of rubble. With the help of San Francisco banks and the insurance pay-outs, a more modern city rose from the smoking ashes.

One serious mistake that was made was the bulldozing of debris from demolished buildings into the bay. This man-made ground was in due course regarded as new land available for development, and housing was built on it. In subsequent earthquakes, this non-solid material has momentarily liquefied, causing the later buildings to sink into it and collapse. But there have so far been no subsequent earthquakes at San Francisco on anything like the scale of the 1906 earthquake. Pressure is building up in the Earth beneath the city and a major earthquake is expected imminently. The inhabitants of San Francisco refer to it as 'the Big One'. It is often treated as a joke, but one day it *will* come.

THE MEETING
BETWEEN
JUNG AND FREUD
(1907)

CARL GUSTAV JUNG studied medicine in Basle and continued his psychology studies in Paris under Pierre Janet. He worked as a physician under Eugen Bleuler at the Bergholtzli mental clinic in Zurich from 1900 until 1909, and lectured in psychology at the University of Zurich from 1905 to 1913. Jung was an incredibly prolific writer, and one of his early publications was *Studies in Word Association*, in which he coined the term 'complex'. He also wrote *The Psychology of Dementia Praecox* (which is now called schizophrenia). These publications led directly to a meeting with Freud in Vienna in 1907.

The two men got on well and Carl Jung became Sigmund Freud's friend, leading disciple and collaborator and in 1910 he was elected president of the newly created International Pschoanalytical Association. Freud saw Jung as a son figure, and unfortunately expected unswerving intellectual loyalty. But Jung was an independent researcher with a mind of his own, and he was soon moving off into new realms of thought of his own.

The moment Jung set out his new ideas on the libido and the unconscious, in 1912, there was tension between the two men as Freud felt his authority was being challenged. Jung became increasingly critical of Freud's insistence on the psychosexual origins of neuroses; to Jung this insistence on the sexual was too narrow and too doctrinaire. Jung substituted his own term, libido, for a general non-specific underlying life force; Freud remained fixed on the sexual drive per se as the root of most psychological problems. They regularly exchanged dreams and analyzed them. When, one day, Freud refused to tell Jung one of his dreams 'because it would undermine his authority', Jung knew that it was time for him to go his own way and in 1913 he parted company with Freud. Jung felt that Freud lacked a philosophical background; Jung himself was steeped in philosophy. He also saw that Freud made a mistake in restricting analysis to the personal. We are all steeped in history and zeitgeist, the spirit of the age we live in; the way our parents treat us and the way we are educated are historical, not personal. I became aware of this recently when a friend and near-contemporary showed me a draft memoir of his childhood. I commented on the amount of beating there was in it - the father routinely hitting his son - and he had until then been unaware of its period feeling, having taken it very much for granted as a child. Parents, on the whole, do not routinely strike their children any more. The zeitgeist has changed.

Freud and Jung exchanged over-emotional letters. Freud made the mistake of analyzing some of the things Jung had said, even pointing out a revealing mistake, a significant mistake of a type that would in time become known as a 'Freudian slip'. Freud knew this shallow analysis would annoy Jung, which is probably why he wrote it. Jung replied at length, criticizing Freud for 'treating his pupils like patients'. Freud was humiliated at being addressed like this and composed a reply, but did not send it. The two great psychologists were actually struggling to understand their own minds and emotions, and unable to understand the strength of their effect upon one other. It was like a tiff between teenage lovers.

A Freudian bystander might have judged that Freud was playing the father, and Jung was reacting badly to this as he had not enjoyed his relationship with his father, so he was playing the ultra-rebellious son. One tyrant-father was quite enough. Probably this is what their colleagues thought, as they watched this personal and professional tragedy unfold. The personal falling-out had a serious effect on most of their subsequent writings, which polarized; they put themselves in positions where they were unable to agree academically. The two great founders of modern psychology had said unforgivable things to each other. After that they had to go their separate ways.

Possibly as a result of this loss, Jung had a serious mental breakdown which lasted for the duration of the First World War. He went on seeing patients during this period but one wonders whether he can have helped them in any significant way. He diagnosed one poor man who went to him as being in the final stages of syphilis and gave him only weeks to live. The patient wisely sought a second opinion; he turned out to be manic-depressive and lived for another 50 years.

Jung and Freud had exchanged dreams and psychoanalyzed one another. Jung knew a lot about the workings of Freud's mind, but even in his final year he was not prepared to divulge what he knew. Jung smiled and said, 'There's such a thing as a professional secret.'

What Jung shared with Freud – and he never deviated from it – was the profound belief in the fundamental importance and truthfulness of dreams. Dreams were a window onto the unconscious mind. Where the two men differed was in the interpretation of dreams. Freud delved into a patient's dream until he found the sexual metaphor, which might be a tree or a tunnel, and was then satisfied that he had reached *the* interpretation; once he had reached a sexual stratum he had interpreted the dream and looked no further. For Jung, the sexual content of a dream might be no more than metaphorical language, and still deeper layers might lie beneath; where Freud stopped, Jung went on delving deeper.

Jung's approach to the human mind is immeasurably richer and more exhilarating than Freud's, which often seems squalid, mundane and over-simplified by comparison. Jung was able to use his analytical method to explain the dreams of disturbed patients, the content of great literature such as Goethe or Shakespeare, or the content of myths and religions; Jung offered a more universal gateway to the mind of man. If Freud opened the door on the twentieth century way of looking at things, Jung opened the door on the twenty-first.

THE CUBIST
EXHIBITION IN PARIS
(1907)

AFTER SETTING HIMSELF up in his Paris studio in 1901, Pablo Picasso, the greatest artist of the twentieth century, quickly absorbed the Neo-Impressionist influences of the Paris school, as seen in the work of Toulouse-Lautrec, Degas and Vuillard, and went on to paint works such as *The Blue Room* (1904). In his blue period, 1902–04, Picasso painted a series of haunting but depressing interiors. In the pink period that followed, 1904–06, he produced a contrasting series of harlequins and acrobats. Toulouse-Lautrec had painted the bars and the music halls, Degas had painted the ballet, now Picasso was painting the circus.

Picasso never stayed in the same waters for long, and he moved on to explore what African art could teach him. He was fascinated by the simplified, reductive forms of African sculpture in particular: simple geometric shapes and plane surfaces. This preoccupation produced the transitional *Two Nudes* (1906), which heralded a major break with traditional styles, and a breakthrough into a series of 'twentieth century' styles. The landmark work was *Les Demoiselles d'Avignon* of 1906, the first full-blown Cubist painting.

The principle of Cubism was to render three-dimensional objects on canvas without resorting to perspective. Instead of describing objects, the new style allowed the artist to analyze them and present what he regarded as their key features; facets as seen from several different vantage points might be re-assembled in the painting to create an entirely new and perhaps unrecognizable form. It was in its way more like music than the nineteenth century concept of visual art, though it was still not quite fully abstract. It was certainly a more thoughtful and thought-provoking approach to visual art than people were used to seeing. Many people hated it and ridiculed Picasso for being incapable of drawing 'properly'. This perception, and the rift that it created between serious artists and the general public, was to prove a problem for many decades. Ordinary people were still ridiculing Picasso long after his death: he could only have painted like that because he couldn't paint 'properly'.

Georges Braque was at the same time experimenting with strong colours, with a group calling themselves Les Fauves, but he joined forces with Picasso in exploring the possibilities of Cubism. Picasso and Braque experimented with collage and mixed media techniques, including incorporating bits of wood and wire in the composition.

Of the older generation, Paul Cezanne was profoundly interested in the way geometrical forms underlay landscapes and figures. He said that painters should 'look for the cone, the sphere and the cylinder in nature'. He was in an important way the great forerunner of Cubism. On 22 October 1906, Cezanne died at Aix-en-Provence. It was appropriate that the first sensational exhibition of Cubist art should come straight after Cezanne's death, and in fact coincided with a Cezanne Retrospective exhibition at the Salon d'Automne. It opened in July 1907, in Paris. Cubism was almost a fruition of what Cezanne had been working towards.

Picasso's great work, *Les Demoiselles d'Avignon*, first shown in 1907, excited interest partly because it was uncompromisingly modern in appearance, yet seemed to derive in part from an old master *Judgement of Paris*, with three female figures posing like the goddesses on the left, but watched by two mysterious spectators on the right, also nude women, but wearing African masks. It was clearly a puzzle picture. The title was a reference to a brothel in Barcelona. All this, and the challenge of a Cubist treatment too, with its geometrical distortion of the human forms, multiple viewpoints and the flatness of the picture-plane. This one picture gave everyone plenty to talk about. It was to be a profoundly influential painting.

Guillaume Apollinaire's comment on it was, 'It's a revolution!' And it was.

In New York, Alfred Stieglitz expanded Gallery 291 in order to display works by the new Cubists and African-American art.

Braque joined Picasso in his Cubist revolution within a matter of months, painting the first true Cubist landscapes, the landscape series set at L'Estaques, for exhibition in 1908.

From 1917, Picasso became associated with Diaghilev's Russian Ballet, designing costumes and stage sets. For these, he used both Cubist and

Neo-Classical styles, which was a clever way of making Cubism more accessible to the public. Picasso's *Three Dancers* (1925) contains grotesque distortions of the human body, following Cubist principles, and prepared the way for the grotesqueness of what has become Picasso's most famous piece of work, *Guernica*. This huge painting, in which Picasso expressed his horror at the deliberate saturation bombing of a Basque town during the Spanish Civil War, and of the horrors of war in general, was painted in 1937 and has become a classic work of art.

It is easy to see the influence of Cubist paintings in the mid-twentieth century sculptures of Henry Moore and Barbara Hepworth. And all of this cultural development had its beginnings in the Paris exhibition of 1907.

THE FOUNDING OF THE BOY SCOUTS MOVEMENT
(1908)

THE BOY SCOUTS movement was founded by Robert Baden-Powell, who was the sixth son of an Oxford professor and had distinguished himself in the Boer War. He had been the chief staff officer in the war against the Matabele, and then had been in command in the defence of Mafeking against a Boer siege, which he maintained for 215 days. He was regarded as a national hero for this, promoted to major-general and then lieutenant-general in 1908. But in spite of these grand-sounding promotions, Baden-Powell was beached; his military career seemed not to be going any further. He needed to find something else to spend his energies on.

It was in 1908 that he founded his Boy Scouts, a movement that provided outdoor activities for boys of all backgrounds. The original boy scouts were the young messengers or scouts used at Mafeking to do a very important and risky job of work, to carry messages, gather information and memorize it, and if necessary go behind enemy lines, and do all of this unobtrusively and invisibly. Baden-Powell himself trained them, and he knew what he was talking about. He was at something of a loose end after the Relief of Mafeking and, not having much money, he wrote a series of pamphlets about the skills these 'boy scouts' needed. They excited an enormous amount of interest among boys back in England, who read them voraciously; the pamphlets were eventually assembled to make the classic book about scouting, *Scouting for Boys*.

He went on to found the Girl Guides with the help of his sister Agnes. Both movements proved to be very popular and spread to many other countries. For his services to youth, Baden-Powell was created a baron in 1929. The Boy Scouts of America, a copy-cat organization, was set up by the painter Daniel Carter Beard in 1910, at about the same time that he published his book *Boy Pioneers and Sons of Daniel Boone*. Beard was impressed and inspired by Baden-Powell's ideas. At the same time another parallel organization, the Camp Fire Girls of America, was founded by Luther Gulick, who was also the co-creator of the game of basketball. Gulick was the Director of Physical Education for the state schools in New York and also a social engineer for the Russell Sage Foundation.

What all of these organizations had in common was the underlying belief that a range of outdoor activities, including sleeping under canvas and learning basic survival techniques was good for children. It was an understandable reaction to accelerating urbanization in Europe and North America. More and more children were growing up in cities with little or no knowledge of the countryside. In the early nineteenth century, children were often sent out to work at a young age, but with the passing of the Education Act of 1870, children were bound to spend longer at school. This meant that there was an interval between childhood and manhood, a gap to fill – and scouting filled it. Enormous numbers of boys joined.

Baden-Powell's idea was to take groups of boys out into the countryside and teach them a few basic scouting skills; how to make a fire, how to put up a shelter, how to recognize animal tracks, how to tie knots, how to signal. The natural competitiveness of children was recognized, and badges were awarded for proficiency in each of the activities. Social skills were developed too, and the sing-song round the camp fire was to become a major focus. It was a brilliantly appealing package.

There was a hint of the beliefs of Rousseau and Wordsworth in all of this, in that exposure to nature was in itself though to be good for children. The process of scouting had its moral side too. Boys were encouraged to develop manly habits, to be restrained and not to smoke. The movement was also classless, and one of the things that impressed George VI, who greatly admired the movement, was that it brought together boys and girls from every conceivable social background; it was a great leveller. To begin with there was a strong military element – that had come from Mafeking, where the scouts were in effect boy soldiers in the nineteenth century tradition – and there was no disguising the movement's intention to train boys for the army. That element of scouting, the paramilitary marching, gradually died out.

The scouting and guiding movements became global and enduring – and they continue still. Some of the original ideas have been discreetly dropped along the way as they seemed less appropriate. In a strongly multi-cultural society, the Christian ethic is no longer assumed, and the elements of patriotism and militarism have been dropped too. Other parallel organizations have adopted some of the principles of scouting, notably the Duke of Edinburgh's Award Scheme.

THE TUNGUSKA
FIREBALL
(1908)

ON THE MORNING of 30 June 1908 a mysterious ball of fire exploded in the air over a remote area of Siberia called Tunguska. The high-energy explosion sent out shock waves that flattened the forest and were felt far away. Virtually every tree within 30km of the explosion was laid flat, the trunks pointing radially away from the blast. It also set large areas of forest on fire. A mushroom cloud went up from the focus of the explosion and a black rain that followed inflicted a skin disease on the herds of reindeer in the area. People 60km away were burnt by the blast, and as much as 600 km away horses were knocked off their feet.

That night and on succeeding nights all round the world the sky was unusually bright and glowing with colour. In England and many other parts of Europe the night sky was so bright that it was possible to read a newspaper outside at midnight. The effect was a bit like the aurora borealis, the northern lights, but the light was steadier and more constant. It was as if the entire atmosphere had been energized by the Tunguska event.

The cause of the explosion was a mystery at the time, and rather surprisingly it continues to be a mystery today. The only thing that comes anywhere near to producing the effects of the Tunguska explosion is a nuclear bomb, but this would have needed to be a very large nuclear bomb and it was in any case over 30 years before the nuclear bomb would be invented. So it could not have been a nuclear bomb. Something fell to Earth that morning, and fell with sufficient force to send earth tremors that were picked up by geologists in Irkutsk, Batavia, Moscow and Washington DC.

The Tunguska area is very remote. No-one was living in the area, and no-one visited it for a long time afterwards. Almost incredibly, it was not until 1927, 19 long years after the event, that Russian scientists went to see what had happened at Tunguska. That suggests a low level of curiosity among scientists; why did they not go before? That 1927 expedition was led by the Soviet scientist L. A. Kulik. One possibility – and this is Kulik's explanation – is that a large meteorite or a small asteroid hit the Earth, causing the earth tremors, but that does not explain the explosion in the sky, and the Russian scientists were unable to find any fragments of a meteorite. Kulik suggested that the meteorite was vaporized or pulverized by the impact and that it was dust from the exploded meteorite that created the 'night dawns'.

Those favouring aliens from outer space have suggested that a crippled alien space vehicle burnt up as it crash landed, and the mushroom cloud shows that the vehicle was power by nuclear energy. Others living on the wilder shores of speculation have suggested that it was a collision between the Earth and anti-matter or a black hole.

Another possibility is that the explosion was caused by a comet colliding with the Earth. Given the number of comets and the number of planets in the solar system and the independence of their orbits round the sun, such things must happen from time to time. Indeed, the collision of a comet with the planet Jupiter was actually filmed in recent years; we saw it happen.

BLERIOT'S CHANNEL CROSSING BY PLANE
(1909)

ON 25 JULY 1909, the English Channel was crossed by plane for the first time. The pilot was a 36 year old French engineer, Louis Bleriot. He himself built the 24-horse power monoplane with its three-cylinder engine and what from the photographs look like pram wheels. He flew the unpromising-looking machine from Sangatte on the French coast near Calais to Dover Castle in just 37 minutes, landing in a field near Dover after a 43 minute flight. In doing so, he won the *Daily Mail* prize of £1,000 for piloting the first heavier-than-air machine across the Channel. His average speed was 64 km per hour (40 mph). It was a huge success in every way, and Bleriot was surrounded by crowds of admirers.

Fellow aviators warned Bleriot that cross-winds could bring his plane down in the Channel, but he was confident that he could do it. He was very sure that his monoplane was a sounder, safer machine than the biplanes that other aviators were using. A French destroyer waited mid-Channel, in case Bleriot was forced to ditch in the sea and needed to be rescued. In fact it was not needed, as Bleriot waited for several days until the weather conditions were just right for the attempt. The flight went without any hitch at all.

This short flight was an historic moment. Britain's main defence, and an incredibly effective defence, had always been the English Channel. Now that it could be crossed by air, there was a new vulnerability. By the time of the Second World War, when aircraft had improved enormously in reliability and range, it would be possible for whole fleets of planes to cross the Channel, bomb the Channel ports and cross South-east England to bomb London itself. The Battle of Britain proved how the new technology put Britain's national security at risk. It was Bleriot's innocent-looking flight that heralded the Battle of Britain.

THE INVENTION OF
BAKELITE
(1909)

THE 46 YEAR old Belgian-American chemist Leo Baekeland created the first plastic in 1909. Baekeland's synthetic shellac polymer was made out of phenol and formaldehyde. He named his new material Bakelite. Baekeland set up a company to market the moulding powder for making Bakelite products.

Bakelite found an immediate use for the fittings on electrical appliances of various kinds. It turned out to be a good material for electrical insulation, so it was very useful for making collars to protect electric light fittings. It is still used in this way. Other uses followed. Once the domestic wireless (radio) was marketed, it seemed natural to make the case in moulded Bakelite, which insulated the electric circuitry inside; it could also be moulded into any shape, and by the 1930s these designs became more adventurous. Bakelite became a substance that was seen in every Western home. It found hundreds of uses.

Bakelite was important in being the first of a whole range of different plastics created for different purposes in the twentieth century. Bakelite was very useful in its way, but it was hard, rigid and brittle. New plastics were developed over the succeeding decades with different properties; the relative softness of alkathene made it suitable for making washing-up bowls; the long chains of molecules in polyethylene made it eminently suitable for making artificial fibres.

THE SINKING OF THE
TITANIC
(1912)

AT 2.20 IN the morning on 15 April 1912, the greatest ship in the world
went to the bottom of the Atlantic Ocean. With her died 1,522 people,
some by drowning, many by hypothermia in the freezing water. There were
705 people saved in the lifeboats, and they were picked up later by the
Cunard liner *Carpathia* after spending four lonely and terrifying hours
freezing in the open boats, drifting among ice floes, not knowing whether
rescue was on its way. It was a second terrible ordeal. A third ordeal was
waiting those four hours or longer to find out whether the rest of the family
had been rescued or not. Ever since the official enquiries into the loss of
the *Titanic*, and there were two – one on each side of the Atlantic, it has
been accepted that the management of the White Star Line, the ship's
owners, were at fault in several ways. There were not enough lifeboats for
all the passengers and crew; Captain Smith was taking the ship at 22 knots
– far too fast – through seas that were known to be strewn with icebergs;
the watertight bulkheads did not rise high enough inside the ship's hull;
the crew were not given enough time to familiarize themselves with the
layout of the ship; and so on.

But even after the disaster had happened, even after the ship had
collided with the iceberg and been fatally damaged, there was one man
who could have saved everyone on board – at least everyone except the
handful of men in the boiler room who had been killed on impact. One
man with the power to save them all.

He was Captain Stanley Lord, captain of the Leyland Line *Californian*,
a 6000-tonne cargo vessel with a licence to carry passengers, bound from
London to Boston. On 14 April 1912, the *Californian* was on a similar
westward course to the *Titanic* but a little to the north. On encountering

sea-ice, Captain Lord wisely stopped his ship until the morning brought a clear view of the hazard. It was at 10.20 pm that Lord stopped his ship and told the wireless operator to send out a general ice report. The ship remained stationary in the water until 5.15 the next morning. In the meantime, not very far away, the *Titanic* steamed catastrophically into an iceberg weighing an estimated 500,000 tonnes, ten times as much as the *Titanic*, and sank with the loss of 1,500 lives. The *Titanic* hit the iceberg at 11.40 pm. Some time after that, perhaps at midnight, the Titanic's Fourth Officer Boxhall went to the bridge to look at a light ahead; through glasses he saw the two masthead lights of a steamer. Boxhall told Captain Smith about the steamer in the distance and told him that he had sent for some distress rockets to attract her attention. Smith told him to carry on. Obviously transferring the passengers to another ship was their best chance of saving lives. As he sent off the rockets – 'between half a dozen and a dozen' – Boxhall thought the steamer was getting closer. The distress rockets were very distinctive: they were bigger than ordinary firework rockets, white, with a luminous tail, they exploded quite loudly and they produced a shower of white stars. They could not be mistaken for anything other than distress rockets. Boxhall thought the steamer was close enough to read the *Titanic's* electric Morse signalling lamp, so he signalled, 'Come at once. We are sinking.' Captain Smith also saw the distant steamer. There was no doubt at all that it was there.

Boxhall left the *Titanic* at about 1.45 am in one of the lifeboats and, although he was now right down at sea level instead of perched up on the ship's sinking bridge, he could still see the lights of the steamer, which he estimated must have been only about 8km away. Second Officer Lightoller also saw the lights of the steamer. He estimated that it was 8 or 9km away. Frustratingly, the distant steamer did not respond in any way. No reply by Morse lamp, no rockets, no attempt to come to the *Titanic's aid*.

At 11 pm, the officer of the watch on the *Californian* was Third Officer Groves. He saw the lights of an unknown steamer approaching from the east. Captain Lord told him to call her with the Morse lamp, but the steamer did not respond. Lord went into the wireless cabin and asked the wireless operator, Evans, who was very inexperienced, if he had had any communication with any other ships. Evans said he had had the *Titanic*, but from the strength of her signal she was 160km away (he thought). Lord told Evans to call the *Titanic* to let her know that the *Californian* was surrounded by ice and stopped. Evans started an inappropriately informal message – 'Say old man we are surrounded by ice and stopped' – but the *Titanic's* chief operator, Phillips, told him to shut up as he was busy. At 11.30 pm Evans listened in to the *Titanic* sending passengers' telegrams to New York. Unfortunately, at 11.35 pm, which was just five minutes before the collision, Evans stopped eavesdropping and turned in. If he had stayed listening for another 10 or 15 minutes he would have picked up the *Titanic's* first call for help.

At 11.40 pm Groves saw that the unknown vessel had stopped and thought he saw the steamer's lights go out. In fact the *Titanic's* lights stayed on for a surprisingly long time during the sinking, so it may be that once the *Titanic* had stopped powering across the Atlantic her sinking bow section was gradually turned by the current so that at a certain point the crew of the *Californian* were looking at her end on and were no longer able to see the huge array of lights along her side. Lord for some reason decided she was not a passenger steamer. Grove disagreed and said she was. At midnight, Second Officer Stone came on duty as officer of the watch, relieving Groves, and met Lord at the wheelhouse. Lord pointed at the steamer and said she had stopped; he would have thought nothing of this, as he himself had stopped his ship for the night and probably thought the other ship had done the same. Stone observed one mast-head light, a red side-light (which suggests that the *Titanic* was after all not being viewed end-on) and one or two indistinct lights round the deck that looked like portholes. Stone thought she was about 8km away.

At 12.15 am, James Gibson, another inexperienced crew member on the *Californian*, arrived on the bridge with coffee. He tried the telegraph, but with no response. Was he actually using the equipment correctly? At 12.45 Stone saw a flash of white in the sky above the mystery steamer and thought it was a shooting star. Then soon afterwards he saw another and realised it was a rocket. In the next half hour he watched three more of these rockets, all of them white. He had the impression they were coming from beyond the steamer.

At 1.15 am Stone whistled down the speaking tube to Captain Lord. Stone told Lord about the rockets. Lord told Stone to call the steamer on the Morse lamp and try to find out more: 'When you get an answer let me know by Gibson'. Gibson and Stone watched as the *Titanic* in desperation sent up three more rockets. They also noticed that the steamer was apparently steaming away to the southwest. In fact she wasn't: she was sinking. By 2 am Stone thought the steamer was moving away from them rapidly. She was now showing only her stern light and one masthead light. In fact what was happening was that the *Titanic* had sunk to the point where the front half of the ship was under the water and the stern was coming up out of the water.

Gibson was sent down to tell Captain Lord that he and Stone had seen eight rockets and that the steamer was moving out of sight. Lord said, 'All right. Are you sure there were no colours in them?' Gibson confirmed that they were all white. In other words, there was no doubt that they were distress rockets. At 2.45 am Stone again whistled down the tube to tell Lord that they couldn't see the lights any more and the ship had gone. It had in fact sunk 25 minutes earlier. Captain Lord's sleep would be disturbed no more by the *Titanic* – not that night, anyway.

Meanwhile, the Cunard passenger liner *Carpathia* had picked up the *Titanic's* distress calls and had been steaming at full speed for a couple of hours through the icefield towards the *Titanic's* last position. Captain Rostron of the *Carpathia* acted exactly as we would all expect a ship's captain to act; he dropped everything, changed course and without regard for anything else at all he raced to the scene of the disaster to offer help. He was the opposite of Captain Lord, who had ample evidence that a ship nearby was in deep trouble and did nothing whatever to help – and he was close enough to have saved everyone. Several witnesses on the *Titanic* and the *Californian* put the distance between the two ships as 8km. The icy night air was unusually clear and it may be that they were deceived. Maybe the distance was greater, but still between 8km and 16km. The *Californian* could have been on the scene of the disaster within half an hour, well before the *Titanic* sank, and taken all the crew and passengers safely on board. Captain Rostron would have done his bit, but Captain Lord would have been the hero of the hour.

As it was, the *Carpathia* arrived at the scene of the sinking far too late to save any of those in the water, but rescued those in the lifeboats.

News of the sinking of the *Titanic* dominated the newspapers in England and North America for the next few days. On 18 April, the *Carpathia* arrived in New York harbour with the survivors to be greeted by chaotic, grief-stricken crowds.

At the enquiry Lord's defence – it became just that – was that the vessel seen from the *Californian* was not the *Titanic* and the vessel seen from the *Titanic* was not the *Californian*. But in spite of extensive enquiries no evidence ever emerged of any third ship in the area at the right time. The big ship that Lord and his officers watched, setting off eight distress rockets and then disappearing can only have been the *Titanic*. The stationary or gradually moving small steamer seen by the officers of the *Titanic* and failing to respond to their desperate please for help by rocket and Morse lamp can only have been the *Californian*.

Lord claimed under cross-examination that he had no recollection of asking about the colours of the rockets. 'I really do not know what was the object of my question,' he said under cross-examination. It was obvious why he asked. It was not a random question asked by someone not fully awake. The significance of the colour was that a white rocket was a distress rocket. He was told that the rockets were white and he was unwilling to admit that he knew all the information he needed to know to justify starting the *Californian's* engines and steaming cautiously towards the rockets.

Captain Lord's career as a ship's master should have ended there and then. Given the damning verdicts of both American and British enquiries, Lord was forced to resign from the Leyland Line. Yet somehow he managed to continue his career at sea until 1927, without any further incident. Both the British Board of Trade enquiry and the US Senate enquiry condemned Captain Lord's behaviour. Both concluded that, 'She (the *Californian*) might have saved many if not all of the lives lost.'

But there were other causes that lay behind this disaster, as unseen as the submerged mass of the iceberg. One was the deficiency of lifeboats. There were only 16: enough for only a fraction of the number of people on board. The White Star Line's answer was that it had supplied the minimum number required by Board of Trade regulations, which had a formula for lifeboat provision that was based on the ship's tonnage, not on the number of people the ship carried. It emerged that there was a more complicated story behind the White Star's decision. Special paired davits had been commissioned from the engineering firm of Welin, which could lower not just one lifeboat to the water, but two, three or four. The original proposal from the designer, Axel Welin, was a stack of four lifeboats beside each pair of davits. This arrangement would have given the *Titanic* 64 lifeboats and room on those lifeboats for everyone on board. Why were the 64 lifeboats whittled down to 16? The arguments White Star offered were that the deck would have become unduly cluttered with lifeboats and that as the ship was regarded as virtually unsinkable she was 'a lifeboat in herself'. The real reason was cost. Even though *Titanic* was the last word in luxury, the company was cutting corners on any cost it considered unnecessary.

And then there was Captain Smith. He was a very experienced skipper, and due to retire after this prestigious final voyage on the *Titanic*. With his great experience and his Father Christmas beard he must have looked like a very safe pair of hands. He wasn't. He was a dangerous driver. There had been several near misses in harbour with this ship or that, even with the *Titanic* on leaving port. He was a captain who liked to sail in style, make a big entrance or a swaggering exit. He sailed in and out of harbours far too fast. On the night in question, he was as usual going too fast in relation to the conditions. Whatever we say about Captain Lord, he had the sense to heave to when there was so much ice about. Captain Smith went full steam ahead – into the iceberg.

The aftershocks of the *Titanic* disaster were to reverberate through the twentieth century. Safety procedures were overhauled. Checks of basic equipment became routine. Lifeboat drill became mandatory on all voyages, so that everyone on board knew where they were to go in an emergency and how to get there. And of course the Board of Trade's rule was changed; from then on there had to be enough space in the lifeboats for everyone on board.

The sinking of the *Titanic* was a watershed in another way. It marked the end of a period of Victorian and Edwardian complacency, the beginning of a century of doubt and scepticism. The newspapers had crowed immediately after the sinking that all the women and children had been saved; but they hadn't. First class women and children had been saved, but very few steerage class women and children survived. The sinking jarred and cracked the British class system. It would be a long time sinking, but its hull had been seriously scraped and perforated; from 1912 on, the class system was a sinking ship.

THE MURDER OF THE ARCHDUKE AT SARAJEVO
(1914)

IN JUNE 1914, the heir to the Austrian throne, the Archduke Franz Ferdinand was on a formal visit to Sarajevo with his wife, the Archduchess. A drive was planned through the streets of the town and the archduke and his wife were driven along it in an open-topped Graf und Stift car. The route was unwisely advertised beforehand and this made it doubly easy for assassins to attack. A group of young Serbian terrorists formed a conspiracy to assassinate the archduke, and they stationed themselves at several points along the route. The plan looked foolproof; if the first assassin missed the target or for some other reason failed, then the next assassin along the route would succeed. One of the youths fired and missed, took poison and jumped into the adjacent river, another youth was unable to respond at the critical moment, and it looked as if the conspiracy had failed. But then the driver took a wrong turning and had to stop and turn the car round. As he did so, one of the assassins, Gavrilo Prinzip, found himself face to face, quite by chance, with the 51 year old archduke and his wife. He shot them both dead and was immediately arrested.

The heir to the Austrian empire was dead at the hands of Serbian extremists. It was just the opportunity the die-hard militarists back in Vienna had been waiting for, an excuse to invade the Balkans. Austria declared war on Serbia in retaliation. The problem was that during the arms race that had been developing over the previous decade, one defensive alliance after another had been forged. Now those alliances were to turn abruptly into offensive alliances. As one state declared war on another, other states standing on the sidelines, the Allies found themselves dragged in by their treaty obligations. A relatively minor incident quickly escalated to a continental war, simply because of the web of alliances.

Germany declared war on Russia on 1 August, and on France two days later. German troops invaded Belgium on 4 August. Because Belgium was neutral and Britain had undertaken to defend Belgian neutrality, Britain was forced to declare war on Germany immediately after that.

In a night attack the German army slipped past the fortifications at Liege, forcing the Belgian troops to fall back to Brussels. France's defensive strategy overlooked the possibility of a German invasion through Belgium, and also assumed that there would be support from a Russian advance in the east. The French army advanced into Lorraine, in the hope of regaining control of territory lost to the Germans during the Franco-Prussian War of 1870–71. The French suffered heavy losses and were driven back by the Germans.

Montenegro declared war on Austria on 5 August; Serbia declared war on Germany and Austria declared war on Russia the following day; Montenegro declared war on Germany on 8 August; Britain and France declared war on Austria on 12 August. Within a very short time, a great swathe of Europe was in a state of war.

The double murder at Sarajevo was a personal tragedy for the Archduke and his wife, and an inexcusable crime for which the assassins should have been punished by due process of law, but it should not have led to the First World War. Europe had been turned into a powder keg by the territorial, military and colonial ambitions of several European countries. Sarajevo was the incidental, almost accidental, discarded lighted match that set it off. Perhaps the most surprising thing of all is that Prinzip survived the immediate mayhem; he died a natural death, of tuberculosis, a few years later.

THE SINKING OF THE
LUSITANIA
(1915)

THE CUNARD LINE passenger ship *Lusitania* was one of the great transatlantic liners of her day, the sister ship of the longer-lived *Mauretania*. She was sailing between North America and Britain, from New York to Liverpool, when she was sunk without any warning just 13km off the Old Head of Kinsale on the south coast of Ireland.

Torpedoes fired from the German U-boat U-20 hit the *Lusitania* just after two o'clock in the afternoon on 7 May 1915. One of the passengers standing on the deck of the *Lusitania*, Ernest Cowper, who was a Canadian journalist, actually saw the submarine's conning tower and the track of the first torpedo. The torpedo hit the ship with a loud explosion and pieces of the hull flew into the air. A few seconds later there was a second explosion, which everyone assumed was a second torpedo. The huge ship sank remarkably quickly, bow first, in just 20 minutes, and 1,198 people were drowned. There was some doubt about the nature of the disaster at the time. Were there two torpedoes or just one? Many survivors were sure that there were two explosions. It now seems likely that the first explosion stirred up a lot of coal dust in an almost empty hold, and the mixture of coal dust and air is known to be very explosive, so this may explain the second explosion.

Apart from being a major disaster and a big news event, the sinking was partly responsible for jolting the United States, at that stage still resolutely neutral, into the First World War. Up until 1915, the United States had remained aloof from what was evidently a European war; there was no reason for them to be involved. But the attack on a civilian passenger ship, and the killing of 128 American citizens was seen in the United States as an undeclared act of war deserving retaliation of some kind.

Among the dead were friends of the American president, the American railroad magnate Alfred Vanderbilt and the New York theatre manager Charles Frohman. The German propaganda machine put out the accusation that the *Lusitania* was armed or carrying munitions. It has been suggested by more than one researcher that the ship was indeed carrying rifle ammunition, shrapnel casings and supplies of food to help the British war effort, and that to some extent the Germans were justified in regarding the ship as something more than just a passenger liner. The captain of the *Lusitania* did not behave as if he thought there was any danger of attack by U-boats. German submarines had been sighted in the area, yet he did not change course and had no escort vessel; that may of course have been sheer bravado.

Three days after the sinking, President Wilson said, 'There is such a thing as a man being too proud to fight. There is such a thing as a nation being so right that it does not need to convince others by force that it is right.' He was arguing against using the sinking as a pretext for war, but the disaster raised such a level of anti-German feeling in the United States that he could not go on ignoring it. A former president, Theodore Roosevelt, condemned the action of the Germans as 'an act of piracy'. On 13 May, a formal protest was sent to Berlin, and the pacifist Secretary of State William Bryan resigned a few weeks later.

What was more, the attacks on neutral passenger ships continued. In February 1917, news that the Cunard liner *Laconia* had been sunk arrived in Washington as Congress was debating measures to combat the continuing menace from German U-boats in the Atlantic. Earlier in the same month, the *Housatonic* had been sunk, making a total of 134 neutral ships sunk in just three weeks. President Wilson asked Congress to authorize the arming of American vessels to 'protect our ships and our people in their legitimate pursuits on the sea.' A declaration of war became inevitable.

The calls for the United States to join in the war against Germany mounted until, in June 1917, the first American troops arrived in French ports to a heroes' welcome; they were there to support the French and the British against the German aggressors. A huge and enthusiastic crowd of French people gathered at the docks to greet them. The first batch of troops was to be commanded by Major-General John Pershing, who was to be independent of the Anglo-French command. The United States formally entered the war in April 1917, when a Selective Service Act allowed Americans between 21 and 30 to be called up.

The sinking of the *Lusitania* was different from the sinking of the Titanic in many significant ways. The *Titanic* had been sunk by an iceberg, and although it is possible to blame human failings of various kinds for making the disaster worse the immediate cause was a natural phenomenon; the *Lusitania* on the other hand had unmistakably and undeniably been sunk deliberately by a German U-boat captain. The *Titanic* sank in the middle of the night; the *Lusitania* sank in the middle of the day. The *Titanic* sank out in the ocean, far from help; the *Lusitania* sank close to the coast, and in sight of land. In fact, a six year old Irish boy who just happened to be on the headland at the time saw the whole tragedy unfold in the distance, though without understanding what was happening. Even though the ship sank within sight of land, it was still impossible to help those who did not manage to get into the lifeboats, and the loss of life was on the same scale.

THE BATTLE OF
JUTLAND
(1916)

THE BATTLE OF Jutland was a two-day set-piece sea battle between the British and German fleets off the coast of Denmark. It was described at the time as the greatest sea battle in history. It took place on 31 May and 1 June 1916. The British fleet was commanded by Lord Jellicoe, once described as 'the only man who could have lost the war in an afternoon'. Both sides sustained heavy losses, both in terms of men and battleships. The sea was awash with the bodies of sailors; a passenger steamer passing the site of the battle shortly afterwards counted 500 bodies floating on the water. The British lost seven ships and almost 7,000 men, while the Germans lost three ships and 2,500 men.

Jutland was a strange battle, in that both sides afterwards claimed it as a victory, but the British were unable to secure a surrender and the German fleet escaped. The British losses, in both ships and men, were significantly greater and that points to a German victory. But the German fleet never again sailed the North Sea; the German fleet was from then until the end of the First World War confined to port. The British claim to dominate the high seas was not challenged after the Battle of Jutland, so from that purely strategic point of view it can be seen as a British victory. From the human point of view it was an orgy of destruction that failed to bring the war to an end, and, was therefore in the same league as the appalling land battle that followed soon afterwards, the Battle of the Somme.

THE BATTLE OF THE
SOMME
(1916)

THE BATTLE OF the Somme was one of the worst and bloodiest battles in human history. It was in itself a mini-war, lasting from July to November 1916. The principle behind the British offensive was that the British guns would bombard the German positions, knocking out German fire while British troops advanced underneath this friendly fire. That initial barrage was the largest military barrage in history, involving 1,437 British guns raining a torrential one-and-a-half million shells on the enemy lines along a front 28km long during the course of seven days.

It did not work, not least because one-third of the British shells were duds, the guns were incorrectly aimed and the shells were not landing in the right place. Advancing British troops were mown down by surviving German guns as they walked across the No-Man's-Land between the fronts. General Douglas Haig, the commander-in-chief of the British forces had insufficient respect for modern weaponry. Shortly before the Battle of the Somme he said, 'The machine gun is a much overrated weapon: two per battalion is more than sufficient.' Like other top officers, Haig did not visit the front line; he considered it his duty not to do so, in case the sight of wounded men should affect his judgement and weaken his resolve. It was this weird detachment from the reality of battle that led to Haig's pouring tens of thousands of British soldiers' lives into one battle after another, and it also led to some major strategic blunders. It was this attitude that led to the long sad columns of names that we still read today on war memorials in towns and villages all over Britain – the ultimate lesson of history.

The first day of the battle, 1 July, was the bloodiest and most disastrous day of all, when the casualties were astronomical. 19,000 Allied soldiers were killed, 35,000 were wounded, 2,000 went missing and 500 were taken prisoner. On the same day the Germans sustained 8,000 casualties. The attack began two minutes after five gigantic mines dug beneath the German lines blew up at 7.28 am. The Boer War veteran General Rawlinson ordered the daylight attack out of consideration for French artillery observers, in spite of the known advantages of attacking at first light. Then 66,000 British troops emerged from their trenches and advanced on the enemy at ceremonial speed, which was about 1m per second. One regiment came out to the sound of bagpipes, while the Surreys came out kicking footballs.

The terrifying booming sound of the bombardment travelled right across the English Channel and was heard all over South-East England, as far north as Hampstead Heath.

The Battle of the Somme was a landmark battle in several ways. It was the first battle in which tanks were used. The newly invented heavily armoured vehicle went into use on 15 September 1916. The tank was invented by Ernest Swinton, a 48 year old veteran of the Boer War.

The Battle of the Somme was only brought to an end by the onset of winter, and with little to show for it except terrible loss of life. The idea of the Somme had been to make an explosive push, to force the Germans back in a 'great break-out'. It failed hopelessly.

Losses on both sides were huge in this incredibly large-scale battle involving 3 million soldiers. The Germans and their allies lost 538,000 men, the British and their allies lost 794,000 men. In terms of human loss, the British lost the Somme, but was it perhaps, like Jutland, some kind of strategic victory? The British succeeded in pushing back the German line a maximum of 11km at one stage in the battle, but it was ground that the Germans would later take back again. After the Somme, the Allies settled back into the squalid routine of life in the trenches with their lice, rats and shell shock, but where they were reasonably safe except for sniper fire and the occasional direct hit by random shells. The Battle of the Somme can only be seen as a defeat for the British and their allies, and as one of the most conspicuous demonstrations of the folly of war in modern times – and there have been more than enough of those.

THE MURDER OF THE
TSAR AND HIS FAMILY
(1918)

THE RUSSIAN REVOLUTION inevitably involved the deposition of the tsar.
Then followed the problem of disposing of the tsar and his family. For a
time, in the immediate aftermath of the revolution, it looked as if the they
would be allowed to leave Russia and live in exile in England. The
invitation extended by George V and the British government was then
withdrawn when Lord Stamfordham, George V's secretary, pointed out to
the king that the tsar was not popular with the British people. The king
had already been pressed to change his own family name, which sounded
far too German, to 'Windsor', and was aware that his own position was not
invulnerable. It was too dangerous – to the British royal family – to be seen
to be harbouring a very unpopular Russian royal family, closely related
though they were. It was better not to be seen to be associated with a tsar
who had been deposed; befriending a man seen as a tyrant was not going
to be good PR in Britain.

Thus it was that the deposed tsar, Nicholas II became stranded in Russia
in the midst of a power struggle between warring factions. He and his family
were being taken by train from Tobolsk to Ufa when Bolsheviks stopped it
and took them off. The captured tsar was then confined in a private house in
Ekaterinburg, which became known as the House of Special Purpose.

As rival 'White Guards' advanced on Ekaterinburg, the local Bolshevik-
dominated soviet became increasingly alarmed that the Whites would
release the Romanovs and use them to their own political advantage.

The local branch of Lenin's secret police, the Cheka, took over guard
duties at the House of Special Purpose. The Romanovs were treated with
progressively less courtesy, consideration and respect, and must have become
very apprehensive about how things would end. One night, on 16 July 1918,

they were told to go down into a basement room, ready to travel elsewhere. Then several men burst in and shot them all – the tsar, the tsarina, the invalid tsarevich and the tsar's four daughters. The Cheka officers wanted to make sure that no-one would survive to tell what had happened that night, so the family's doctor, valet, cook, maid and even dog were killed too.

The Bolshevik leadership in Moscow put it about that the decision to kill the royal family was made locally. This seems scarcely possible. Moscow saw the Romanovs as a possible rallying-point for anti-Bolshevik groups and made it clear, possibly through the Cheka, that the murder of the Romanovs would not be unwelcome.

Rumours persisted for decades that one or more of the Romanovs had survived the shooting – another example of Sebastianism – and there were several 'pretenders', one of whom famously claimed to be the Grand Duchess Anastasia. The discovery of a collection of bones near Ekaterinburg and the use of DNA tests proved that most of the family had indeed died. But the skeletons of the tsarevich and one of the girls were missing. This does not prove that Anastasia really survived, but that mystery is still unresolved.

THE END OF THE FIRST WORLD WAR

(1918)

THE FIRST WORLD War ended in November 1918. For the first time in over four years, the guns were silent along the Western Front. And when it came, the end of the war arrived with surprising suddenness. The French Allied Commander, Foch, had been asking for reinforcements only a fortnight before, and the Americans were developing plans for a new offensive in 1919. What brought it to this sudden end was a sense of desperation behind the German lines and a change of leadership. Ludendorff was replaced by the more level-headed General Groener, who had bluntly told the kaiser that he must either abdicate or shoot himself.

The German troops were reeling, but the starving civilians in Germany were the ones who were really signalling defeat. At dawn on 11 November 1918, in a railway carriage in the forest of Compiegne, Foch and the British Admiral Wemyss received a German delegation that included two generals. They accepted the German surrender. Six hours after this dawn meeting, the armistice formally took effect. Germany was to surrender 5,000 heavy guns, 30,000 machine guns, 2,000 planes, all of its U-boats; the German navy was to be interned in British waters. The Germans were so incensed by this humiliation that they scuttled their fleet in Scapa Flow rather than allow the British to have it.

The terms were severe, and that in itself set up problems for the future. Germans who had been fighting at the front had not seen themselves as losing the war at all, so they did not understand the surrender; they certainly did not accept the defeat. This was how the Second World War became, for many Germans, a continuation of the First.

After the defeat, Germany collapsed into chaos. The kaiser fled to Holland. Angry political agitators took to the streets, sailors mutinied, soldiers seized their command posts. Friedrich Ebert, a trade union leader and Social Democrat, attempted to restore order. He told the Reichstag that a republic had been declared. Ebert's Minister of Defence, Gustav Noske, collaborated with General Groener to form volunteer units of anti-revolutionary soldiers. Meanwhile extreme left-wingers such as Rosa Luxembourg and Karl Liebknecht called for a 'free socialist republic'. There were also extreme right-wing elements in the army who wanted to take power and plotted the murder of people such as Liebknecht and Luxembourg, who were in due course murdered while being transferred from military headquarters to prison after their arrest in Berlin for insurrection.

It was out of this chaos that Nazism and the Third Reich were born.

There were other consequences too. The political map of Europe was re-drawn. A small part of eastern Germany, including Danzig, was handed over to Poland. More devastatingly, the Austro-Hungarian Empire was divided up to form the new states of Yugoslavia, Austria, Hungary, Czechoslovakia and Romania.

The First World War had other repercussions. The immediate post-war years were dominated by the process of demobilization: the return of sailors and soldiers to their civilian lives. This was often a very difficult change for them to make. Their experiences in the trenches had been searing and life-changing for the soldiers who lived through it. When they returned to their peace-time jobs, they found that many people at home were unmoved and unchanged by the war; many had no idea what it might have been like – censorship had seen to it that they should not. In Britain there was a good deal of industrial unrest. In France, inflation destroyed the value of people's savings.

About nine million men had been killed, 17 million had been wounded, four million women had lost their husbands, eight million children had lost their fathers. Not since the Black Death in the fourteenth century had Europe suffered such a haemorrhage of human lives. The physical and emotional suffering involved is on unimaginable scale. There was a huge shortage of men, which in turn created a shortage of labour, and also a shortage of husbands. The generation of women deprived of partners, whether husbands, lovers or boy friends, by the First World War is now dead, but the last of them – one of them was a close friend of mine – have only recently died. The First World War, at the time believed to be 'the war to end wars' cast a very long shadow – a shadow that reached the length of the twentieth century.

THE SPANISH FLU EPIDEMIC
(1918)

THE FIRST WORLD War claimed an estimated nine million lives in four years. But a disastrous pandemic of influenza known as 'Spanish flu' killed more people than that in the year 1918 alone. The pandemic, which was more deadly than the Black Death, claimed more and more lives. In 1919, even more people died, taking the total death toll to over 20 million.

The strain of influenza was unusually virulent in itself, but it also carried with it the added risk of bacterial infection in the lungs, which caused an equally deadly pneumonia.

The name was misleading, as it did not come from Spain, but originated in Asia, where the death toll was highest. The countries suffering most were India and China, where the disease started. From there the disease spread to North America and Europe. In Spain, 80 percent of the population were affected by the disease – hence the name. The first American cases appeared in Boston in August 1918, when two sailors reported sick; within four days there were 106 cases. Within a month the illness had spread all along the East Coast of North America. Altogether 500,000 Americans died, including 19,000 in New York alone. Schools were closed, hospitals filled to overflowing, and supplies of coffins ran out.

Spanish flu is now seen almost as an historical footnote, but the death rate in itself tells us that this was an event that, in demographic terms, was on a level with the First World War. It killed 21,640,000 people, more than one percent of the world's population. It was one of those major world-changing events that for some reason we look past.

THE TREATY OF VERSAILLES
(1919)

THE VERSAILLES PEACE Conference opened on 18 January 1919, with delegates from the 27 nations that were on the winning side in the First World War. A week later, the conference adopted a unanimous resolution to create a League of Nations, which will protect members against aggression and devote itself to such matters as disarmament, labour legislation and world health.

On 28 June, the Treaty of Versailles was signed. This obliged Germany to accept sole responsibility for causing the First World War. Germany was forced to return to France the territories conquered in 1870–71, Alsace and Lorraine, and to cede territory to Poland and Belgium. The loss of Alsace-Lorraine, meant the loss of 72 percent of Germany's iron ore reserves; this in turn meant that from this point on Germany's industrial development became more and more concentrated in her largest coalfield, the Ruhr.

The humiliation was completed by taking Germany's colonies away from her to be administered by the Allies as mandates under the League of Nations. This part of the Treaty was in reality just another round in the Scramble for Africa. But even that was not the end of it. Germany was to pay for the war – in cash.

Huge sums in reparations were to be paid to the Allies to compensate for their financial losses in the war. This was fair, but turned out to be uneconomic and unmanageable – and also very dangerous politically. Even the United States coming into the war three-quarters of the way through, had lost 22 billion dollars. Morally, Germany certainly should have compensated the Allies for their losses, but the German economy was in a mess, and with the political instability resulting from the war as well, it was impossible for Germany to pay the reparations.

Following the Versailles Treaty came the Treaty of Saint-Germain, in September, which dealt with the splitting-up of the old Austro-Hungarian Empire. This ancillary treaty obliged Austria to recognized the independence of Czechoslovakia, Hungary, Poland and Yugoslavia. Austria was also obliged to pay heavy reparations and ceded territories to Italy.

By 1922, the Reparations Commission was adopting a Belgian proposal that Germany should be allowed to pay in instalments. The French came to an agreement with Germany to allow Germany to pay in commodities such as coal instead of cash, but the German economy was in such a bad way that its stock market collapsed in August 1922. The mark fell in value from 162 to the dollar to 7,000 to the dollar, and then the following year it fell to 13 million to the dollar by September and to 4 trillion at the end of November. Germans switched to bartering in basic commodities.

The frustration that many Germans felt at the impossible burden of paying war reparations boiled over into an even more militant nationalism than before. It was a frustration that Adolf Hitler was able to exploit to great effect.

THE AMRITSAR MASSACRE
(1919)

ON 10 APRIL 1919, Indians demonstrating for self-government at Amritsar, the holy city of the Sikhs, prompted a ferocious response from the British troops under General Dyer. General Reginald Dyer was Anglo-Irish, born in the Punjab in 1864. In the First World War, he had commanded the 45th Infantry Brigade. In 1919, he was brigade commander at Jullundur; when the demonstration at Amritsar appeared to be getting too lively, he was called out with his Gurkha troops. Without giving the demonstrators any warning Dyer ordered his men to fire on them, even though they were unarmed civilians. He killed 379 people and wounded 1,200.

A commission of enquiry was set up and Dyer was discreetly removed. He eventually retired from the army and died in retirement in Bristol in 1927.

There was widespread hostility to the British action throughout India. The British imposed emergency war regulations, fearing an uprising. The talks that had been under way regarding provincial self-government were shelved. There had also been plans to 'Indianize' the army and the civil service, and these too were shelved.

The effect of the Amritsar massacre within India was far-reaching. The Indian National Council bought the Jallianwala Bagh, the site of the massacre, as a memorial to the martyrs who had died there; it became a site of pilgrimage. Many Indians who had been supportive of the idea of self-government for India had favoured using peaceful means. The response of the colonial power to this fairly harmless demonstration showed that Britain was not a power with which they could negotiate; nor was it one that they could trust. Amritsar led to a hardening of attitude, and a more aggressive approach to the Indian campaign for independence. Above all, the Amritsar massacre proved that India needed independence from Britain.

THE BEGINNING OF RADIO BROADCASTING
(1921)

THE FIRST EXPERIMENTAL radio broadcasts were made in Britain in 1921. They led to the formation a few months later of the British Broadcasting Company (later Corporation). This was at the instigation of the General Post Office (GPO), who wanted to see the formation of a single consortium of wireless equipment manufacturers and broadcasters, specifically to avoid the major confusion that had arisen in North America, where there were 500 rival stations. The new company worked under John Reith, an engineer from Aberdeen who was the company's general manager for its first 16 years. Under Reith's leadership, the BBC became a major national institution. The broadcasts were entirely live, and Reith insisted on a high level of formality, in spoken English, behaviour and dress, traditions which have unfortunately been thrown to the four winds in recent years.

The London broadcasting station, known as 2LO, went on the air on 14 November 1922 as the British Broadcasting Company. A news bulletin was read by Arthur Burrows of the Marconi Company. The initial broadcasts were fairly short, but soon lengthened to four hours a day of news, talks and concerts.

The BBC was supported financially by licence fees paid for by the users. They had to pay ten shillings a year (50 pence) for the privilege of operating a receiver. The same system was used when television was introduced, also by the BBC.

At the same time in North America, the first commercial radio was being broadcast. The New York station, WEAF, broadcast the first radio commercials. This different approach to broadcasting was to become the set pattern in North America – private control of the airwaves and programmes dominated by sponsors. The radio pioneer Lee De Forest asked,

What have you done with my child? You have sent him out on the street in rags of ragtime to collect money from all and sundry. You have made of him a laughing stock of intelligence, surely a stench in the nostrils of the gods of the ionosphere.

In 1923, the BBC began publishing its magazine, the *Radio Times*, so that listeners would know in advance what programmes were to be broadcast; this too became a long-continuing practice.

By 1926, radio ownership in the United States reached three million; most of these radios required listeners to wear earphones. In 1926, NBC (the National Broadcasting Company) was founded by David Sarnoff; this ambitious project had nine stations.

The first experiments with television followed hard on the heels of radio. It was in 1926 that John Logie Baird gave his first public demonstration of television, but the system he used was based on the rotating disc invented by van Nipkov in 1886 and had serious limitations. Television had its first American demonstration in 1927 in the auditorium of New York's Bell Telephone Laboratories. Walter Gifford showed a large audience Commerce Secretary Herbert Hoover in his office in Washington while Hoover's voice was transmitted over telephone wires. The development of television was seriously inhibited by the fact that it needed a frequency band of four million cycles compared with only 400 for a radio; this was because of the need to transmit 250,000 elements required to build a clear picture on the screen.

The first regularly scheduled TV programmes started on 11 May 1928. General Electric's station in New York broadcast the first programmes.

Another contributing development was the invention of the first tape recorder. The blattnerphone designed by the German film producer Louis Blattner used magnetized steel tape. Blattner himself used his invention to supply synchronized sound tracks to the films he was making at Elstree Studios. The BBC saw straight away that the tape recorder was going to be invaluable to them, not least for making recorded programmes, and acquired the first commercially produced blattnerphone in 1931.

Both radio and television continued to develop. In the United States 75,000 radio sets were sold in 1921; by the end of the decade sales had increased to over 13 million. It had become a major communicator. It had also become big business. American advertizers were spending 60 million dollars on radio commercials.

THE OPENING OF THE FIRST AUTOBAHN
(1921)

ON 10 SEPTEMBER, the first motorway in the world was opened. It was the Avus autobahn in Berlin. It was first planned as early as 1909, and building work began shortly after that. When the First World War broke out in 1914 it was almost complete, but work on it stopped and it was not completed until after the war was over.

The revolutionary new autobahn was the first road in the world to be designed exclusively for the motor car and with controlled and restricted access. It was nevertheless rather short. It ran for just over 9km from the Grunewald to the suburb of Wannsee. The two carriageways, each 8m wide, were separated by an 8m wide central reservation to separate the two flows of traffic and improve safety. The road was spanned by ten ferro-concrete bridges.

The design was to be copied again and again during the next half century, first in Germany, and then in other countries. Hitler is popularly supposed to have created the autobahn system in Germany, but autobahns were already being built before Hitler came to power. It is one of the many 'historic legends' that are peddled by non-historians; a parallel one is that Mussolini made the trains run on time. Another is that Queen Victoria was 'not amused', when in fact she laughed and giggled a lot.

Britain was rather slow by comparison with Germany and did not get its first motorway until the 1950s. Many of the design features of the first autobahn were kept in subsequent motorways. The concept of relatively infrequent access points and exits was an important one; it kept the traffic moving fast. The concept of reinforced concrete bridges to take minor roads over the top of the motorway without interrupting the traffic flow was another. The central reservation is another idea that we take for granted now, but that too was part of the original design of the autobahn.

THE APPOINTMENT OF MUSSOLINI

(1922)

A FASCIST DICTATORSHIP was launched in Italy in November 1922. The King of Italy, Victor Emmanuel III, summoned Benito Mussolini to form a ministry, granting him dictatorial powers. The King's intention was that Mussolini would restore order in Italy and bring about reform.

Mussolini had campaigned in his *Popolo d'Italia* against Communism, and organized his own Fascist organization into a political party. Mussolini managed to win a great deal of support from businessmen who were afraid of Communism. The King too feared a Communist takeover. On 4 August 1922, Mussolini and his Fascisti violently broke the Communist-led strike in Milan and took control of the city. Sixteen trucks filled with Blackshirts converged on the Communist-occupied town hall in Milan at the same time as crowds of Blackshirts on foot. One of the trucks was used to smash down the front doors of the town hall. The few guards were quickly overcome and the building was taken over. The Bolshevik red flag was thrown down and the national flag put in its place.

This episode was a marvellous piece of street theatre and it greatly strengthened Mussolini's image as a man of action. The result was that when the Fascisti staged a March on Rome at the end of October, he was given the political power to resist the Communists. It is interesting that in spite of his image Mussolini did not have the physical courage to lead this march. He thought it might fail and put him in danger. He waited in Milan, ready to speed northwards into Switzerland if the plan should fail. In fact the Fascisti were cheered by the crowds in Rome. The king saw that the only way forward, short of a civil war that might well destroy the monarchy, was to give Mussolini formal power. He sent a special train to collect Mussolini. Government troops blew up the track, so he had to complete the journey by car.

The king intended Mussolini's dictatorship to end after a year. What Mussolini did was to dissolve the opposition parties. He then forced a law through the Italian Parliament in November 1923, which said that any party winning the largest number of votes in an election should have two-thirds of the seats, regardless of the percentage of the electorate it represented. In 1924, he took control of the electoral machinery and saw to it that his Fascisti gained 65 percent of the vote.

Behind the scenes, Mussolini was less scrupulous. The Italian Socialist Deputy Giacomo Matteotti was murdered on 10 June by Mussolini's Fascisti. He claimed to know nothing about the murder, imposed strict press censorship and two months later banned opposition meetings. Step by step, Mussolini strengthened his position as Italy's dictator, and he managed to remain in power for 20 years. In some ways, Mussolini looks like a pale reflection of Hitler, a back-street bully, but he did succeed in staying in power as a national leader for 20 years compared with Hitler's 12. It was also a major prop for Hitler to have an ally in the Mediterranean. But – could Victor Emmanuel have done anything to stop Mussolini?

WALT DISNEY'S
STEAMBOAT WILLIE
(1928)

AT THE YOUNG age of 17 Walt Disney became an ambulance driver for the Red Cross with the American troops in France in 1918. After the war he worked as a commercial artist for a couple of years, before becoming a cartoonist for the Kansas City Film Advertising from 1920 to 1922.

Disney experimented with a number of animated cartoon films in Hollywood, creating the *Alice* comedies. He created and produced the first Oswald the Rabbit cartoons in 1926. Disney created his first successful sound picture, *Steamboat Willie*, in 1928. It was in *Steamboat Willie* that Mickey Mouse, probably the best-loved cartoon character of all time, made his first appearance. From then on Mickey Mouse became a firm favourite with audiences. In the short *Silly Symphony* cartoons in colour, Disney introduced Donald Duck, Pluto and other cartoon characters that quickly became very popular. In fact these colour cartoons were the most popular entertainment on the screen.

Mickey Mouse became something more too. Disney had a strong commercial sense, and Mickey Mouse was the springboard for a huge and lucrative merchandising empire.

Disney broke new ground with his full-length colour cartoon films. They required enormous numbers of hand-drawn images, and this work was shared among a team of dedicated artists. Disney was a hard taskmaster and demanded incredibly high standards from his staff. The first of these very ambitious projects was *Snow White and the Seven Dwarfs*, which was first shown in 1937. The film was – and still is – very popular. The reception of this film encouraged Disney to go on to make more feature-length cartoon films: *Pinocchio*, *Dumbo*, *Bambi*, *Lady and the Tramp* and *Sleeping Beauty*. All became twentieth century classics.

Fantasia was a different experiment. Disney took an orchestral score, conducted by Leopold Stokowski, and made an animated animal cartoon film to synchronize with the music. Many of the effects were surreal, and as a piece of craftsmanship it is an outstanding piece of work, but *Fantasia* lacks a story line and has never had the same popular following as *Snow White*. After the war, Disney resumed full-length cartoon films, with two more huge successes: *Cinderella* in 1950 and *Alice in Wonderland* in 1951.

Another major feature of Walt Disney's activity was his strong and voracious business sense. He was intent on making as much money as possible out of each project, and there were always tie-in books, toys and other merchandise that developed into as big a business as the films.

The most spectacular tie-in projects were the theme parks: the Disneyland amusement park built in California in 1955, and its spin-off theme parks in Florida and Paris.

With *Steamboat Willie* Disney launched a minor art form, the black and white short cartoon film, and developed it into a major art form that became large-scale mass entertainment. It was a revolution in popular entertainment. He introduced a range of cartoon characters that have become icons of twentieth century popular culture, but of all of them there is no question that the irrepressibly good-natured and optimistic Mickey Mouse was the central and most popular of them all, and he made his first appearance in *Steamboat Willie*. In his various transformations, whether on film, on car stickers, or 'in person' at Disneyland, Mickey Mouse became a celebrity. Perhaps his hour of triumph was meeting Hirohito, the defeated Emperor of Japan, at a photo opportunity – and there really is a photograph to prove it. That is international celebrity.

THE
COLLECTIVIZATION OF
SOVIET AGRICULTURE
(1928)

IN THE LAST few months of 1927, the Russian dictator Stalin decisively suppressed any possible opposition. He expelled Leon Trotsky and Grigori Zinoviev from the Soviet Communist Party and routed his opponents. Trotsky had been a close colleague of Lenin's during the Bolshevik revolution, but this link with the historic past actually counted against him as far as Stalin was concerned. He wanted no near-equals, or possible rivals. Trotsky dangerously criticized Stalin for a lack of foresight, efficiency and determination. Stalin simply got rid of him, initially by sending him to the Soviet-Chinese border.

The way was clear for Stalin's unopposed dictatorship. In October 1928, Stalin's first Five-Year Plan went into operation. This was an ambitious scheme to catapult the Soviet Union into the forefront of developed nations. The development of heavy industry was a major priority, with its emphasis on steel and armaments. The aim was rapid industrialization. The other major aim was the modernization of agriculture. The countryside was to be transformed. Peasant smallholdings were to be combined into collective farms, which would belong to villages as a whole; they would be farmed by modern methods.

The collectivization programme was very unpopular with the peasant farmers. Without any stake in the land, they had no incentive to work hard. Stalin went ahead regardless. In January 1930, Stalin extended the collectivization programme through the entire Soviet Union. He saw the movement as successful and ignored evidence to the contrary. Tens of thousands of agents were sent out into the rural areas to deal with kulaks, or rich peasants, who were resisting the process.

Stalin was driven to this desperately radical measure by the threat of famine. He offered poor farmers rewards for going along with collectivization. Each family opting in was allowed to own a house, garden, stable and car. The family was also allowed to keep any income from the sale of their vegetables.

There was continuing resistance, but what Stalin was doing was far more revolutionary than anything so far attempted. It was more than economic engineering, it was social engineering too. It also had the advantage of strengthening the Communist Party's control over the traditionally undisciplined Russian peasant. But the process was not given any time to evolve. Stalin insisted on immediate collaboration. The better-off kulaks resisted. By February 1930 it was reported that Stalin's agents were murdering an average of 40 kulaks every day. Thousands fled to Poland to escape the collectivization process.

The problem with the collective farms was that individuals had too little incentive to work hard and produce as much food as possible. Ultimately, it was an experiment that was bound to fail. The Soviet Union under Stalin and his successors suffered continual crop failures and food shortages. This was bad for the people who suffered in the famines that followed, and it weakened the Soviet Union in the Cold War; the United States was able to use its grain surplus as a major political lever.

THE DISCOVERY OF PENICILLIN
(1928)

IN 1928, PROFESSOR Alexander Fleming of Queen Mary's Hospital in London accidentally discovered a mould that could attack harmful bacteria.

He left a plate of staphylococcus bacteria out in his laboratory for a few days. Staphylococcus bacteria are responsible for many infections that afflict people. When he had a look at the plate he noticed that it had become contaminated with mould. He also noticed that around the mould there were rings that were cleared of bacteria. It looked as if the mould must be producing a chemical that was killing the bacteria.

Fleming identified the mould as *Penicillin notatum*, which is the common mould that grows on bread. It kills many types of bacteria, not just staphylococcus, and does no harm to the white blood cells found in human blood, and this was an early indication that it was going to be safe to use on people. Fleming had difficulty in isolating the chemical from the mould, and it was to be some time before penicillin extracted from mould would be available to treat infections.

On 9 January 1929, Fleming made his first trial use of penicillin on a human being. One of his assistants had an infected sinus. Fleming washed the man's sinus out with a broth of diluted penicillin. This was very successful in destroying most of the staphylococci. In 1931, penicillin was used on two children at the Royal Infirmary in Sheffield. They had contracted gonorrhoea from their mothers at birth and were suffering from gonococcal ophthalmitis. Penicillin reduced the infection. The new discovery was also used at Sheffield on a colliery manager with an eye infection.

With these first tentative treatments, the new age of antibiotics had arrived. But the use of the new drug was slow to take off in the 1930s. Then in 1940, the Australian-British pathologist Howard Florey published an article in *The Lancet*, '*Penicillin as a Chemotherapeutic agent*'. Together with his refugee collaborator Ernest Chaim, Florey had developed Fleming's penicillin into an agent that would become a major weapon against infections and diseases. The three of them, Fleming, Florey and Chaim, were to be awarded the Nobel Prize for Medicine. But for the time being penicillin was in extremely short supply. The entire world supply of penicillin as it stood in 1942 was barely enough to treat just one case of meningitis. Only in 1945 did an Anglo-American research team develop a way of mass-producing penicillin so that it could be distributed on a commercial basis. After that, antibiotics became increasingly available to cure a very wide range of infections. It was a great leap forward in modern medicine.

THE WALL STREET CRASH

(1929)

THE AMERICAN STOCK market had been booming during the 1920s. In the early 1920s, around 250 million shares were sold per year; by the end of the decade that figure had quadrupled. The Dow Jones Industrial Average reached its peak of 381 on Wall Street, the New York Stock Exchange, in September 1929. After that things started to go wrong. American iron and steel production fell. At the same time British interest rates rose to over 6 percent, which attracted investors, and this pulled European money out of the American money market.

24 October 1929, 'Black Thursday', saw a wave of panic sweep through Wall Street. Thirteen million shares changed hands. Dazed brokers wandered around clutching clients' orders to 'sell at any price'. People tried to get rid of their shares before they became worthless. The sheer volume of selling caused share prices to plummet. Police were called to disperse hysterical crowds gathering in Wall Street. At midday, New York's leading bankers held a meeting to discuss the situation. Because investors thought this meant an intervention, a rescue of some kind, they started buying again, and there was a recovery during the afternoon. The bankers saw nothing in the business world to justify the loss of confidence and put the problem down to the inadequacy of the ticker-tape machine, which was not designed to cope with these very fast rates of buying and selling. They tried to stop the slide by assuring traders that there was no real business depression. But confidence in Wall Street shares had vanished and the selling continued – and the value of the shares fell accordingly.

Many small investors lost everything. Eleven people committed suicide. Thirty billion dollars simply disappeared, a huge sum roughly equivalent to the cost of the First World War to North America.

By the spring of 1930, confidence began to return and share prices rose, but by May a long decline resumed. A general world economic depression set in. World trade declined, industrial production fell, unemployment increased. In the United States, unemployment reached 4.5 million and the Gross Domestic Product fell from 81 billion dollars to 68 billion dollars. Over a thousand banks closed in the United States during 1930. President Hoover requested 150 million dollars from Congress for public works projects, and in December Congress granted 116 million dollars. The intention was to generate economic activity and create jobs.

The Wall Street Crash was not only a disaster for the United States, but also for the rest of the world. Investment depended on confidence and the confidence had evaporated. The ripples of fear spread endlessly outwards. A pandemic of financial panic spread round the world. In Vienna in 1931, a major bank closed and the panic spread to Germany, where another bank closed. The situation in Britain was shaky and the pound was devalued. In 1932 Britain abandoned free trade for the first time since 1849, imposing a ten percent tariff on imported goods, exempting Commonwealth imports. Unemployment rose to 2.5 million in Britain. In Germany unemployment rose to 5.6 million, stirring up the dissatisfaction that would feed Nazism. The repercussions of the Wall Street Crash were far-reaching.

THE VATICAN BAN ON CONTRACEPTION

(1930)

ON 31 DECEMBER 1930, Pope Pius XI issued an encyclical entitled *Casti connubii*. It read:

> *Any use whatsoever of matrimony exercised in such a way that the [sex] act is deliberately frustrated in its natural power to generate life is an offence against the law of God and of nature, and those who indulge in such are branded with the guilt of a grave sin.*

This stern and uncompromising statement amounted to an absolute ban on the use of artificial contraception within marriage. The Vatican nevertheless allowed married couples to use the so-called rhythm system of birth control, though this was known to be an unreliable and ineffective technique.

The Vatican went on opposing the use of artificial contraceptive methods, and has gone on opposing it to the present day. One effect of this has been to push 'thinking Catholics' into making their own decision to use contraceptives, which has to an extent undermined the authority of the Vatican. Another effect has been to maintain high birth rates in less economically developed countries, and therefore also to maintain high levels of poverty. When Pius XI imposed his ban on contraception in 1930, there were two billion people in the world. Now there are well over six billion, and there would have been a better chance of improving living standards in the Third World if the rate of population growth had been slower.

THE INVENTION OF
THE ELECTRON
MICROSCOPE
(1932)

IT WAS ANTHONY van Leeuwenhoek, at the end of the seventeenth century, who ground small high-power lenses for the first time with a view to observing small objects with them. With his carefully ground lenses, van Leeuwenhoek was able to see objects a 100 times smaller than could be observed with the naked eye. The modern microscope was not immediately to follow; the lenses refracted and split light and it was not until the early nineteenth century that lenses could be corrected and the image sharpened up. Then there was great optimism that the optical microscope could be improved and improved until even the smallest object would become visible. Gradually it became apparent that there were physical limits to the optical microscope and that some other type of technology would be necessary to deal with very small objects.

In 1924, the wavelike nature of moving electrons was discovered. Then it became clear that magnetic or electrical fields could be used to act as lenses for electrons or other charged particles. Instead of light, streams of charged particles would be used.

The first electron microscope in the world was invented by the German engineers M. Knoll and Ernst Ruska in 1932. Knoll and Ruska confidently claimed that an electron microscope using high-velocity electrons would be able to surpass the magnification of the optical microscope. In fact their electron microscope could not exceed the magnification possible with the most powerful optical microscopes. Two other workers, Driest and Muller, modified their microscope and achieved significant increases in magnification. The new instrument could achieve a magnification of

12,000 times. Two years later commercial production of electron microscopes started in England. By 1938, a scanning electron microscope was being built by the German physicist Manfred von Ardenne.

The first powerful modern electron microscope was put on show on 1 April 1940 at the RCA Laboratories at Camden in New Jersey. The new microscope, which could achieve a magnification of up to 100,000 times, was developed by RCA engineers under the supervision of the 50 year old Russian-American Vladimir Zworykin. It was Zworykin who, back in the 1920s, had invented the television screen. The new electron microscope was bulky; it stood an imposing 3m high and weighed 350kg.

The electron microscope made all kinds of new scientific investigations possible, such as the organization of molecules into crystal lattices. The electron microscope fills the gap between the light microscope and the molecule. It has been of enormous value in chemistry, in studying materials with distinctive structures such as cellulose and vulcanized rubber. In the field of biology, it has been possible to examine viruses, bacteria and even the internal organs of insects. Without the electron microscope it would not have been possible to observe the protein molecules, and it would not have been possible to explore the structure of DNA.

Above all, the electron microscope made it possible for us to explore the inner universe of the very small and very close to home, in the same way that the more powerful modern telescopes and space probes have enabled us to explore the outer universe of the very large and very distant.

HITLER'S APPOINTMENT AS CHANCELLOR
(1933)

AT MIDDAY ON 30 January 1933, Adolf Hitler came to power as Chancellor of Germany on a rising tide of economic unrest and German nationalism. Hitler emerged from the First World a great German patriot, even though he was not actually a German, and he continued to believe along with many others who had fought on the Western Front that Germany had not really been defeated. His early followers included Rudolf Hess, Hermann Goering, Ernst Röhm and Field-Marshal Erich Lüdendorff. Hitler used Lüdendorff as a front in an absurd attempt to seize power on 8 November 1923. In this 'Beer Hall Putsch', the Nazis marched from a beer hall to the Bavarian War Ministry, with the intention of overthrowing the Bavarian government, and then marching on Berlin. They were quickly dispersed by soldiers and Hitler was arrested and tried for treason.

In April 1924, he was sentenced to five years in prison, where he dictated *Mein Kampf* to the loyal Hess. This rambling autobiography contains Hitler's alarming views on race, history and the Jews, and includes threats against his enemies if he should win power. It was natural that no-one should have taken any notice. Hitler was considered a harmless crank and released early.

Hitler was able to build on a widespread sense of injured national pride, caused by the Treaty of Versailles imposed on Germany. Huge reparations were exacted from Germany to pay for the war. Most Germans bitterly resented having to pay, particularly since they did not consider that they had lost. The second turning point in Hitler's career came when the Depression hit Germany in 1930. The traditional parties were unable to deal with the unprecedented shock of the Depression, and in the September 1930 elections the Nazis won 107 seats in the Reichstag, becoming the second largest party. In the July 1932 elections, they won 230 seats, making them the largest party. Behind the scenes, conspirators persuaded Hindenburg to appoint Hitler chancellor, which he did in January 1933. This was the start of Hitler's dictatorship. It is hard now to believe that it lasted only 12 years, given how much Hitler destroyed in that short time.

Using the pretext of the Reichstag fire of 27 February 1933, which may actually have been started by the Nazis themselves, Hitler issued a decree suppressing civil rights in the interests of national security. The Communist leaders and other opponents of Hitler's regime found themselves in prison.

In the space of a few months, Hitler achieved authoritarian control over Germany by more or less legal means and without suspending the Weimar constitution. But democracy in Germany was over and the escalation of evil had begun. With Goebbels as his propaganda chief, Hitler was able to persuade most Germans that he was their saviour. Those who were not persuaded were rounded up by the SA, the SS and the Gestapo, the Secret State Police. Thousands were to disappear into concentration camps. Thousands more, including half of Germany's Jewish population, emigrated in order to escape the Holocaust that was clearly coming. Those Jews who had not emigrated soon regretted their decision to stay. Under Hitler's 1935 Nuremberg Laws, they lost their status as citizens and were thrown out of all government employment, the professions and many other jobs too. From 1941 Jews were subjected to the further humiliation of wearing a yellow star in public places. Hitler was the evil behind this, but the Christian churches, riddled as they were with anti-semitism, stayed silent.

Hitler's foreign policy was to prove astonishingly aggressive, whipping up a world war that no-one else in Europe or North America wanted. He provoked it by invading one country after another.

The Second World War was only started because of Adolf Hitler's megalomania. It was only drawn out for a final unnecessary year because he had lost touch with reality. The cost in human misery and human life was incalculable. The Second World War was in large part due to the actions of this one man, and that war is estimated to have cost 50 million lives. The only comparable blood-letting in the past century has been Mao Zedong's regime in China, which cost 48 million lives.

The 85-year-old Hindenburg made a mistake in appointing Hitler as chancellor. In fact he had already rejected the idea in November 1932, because he knew that Hitler's cabinet would be 'bound to develop into a party dictatorship.' The reason why Hindenburg changed his mind was that parliamentary government was collapsing and every day that passed brought civil war closer. There were daily street battles between Communists and Nazis. Hindenburg decided that making Hitler chancellor was the lesser of the two evils. From our present vantage point, with the benefit of hindsight, it is very hard to see how things could have turned out worse.

THE DISCOVERY THAT CIGARETTE SMOKE CAUSES CANCER
(1933)

ERNEST KENNAWAY, A British biochemist, isolated the first pure cancer-causing chemical. He also showed in laboratory tests in 1933 that a hydrocarbon produced from incomplete combustion can cause cancer in animals. These hydrocarbons were to be found in the exhaust fumes of cars and lorries and in cigarette smoke. Inhaling cigarette smoke increased the risk of developing cancer.

This appears to be the first medical evidence that the much-maligned King James I of England was right, after all, about the harmful effects of smoking tobacco. Over the next 30 or 40 years, more and more evidence was to emerge from medical research that smoking was harmful. By 1953, the popular magazine *Reader's Digest* published an article on the harmful effects of smoking; its title said it all: 'Cancer by the Carton'. The following year the American National Cancer Institute said that there was a link between smoking and lung cancer. In 1960, the American Heart Association published its finding that smokers were 50 to 150 percent likelier to die from coronary heart disease than non-smokers. More research along the same lines and with the same result came out the following year.

In 1963, the American Heart Association launched its first campaign against tobacco smoking. In 1964, the American Surgeon-General Luther Terry brought out a report entitled *Smoking and Health*; this confirmed that smoking was dangerous and that both lung cancer and heart disease could result from it. Within two years, packets of cigarettes were carrying health warnings.

People nevertheless carried on smoking as if this information and advice did not exist. In the mid-1960s, the average American smoked ten cigarettes a day. In 1971, the Royal College of Surgeons in Britain reported that smoking cigarettes was causing as many deaths as the typhoid and cholera epidemics of the nineteenth century.

A new slant on tobacco smoking appeared in 1972, when the American surgeon-general reported that passive smoking was a severe health hazard. This had not previously been thought of as dangerous, and it led to increasingly vociferous calls to ban smoking in public places such as restaurants, offices and planes. The very next year the state of Arizona imposed a ban on smoking in public places, in order to protect the health of people who had decided not to smoke.

The evidence that cigarette smoking causes a range of health problems, both to the smokers and those around them, has been gradually mounting. Some of the illnesses that result are extremely serious, the worst of them being heart disease and lung cancer. Curiously, many seasoned smokers continue to maintain that they had no idea when they took it up that smoking could be harmful, but it is clear that as early as 1933 the information that smoking could cause cancer was already available; any smoker below the age of 75 and able to read a newspaper had access to it.

THE INVENTION OF THE RADIO TELESCOPE
(1937)

IN 1931, THE American engineer Karl Kansky discovered that interference in telephone communications was being caused by radio emissions from the Milky Way. This remarkable discovery, that radio waves are reaching the Earth from outer space, opened the way to a new era in astronomy – radio astronomy.

The 25 year old American astronomer Grote Reber built the world's first radio telescope at Wheaton, Illinois, in 1937. It had a parabolic reflector nine metres across. For almost a decade, Reber was to be the only radio astronomer in the world.

The areas of maximum emissions were located and mapped on the celestial sphere with the aid of the new generation of radio telescopes. In 1942, Grote Reber made the first radio maps of the sky. In the 1950s astronomers found themselves confronted with the problem of identifying these newly discovered 'radio stars', or whatever the objects might be that were the sources of the radio signals. In 1955, the American astronomer B. F. Burk discovered that not all of the emissions were coming from outside the solar system; even the planet Jupiter was giving off radio waves. In 1958, radio astronomers picked up radio waves that had been reflected from the surface of the planet Venus, and found that this 'bouncing' of radio waves could be used to measure the distance of the planets more accurately than before.

The radio telescope gave astronomers a new way of looking at and listening to the universe. Revolutionary though they were in their day, the old 'Galilean' telescopes simply magnified and enhanced what was already visible from the Earth. The new radio telescopes made it possible to detect things that were completely invisible, beyond the reach of ordinary telescopes. They have enabled us to 'see' further out into the universe than ever before.

PICASSO'S *GUERNICA*
(1937)

PABLO PICASSO, WHO was probably the greatest artist of the twentieth century, developed his Cubist style early on. The early Cubist paintings prepared the way for Picasso's most famous piece of work, *Guernica*.

Guernica was painted in 1937. It is a huge canvas, on which Picasso expressed his horror at the bombing of a Basque town during the Spanish Civil War, and of the horrors of war in general. The town of Guernica was entirely undefended and defenceless; but it was a communications centre and it had a munitions factory. On the afternoon of 26 April 1937, it was bombed relentlessly with high explosives and incendiary bombs for over three hours by German Junker and Heinkel bombers sent by Hitler to help Franco. It was market day and the square was crowded with people. Civilians fleeing out into the surrounding fields were strafed by Heinkel fighter planes. Afterwards soldiers went in to pick up the charred bodies. A reporter arriving shortly afterwards said, 'It was impossible to go down many of the streets, because they were walls of flame. Debris was piled high. The shocked survivors all had the same story to tell: aeroplanes, bullets, bombs, fire.'

The painting *Guernica* was Picasso's response to that war crime. The colours he used are extremely muted, black and slightly tinted greys; the effect is distinctly monochrome, which gives the picture an extraordinary gravity and seriousness. It has become a classic art work, with the same status as Leonardo's *Mona Lisa*, Michelangelo's *David* or Constable's *The Hay Wain*; it is recognized as great art.

After the Second World War he became a communist, but neither the visual nightmare of *Guernica* nor his portrait of Stalin painted in 1953 endeared him to the Communist Party. His was not the art of the people, by a long way. Even so, people have become gradually more and more familiar with the expressive power of *Guernica*, and it is a work of art that has somehow grown in stature over the decades. It has increased in power.

THE ASSASSINATION OF VOM RATH
(1938)

IN OCTOBER 1938 the Polish government passed a law to the effect that any Poles living abroad for more than five years would not be re-admitted. This was a measure to defend Poland from being flooded by the thousands of Jews of Polish origin who were currently living outside Poland and who were being ejected from Germany and Austria. The German response to this was to deliver 15,000 Jews to the Polish frontier on 27 October and cold-bloodedly leave them there. They were not allowed to enter Poland; they were not allowed to return to Germany. Some managed to escape into Poland, but many did not. The rest languished there for three months, many dying, some going insane, some committing suicide. Eventually it was the Germans (not the Poles) who relented and took the survivors back; some of them reached Britain or North America.

Herschel Grynspan, a 17 year old Jewish youth, left Hanover in 1936 intending to emigrate to Palestine, but ended up in Paris, where he lived with an aunt and uncle. In August 1938, he was served with an expulsion order by the French government; after that his uncle sheltered him illegally. On 3 November, he received a postcard from his sister telling him of his family's deportation and suffering on the Polish border, a postcard which she may later have regretted sending. Four days later, Grynspan bought a revolver and walked into the German embassy, asking to see the first secretary. Instead, he was shown in to the third secretary's office.

The third secretary was a German diplomat called Ernst vom Rath. Grynspan protested about the treatment of the Jews at the Polish frontier and then fired five shots, two of which hit vom Rath. Herschel Grynspan made no attempt to escape, and vom Rath died two days later.

Because Grynspan was Jewish, there was a large-scale and well co-ordinated reprisal levelled at the Jews in general. And the reprisal, on 9 November, was the infamous Kristallnacht (Crystal Night), so called by the Nazis because of the huge expanses of broken glass from the smashed windows of Jewish-owned shops left in the streets the following morning. Jewish people, shops and business premises were viciously attacked all over Germany. Hundreds of synagogues were burnt down. Countless Jews died. In Berlin, fashionably dressed women laughed and clapped as they watched Jews being beaten senseless by youths with lengths of lead piping. Over 7,000 shops were looted. The attacks were evidently carefully co-ordinated as they broke out simultaneously in towns and cities throughout Germany. Broken glass accounted for millions of marks' worth of damage. Goering was annoyed when he heard that the replacement glass would have to be imported and paid for in foreign currency. He said, 'They should have killed more Jews and broken less glass.'

The story of Grynspan's futile gesture and its terrible consequences – the pure blind collective sadism of the pogrom – inspired Michael Tippett's *A Child of Our Time*. Tippett borrowed the title from the last novel by Horvath, which tells the story of an embittered soldier who murders the wrong person in a futile gesture and then dies, frozen to death in the snow. Tippett was interested in scapegoats, people who are in themselves innocent but are sacrificed in some cause or other. The soldier in Horvath's last novel, and then Grynspan: the story seemed to repeat. Tippett was also intrigued by a poem by Wilfred Owen in which the Old Testament story of Abraham and Isaac was given a savage, modern, ironic twist. The angel stays Abraham's hand and tells him not to kill Isaac but the Ram of Pride instead. 'But the old man would not so, but slew his son, - And half the seed of Europe, one by one.'

Benjamin Britten would later set that poem vividly to music as part of his *War Requiem*. Tippett might have done that, but he wanted his friend T. S. Eliot to supply new words for his war oratorio. Eliot read Tippett's sketch, and then surprised Tippett by advising him to write his own words. The result was a great modern classic, which sums up 'the pity of war.' For Tippett it was a turning-point in his career as a composer. He knew when he eventually heard it for the first time, in 1944, that he had found his true role. And the trigger had been the shooting incident in Paris in 1938.

And what of the young man who caught Michael Tippett's

imagination? For Herschel Grynspan one might have expected a quick trial followed by immediate execution, but things did not turn out that way. The trial of Grynspan was delayed, because the Nazis wanted the French to try him in secret, and Grynspan's supporters in North America pressed for a public trial. Then the war broke out. Grynspan wrote to the French Minister of Justice from prison, asking to be released so that he could fight the Nazis. Along with other prisoners he was moved, because of the German advance, away from Paris. He was first encouraged to escape by his guards. For some reason he was uneasy about doing this, perhaps suspecting that this was a trick to justify shooting him. But other prisoners were also being encouraged to disappear by their guards and Grynspan had finally to be ordered to escape.

When France was overrun by the Germans and occupied, Grynspan was traced and caught under the Vichy regime in 1940. He was tried and sentenced to 20 years in prison. In 1941, he was sent to Berlin and then to Sachsenhausen concentration camp. He was treated well by the Germans, because they wanted him to look well in the show trial they were planning. The trial was fixed for May 1942, but it never took place. Grynspan claimed that he had been sexually abused by vom Rath. This was probably untrue – he had after all asked to see the first secretary at the embassy, when von Rath was the *third* secretary – but Goebbels recognized that the show trial would not after all be any good for public relations. Incredibly, Grynspan had outwitted Goebbels.

It is not known for certain what became of Herschel Grynspan after that. Somehow, in the turmoil of the Second World War, Grynspan was forgotten. He vanished, and it is possible that he was executed in secret with no trial. But there is good evidence to believe that he survived the war, changed his name and started a fresh life in the new state of Israel. Probably Herschel Grynspan is dead now, but he did not die as one might have expected, in 1938.

THE START OF THE SECOND WORLD WAR
(1939)

IN A SENSE the Second World War was a continuation of the First. Many Germans who had fought in the Great War thought they were winning in 1918, and felt betrayed by the politicians far behind the lines, who surrendered on their behalf. As far as they were concerned Germany's status had not been truly recognized. Hitler and Mussolini both knew that foreign wars and conquests were politically strengthening at home. Mussolini accordingly occupied Albania in April 1938 and in May Italy and Germany signed a 'Pact of Steel' alliance. The two countries were 'resolved to fight side by side and with united forces to secure their living space.' The alliance was from the start uneasy. Mussolini was wary of Germany's blatant territorial ambitions, and feared that after the Nazi putsch in Vienna in 1934 the Germans might come south into Italy; he was so uneasy that he sent Italian troops to guard the frontier with Austria – a very significant precaution.

The British knew by early 1939 that war with Germany was inevitable, and overtures were made in May to Stalin. Britain wanted an alliance with Russia to stop German expansion. Stalin was in two minds about his European policy, and he was actually negotiating with Hitler with a view to a Russo-German collaboration.

In July, Hitler's plan to invade Poland became clearer as he prepared to take back Danzig. At the Treaty of Versailles, this area of Germany had been handed over to Poland; Hitler was clearly preparing to take it back. The British government explicitly guaranteed Poland its support. Chamberlain said that if Poland felt it necessary to use force to maintain the status quo in Danzig Britain would help.

In August, Stalin decided to sign a Non-Aggression Pact with Germany.

This deeply shocked the Western Powers, who hoped that Stalin might fall in with them. Hitler and Stalin had been vilifying one another for the last six years, so this oath of friendship was indeed surprising. It was a kind of poker game that the two dictators were playing with one another, and a brilliant political cartoon of the time shows the dictators as two card sharps in a Western saloon, both holding guns out of sight under the table, both ready to shoot. In fact what had been secretly agreed was a partition of Poland between Germany and Russia.

By the end of August, Poland had mobilized its troops, expecting imminent invasion. The British rejected Hitler's offer of a deal; if Britain would help Hitler take Danzig, he would defend the British Empire. The British pointed out that they were already bound by treaty to defend Poland. War was now inevitable and imminent. In Britain, children were evacuated from industrial cities where bombing by German aircraft was expected, and exhibits in art galleries and museums were taken down and put into storage. Even the Coronation chair was moved from Westminster Abbey and taken to a place of safety.

On 1 September, the double invasion of Poland, by Germany and Russia, actually happened. Russia was expelled from the League of Nations. The German style of invasion was terrifyingly effective. Known as 'blitzkrieg' (lightning war), it consisted of waves of aircraft going in to knock out the Polish gun emplacements with heavy bombing, then ground forces comprising fleets of tanks going in. Hitler used this technique again and again, invading country after country. About 60,000 Poles were killed, 200,000 were wounded and another 700,000 were taken prisoner.

Then, as in the First World War, one by one the alliances dragged in the other countries. On 3 September, both France and Britain declared war on Germany. Half an hour after the declaration by Neville Chamberlain a plane was sighted approaching the south coast and the air raid sirens sounded in London. But the war in Britain was not so quick to get going; the Battle of Britain was not to come for a few months.

Italy oddly declared neutrality, and so did the United States, just as President Wilson did in 1914. Sweden and Norway hoped to remain neutral. The Commonwealth countries joined Britain in the war against Germany.

The outbreak of the Second World War led on, by a complex and explosive chain reaction, to a further redrawing of the map of Europe in the

1940s. It also led to a loosening of Britain's grip on its colonies. In India, the separatists were busily planning a new India free of British rule during the European diversion, and the post-war world would see the end of the Empire, with one country after another demanding its independence.

The Cold War was in itself an outcome of the Second World War. Stalin had started the war doing a deal with Hitler to take half of Poland, and ended it doing a deal with Churchill to have a free hand in eastern Europe. Because of the wider-ranging nature of the Second World War, to include the Pacific basin, its effects were enormous. It was not only the biggest and most destructive war of all time, it had the most far-reaching effects, which still operate today. But for the Second World War, it is unlikely that the European Union would exist.

SPLITTING THE ATOM
(1939)

IN 1934, THE Italian physicist Enrico Fermi began experimenting with the bombardment of uranium with neutrons. Using this technique, he succeeded in producing new 'trans-uranium' elements. Using a cyclotron invented by John Dunning at Columbia University's Physics Laboratory, Fermi was the first to split an atom in January 1939, establishing the phenomenon of atomic fission.

The experiment had many implications, not least the possibility of self-sustaining nuclear fission. When the cyclotron was shut down, it was found that stable cobalt-59 inside it had produced unstable cobalt-60, emitting gamma rays. Dunning repeated the experiment in March, in collaboration with Enrico Fermi, Leo Szilard, Walter Zinn and C. B. Pegram, with the same result.

The experiments confirmed that the absorption of a neutron by a uranium atom sometimes causes the atom to split in two, with the release of enormous amounts of energy. This energy became the focus of attention. If the energy contained inside atoms could be released, then presumably it might be harnessed as a power source. But the experiments had other implications too. Albert Einstein wrote to President Roosevelt.

Some recent work by E. Fermi and L. Szilard, which has been communicated to me in manuscript, leads me to expect that the element uranium may be turned into a new and important source of energy in the near future. Certain aspects of the situation which has arisen seem to call for watchfulness and, if necessary, quick action on the part of the administration. In the course of the last four months it has made me almost certain that it may be possible to set up a nuclear chain reaction in a large mass of uranium, by which vast amounts of power would be generated. This new phenomenon would lead also to the construction of bombs.

The construction of bombs. President Roosevelt evidently took what Einstein said seriously, as well he might, and appointed an advisory committee – though only after he heard the news that a *German* physicist, Otto Hahn, had also succeeded in splitting the uranium atom by bombarding it with neutrons. Hahn's work was reported by a former colleague, Lise Meitner, who had fled to Sweden. Hahn, Meitner and Fritz Strassmann had repeated Fermi's experiments and come to the same conclusions about the implications.

In December 1942, Fermi and his colleagues at the University of Chicago used layers of uranium oxide and graphite to create the first nuclear pile, and used it to initiate a controlled chain reaction, It was the very first nuclear reactor. Fermi died, aged 53, in 1954, as the first generation of nuclear power stations was being planned. The new physics had been able to produce a terrifyingly dangerous new generation of weapons, the atom and hydrogen bombs, and also a new generation of power stations, which though promising unlimited energy would also turn out to be dangerous in their own way. Only time will tell whether these discoveries were a 'good thing' so far they seem to have created more problems than they have solved.

THE DISCOVERY OF THE LASCAUX CAVE PAINTINGS
(1940)

SOME SPECTACULAR AND entirely unsuspected prehistoric paintings were discovered quite by chance by Jacques Marsal, a French schoolboy, in a cave at Lascaux near Périgueux in 1940. What the boy saw, along both sides of the corridor-like cave passage was a painted frieze of prehistoric animals. The discovery was an historic moment. There is a popular tendency to see the history of archaeology as a sequence of great discoveries: the tomb of Tutankhamun in Egypt, the lost Maya cities of Mexico, the painted caves of the Old Stone Age. The discovery of the Lascaux paintings was certainly one of those popular historic landmarks.

For some reason there seems to have been a surge of artistic creativity at around the time when the late-glacial ice sheets reached their largest extent. The European cave paintings, such as Lascaux in southern France and Altamira in northern Spain, date from the period 20,000–15,000 BC. The coldest point, the time when the ice was at its greatest extent and the sea level was at its lowest, was 16,000 BC. It is tempting to see the burst of creativity as a response to extremely adverse environmental conditions. This was a climatic crisis far worse than the global warming that is the big scare story of the twenty-first century, with huge areas of northern Europe completely entombed in ice. It may well be that people were responding to the climatic crisis with some religious appeal for help. But we must not argue too far in that direction; the number of dated finds is really too small to draw that inference, and some pieces of artwork have been found from significantly earlier times, when the climate was milder.

It is very difficult to be sure what the drawings and paintings of animals were for. One possibility that has been proposed is that the major centres of art production, such as Altamira and Lascaux, served as major religious or ceremonial centres, and were the scene of important ceremonies that took place during regular annual gatherings of the people of each area. Or it may be that the production of the art was in the hands of particular chiefs or religious leaders, and that they used the creation of the art and the ceremonies that went with it to legitimize their authority. But this is all very speculative. One thing that is clear is that the art is not to be found uniformly across Europe, but concentrated in the areas that are known to have been most densely populated around 16,000 BC.

One of the painted panels at Lascaux shows a sequence of vigorous overlapping images of wild cattle, horses, ibex and red deer, painted in red ochre and black manganese dioxide. The Chauvet cave, discovered in southern France half a century later, also has overlapping animal images; it was for a time seriously thought that the spectacularly vivid Chauvet paintings must be a modern forgery – but they are not.

Another image at Lascaux shows a wounded bison apparently knocking over a naked man. Nearby another bison defecates and there is a bird on a stick. There are also some enigmatic dots and rectangles. It is very hard to work out what the image is about, but it appears to be connected with hunting magic. Other cave art also has animals that might well have been targeted for hunting as the main focus of interest. The pictures are certainly not landscape art in any sense that we understand.

Most of the cave and rock shelter art so far recognized comes from northern Spain and southern France, but that may only be because we have not been looking hard enough elsewhere, and there are lots of caves all over Europe. In fact, recently some prehistoric cave sketches or engravings have been discovered in caves in England, first in Derbyshire, then at Cheddar – and there may be more. Some caves are accessible enough, and young Jacques was able to walk straight into the Lascaux cave. But others are far less accessible. The Cosquer cave near Marseilles has its entrance fully 37m below present sea level, and it was only discovered by a professional diver in 1985. The Cosquer entrance passage must have been well above sea level at the time when the art work was done so that the stone age artists could get into it – and sea level was indeed very low in 16,000 BC, around 110m lower than it is today. The Cosquer cave is particularly interesting because it is full of stencils of handprints. The cave environment seems to favour the preservation of paintings and other remains; it was a great surprise to archaeologists to find the remains of a length of prehistoric rope, twisted by a right-handed person, in the Lascaux cave. There was also evidence, in the form of sockets in the gallery walls for beams, that wooden scaffolding had been put up in the cave to enable the artist to paint the images. Even so, an experiment by Michel Lorblanchet showed that an entire frieze of animals could be painted in just one hour.

The famous 'Venus' figurines date from about the same time or a little earlier. These have been found at about 25 sites scattered right across Europe from the Pyrenees to the Ukraine. They show a stylized, fleshy female form that may conceivably have been some ideal of womanhood or a celebration of human fertility. The art is conceptual rather than representational, and has more in common with twentieth century Cubist art than with any art form the intervening centuries.

The simple, stylized drawings of animals discovered at Lascaux gave modern people an insight into the way people lived and the things that mattered to them at the time when they were created, 17,000 or more years ago. Like many other such discoveries, the Lascaux paintings enrich and extend us by putting us in touch not just with our remote ancestors but, in a sense, with ourselves as we were then. That reflection on where we have come from, and how we have travelled, is vitally important in telling us where we are and even where we might be heading. The recovery of the past is one of the most important things we human beings do; no other species does it.

PEARL HARBOUR
(1941)

THE SECOND WORLD War was really an exclusively European conflict from 1939 until 1941, a war rather similar to the First World War in its scope. With the Japanese attack on Pearl Harbour, it was to erupt into a global conflict.

Pearl Harbour was an American naval base on the Hawaiian island of Oahu. On the morning of 7 December 1941 (or 8 December Tokyo time), the Japanese launched an unprovoked attack on it without a formal declaration of war. Mitsuo Fuchida led 360 carrier-based aircraft and attacked the warships at anchor in the harbour. Only 29 Japanese planes were lost in the action, which left the US Pacific fleet crippled. The battleships USS *Arizona, Oklahoma, California, Nevada* and *West Virginia* were all sunk and three other battleships were damaged. Three cruisers and three destroyers also suffered major damage. There were 200 American planes destroyed and over 2,300 American servicemen were killed. The damage inflicted, all the greater because of the element of surprise, was so enormous that the American government felt that it could not reveal its true extent to the public; the attack was announced and the fact that the *Arizona* had been sunk.

The attack, which came shortly after midday Washington time, was made without a declaration of war. The Japanese foreign minister had been given the task of issuing the formal declaration of war to the American embassy in Tokyo, which was deliberately made at the last minute. The American embassy officials suspected that he was on some such mission and deliberately kept him waiting. He was therefore only able to reveal the Japanese declaration of war at nine in the evening, many hours after the attack took place. The declaration of war was not entirely unexpected, and the American diplomats' delaying tactic had the effect of changing the character of the Pearl Harbour attack.

Instead of being seen in the world's eyes as a dazzlingly brilliant and effective first strike in a formal war, it was seen as a deceitful, shabby and dishonourable act that would set the tone for the behaviour of the Japanese throughout the war – dishonourable behaviour that would extend to the systematic maltreatment, torture and murder of prisoners of war. Japan's reputation has still not fully recovered from this shameful four-year episode.

Above all, the attack on Pearl Harbour ensured a vigorous American counter-attack, which would sweep across the Pacific and finally defeat the Japanese utterly. The disgraceful attack on Pearl Harbour ensured that the American people were whole-heartedly behind the war effort, in a way that they would never be behind the involvement in Vietnam. The nature of the Japanese 'victory' at Pearl Harbour guaranteed an American commitment to defeat them.

THE BATTLE OF STALINGRAD
(1942)

IN MAY 1942, the German push to the east, the ill-conceived war against Russia, was well under way. A tremendous battle raged for the Donetz river crossings south of Kharkov. The town of Kharkov itself had been in German hands for eight months, and the Russians fought hard to retake it. The two opposing armies under General von Bock and Marshal Timoshenko clashed in fierce hand-to-hand fighting. The Russians reported that 14 waves of German tanks had been hurled back. The spring offensive on the Crimea, to which Hitler gave much publicity, opened on 12 May, with the usual blitzkrieg, an onslaught that smashed into the Russian lines with bombers and tanks. But the Russians outflanked the main German attack by striking out towards Kharkov, where the occupying German troops were still holed up in their winter positions.

The Germans captured the great Russian Black Sea fortress of Sebastopol in the Crimea on 2 July after a nine-month siege, though only after suffering the loss of more than 300,000 men, killed or wounded. During the last-ditch resistance, the Russian defenders were reduced to fighting wearing gas masks because of the terrible smell of unburied bodies decomposing in the summer heat.

After that the Germans launched an offensive against the major city of Stalingrad, a centre on the River Volga for the shipment of oil from the Baku oilfield. The Germans expected to succeed; they had taken Kerch, Kharkov and Sebastopol and saw no reason why they should not take Stalingrad too. The battle for the city of Stalingrad was a very fierce one, lasting a full five months. During the course of it the population of 500,000 dwindled to only 1,000.

The Germans had to take Stalingrad in order to take possession of the

Baku oilfield, a key resource without which Hitler could not continue fighting elsewhere. He had not expected such ferocious resistance from the Russian army. The death toll in this barbaric battle reached astonishing levels. The Russians lost 750,000 men, the Germans lost 400,000, the Romanians 200,000, the Italians 130,000, the Hungarians 120,000.

The Battle of Stalingrad began on 22 August 1942. Two Russian relief columns joined forces near Kalach to the west of Stalingrad, behind the German Sixth Army commanded by General von Paulus, in effect surrounding the Germans. The Russians advanced on the Germans so rapidly that many German soldiers were shot in the back as they tried to retreat. Many other German soldiers, cut off from their supplies, froze or starved to death during the winter. The massive Russian counter-offensive, led by General Chukov, went on until the Germans were forced to surrender at the end of January 1943. General von Paulus and 15 other generals surrendered. Von Paulus was completely traumatized by the experience. Hitler had expressly forbidden him to surrender, promoting him to the rank of Field Marshal because no German Field Marshal had ever surrendered. But by 31 January, von Paulus was unable to go on obeying Hitler's orders; too many men had been lost and the situation was hopeless. By then, the German troops had been encircled for about three weeks, during which time 50,000 of them died. Axis survivors had been reduced to eating each other, and there were only 22 German divisions left, consisting of only 80,000 men.

The Battle of Stalingrad was a turning-point in the war. While Hitler was fighting a war on one front, the Western Front, he had a chance of winning. Opening a second front, an Eastern Front, was a big mistake. In fact it was the classic military error. But the lure of the Baku oilfield was irresistible, and Hitler was determined to have it. Stalin was even more determined that Hitler should not get it. The huge German losses could not be made good; from then on the German army was depleted. The Germans had also been shown that they were not invincible.

D-DAY
(1944)

ON 6 JUNE 1944, D-Day, the long-awaited Allied invasion of Europe began. The American General Eisenhower's headquarters announced: 'Allied naval forces supported by strong air forces began landing Allied armies this morning on the northern coast of France.' No details were broadcast, so as to offer the Germans no help, but the landings in Normandy, at beaches code-named Utah, Omaha, Gold, Juno and Sword, were the biggest combined land-sea and air operation of all time.

It began with airborne troops taking off from airfields along the south coast of England the previous evening, and landing by parachute or glider behind enemy lines at dawn. Through the night RAF bombers pounded German batteries along the French coast; then at dawn heavy bombers took over. Then a sea-borne force of several thousand ships arrived from many widely-scattered ports in Britain converged on the Normandy beaches at around 5am. The weather was not ideal. A strong north-westerly wind made the sea rougher than desirable for safe landings.

The Germans believed that the Normandy invasion was a bluff, that the real invasion was going to happen somewhere else. In fact Churchill had hoped to persuade the Americans that a two-pronged invasion, with a second invasion force landing somewhere else would be effective, but he was overruled by the Americans and the invasion of Italy from the Mediterranean had in any case already taken place.

Within a few weeks the invasion was consolidated. In the west, the key French port of Cherbourg was captured along with its naval forts and arsenal, and General Karl von Schlieben surrendered. Inland, the town of Bayeux was captured and Allied forces under Montgomery swung round behind the heavily defended town of Caen. The German defence was weakened by poor weaponry. The Germans were using the usual Panzer tanks, but also obsolete French tanks, which were useless against the latest

Allied guns. The Germans even so put up a stubborn resistance, determined to hold the key town of Caen, which was at the hub of 12 roads. In the end, they were defeated by a pincer movement, with the British coming at them from one side and the Canadians from the other.

The Free French leader, General de Gaulle, visited Bayeux, and although already incredibly tall stood on a café table to lead the crowd in singing the *Marseillaise*. George VI crossed the Channel to the Normandy beaches, where he was welcomed by Field-Marshal Montgomery, in order to present officers with medals.

The D-Day landings were incredibly hard-won. In the first 15 days of the invasion, around 10,000 Allied servicemen were killed and twice as many were wounded. But the invasion was successful. It achieved its goal, and the Allied troops worked swiftly inland from the coast to liberate Paris on 25 August. The Nazi swastika was pulled down from the Eiffel Tower and replaced by the French Tricolour. The end of the Second World War in Europe was in sight.

HIROSHIMA
(1945)

TO MOST PEOPLE the single word 'Hiroshima' means an event, not just a place. It means the blowing-up of the Japanese city of Hiroshima by a single bomb in 1945. It was an extremely controversial event at the time, and it has remained so ever since.

The atom bomb dropped on Hiroshima on 6 August 1945 was a 3 m-long device with the explosive power of 20,000 tonnes of TNT. This was the bomb that Einstein had in mind when he wrote to the American President about the possible 'construction of bombs'. The atom bomb was delivered by the US Army Air Force Boeing B-29 bomber *Enola Gay*, piloted by Paul Tibbets, who flew the plane from the Pacific atoll of Tinian.

The bomb was dropped from an altitude of 10,000m and exploded in the air 200m above the city. The energy released was so great that 8 km^2 of Hiroshima were completely flattened. Of the people living in Hiroshima, 1,000,000 were killed outright. Many of the survivors, perhaps another 100,000 people, were horribly burnt or affected by radiation sickness and died later. Many more were disfigured.

The Japanese government refused to respond to the Hiroshima bomb, code-named 'Little Boy' by the Americans, with a formal surrender. Emperor Hirohito visited the scene of unparalleled destruction and said, 'There seems to have been considerable damage here.' It was scarcely an adequate response.

In view of the Japanese failure to surrender, the Americans decided three days later to give a second Japanese city the same treatment. The second bomb, code-named 'Big Boy', was dropped on Nagasaki on 9 August. This bomb, with the same power as the Hiroshima bomb, was delivered by another B-29 bomber, *Bock's Car*. It killed 75,000 Japanese civilians outright, and as many again died lingering deaths afterwards of burns and radiation sickness. The long-term effects of radiation were not yet

509

understood. This time the Japanese government responded, the very next day, with a request for peace. The negotiation of surrender terms had begun.

Reactions to the American attack on Hiroshima and Nagasaki were divided. Some argued that the Japanese deserved to be beaten into surrender; they had been militarily defeated and yet had still refused to surrender. Direct and overwhelming onslaughts on civilian populations were the only answer. But others argued that the cold and deliberate annihilation of civilians was nothing short of a war crime, and morally indefensible. The Americans were also suspected of using the termination of the war as an excuse to experiment with their new bomb. Those responsible for developing the bomb, Robert Oppenheimer in particular, were horrified at what they had invented.

The decision to devastate Japanese cities was not taken lightly. There had been prison camps scattered all over the East until close to the end of the Second World War. Workers on the Burma Railway – the famous Bridge on the River Kwai project – were naturally held in camps in South-East Asia. But as the Americans closed in on Japan and it looked as if direct attacks on Japan itself were imminent, the Japanese launched on a sinister programme of prisoner transfer. They transferred British, American and other Allied prisoners to camps in Japan. They were deliberately and cold-bloodedly gathering them as a human shield, as hostages. I knew one of the men who were held in this way, under appalling near-starvation conditions. He was convinced, at the time and afterwards, that if a conventional Allied invasion of Japan had taken place, the prisoners of war would have been slaughtered as a final revenge for the defeat.

What actually happened in his prisoner-of-war camp was that one day the guards were simply not there. It was very quiet. The gates had been left open and there were no Japanese soldiers on duty. He and the other prisoners thought it was a trick, that the Japanese guards were hiding and tempting them to try to escape so that they had an excuse to shoot them all. They stayed in the compound. A day passed, then another. It was eerily quiet. Then Japanese civilians started to appear, trudging along the road past the camp, filthy, injured, traumatized, totally silent; something terrible had happened to them. First there were just a few, then scores, then hundreds of them. They passed the camp in silence. It was only much later that my friend realized that these were the survivors of Hiroshima. The prison camp was far enough from the city for them not to have heard the bomb itself, or felt the shock wave. But they saw the survivors streaming away from the scene of the nightmare. Shortly after that American planes flew over, indiscriminately dropping sacks of food on the camp. Several prisoners were killed by this friendly bombing. They had survived working on the Burma Railway, all kinds of maltreatment by the Japanese guards, and even near misses by two atom bombs - only to be killed by sacks of American food.

The two atom bombs did have the effect of bringing the war on Japan to a swift end. They probably saved the lives of the surviving prisoners of war. President Truman proclaimed victory over Japan on 14 August, which became known as VJ-Day. Later in the month, American troops landed in Japan led by General MacArthur. The two bombs brought the Second World War finally to an end after six traumatic years in which it is estimated that 55 million people died.

The Hiroshima bomb has nevertheless given Japan a false view of itself as a victim. The war crime, if that is what it was, was committed under extreme provocation and it pales into insignificance beside the multitude of terrible acts committed by the Japanese during the war. It has been pointed out recently that many Japanese people are still readier to dwell on the sufferings of Japanese civilians at Hiroshima and Nagasaki than to admit the guilt of Japan in causing the war.

To the world as a whole, Hiroshima meant something more than the end of the Second World War. It became a terrible warning of what a *Third World War* would be like. The images of the annihilated city and its afflicted people haunted the post-war generation. This was what nuclear war would be like. The nuclear bombs that were developed and stockpiled during the next few decades would be even more powerful and do even more damage. Each time there was a bomb test, journalists described it as being so many times more powerful than the Hiroshima bomb; it was an index of horror. As the Cold War developed, it was the memory of Hiroshima that put the fear of God into the superpowers and all their allies.

THE INDEPENDENCE OF INDIA
(1947)

ON 15 AUGUST 1947, after a long struggle India at last became independent. In 1928, Nehru was elected President of the Indian National Congress, an office he held intermittently and frequently. He was the acknowledged leader of the movement's socialist wing. In the 1930s, while in prison, Nehru wrote two books, *Glimpses of World History* and *Autobiography*. He himself organized the campaign that swept Congress to power in most of the provinces of India in the elections in the 1930s.

Nehru was sympathetic to the British cause in the Second World War, but along with other Congress leaders he refused to co-operate with the British while they withheld independence from India. When Stafford Cripps, for the British government, made his offer of dominion status in 1942, Nehru turned it down.

On 15 August 1947, when India achieved full independence, Nehru was sworn in as the first Prime Minister of India. Independence was accompanied by a great deal of rioting and fighting between Hindu and Muslim communities. Partition was the only solution – the creation of a separate Muslim state of Pakistan. A large-scale, two-way migration took place on partition, as Muslims made their way into East or West Pakistan and Hindus headed for India. There were skirmishes, assaults and murders as they massed.

As a colony, India had not needed a foreign policy; now that the country was independent, it was free to pursue any foreign policy it likes. Nehru created India's foreign policy himself, from scratch, and it was both inspired and progressive. He followed a policy of studied and statesman-like neutrality through the Cold War, often acting as a go-between among the leaders of the great powers. He pursued a global campaign against colonialism, which meant that the British Empire or Commonwealth was under constant attack from him, and ensuring that other colonies would one by one be granted independence. India had been a very high-profile British colony, and once it was independent its was certain that other colonies would press for independence too.

India pursued the enlightened policy of non-alignment, refusing to side with the West or with the Soviet Union. To compensate for the attitudes of the West, Nehru campaigned for China to be given its place in world councils. Following Nehru's principles, India has maintained its non-aligned place in the post-war, post-independence world.

THE START OF THE COLD WAR
(1948)

AFTER THE SECOND World War the responsibility for supervising the defeated Germany was divided among the Allied victors. West Germany was occupied by British and American troops, while East Germany was occupied by Russian troops. Berlin, the capital of Germany, was also divided into West and East, but embedded within East German territory.

On 24 July 1948, Soviet troops set up a blockade, severing the road and rail links between West Germany and Berlin. It was a calculated act of aggression against the West, and was felt as such. The West came close to declaring war on Russia and was only put off by the thought of Stalingrad. In fact it later turned out that Stalin did not have sufficient troops or equipment in the Russian Sector (later East Germany) to launch a war on the British and American Sectors (later West Germany), so it was a bluff. If the British and American troops had fought their way through the Soviet blockade, there would *probably* have been no further military action from Moscow, but at the time the level of risk was unknown.

The day after the Berlin blockade started an airlift began, with British and American aircraft flying in food and supplies for the people living in West Berlin – two million of them. The blockade continued and by September the aircraft were ferrying in 4,500 tonnes of supplies per day. The blockade was maintained for a year and a half.

Relations between the West and the Soviet Union naturally cooled over the Berlin blockade. The US Presidential adviser Bernard Baruch described the situation as a 'Cold War', coining the phrase that would characterize the state of the world for the next half-century. The Soviets were not firing guns at anybody, but their behaviour was certainly hostile and intimidating.

This state of frozen hostility went on for over 40 years. It led directly to a dangerous arms race in which the latest atomic weapons were stockpiled. As the science of rocketry developed, the United States and the Soviet Union equipped their arsenals with rockets that could carry nuclear warheads right across the Arctic Ocean or from one side of Europe to the other, inter-continental ballistic missiles. The cost of these armaments was enormous, a huge drain on the economic resources of the countries involved.

A climate of fear was generated. Both sides wanted to test their latest nuclear bombs, and the bomb test explosions were in themselves intended to deter the enemy. By the late 1950s, it was evident that dangerous levels of radiation were being pumped into the atmosphere by these test explosions, and people worried that their life expectancy was being shortened by the increased risk of cancer. In the West, there was also a heightened fear that real, full-scale war would break out, a Third World War that might be shorter but far more violent than the two previous world wars, a war that could destroy both sides utterly.

Perhaps in the knowledge that an old-style military war would probably destroy everyone involved, the United States and the Soviet Union played out their rivalry in a space race. The competition to launch satellites, space probes and land men on the Moon was a kind of displacement activity, an acting-out of the Cold War in a contest of peaceful space technology.

MAO COMES TO POWER IN CHINA
(1949)

MAO SPENT THE early 1920s travelling round China, eventually returning to Hunan, where he took the lead in promoting worker's rights and collective action. In 1921, when he was 27, Mao attended the First Congress of the Communist Party of China in Shanghai, and two years after that he was elected to the Party's Central Committee, and then became director of the Peasant Training Institute. In 1927, he was sent to Hunan province to report on recent peasant risings; his report is regarded as the first important statement of Maoist theory. It was at this time that Mao developed many of his political theories, the most important one being that peasants are the source of revolution. The traditional thinking of Marx and Lenin held that it was urban workers who led the way to revolution, but Mao argued that in China it would be the rural peasants. He also developed a three-stage theory of guerrilla warfare and a concept of a 'people's democratic dictatorship'.

The first attempt at revolution was a failure. He led the Autumn Harvest Rising at Changsa in Hunan in 1927, and was lucky to survive. He was being led to execution when he managed to escape from his guards. Together with a band of guerrillas, he took refuge in the Jinggang Mountains in south-east China. There, between 1931 and 1934, he helped set up the Chinese Soviet Republic and was elected its chairman.

By now Chiang Kai-shek, who had assumed partial control of China, was determined to eradicate the Communists. To avoid being encircled by Chiang Kai-shek's KMT forces, the Communists set off on 'The Long March', which was in effect a retreat from Jiangxi in south-east China to Shaanxi in the north-west. It was during this arduous journey, almost 10,000km long, that Mao emerged as the natural leader.

After China defeated Japan, the country disintegrated into civil war, in which the Communists defeated the Kuomintang and set up the People's Republic of China in October 1949. It had taken Mao and the Communist Party 20 years to achieve it. Mao became Chairman of the new republic. His main programme now was a phase of fast, forced collectivization, which went on until 1958. Mao also indicated that he was willing to consider different views about the way China should be ruled. Given this opportunity, Many Chinese people voiced their doubts about the dogmas of the Communist Party. Mao reversed his policy and rounded up his critics in an Anti-Rightist Movement.

Then came Mao's Great Leap Forward, which was supposed to be a programme of economic growth based on different principles from the Soviet model, which had depended on the development of heavy industry. True to his initial beliefs, Mao based his Great Leap on agricultural growth and the development of small-scale industry. In the midst of this, Khrushchev withdrew the technical support that the Soviet Union had been supplying, because Mao was too aggressive in his demands to precipitate world-wide Communist revolution. Mao was in still greater difficulties because of droughts. The Great Leap came to an end in 1960. Both Chinese and outside observers now see the Great Leap Forward as a fiasco that led to millions of deaths.

In the light of all of these economic, social and political failures, other Communist Party members decided that Mao should relinquish power. Mao's response to this palace coup was to try to rally the Chinese people in a quite extraordinary way. In his Cultural Revolution, power was given directly to the Red Guards, groups of young people who set up their own tribunals. The Cultural Revolution was an even bigger catastrophe than the Great Leap Forward. It led to the destruction of much of China's heritage, the pointless imprisonment of huge numbers of Chinese academics, and general social chaos.

Mao's legacy as China's leader is complex. The Great Leap was a terrible economic and social failure. The Cultural Revolution was an even bigger failure. Huge numbers of people died in the aftermath of the Chinese civil war. On the other hand, the numbers of deaths were small compared with those resulting from famine, anarchy and foreign invasion in the period before the Communists took over, and Mao did give China a period free of foreign domination, which it had not enjoyed for a very long time.

During Mao's time literacy rates rose from 20 to 93 percent and life expectancy had risen to over 70 years.

The improvement in life expectancy may not have been due to Communism, though; there were similar improvements in Taiwan, which was ruled by Mao's political enemies. Mao has been denounced for failing to promote birth control; this failure led to a rapid and unmanageable population increase which forced later Chinese leaders to adopt the over-strenuous one-child policy. Another harmful effect of Mao's life has been the imitation of Maoism in communist countries around the world, spawning aggressive revolutionary movements such as the Shining Path in Peru and the Khmer Rouge in Cambodia. While other less economically developed countries have been busily (and often very destructively) imitating Mao and trying to follow his principles, China itself has moved sharply away from Maoism.

THE DECIPHERMENT
OF LINEAR B
(1952)

THE MYCENAEANS OF bronze age Greece and the earlier Minoans of bronze age Crete are famous for having been literate. At least some of them were literate, and they could write and read a syllabic script known to archaeologists as Linear B. It had 89 different signs. Sir Arthur Evans discovered the first clay tablets with Minoan 'hieroglyphics' at Knossos on Crete and published a selection of them in his huge book on Knossos, *The Palace of Minos*, though not enough to allow anyone else the chance of deciphering them. He clung to the hope that he could do that himself.

When he died at an advanced age in 1941, Evans had got no further forward. Once Evans was dead, other scholars might have had access to the inscriptions, and systematic work on deciphering them could begin. In fact it was not until 1952, 11 years after Evans's death, and half a century after the first tablets were discovered, that they were published.

In 1939, Carl Blegen struck the Archive Room at Pylos on the mainland of Greece with his first trench and found a huge cache of Linear B tablets. These extra documents made the decipherment much easier.

Michael Ventris was a young architect who developed an obsession with the untranslated tablets. He realized that some signs represented vowels, like a, and others represented vowels with consonants, like *pa*. The signs were written in horizontal lines from left to right, just like modern Western writing; we know this because all the lines inscribed on the clay tablets were left-justified. Groups of signs were separated by a short bar, which implied that the sign groups were words. An early barrier to decipherment was the widespread belief that the Linear B language was *not* Greek but an older, Minoan, language. But there were some scholars who thought differently. They cleverly saw the frequency of Greek names in Homer as a sign that the Mycenaean world Homer described was also a Greek-speaking world.

Ventris, in collaboration with the Cambridge University academic John Chadwick, guessed that some words on the Cretan tablets might be the names of Cretan towns. *Ko-no-so* might be Knossos, *A-mi-ni-so* Amnisos, *Tu-ri-so* Tylissos. There were too many of these parallels to be a coincidence. Even so, it was remarkable that tablets written in the 200 years before 1200 BC should refer to towns and villages by their modern names; it was a little like finding that a contemporary early bronze age inscription on one of the stones at Stonehenge read 'Stonehenge near Amesbury'. It implied an astonishing continuity of language and memory.

The hypothesis that the language was Greek led to the emergence of more and more Greek words on the tablets. It was vindicated in 1953 when Blegen studied some newly discovered tablets from Pylos. One of them had picture-signs showing three-legged cauldrons. When Blegen substituted the syllables Ventris and Chadwick had proposed for the signs, he was astonished to see the word *ti-ri-po-de* appearing – the Greek word meaning 'tripods'.

After a great many exchanges of ideas – Ventris was very keen on circulating his ideas on neatly hand-written pamphlets – more and more Greek or near-Greek words emerged on the tablets. *Korwos* (boy) was very close to the later Greek word, *kouros*. *Guasileus* (chief) was close to the later Greek word for king, *basileus*.

The decipherment of the tablets has enabled us to read the archives of the Minoans and the Mycenaeans and get a greater insight into the nature of the two civilizations. One very significant fact is that the Mycenaeans were Greeks, even though their civilization ended in about 1200 BC and was followed by a 500 year long dark age when there was no writing. Only after that did Homer write some of their story down in Greek. The Greek language links the two together in a significant way. Homer wrote about the Trojan War in Greek. The Greeks at the time of the Trojan War also spoke and wrote in Greek. With the translation of Linear B, a door swings open on the world of Agamemnon and Achilles.

THE DISCOVERY OF THE STRUCTURE OF DNA

(1952)

FROM 1949 ONWARDS Francis Crick was researching into molecular biology at the Cavendish Laboratory. In 1953, in collaboration with James D. Watson, a young American biologist who had joined the laboratory two years earlier at the age of only 23, he constructed a molecular model of the extremely complex genetic material known as DNA (deoxyribonucleic acid). The molecular model was in the form of a double helix. The new discovery was published in *Nature* in 1953. The one-page article opened modestly: 'We wish to suggest a structure for the salt of DNA. This structure has novel features that are of considerable biological interest.' Watson and Crick went on to demonstrate that chromosomes consist of long helical strands of DNA contained the codified genetic material that determines how animal and human cells develop. These exciting new findings were confirmed by experiments by other scientists round the world.

Later Crick went on to research the nucleic acids, making far-reaching discoveries about the genetic code they contain. When Crick died in 2004, James Watson said, 'I will always remember Francis for his extraordinary focused intelligence. He treated me as though I were a member of his family. I always looked forward to being with him and speaking to him.'

Crick was awarded the Nobel Prize for medicine and physiology in 1962, jointly with James Watson and Maurice Wilkins, his co-workers. James Watson returned to the United States, where he became director of the Cold Spring Biological Laboratories in New York.

The discovery of the structure of DNA and its significance was one of the great scientific breakthroughs of the second half of the twentieth century. It was a discovery with lots of ramifications. When it emerged that everyone has different DNA, the possibility of using it for identification presented itself. DNA analysis has since become a major forensic tool. A criminal has now to leave only a few traces of human tissue at the scene of a crime, and he or she can be identified. This new technique has made it possible to solve some crimes committed decades ago and also, disturbingly, prove that some people serving very long prison sentences really did not commit the crimes for which they were convicted. At least DNA has ensured their release.

Family members have related DNA, so DNA analysis can establish kinship links; this was how the remains of the last Tsar of Russia and his family were identified. This kinship feature can also help to resolve cases of disputed paternity. Since DNA can survive for a long time after death, it has also proved invaluable to historians, archaeologists and anthropologists in establishing kinship groups. DNA has created a whole sequence of new possibilities – including the prevention of genetically communicated disorders.

THE INVENTION OF CALCULATORS FOR BUSINESS USE

(1954)

IN 1954, SEVERAL significant steps forward were made in the computer industry. One of these was the introduction of the first practical silicon transistors. They were manufactured and sold by Texas Instruments. They were cheaper than germanium transistors and because of this they would lead to a sharp increase in the use of solid-state electronic components. They also led to a sales boom for Texas Instruments.

Another of these steps forward was the introduction of electronic computers in a business context. This was a halfway house to the personal computer.

A third was the brainchild of the computer engineer An Wang, who founded Wang Laboratories at Lowell, Massachusetts, to manufacture small business calculators. Wang undertook pioneering work on magnetic core memory, which became the basis for all modern computer technology.

The calculator was at first a very expensive item, but in time they were made more and more cheaply until everyone could afford them. They became indispensable aids to every kind of accounting, from business to domestic, from schoolwork to VAT. In research, too, they facilitated statistical analysis. Calculating a correlation coefficient without a calculator could take all afternoon; with a calculator it became the work of ten minutes. This meant that many more runs of statistical tests became feasible. The quality of research results rose accordingly. The calculators that we take so much for granted now were an unobtrusive revolution.

THE HUNGARIAN REVOLUTION

(1956)

IN OCTOBER 1956, Hungary rose in rebellion against Russian domination. The rising began on 23 October, with ordinary Hungarians pitting themselves, often with their bare hands, against Soviet tanks and the hated security police, the AVH, and demanding freedom from Moscow. They succeeded in putting out the illuminated Red Star on the Parliament buildings and replacing it with the national flag. In Stalin Square in Budapest, rebels succeeded in destroying the most hated symbol of Russian domination, the huge bronze statue of Stalin. Unfortunately it took more than flags and grand symbolic gestures to succeed in breaking away from the Soviet Union, and 3,000 Hungarians were killed in the first three days of the revolution. In some areas of Budapest, the fighting was so heavy that the streets looked just as they had after the siege of the city when it fell to the Red Army in 1945. The streets were littered with debris, the Astoria Hotel had all its windows broken, trams were derailed and used as barricades.

There was some hope of the revolution succeeding as Hungarian soldiers among the Soviet forces joined the revolutionary cause. The revolution was not just confined to Budapest, either. Large areas of Hungary were in rebel hands, in spite of savage treatment by the Russian invaders, but the situation was very chaotic. Some tanks were seen opening fire on unarmed demonstrators. Others were seen with Hungarian civilians riding on top of them because the Russian crews had said they had no intention of firing on them.

On 26 October, Imre Nagy, the new Prime Minister, declared in a broadcast that he was negotiating for 'the withdrawal of all Soviet troops stationed in Hungary', but that this was conditional on all armed revolt ceasing. He admitted that some workers had joined the revolt, but that this was due to mistakes made by the Hungarian government. In other words no blame attached to Moscow for the revolt; only Hungarians were to blame. All Hungarians were urged to 'go home and stay there'.

Then Moscow ordered more armoured forces in. Five divisions were brought up to the Hungarian frontier from East Germany. On 31 October, Hungarian rebels freed Cardinal Mindszenty, the Roman Catholic primate of Hungary who had been held as a political prisoner for eight years. The cardinal's first act when he returned to Budapest was to celebrate Mass. He said, 'I send my blessing to the Hungarian weapons that have won this glorious victory.'

On 2 November, Nagy told the Soviet ambassador Yuri Andropov that Hungary was leaving the Warsaw Pact and becoming neutral. Only three days later, the revolution was over, and it was not, as Nagy and Mindszenty had believed, a victory for the Hungarian rebels. The Red Army crushed the rebellion with 1,000 extra tanks, rolling into Hungary before dawn on 5 November. The Parliament building fell. The last words from Nagy were heard over the radio at 5am, when he told Hungary and the rest of the world of the Russian attack. Within a few hours all the key installations in Budapest were in Russian hands.

The Russian invasion of Hungary shook the rest of the world, and on 9 November the United Nations told the Soviet Union to withdraw its troops from Hungary. Later in the month, Austrian troops clashed with Soviet troops who were pursuing Hungarians as they escaped across the Austrian border. But the international protests had no effect. What had seemed like the beginning of a new life for eastern Europe was a false dawn. The Soviet Union showed itself to be an old-style empire maintained by military force. Hungary would not gain its freedom for a long time to come; the other Iron Curtain countries would also have to wait for several decades for their freedom. The brutal suppression of the Hungarian Revolution marked another refrigeration stage in the Cold War.

THE STRUGGLE FOR CLEAN AIR

(1956)

IN OCTOBER 1955, the British Parliament passed the Clean Air Act. This identified areas in British cities suffering particularly high levels of atmospheric pollution and turned them into smoke-free zones. Within them it became illegal, from 1956 onwards, to burn untreated house coal and other fuels likely to produce smoke.

This measure was partly a response to the killer smogs of 1952, when the billions of dust particles in the London air acted as condensation nuclei to make a fog that was known as a 'pea-souper'. People with respiratory problems associated with asthma, bronchitis or pneumonia were in great difficulty and many of them died.

But there had been an air pollution problem in London and other industrial cities for hundreds of years. Even in the middle ages, city-dwellers suffered from the effects of pollution, and there were very severe punishments for householders who burned coal in their grates in London. Even then, coal was regarded as a filthy fuel. But with the Industrial Revolution, and the mass production of coal, it became the normal fuel for both home and factory. The output of smoke in the industrial cities of the nineteenth century was horrific. Dickens described the typical London fogs that reduced visibility in the poorly lit streets almost to zero. They made breathing difficult and unpleasant; they made walking dangerous; they provided cover for criminals. The soot and chemicals raining down on the city also did an enormous amount of corrosive damage to the fabric of the city. The damage to the buildings of London alone was estimated to cost two million pounds a year to repair. Many of them remained streaked and blackened with a crust of soot. Some ancient and historic buildings were coated with layers of soot over 20cm thick.

After the Clean Air Act, an intensive campaign to clean the public buildings was put under way. It came as a revelation to both Londoners and visitors to London to discover that St Paul's was not black but made of a pale grey limestone. Sir Christopher Wren's preference for Portland stone became part of the urban landscape once again, after 300 years of blackening by atmospheric pollution. Then, suddenly the architectural detail was visible. London gradually emerged as a far more attractive city to look at than anyone could remember.

The reduction in air pollution meant that London and other British cities became lighter. As much as 80 percent more sunshine was able to reach the pavements than before. Grass was able to grow. Birds returned. The British attack on urban atmospheric pollution was a huge success, and it acted as a model for urban clean-up. The British approach was to be widely copied in industrial cities in other developed countries.

THE FIRST MAN-MADE SATELLITE (1957)

On 4 October 1957, the Russians launched the first man-made satellite ever to go into orbit round the Earth. This tiny artificial moon was known as Sputnik-1 and it went into orbit 800km above the Earth, taking 95 minutes to complete a circuit. It travelled at an astonishing 29,000km an hour.

The satellite was a simple device, a metal globe not much bigger than a football, and trailing radio antennae. Inside were two radio transmitters which sent out a distinctive intermittent piping sound that could be picked up by ground-based radio stations. The bleep was an extremely clever publicity device, in that it performed no function whatever other than to remind people that it was there. The radio signal was first picked up by Geoffrey Perry, a science teacher at Kettering Grammar School in England; he had a gift for picking up the radio signals from this and many subsequent satellites long before the professionals and became a minor media celebrity on the strength of it.

The Sputnik weighed 84kg, which implied that the Russians had developed a fairly powerful launching rocket. The Sputnik was six times heavier than the satellite the Americans were planning to launch in 1958. The Russians had won the first round in the space race by getting their satellite into orbit first.

Throughout the Cold War, the Russians were extremely secretive about their planned projects, only announcing successes afterwards, and sometimes concealing failed missions altogether. By contrast, the Americans were very open about their missions, and both the successes and the failures were very public. After the launch of the Sputnik the Russians proudly issued a detailed statement of their achievement, giving the specifications of the satellite. The Americans acknowledged that it was a great achievement.

Dr Joseph Kaplan, who was Chairman of the US National Committee for the International Geophysical Year (1958), said the Russian achievement was 'fantastic'. But it was a great blow to American pride to be beaten in the space race in this way. The Pentagon was too stunned to respond immediately, saying only that it needed time to study the Russian report in detail.

Apart from being a technical and political landmark, the first artificial satellite marked the start of an era of what has been called 'remote sensing'. There are now scores of satellites circling the Earth, some of them geo-stationary, rotating with the Earth and therefore staying above the same place on the earth's surface all the time, but all of them doing something useful. They send back all kinds of information. There is Meteosat, a weather satellite that every quarter of an hour sends down a photograph of the current cloud patterns; sequences of these photographs are very useful to meteorologists in helping them to understand weather systems and forecast weather. The sequences of photographs from the satellite are often used on television weather forecasts. There is also Landsat, which sends down detailed true-colour photographs of the landscape and can be used as an aid to topographical and vegetation mapping.

Satellites can be used to spot forest fires in the Amazon Basin, and are useful in policing illegal burning. They can even be used to identify what crops farmers are growing. In the European Union, where subsidies are available for growing some crops, there is always the possibility of farmers making false claims about what they are growing on their land. The 'spy in the sky' can be used by EU officials to find out exactly what they are growing.

Satellites can be used for more conventional spying too. Expert interpreters are able to identify missile silos, armaments factories, and even divisions of tanks on the move, so the satellite has become a new weapon in modern warfare.

Satellites can also give unparalleled detail of changes in river channels. Mapping a rapidly changing multi-channel river such as the Brahmaputra in India was very difficult to do from ground level. Satellite photographs enable maps to be updated instantly. They also enable geographers to understand how such systems change through time. Infra-red photography can give information on the health of vegetation, and give us information on the impact of acid rain on forests in Scandinavia.

The launching of the first satellite was the launching of a new age of data-gathering. Thanks to satellites, we can find out much more about the world – and how fast it is changing.

THE CAMPAIGN FOR NUCLEAR DISARMAMENT
(1958)

MANY ORDINARY PEOPLE became very alarmed at the Cold War arms race. It looked as if the stockpiling of nuclear weapons could only lead to the outbreak of a catastrophic world war. In a meeting at Westminster's Central Hall on 17 February 1958 British protesters formed the Campaign for Nuclear Disarmament. It was created out of the National Council for Abolition of Nuclear Weapons Tests, which was formed only the previous year but proved to be extremely popular, attracting thousands of people who wanted to see an end to nuclear bomb tests.

The new CND was led by a steering committee consisting of the Labour MP Michael Foot, the distinguished philosopher Bertrand Russell, the author J. B. Priestley and the journalist James Cameron. It was given free office space in Fleet Street by Horizon Holidays. Russell, who often spoke at protest rallies, introduced a distinctive logo for CND, a downward-pointing trident inside a circle. It was a very simple device, easy to draw and instantly recognizable. The CND marchers also had a simple and effective slogan: 'Ban the bomb!'

On 4 April 1958, 3,000 anti-nuclear protesters gathered London to give a send-off to 600 'hard core' marchers who started a three-day march to the Atomic Weapons Research Establishment at Aldermaston. They arrived to the sound of a skiffle group playing *When the Saints Go Marching In*. Altogether 12,000 protesters assembled the rally at the gates of the establishment. There were speeches and a pledge was passed urging Britain, Russia and the United States to stop making, testing and storing nuclear weapons. A loudspeaker car intercepted the marchers at one point, to tell them that they were 'playing Khrushchev's game'. The marchers duly set about the van, but that was the only violence involved.

The demonstrations and the marches continued, year after year. In September 1958, the cleric Donald Soper, later Lord Soper, addressed the crowd at Aldermaston. In December 1958, violence broke out as the police clashed with demonstrators at the Swaffham missile base. There were 21 protesters arrested.

In October 1960, Bertrand Russell resigned as leader of CND.

It is hard to tell what effect if any this campaign had on politicians. Certainly all the politicians of the day appeared to be unaffected by it. The campaign itself seemed to run itself out of steam. Bertrand Russell was undoubtedly deeply committed to it, but he was extremely old and had to give it up. The campaign was in the late 1960s in danger of being overtaken by another campaign, the campaign to stop the war in Vietnam. Like CND, this was a pro-peace cause, but not related to nuclear weapons in any way.

But CND went on, its support undiminished. On 24 October 1981, a huge rally in Hyde Park was the biggest anti-nuclear rally in 20 years. Over 150,000 people protested at the siting of American Cruise missiles in Britain – not least because they automatically made Britain a target for Russian missiles. The procession of marchers walking to Hyde Park was so long that many reached the park long after the speeches by Michael Foot and Bruce Kent were over.

Similar large-scale demonstrations against nuclear weapons were mounted in other European cities. The campaign was now international in scale.

In March 1978, President Jimmy Carter signed a Nuclear Non-Proliferation Act. This imposed new controls on the export of American nuclear technology. The idea was to stop the spread of nuclear weapon technology to more nations. But this was a long way short of nuclear disarmament. That was not to come until the Gorbachev-Reagan era. Then the issue was one of cost. The Soviet Union was not strong economically to maintain its nuclear weaponry. So, in the end the nuclear disarmament had no ethical or moral basis – only a financial one.

But the campaign did have the effect of nudging politicians towards negotiating. One month after the huge rally in Hyde Park in 1981, the NATO and Warsaw Pact countries started talks in Geneva on limiting medium-range nuclear missiles. That, with hindsight, marked the beginning of the end of the Cold War.

THE CUBAN
REVOLUTION
(1959)

THE CUBAN REVOLUTION of 1959 was masterminded by Fidel Castro. Castro was the son of a successful sugar planter, and practised as a lawyer in Havana. He specialized in cases that involved fighting on behalf of poor people against official corruption under the oppressive rule of President Batista.

In July 1953, Fidel and his brother Raul led a revolution against Batista. It was unsuccessful and Castro was sentenced to 15 years in prison. Under an amnesty, he was free within the year and he took refuge in the United States. Then he went on to Mexico, where he set to work organizing anti-Batista activities.

In 1956, Castro and a small band of revolutionaries landed in Cuba, but they were betrayed, ambushed and barely escaped into the mountains. From there he waged an ongoing guerrilla warfare campaign. As Cuba degenerated into a police state, more and more young men drifted over to the revolutionary cause. By December 1958, Castro was able to mount a full-scale attack that was strong enough to force Batista to flee. He was assisted by Che Guevara.

In February 1959, Fidel Castro became Prime Minister of Cuba, announcing a Marxist-Leninist programme adapted to suit Cuba's needs. He initiated sweeping reforms in agriculture, education and industry. These were not all successful, but enough of his reforms worked for his new regime to gain support. He managed to overthrow the dominance of the United States in the Cuban economy. The American response to the Communist regime in its backyard was an invasion. Luckily for Castro, the Bay of Pigs invasion in April 1961 was a high-profile disaster for the Americans and a propaganda victory for Castro.

Following the Bay of Pigs, the Cubans depended on Soviet support against the ever-present threat from the United States. This led directly to confrontation between the super-powers and the near-catastrophe of the Cuban missile crisis of 1962.

Castro has had ongoing problems in managing the Cuban economy. Sugar and tobacco production have not proved reliable. In spite of many problems, Fidel Castro's personal popularity remained high.

There have been many attempts by the Americans, both open and covert, to get rid of Castro, but all have failed. It is not known how many attempts the Americans made to assassinate Castro, but in 1975 a committee set up by the US Senate to investigate the CIA found documentary proof that the CIA had planned to assassinate Castro. Given the power and wealth of the United States, and give how much the American authorities have hated having him as a next-door neighbour, his survival is in itself a remarkable achievement. Castro has denied any involvement in the assassination of President John F. Kennedy, and there is no reason to doubt his denial. Castro succeeded, against huge odds, in overthrowing the Batista regime, in reorganizing the Cuban economy along Marxist-Leninist lines, and in staving off American intervention. His actions led indirectly to the Cuban missile crisis, but the principal blame for that must rest with Kennedy.

THE INVENTION OF THE MICROCHIP
(1959)

TWO AMERICAN ENGINEERS were responsible for inventing the microchip. Jack Kilby worked for Texas Instruments and Robert Noyce worked for Fairchild Semiconductor. The microchip made it possible to install a large amount of circuitry in a very small space. This led the way to the manufacture of a range of miniaturized products such as electronic wristwatches and electronic clock mechanisms.

Working independently, Kilby successfully encased an integrated circuit in a single silicon wafer. Noyce's contribution was to find a way of joining the circuits by printing, which eliminated thousands of man-hours of labour and made mass production possible. These two breakthroughs together drastically reduced the size, weight and cost of electronic components. Robert Noyce went on to found the Intel Corporation, which was to give the microchip memory and logic functions to produce the microprocessor. This in turn would make possible the development of the personal computer.

Today we take the manageable size of our desktop and laptop computers for granted. But before the invention of miniature printed circuits, before the invention of the silicon chip, computers were bulky, heavy and hugely expensive. The work of Kilby and Noyce made the democratization of computing possible.

THE KENNEDY-NIXON
TV DEBATE
(1960)

IN JUNE 1956, John F. Kennedy launched a campaign to win the vice-presidential nomination. Then in 1960 came his opportunity to become president of the United States. In the run-up to this, he and his opponent Richard Nixon took part in the first television debate between presidential candidates. Afterwards, voters said that the televised debate made no difference to the way they voted, but it was clear that Kennedy looked better than Nixon, who appeared unshaven and shifty. It was also highly significant that those who heard the debate on radio and therefore were unconscious of the difference in appearance between the two men considered that Nixon had won. The fact that it was Kennedy who won that election in 1960, even if by a narrow margin, suggests that it was his appearance on television that tipped the balance in his favour.

From that moment on, television took on a more significant role in world politics, and Kennedy in particular consciously and deliberately exploited the media. He knew that he was photogenic and he knew that his wife Jackie was photogenic too. He and his aides took great care over his public image and the photo opportunities and the formal family photographs were an important part of this. From then on, leading politicians in many countries have followed the same path of careful self-presentation through the media, often using professional media consultants. Politicians who looked good such as Tony Blair did well. Politicians who didn't such as Alec Douglas-Home did badly. Only very rarely do politicians flourish in spite of a poor media image; Sir Edward Heath is a case in point.

THE PILL
(1960)

Gregory Pincus was a consultant in experimental biology at Shrewsbury in Massachusetts. In 1951, he was persuaded by the birth control campaigner Margaret Sanger to focus his work on reproductive biology. Pincus worked with M. C. Chang and John Rock, and together they studied the negative effect of steroid hormones on the fertility of mammals. Synthetic hormones became available during the 1950s, and Pincus organized some field trials of the effect on human fertility of doses of these hormones. The trials, which were conducted in Haiti and Puerto Rico in 1954, were overwhelmingly successful.

Since then, oral contraceptives – generally referred to as 'The Pill' – have gone into general use in all the more economically developed countries of the world. There have been some concerns about the side effects of taking the pill, especially for many years at a time, but the popularity of oral contraception as the major birth control technique is undiminished. The success of oral contraception is a pharmaceutical rarity. It is very uncommon for synthetic chemical agents to have a 100 percent effectiveness in controlling human physiology.

The sociological effects have been phenomenal. The main birth control technique until the arrival of the pill was the condom; it was worn by men, so whether it was worn or not was a decision made by men. The oral contraceptive, taken discreetly by women, was something about which women could make their own decisions. For the first time in human history, women could decided when, or even whether, they would become pregnant. As a result, women have been freed to work, to have professional careers, and families have become smaller, enabling parents to give more care and attention to each child. The effects of this social, economic and demographic revolution have spread out first through the richer countries, and now through the poorer countries too. Many human geographers see this process of reducing the birth rate as a major way of improving the quality of life for both women and children throughout the world. The contraceptive pill has changed the world on a very large scale, by staving off the 'population explosion' that pessimists were predicting in the 1960s.

THE CUBAN MISSILE CRISIS
(1962)

IN FOREIGN POLICY, President Kennedy was firm and intolerant. He took the traditional American view that the Caribbean was the United State's backyard, and that it was their right to police it. Along with a great many other Americans, Kennedy hated the presence of a Marxist regime in Cuba, under Fidel Castro. In 1961, Kennedy's 'Bay of Pigs' invasion of Fidel Castro's Cuba was a complete fiasco. Kennedy seemed to learn little from this mistake. In October 1962, he risked nuclear war with the Soviet Union by insisting that the Soviets withdraw missiles from Cuba. He was lucky - and so was the rest of the world – that the Soviet leader, Khrushchev, backed down. In 1963, he followed this by negotiating a partial nuclear test ban treaty with the Soviet Union.

John F. Kennedy's reputation remained high partly because of his assassination. Had he lived, the inadequacy of some of his policies and strategies might have been seen and the reputation tarnished. Cut off in his prime, he seemed to have infinite promise. The foreign policy was disastrous, and the Cuban missile crisis could have ended in a catastrophe of global proportions; no president should take such risks.

THE ANCHORAGE EARTHQUAKE
(1964)

A MAJOR EARTHQUAKE hit Alaska on 28 March 1964. It reached 9.2 on the Richter scale, making it one of the biggest earthquakes in modern times, on the same level as the big Chile earthquake of 1960. The earthquake generated a spectacular tsunami, which was filmed from a vessel in the harbour at Anchorage. The indistinct and naturally rather shaky film shows the water drawing back and draining down into fissures opening up in the rock on the seabed; then a huge wave rolls into the harbour.

The tsunami was on a grand scale. Reaching a maximum height of 55m, it was the largest tsunami ever measured.

Fieldwork in the area round Anchorage has shown that the relative land-sea levels in the area changed considerably as a result of the earthquake. This is explained by the earthquake releasing one crustal plate that was jammed up against another. The actual shape of the land surface changed as a result of the pressure release, with some areas that were at sea level now a couple of metres above sea level and other areas that were well above sea level (and forested) now lowered and waterlogged.

Events such as the Anchorage earthquake are intermittent reminders of the extraordinary forces at work inside the Earth, and the ways in which they can suddenly break out.

DESEGREGATION IN THE AMERICAN SOUTH
(1964)

SEGREGATION IN THE American South meant treating black people separately and differently; it was fundamentally the same idea as the South African policy of apartheid, separate development. What segregation meant in practice was that black people were not allowed on whites-only buses, and they were excluded from whites-only schools and universities. Desegregation was the abolition of segregation. It was in effect finishing the work that Abraham Lincoln had begun. Slavery might have become a thing of the past in twentieth century North America, but treating black people as inferior was certainly not a thing of the past. The civil rights movement, conspicuously led by Martin Luther King Jr, aimed to get equal rights for black people, and that included desegregation.

President Eisenhower gave weak support to the civil rights movement with the words, 'It is incumbent on all the South to show some progress toward racial integration.' It was not nearly enough.

As early as 1954, the US Supreme Court declared that separate schools were unconstitutional and the following year ordered the desegregation of public parks and recreation facilities. A black woman was arrested after refusing to give up her seat on a bus to a white man, and this incident galvanized the civil rights movement.

James Meredith was the first black person to brave the colour bar at the University of Mississippi in 1962. While he was at university, he was given continuous protection by the Federal Guard.

Martin Luther King Jr helped to found the Southern Christian Leadership Conference in 1957, which set up civil rights activities throughout the country. King was therefore responsible for stimulating both the black and white populations of the United States into confronting

540

the unfair treatment of black people. He was the central figure. He became a natural target for discrimination. In 1958, he was arrested 'for loitering' and beaten up by the police. Two years later he was arrested for falsifying his income tax return, but later acquitted.

Martin Luther King Jr was a powerful orator, addressing public meetings and energizing the civil rights movement, which was firmly based on non-violent principles. The movement led to the great march through Washington in 1963, attended by over 200,000 black and white demonstrators, among them Marlon Brando, Judy Garland, Bob Dylan and Burt Lancaster. At this, the biggest-ever demonstration for civil rights, Martin Luther King Jr asked people not to 'drink from the cup of hatred and bitterness'. He told them:

'I still have a dream. It is a dream chiefly rooted in the American dream. I have a dream that one day this nation will rise up and live out the true meaning of its creed: We hold these truths to be self-evident, that all men are created equal.'

In April 1963, King was arrested for leading another civil rights march in Alabama. Shortly afterwards, 1,000 black people were arrested on another march, prompting President Kennedy to visit the South in person and praise the work of the demonstrators. In June, Kennedy challenged Congress to enact major civil rights legislation, making it compulsory to end the segregation of all public facilities, including those privately owned. But in September Governor Wallace of Alabama ordered his state troops to halt integration at a high school. A week later, the president took control of the Alabama state militia in order to allow integration to proceed. Kennedy ordered in the National Guard to usher students into the school buildings, compelling the desegregation of the campus against the express order of the state governor. It was a major trial of strength between president and governor.

In 1964, he saw success on a grand scale. Martin Luther King Jr was there to shake hands with President Johnson after Johnson signed the Civil Rights Act, which enshrined in law all the things for which King had been campaigning. Kennedy had been preparing the legislation as the time of his own assassination approached. Johnson saw it through, ensuring that the US Congress did not weaken it. Johnson called on Americans to 'eliminate the last vestiges of injustice in America.' That year, King was given an honorary doctorate by Yale University, the Kennedy Peace Prize and the Nobel Peace Prize.

The struggle was not over; racial tensions in the United States generally ran high. In February 1965, another black civil rights leader, Malcolm X, was shot dead as he prepared to address an audience in Harlem on the need for blacks and whites to live peacefully together. King led yet another march in Montgomery to protest about bombs found on the premises of various black organizations. In March, the white civil rights activist Viola Liuzzo was chased and shot dead by four Ku Klux Klansmen. On 6 June 1966, James Meredith, the first black graduate from Mississippi, was taking part in one of King's civil rights marches from Memphis to Jackson when he was shot in the back and legs. He was carrying only a Bible. Just moments before he was shot he said, 'There are a million negroes in Mississippi. I think they'll take care of me.' The shots were fired from a wood shortly after a car full of white men waving the Confederate flag had passed the marchers. Meredith was taken to hospital after the shooting and made a full recovery.

The next day, Martin Luther King led the march, resuming at the point where Meredith had been shot. Meredith said he wanted to rejoin the march as soon as he was well enough, adding, 'The day for the negro man being a coward is over.' The United States was seething with racial tension. A month of race riots and looting broke out in June in Cleveland. There were riots in Chicago and Atlanta.

But Atlanta was the first city in the South to integrate its state school without any disturbance; the race riot happened afterwards, in the black Summerhill district of the city. Desegregation really was under way.

Martin Luther King Jr's career came to an abrupt end in 1968, when he was assassinated in Memphis, Tennessee, where he had gone to lead a dustmen's strike.

THE GREEN REVOLUTION (1964)

IN 1964 HIGH-YIELDING dwarf strains of *indica* rice were introduced. The International Rice Research Institute at Los Banos in the Philippines was responsible for developing these new strains, which were still at an experimental stage. The principle behind the development of the new strains was that by having a short stem, the plant would waste less energy in building the stem, that more of the nutrients would go into forming the grain. Short stems on cereals are also better because they are less likely to be blown or washed over, or beaten down by heavy rainfall. The new dwarf rice strains were known by their experimental names, IR5 and IR8. They produced up to five times as much grain per hectare as traditional strains.

This development was highly significant to the poorer countries of the world. If a given area of land could be made to produce five times as much food, it could support five times as many people. This was something that Thomas Malthus had not envisaged when he wrote of population growth outstripping the growth of food supply. Population might grow, but food supplies also can be extended, and extended by a major step-change. The production of new strains of rice was not an isolated development, either. Other cereal crops were also selectively bred to produce strains with a variety of desirable qualities, such as short stem, large grain size, disease resistance, easy milling properties, and so on. All round the world a quiet revolution in food supply was going on. It was called the Green Revolution.

The intention of the scientists working on these projects was not so much to encourage the population to quadruple as to provide better and more reliable food supplies for existing populations; people in the poorer countries of the world had inadequate diets and inadequate amounts of food. But at the same time, the expansion of the food supply meant that the gloom-and-doom scenarios about a population explosion or a population bomb were no more than scare stories.

THE FIRST HEART TRANSPLANT
(1967)

THE FIRST HEART transplant operation was undertaken by the South African surgeon, Christian Barnard, on 3 December 1967. The operation was a global media sensation. It was a major breakthrough in medical science. The euphoria diminished somewhat when the patient, Louis Washkansky, died only 18 days after the operation. Evidently replacing the human heart was not as straightforward as it had appeared. The second heart transplant took place at the National Heart Hospital in London on 3 May 1968. The patient, Frederick West, survived for 45 days, which was a significant advance and showed that the technique had at least the possibility of working.

One implication of this new development in transplant surgery was that guidelines were urgently needed to establish when a patient was dead. The American Medical Association adopted a new standard for declaring a potential organ donor 'dead' – it was when two doctors independently declare the patient's death irreversible, that is, beyond hope of resuscitation. The debate continued, as it is by no means obvious when death has finally occurred; a patient's brain may go on functioning for some time after the patient has stopped breathing and after the heart has stopped beating. Eventually the idea of 'brain death' was introduced.

Another implication was that certain patients, such as young traffic accident victims, might be seen as quarries for transplant organs and that surgeons might become more interested in pronouncing death than saving life. There was also the problem of permission. Close relatives of the recently dead are usually in no state to be asked whether they agree to their loved ones' organs being removed. The idea of an organ donor card seemed like a better option. The problem of donors would disappear if artificial hearts could be manufactured. At the University of Utah Medical Centre, an artificial heart was successfully implanted into a patient, Barney Clark, who lived for 112 days. The artificial heart was designed by Robert Jarvik. Even more controversial was the experimental transplant of a baboon's heart into a two-week-old baby girl at the Loma Linda University Medical Centre in California. The baby survived with the baboon's heart for 20 days.

On 17 December 1986, one of the most ambitious organ transplant operations was attempted. The first triple transplant, of heart, lungs and liver, was undertaken at Papworth Hospital, Cambridge, by John Wallwork and Roy Calne. Five years later, surgeons found that they could repair damaged hearts by using muscles removed from other areas of the patient's body.

The first heart transplant was greeted with great excitement, followed by disappointment when the patient died. The major problem is that of rejection. The human body is designed to 'fight off' foreign tissue of any kind: it is part of the body's natural defence against infection. It is possible to feed the transplant patient drugs that will reduce this natural defence, but this in turn reduces the body's immune system and makes it vulnerable to infections. These problems may be overcome in time, but the early promise of organ transplant has not yet been realized. It is still not a very reliable or safe procedure.

THE FIRST MOON LANDING
(1969)

ON 21 JULY 1969, a man walked on the Moon for the first time. It happened at 3.56 am British Summer Time. US astronaut Neil Armstrong stepped out of Eagle, the lunar module from Apollo 11, and warily descended a ladder onto the pale grey dusty surface of the Moon. As he planted the first human footprint on the Moon, he said, 'That's one small step for a man, one giant leap for mankind.' Shortly afterwards he was joined by his fellow astronaut Buzz Aldrin and the two of them experimented with moving about under the low gravity conditions. The moment was watched on television all over the world, by hundreds of millions of people. Armstrong was intrigued by the texture under foot. 'The surface is like a fine powder. It has a soft beauty all its own, like some desert of the United States.'

The Moon landing came as the climax of the Apollo 11 mission, four days after blasting off from Cape Canaveral (or Cape Kennedy). After an uneventful flight, the Apollo went into orbit round the Moon. Armstrong and Aldrin transferred to the lunar module and started their descent to the Moon. There was a tense final moment, when without much fuel left they had to avoid a boulder-filled crater. The two astronauts stayed on the Moon for less than one day before lifting off to rendezvous with Apollo 11, still orbiting the Moon.

Five days later, scientists put the rocks collected on the Moon into quarantine for two months. For the moment frustrated geologists were only allowed to look at them through a window. The quarantine procedure was a precaution, just in case there were organisms of any kind on the Moon that could infect plants or animals on Earth. In fact the rocks turned out to be sterile. They also, in due course, when dated, turned out to be very old. They turned out to be 4.5 billion years old, which is the date when the solar system was created. Rocks exposed at the surface of the Earth are much younger, because the Earth is a more active planet and the surface rocks have been recycled many times. The Moon's surface shows every sign of being a very ancient landscape, little changed since its creation apart from the bombardment by meteorites.

For some reason, millions of Americans were persuaded that they were watching a simulation staged in a film studio, or in fact some desert of the United States, to divert their attention away from the Vietnam War. Conspiracy theories multiplied. Millions more were concerned about the huge sum of money spent on the Moon landing, believing that the money could have been spent more usefully. So, even as the event happened, people were reading a variety of subtexts into the event.

The Moon landing was also, in part, a contribution to the Cold War. Americans had reached the Moon before the Russians. The Russians had been beaten. It was not actually said, but it didn't need to be.

The visit to the Moon was man's first step away from the Earth out into the solar system, and undoubtedly more symbolic than useful, as the rock samples could more cheaply have been collected by a robot. But it marked a critical stage in man's interest in the cosmos. People speculated about journeys further afield, and there was talk of a mission to Mars. The danger and the ever-increasing cost ruled that out, and subsequent explorations have been undertaken by unmanned vehicles. Even the outer planets and their satellites have been flown past now, and the photographs taken during those close encounters have been carefully analyzed in order to reconstruct the nature of the planets. The most striking thing is their diversity. Given their common origin, they are surprisingly different and individual. Another surprise was the unexpected jewel-like beauty of the Earth, seen from the Moon.

The Apollo 11 mission to the Moon may have been a politically motivated stunt to show the Soviets that the United States was ahead, but it really did demonstrate the sophistication and precision that was possible in modern rocket science. Devices, whether manned or unmanned, could be sent scouting round the solar system to gather data - and brought safely back again. It was very much the beginning of a new age, an age of physical reaching-out into the cosmos.

WATERGATE
(1972)

IT WAS IN June 1972 that the biggest constitutional crisis in American history since independence began. Specifically, it began at two in the morning of 17 June, when police alerted by a young security guard arrested five men inside the national headquarters of the Democratic Party, the Watergate complex. The five were Bernard Barker, James McCord, Eugenio Martinez, Frank Sturgis and Virgilio Gonzalez. They had cameras and surveillance equipment with them and the overwhelming suspicion was that President Nixon or his associates had ordered this surveillance. Nixon's campaign manager denied it, but Nixon's office admitted that one of the men, Barker, had met CIA agent E. Howard Hunt. The reason for the break-in at the Watergate complex was still unclear.

The incident seemed peculiar, but perhaps not of national importance. But the story was pursued with great persistence and determination by two *Washington Post* reporters, Carl Bernstein and Bob Woodward. Thanks to them, more and more of the ramifications of the conspiracy came out – and eventually brought down the president of the United States.

In 1973, one of the five men, James McCord, who was a former CIA employee, implicated Republican Party officials in the Watergate break-in of the previous year. Nixon announced what he called 'major developments' in the Watergate case on 17 April. In the wake of this manoeuvre, Nixon's aides, Bob Haldeman and John Ehrlichman were forced to resign. Nixon evidently expected them to take the blame, which was a very short-term solution; he could not seriously have expected them to remain silent in the face of prison sentences and wrecked careers. John Dean, a former White House legal aide, who was expected to make the same sacrifice, implicated other associates of Nixon's under questioning. He also said in his testimony that Nixon had taken part in the cover-up of illegal acts. Dean said he had warned Nixon that the effort to cover up the White House's involvement in the Watergate break-in was 'a cancer growing in his presidency'. He confirmed that Haldeman and Ehrlichman had organized the cover-up. He accused the president of saying that it would be possible to find one million dollars in hush money. He accused the president of trying to get other people to take the rap. Dean's courageous testimony had an explosive effect.

In July 1973, it emerged that Nixon had installed listening devices in the Oval Office at the White House. Alexander Butterfield, who was in charge of routine administration in the White House, testified that the listening devices had been installed three years earlier in the Oval Office and on the phones used by the president. Then it became clear that a large-scale constitutional crisis was looming. Would the Senate investigating committee be able to insist on having access to the president's tape recordings? The tapes would reveal whether the president had been telling the truth or not.

The special Watergate prosecutor, Professor Archibald Cox, tried to insist that Nixon must hand over the tape recordings of conversations with his aides to Judge Sirica. For this he was dismissed. The Attorney General, Elliott Richardson, who was ordered by Nixon to sack Cox, refused and promptly resigned in protest. Nixon then ordered his deputy, William Ruckelshaus, to sack Professor Cox; he too refused. Finally the Solicitor-General, Robert Bork, agreed to sack Cox. Nixon replaced Cox with Leon Jaworski as prosecutor. This remarkable episode was described in the press as 'the Saturday Night Massacre'. Nixon then released the tapes, but it became apparent that they had gaps; the White House claimed that the missing tapes did not exist.

By March 1974, a federal grand jury came to the conclusion that President was up to his neck in the conspiracy, that he was an 'unindicted co-conspirator'.

In July 1974, the Supreme Court ruled that Nixon must hand over the 64 White House tape recordings to a special prosecutor. The House Judiciary Committee voted to impeach Nixon on three counts of obstructing justice, failure to uphold laws and refusal to produce material that the committee had formally asked for. On 9 August 1974, Nixon was forced to resign in disgrace. It was that or remain in office and face impeachment.

Sworn in on 9 August, Gerald Ford said, 'The long nightmare is over.' A month later he granted Nixon a 'full, free and absolute pardon' for all the crimes he had or might have committed. Ford did this to spare both Nixon and the United States further punishment. Ford incredibly also asked Congress to grant Nixon 850,000 dollars to ease him into private life, presumably seeing that Nixon was totally unemployable; Congress was shocked by the size of the sum and trimmed it back to 200,000 dollars.

The Watergate scandal was a punishing experience for many Americans. It showed that presidents could be fatally flawed, shabby, seedy, corrupt, disloyal, ungrateful and ready to behave entirely unscrupulously in the pursuit of personal power. Many Americans were shocked to discover that behind the scenes their president had behaved like a cheap gangster. Watergate was an American rite of passage.

THE OIL CRISIS
(1973)

IN 1973, THE world was gripped by a fear that finite energy sources were running out. The Arab oil producers became aware that their oil reserves might run out in 100–200 years and tried to slow down consumption rates in order to ensure the long-term prosperity of the Middle East. They decided to double the price of crude oil, with a view to inhibiting Western consumption. This well-intentioned move was a failure. The oil-dependent economies of the West were unable or unprepared to make this adjustment, and went on consuming at the same rate, but paying double. The oil producers doubled the price of oil again about one year later, and this still did not reduce consumption.

The effect was simply to weaken the Western economies, while flooding the Arab producers with untold wealth. The Arabs did not know what to do with it, so much of it ended up in banks. The World Bank, flooded with Arab oil money, was similarly embarrassed and looked around for projects that required large-scale investment. The result of that was a number of multi-million dollar schemes in less economically developed countries, schemes that sounded as if they would assist development but which instead created a huge burden of debt.

In the United States, President Nixon ended the oil import quota that had been in place since 1959, and created tax incentives to subsidize the oil industry's oil exploration programme. Nixon urged Americans to use coal, even if it caused atmospheric pollution, and also to save energy. Nixon told Congress, 'America faces a serious energy problem. While we have 6 percent of the world's population, we consume one-third of the world's energy output. The supply of domestic energy resources available to us is not keeping pace with our ever-growing demand.' American demand was running at 17 million barrels per day, while domestic production (from American oilfields) was 11 million barrels per day.

Part of the anxiety was to do with the prospect of becoming dependent, one day, on foreign supplies of oil. The spectre of political dependence on an unstable Middle East loomed. And here was the ultimate explanation for American interest in the Middle East, and for seeking to control Middle Eastern states.

In Britain too, people were encouraged to save electricity in every way possible. As oil prices rose, competitor resources looked more favourable. In many countries coal was the obvious alternative. In Britain, that did not happen. For political reasons, the British government wanted to wind up the coal industry. So, even though there were reserves of coal underground in Britain to last 300 years, the pit closures continued.

Environmental organizations publicized the idea that many of the world's oilfields would run dry in the space of 25–50 years. Eventually it emerged that this scare story originated in a misreading of oil geologists' reports. The oil companies had commissioned a survey to check that there were sufficient oil reserves to supply the industry for the next 50 years. What the geologists did was just that, and they reported back that there was enough oil in the world to sustain consumption at current levels until 2025. This was interpreted – misinterpreted – as meaning that the oil would run out in 2025. For some reason it took 20 years for this error to emerge and be corrected. It was a hue and cry for nothing. Perhaps it suited the oil companies to have this mistake aired, as it seemed to justify raising prices. The scarcer the resource, the higher the price that could be charged for it.

Meanwhile, in 1974, there was a world economic recession following the oil price rises. Transport costs rose and therefore the retail prices of most goods. In the United States, the Consumer Price Index rose 12 percent, compared with around 2 or 3 percent in most previous years.

One positive outcome of the energy crisis was that people started looking more seriously at the possibility of using renewable sources of energy, such as wind, solar and tidal energy. Architects looked more closely at ways of designing energy-saving houses; better insulation and double-glazing were to make a huge difference not only to energy consumption but to people's domestic comfort.

THE ATTEMPTED ASSASSINATION OF POPE JOHN PAUL II (1981)

KAROL WOJTYLA WAS ordained in 1946, became Archbishop of Cracow in 1964 and was made a cardinal in 1967. In 1978, he became the first non-Italian pope for 450 years. After eight ballots, his election was a victory for the Third World cardinals who wanted a non-Italian pope. He had no expectation of becoming pope and had actually taken something to read into the conclave to choose the new pope; he had not anticipated any personal involvement in the process. He was very surprised by his own election. The thousands of Italians waiting for the result in St Peter's Square were also surprised, and for some time they were stunned by the news.

A few months later, in June 1979, he made his visit 'home', to Poland. It was an historic visit in that it was the first time a pope had visited a Communist country. Later he told journalists in Poland, 'Communism and capitalism are realities, but underneath stand the people. This is a human reality.'

In May 1980, Pope John Paul went on an African tour. He was well aware, because of the circumstances of his election, that the Catholic congregations round the world were alienated, feeling that the Vatican was 'too Italian' and inward-looking, and he made global outreach the outstanding feature of his papacy. He wanted people everywhere to know that he was *their* pope, not just Italy's pope.

It was in May 1981 that he was shot while being driven in a white open-topped jeep through a crowd of 20,000 people in St Peter's Square. The pope was hit by four bullets, two of which lodged in his intestines; he was incredibly lucky to survive this attack, which was meant to kill him. He was seriously wounded but after a five-hour operation he made a full recovery.

The attacker was a Turk called Mehmet Ali Agca, and it is possible that he was a hitman hired by Bulgarians. In his boarding house close to the Vatican Agca left a letter, in which he wrote that he wanted 'to demonstrate to the world the imperialistic crimes of the Soviet Union and the United States.' Whatever view one takes of John Paul, it is hard to see how he could be held responsible for any crimes perpetrated by the Great Powers. It was a peculiar reason for killing him and some other motive must really have lain behind Agca's assassination attempt. Perhaps it was a Soviet revenge attack for John Paul's support for Solidarity in Poland; he had made it very clear that he was going to be a strong ally for the Polish dissidents.

If the assassination attempt had succeeded, no doubt the conspiracy behind it would have been followed up more thoroughly and the ultimate culprits, Agca's masters, would have been exposed. John Paul himself would have been seen as a martyr, which would have put him on the fast track to canonization.

Against the odds, he survived the murderous attack and continued to be the most energetic pope in recent memory, just as he had been an energetic cardinal. As pope he travelled to many foreign countries, preaching wherever he went, and becoming a kind of superstar. He championed economic justice and was an outspoken defender of the Church in Communist countries; in this he was of course speaking from his own bitter experience as a Christian priest in an Eastern European Communist state – Poland. In 1981, he publicly declared his hand; 'Trade unions are indispensable in the struggle for social justice.' He repeated this two years later when he held meetings with Lech Walesa, the leader of Solidarity. He said that people had the right to belong to trade unions. 'This right is not given to us by the State. It is a right given by the Creator.' He also held meetings with Mikhail Gorbachev, the Soviet leader. By these startlingly direct interventions, John Paul greatly assisted the trade union movement in general, Solidarity in particular, and promoted Polish independence, which was achieved in 1989. He went even further than this, making a huge sum of money available for Solidarity. Maybe the incident in St Peter's Square had made him even more determined to help Poland.

From 1996 onwards, John Paul's health declined intermittently; the wounds inflicted in the assassination attempt had taken their toll. His death in 2004 prompted eulogies from every quarter of the world. It is tempting to wonder whether the independence of Poland would have been achieved without John Paul. If he had died in 1981, would Solidarity have failed and would Poland have remained under Soviet rule? And if Poland had failed to gain its independence, might the Baltic states have been more timid about clamouring for it? It is just possible that if Pope John Paul had been assassinated in 1981 the Soviet Union might have continued and not have collapsed in 1991.

THE START OF THE AIDS PANDEMIC
(1981)

IN 1981, AIDS (Acquired Immune Deficiency Syndrome) began to make a serious impact on the world. The disease spread so quickly and easily from country to country that it was soon being compared to the Black Death pandemic of the fourteenth century. Curiously it is still not known how or where the disease began, though lots of theories have been aired.

In terms of identification and diagnosis, AIDS began as a sexually transmitted disease passed on by homosexual American men. In San Francisco and New York, doctors reported that several dozen previously healthy homosexual men had died of Kaposi's sarcoma, a form of cancer that was endemic in Africa but rare in other continents. The men suffered deficiencies of their immune systems. The doctors realized that these mystery cases were recurring. At first they were widely separated in time, but by 1981 they were occurring frequently enough to be identifiably similar.

Every month there were more reported cases. Then it became clear that it was not just homosexuals who were affected by AIDS, but drug addicts using contaminated needles too. At first these new victims were mostly Hispanic or black, and mainly in the cities of the United States. The key process in the transmission of the disease seemed to be an exchange of body fluids. In each case, the immune system collapsed and the victims frequently died of pneumonia. AIDS was always fatal, sooner or later.

By 1987, more than 32,000 Americans had been diagnosed as having AIDS. But AIDS was not just an American problem. It struck Europe and took an ever-increasing toll in Africa, where it was spread mainly by heterosexuals. African men going off to work in the towns picked up AIDS from prostitutes there, then gave the disease to their wives when they returned home. In Africa, there are as many females afflicted with AIDS as males; in some cases, whole families are affected. The disease has now spread to Southern Asia, where there has been a reluctance to admit to the problem.

The AIDS pandemic has become the major health problem in the Third World countries. There are drugs that will keep AIDS at bay for years, but they are expensive. AZT was a drug that came into use in 1987. It could not cure AIDS but relieved some of the symptoms and kept patients alive for longer. On the other hand the side effects were unpleasant and it was costly.

AIDS has had a huge impact on African society, health care and living standards. Some African countries have such high percentages of people with AIDS that they seem to be heading for population collapse. It has also had an effect, though a rather different effect, on Western society. Whereas 15 years earlier there had been a liberalization in attitudes towards homosexuality, AIDS precipitated a backlash of intolerance. After the greater sexual freedom of the Sixties, there was also a general 'retreat' to a more careful attitude to heterosexual behaviour. Moralists were able to exploit the situation, encouraging the young to remain chaste. And instead of free love, there was now protected sex.

MICHAEL BUERK'S REPORT ON THE FAMINE IN ETHIOPIA
(1985)

IN 1985, FAMINE struck Ethiopia. Michael Buerk was one of the leading TV journalists covering the famine, and he sent back a powerful TV news report that was watched by millions of people in Britain. The images of children starving to death in a bleached, dusty and sterile African landscape were in themselves haunting and moving. Michael Buerk's commentary was even more compelling. The impact of this extended news coverage was enormous.

One of the people who watched it and felt he had to do something about it was the singer Bob Geldof. It changed the direction of his life. He was moved by the plight of starving Africans and struck by his own relative comfort. Geldof decided to make a record as a means of raising money to relieve the famine. Some of the bands he approached were understandably suspicious of his motives, but Geldof was on a mission.

Geldof and his collaborators produced a record entitled *Do they know it's Christmas?* with its chorus 'Feed the World'. It was a great success, raising £8 million to alleviate the famine in Ethiopia. Other charities saw Geldof's initiative as a threat, so his associates persuaded Geldof to go to Africa to make sure the aid reached the needy. He went, and managed to meet the Ethiopian head of state and tell him in forthright terms what he thought of him, although the translator discreetly stopped translating at that point. Later, when he met Margaret Thatcher, there was no need for a translator.

The success of the British aid record prompted an American copy-cat record, called *We are the World*. This featured a host of American black singers, including Michael Jackson.

Geldof went on to organize a massive fund-raising event, the Live Aid concert. Many pop musicians offered their services free in order to mount the concert at Wembley on 13 July 1985, which featured 25 bands on stage. A parallel and simultaneous event was mounted across the Atlantic in Philadelphia, and a total of 58 bands played live. Many critics predicted that it would be chaotic, but it was a huge success. A huge sum was raised – £50 million – and this was distributed in Africa to alleviate distress. In 1986, he organized a similar Sport Aid event, which raised a further £50 million.

Bob Geldof staged another event 20 years later, Live8, to coincide with a G8 meeting of politicians from eight rich countries in July 2005.

Bob Geldof has been criticized by the major aid organizations. While he has succeeded in raising huge sums of money as gifts from the general public, these 'one-off' fund-raising initiatives have resulted in a reduction in the income of organizations such as Oxfam and Christian Aid. There is also a danger that emotional appeals made through TV and the press in the wake of a particularly 'photogenic' emergency may produce a lop-sided financial response. This seems to have been the case with the Boxing Day tsunami disaster in 2004, when the global response to an appeal for financial aid was overwhelming and excessive – in relation to the hundreds of smaller tragedies unfolding round the world all the time.

Development experts argue that aid beyond a certain level is unhelpful. Some countries have become aid-dependent, waiting for the next hand-out from the rich countries instead of seeking radical self-help solutions within their own frontiers. There is also the thought that there is an air of patronage and condescension about giving money to the poor; it is a piece of cultural chauvinism. The best way to deal with a beggar is not to give him food but to show him how to produce his own food; then he can be permanently self-sufficient.

Any effort to alleviate the destitution of Africa must be welcomed, and Geldof's initiatives are certainly a positive effort in that direction. But populist initiatives such as Live Aid and Live8 do nothing to address the main problems that bedevil the continent. One is what has been described as the 'criminal incompetence of Africa's post-colonial black elites.' It is this more than anything else that prevents the poor countries of Africa from lifting themselves out of poverty in the way that their Asian equivalents have done. South Korea was a much poorer country than Senegal or Ghana back in 1964, yet it is now 40 times richer than both of those countries put together, both in total wealth and in per capita income. In a similar way, Thailand has become richer than most African countries, simply as a result of efficient government. The key to development is not aid from rich outsiders but systematic spending on education. High spending on education helps the poor to make the most of their abilities; it also leads to the evolution of a middle class, and African countries lack middle classes. The leaders of South Korea realized they had to invest in their people, educated them, and the country as a whole has reaped the benefits, in both social and economic development. The political elites in the poorer countries in Africa have shown no interest in helping their people to better themselves – only in enriching themselves and remaining in power as long as possible in order to do so.

Even so, Bob Geldof has made many ordinary people feel that they can directly improve the lives of other people less fortunate than themselves. The challenge to politicians to explain their actions has also been refreshing.

The whole fund-raising movement had its origins in that first news report in 1985, and its powerful impact is something that I and many others can still vividly remember. Michael Buerk's view of what was happening in Africa in 1985 has changed radically over the years. At the time he thought the famine was caused by population pressure and environmental failure – a natural disaster. Now he sees it as the result of warfare; it was fighting in the region that interrupted food production and caused the displacement of people, so the cause of the famine was political. Either way, that brilliant piece of TV journalism from Ethiopia by Michael Buerk changed the way people saw the world in one very significant way. It roused people's consciences, their sense of responsibility towards those much worse off than themselves.

THE CHERNOBYL DISASTER
(1986)

ON 30 APRIL 1986, it was announced by Moscow that there had been a major accident at the Chernobyl nuclear power station near Kiev in the Ukraine. The announcement came after abnormally high levels of radiation were reported in Sweden, Denmark and Finland; they had to be explained. Moscow admitted that Chernobyl, far away to the south-east, was the source of the radiation. An explosion had blown the roof off Number four reactor at Chernobyl four days earlier, on 26 April, and sent clouds of dangerous radioactive fall-out across much of northern Europe. At Chernobyl itself fire broke out in the graphite moderator and the other three reactors were shut down. How much radioactivity escaped is not known, but since the core was exposed, as American satellite photographs showed, the leakage must have been substantial.

Shortly after the accident over 30 power station workers and fire-fighters died as a result of exposure to high levels of radiation. Over the next few years, somewhere between 7,000 and 45,000 people are thought to have died in the Chernobyl area from cancer as a result of the radiation. There were also reports of increased rates of genetic defects among children born during the years following the explosion.

The reactor was entombed in concrete in an attempt to confine the radiation, but Chernobyl had to be abandoned and a large area round it will be uninhabitable and impossible to farm for thousands of years. The accident created a bleak wasteland.

The south-east wind blowing at the time of the radiation leak took high levels of radiation across eastern Europe, Scandinavia and northern Britain. Sheep that were grazing on the hillsides at the time of the leak were considered unfit for human consumption.

There had always been a background anxiety about nuclear power stations. Fear of radiation leaks from them led to a belief that it was unsafe to live near them. In Britain, nuclear power stations were built in relatively isolated places, but Britain is a densely populated country and nowhere in Britain is very far from towns and cities. What the Chernobyl disaster showed was that the risk is not only greater and more real than had been thought, but much farther-reaching geographically. The insidious radiation pollution could reach right across countries, right across a whole continent. The Soviet reactors were not housed in containment buildings, like most Western nuclear reactors, and the presence of a containment building would have greatly reduced the leakage; Western supporters of nuclear energy took some comfort from this thought.

All over Europe there were questions about the safety of meat and milk produced in a contaminated environment, and about the consequent risks to people. That summer, the summer of 1986, there was a noticeable decrease in the number of American tourists in Europe.

Chernobyl was a watershed in the power production industry in Europe. It showed, beyond any doubt, that nuclear energy is not safe enough. When the first nuclear power stations were built there was great excitement. Some scientists even suggested that once the power stations were built the electricity would be virtually free, and certainly much cheaper than electricity produced in coal-fired power stations. This enthusiasm led successive British governments to wind down the coal industry – coal would not be needed in the future. But the danger of radiation and the costly safety measures that had to be incorporated into power station design and management raised the cost of the electricity to the same as the electricity derived from coal. So nuclear energy turned out to be no cheaper, and there was still the problem, the very expensive and so far unsolved problem, of disposing of the nuclear waste.

TIANANMEN SQUARE
(1989)

THE CHINESE POLITBURO member Hu Yaobang was criticized by hard-liners for not cracking down sufficiently on mounting student unrest. There was a younger generation in China wanting more freedom, more democracy, and was not afraid to campaign for it. Hu was forced by the hard-liners to resign as general secretary of the Politburo in January 1987. When Hu Yaobang died two years later at the age of 73, on 15 April 1989, students gathered in Tiananmen Square, on the face of it to mourn Hu's death.

In fact it was a pretext. The real purpose of the rally was to demand more democracy and to protest against the abuses of corrupt government officials. The crowd of young people alarmed the authorities by staying in the square night and day for weeks on end. The protest spread to other Chinese cities. In at least six other cities, students demanded political reforms – and the resignation of the Chinese premier, Li Peng. Troops were sent into Tiananmen Square to disperse the students, but were won over by the students' arguments.

Finally, on 3 June 1989, People's Liberation Army tanks moved into Tiananmen Square. There is a memorable piece of film of a demonstrator, just one young man, dancing about in front of a tank, and the tank crew, evidently not wanting to run him down, trying to get past him first one side, then the other; it is a vivid image of the complexity of the confrontation. Three days later Deng Xiaoping sent in not Chinese but Mongolian soldiers who were prepared to fire into the crowd with AK-47 assault rifles. It is not known for sure how many young pro-democracy demonstrators they killed, but it is estimated to have been as many as 2,000 deaths. The leaders of the pro-democracy movement were executed, in spite of appeals from the West for leniency. It was a savage and unnecessary act of state violence. All states are capable of it, and it is never excusable. A more recent example is the murder in 2005 of an innocent Brazilian electrician at the Stockwell underground station in London – and that crime was committed by British policemen.

The US Congress imposed sanctions against China, but President Bush undermined these sanctions imposed by his own Congress by sending a secret emissary in July to meet Chinese leaders. In December 1989, Bush acted to veto a bill that would extend the visas of 40,000 Chinese students visiting the United States and waived some of the Congressional sanctions. Bush was evidently siding with the Chinese leaders and approving of the massacre. Refusing to extend the visas meant that some young Chinese could be returning to face considerable danger in China.

The Tiananmen Square massacre showed that the upper echelons of the Chinese government were unreconstructed. It showed that the 'westernization' process was only superficial, and that there was still scant regard for human rights as construed in the West. It was a warning to the West that the East was still a very different place.

THE RELEASE OF NELSON MANDELA

(1990)

FOR 20 LONG years, Nelson Mandela directed a sustained and courageous campaign of defiance against the government of South Africa, in protest against its aggressive racist policies. In May 1961, he organized a three-day national strike. The police tried to head it off by carrying out mass arrests of black activists; in all nearly 10,000 black people were detained. The police tried to arrest Mandela too, but when they called at his home in Orlando, near Johannesburg, he was out. He became known as the Black Pimpernel for his skill at avoiding arrest. But he was eventually arrested and brought to trial on 22 October 1962. He was accused specifically of being the mastermind behind the call for a national strike. He pleaded not guilty. A few weeks later he was found guilty and imprisoned for five years for incitement.

When the strike failed, Nelson Mandela despaired of using non-violent means of overturning the racist regime; he turned instead to violence and helped to found the Spear of the Nation movement.

Inevitably, the South African authorities retaliated, re-arresting Mandela and putting him on trial for more serious political offences. While he was in prison, the police raided the ANC's underground headquarters, where they found Mandela's diaries, containing notes on guerrilla warfare. In April 1964, he went on trial for treason. He was accused of sabotage and trying to overthrow the South African government by revolution. Mandela bravely told the court in Pretoria that his purpose was to rid the country of white domination. 'I do not deny that I planned sabotage. We had either to accept inferiority or fight against it by violence.' In spite of his eloquent defence, he was sentenced to life imprisonment. He then spent many years at the penal colony on Robben

Island. This has a strong current of cold Antarctic water sweeping past it, and escape was reckoned to be impossible.

Nelson Mandela continued to be a political force while in prison. In fact he became a potent symbol of the subjugation of the black population of South Africa, a rallying point. The symbolism of Mandela's captivity became a world-wide phenomenon, and a co-ordinated international campaign for his release was launched. His captivity became an increasing political embarrassment to the government of South Africa.

Side by side with the campaign to release Mandela, there was a world-wide campaign for the South African government to end its system of apartheid, the anti-black racial discrimination that permeated every aspect of South African life. Economic sanctions were applied, with many countries refusing to trade with South Africa. For a long time these sanctions had little effect, and the white South Africans seemed set to maintain their privileged position for ever, but suddenly in the 1980s sanctions began to bite.

President F. W. de Klerk took office in 1989, and introduced liberalizing measures that started the process of dismantling apartheid. Within months of his election, President de Klerk visited Mandela in prison, preparing him for freedom and the new role he was about to play. The ban on the ANC was lifted, restrictions on political meetings were removed.

On de Klerk's orders, Nelson Mandela was released in February 1990. There was world-wide rejoicing. At the age of 71, Mandela was free. At the same time the white supremacy within the South African government crumbled, and the whole country was on the threshold of a massive political and cultural transformation. Mandela was made president of the ANC, and he opened negotiations with de Klerk about the country's future. He pressed the governments of other countries to continue applying pressure; apartheid had to be abolished completely. In 1993, Mandela and de Klerk were jointly awarded the Nobel Peace Prize for their work on the process of reform, and the following year Mandela became the first black president of South Africa.

Some anticipated a bloodbath, in which many old scores against the white community would be settled by the newly-empowered blacks. Mandela was the natural figurehead for the newly emergent black South Africa, and it would have been understandable if he had used his new-found power to punish, humiliate or even destroy his ex-jailers. In fact Mandela showed incredible restraint and magnanimity, encouraging people to confess and come to terms with the bad events of the past, but without undue recrimination, without revenge.

Nelson Mandela won the respect of the whole world for the statesman-like way in which he accepted and wielded political power in the new South Africa. Thanks to his leadership, there were no revenge killings, there was no bloodbath. Against all expectations, the liberation of black South Africa proved to be a happy rite of passage. The revenge killing instead happened elsewhere in southern Africa; it was in Zimbabwe, where trouble had not been anticipated, that a black tyrant unleashed a destructive programme of anti-white discrimination in his own country.

THE COLLAPSE OF THE SOVIET UNION
(1991)

FOR MUCH OF the Cold War, the West saw the Soviet Union as strong, still the nineteenth century Russian bear. In fact there were warning signs, which some of us picked up ten years before the collapse, that the Soviet Union's economy was crippled. It is common for less economically developed countries to find themselves massively in debt to other countries. Brazil built up huge debts in its efforts to speed economic development. The Soviet Union was another country that had a huge debt, and that should have warned more Western observers that the Soviet economy could implode.

, Some of the member states within the Soviet Union sensed that the centre was weakening. The Baltic states, Estonia, Latvia and Lithuania, started agitating for their independence. They were greatly heartened by Poland's success in gaining its independence. In January 1991, Soviet paratroopers were sent in following independence demonstrations; they stormed the television station in Vilnius in Lithuania, killing 13 independence demonstrators. A similar Russian raid on Riga in Latvia led to the killing of four demonstrators. In February, a referendum in Lithuania produced a majority in favour of independence from Russia. The following month referendums in Latvia and Estonia produced the same result.

In Moscow, President Gorbachev struggled to hold the Soviet Union together. He knew that if the Baltic states broke free other states would also agitate for their independence and the Soviet Union would be finished. He tried a desperate remedy. On 17 March, a referendum held throughout the USSR approved Gorbachev's proposal for a new federation of socialist republics that would give member states greater autonomy. Later that month the Warsaw Pact was formally dissolved; this was a military pact between the USSR and the Communist countries of Eastern Europe. In April, a referendum in Georgia produced a vote for independence.

That summer, chaos broke out in the Soviet Union. On 19 August, reactionary Communists led by Gennady Yanayev staged a coup against Gorbachev, who was removed and put under house arrest in the Crimea. But the fragmentation was irresistibly under way; the very next day Estonia declared its independence. The following day the coup in Moscow collapsed and Gorbachev returned from the Crimea. On 21 August, Latvia declared its independence. On 24 August, Gorbachev resigned as general secretary of the Communist Party of the Soviet Union, condemning its role in the recent attempted coup. Two days after that, Gorbachev dismissed the Soviet government and disbanded the leadership of the KGB, the Soviet secret police. On 30 August, Azerbaijan declared its independence. The central government was disintegrating and increasing numbers of member states were opting out.

The time had come to acknowledge what was happening and in early September Moscow made a beginning by acknowledging the independence of the Baltic states. The city of Leningrad, named after the Russian Revolutionary leader, reverted to its pre-Revolution name of St Petersburg; it was an important gesture signifying that the Communist era was over. By the end of 1991, the old Soviet Union itself was abolished and replaced by a looser alliance of independent states. Gorbachev resigned and was succeeded by Boris Yeltsin.

The swift collapse of the Soviet Union sent shock waves through eastern Europe, which had been dominated by Moscow for several decades. The Berlin Wall had come down in 1989, symbolizing the end of the division of Germany into a capitalist West and a Communist East. In eastern Europe, Communist power was challenged and in many cases replaced by liberal Western-style regimes. The map of Eurasia had comprehensively changed. The new Russian Federation is a smaller, less threatening state than the old Soviet Union. Round its borders is a ring of newly independent states, finding their feet, and some, such as Chechnya still struggling to gain their freedom. The map of Europe looks very different indeed. There is no longer an Iron Curtain separating East from West. Instead there is a queue of new countries wanting to join the European Union.

SEPTEMBER 11
(2001)

NINE-ELEVEN – THE American emergency call number, and also the American-style date of the worst terrorist attack on the United States. The Al Qaeda attacks on Washington and New York on 11 September 2001, in which about 3,000 people died, was an expression of frustration by Muslim extremists with the globalization originating in the West. Globalization replaces old ways of life with consumerism and the pursuit of wealth, which many traditional Muslims resist. The West wants to deal with the situation as a 'war against terrorism', but the underlying problem is a clash of civilizations.

In February 1998, the Al Qaeda leader Osama bin Laden issued a fatwa against all American citizens – military and civilian.

The ruling to kill the Americans and their allies – civilian and military – is an individual duty for every Muslim who can do it in any country in which it is possible to do it, in order to liberate the al-Asqua Mosque (Jerusalem) and the holy mosque (Mecca) from their grip, and in order for their armies to move out of all lands of Islam, defeated and unable to threaten any Muslim.

In June 1999, bin Laden was added to the FBI's Ten Most Wanted List and a $5 million reward was offered. Bin Laden has extraordinary mobility. During his time in Afghanistan, bin Laden was able to disguise his movements from the fifty US special officers who worked full-time on tracing his movements by regularly varying his style of movement. He varied the number of vehicles in his convoy, and varied the type of vehicle. Sometimes he gave his entourage hours of notice, sometimes only minutes. Since September 11, US officials have been more determined than ever to find him, yet far less has been known about his movements. It is thought that only 20 dedicated guards know exactly where he is and that they are pledged to die rather than reveal where he is.

During the war in Afghanistan it seemed impossible that he could survive the systematic ambush in the Tora Bora hills, and yet he escaped. The last time he was heard of for sure was close to the Pakistan border. Most analysts think he is now in Pakistan.

Bin Laden's organization is meticulous in its organizational methods. Operations are planned months and even years ahead. Sites are often carefully researched using fieldwork. The 1995 assassination attempt against the President of Egypt, Hosni Mubarak, in Addis Ababa was based on surveillance of Mubarak's security arrangements in Ethiopia two years earlier. The East African embassy bombers phoned in credible but hoax threats to the embassies and then observed the embassy response; this was an operation that was planned over the course of five years.

The terrorist attacks are relatively cheap. It has been estimated that the 1993 World Trade Centre attack cost Al-Qaeda 18,000 dollars altogether, excluding 6,000 dollars in unpaid phone bills. It was once assumed that bin Laden's huge personal fortune enabled him to finance these lavish projects, but it is not so. His personal fortune is not as great as was once thought, though still tens of millions of dollars, and his operations are relatively inexpensive.

The Americans are naturally disappointed not to have apprehended or killed bin Laden, but several senior Al-Qaeda officials have been eliminated, imprisoned or detained. There were also some successes in foiling several planned attacks, but pride in those successes diminished considerably after the September 11th catastrophe in 2001. The more recent train bombings in Madrid in March 2004, when 199 people were killed and the train and bus bombings in London in July 2005, when 56 were killed, are grim reminders that bin Laden is still a force to be reckoned with.

The thing that will never be forgotten about this misguided man is that he bears the ultimate responsibility for the attacks on the World Trade Centre and the Pentagon on 11 September, 2001, attacks in which over 3,000 innocent people died unnecessarily.

The world was changed significantly by the 9–11 attack. It has become a much more dangerous, frightening and uncertain place to live in. There is a certain irony in the way the history of the last 50 years has unfolded. For much of that time we lived in a Cold War world, in the shadow of the atomic bomb. With the collapse of the old Soviet Union and the ending of the Cold War, we should have emerged into the sunlight. Instead of that a new demon has appeared, casting a new and possibly longer shadow.

THE BOXING DAY TSUNAMI
(2004)

CHRISTMAS DAY IN 2004 came to a peaceful end, but not long after midnight the worst natural disaster of modern times was under way. A cousin of mine who always spends Christmas with us suddenly and completely out of the blue, started talking about tsunamis. At the time, on the afternoon of Christmas Day, I just thought it was a bit wayward. With hindsight I wonder whether it was an example of those odd intuitions that some animals seem to have immediately before an earthquake; it certainly seems like second sight.

At 12.59 am Greenwich Mean Time on Boxing Day, on the seabed 150km west of Sumatra a colossal earthquake was unleashed as two of the Earth's plates slipped past each other along a split 250m long. It measured 9.1 on the Richter Scale, making it the biggest since the Anchorage earthquake of 1964 and the fourth biggest since recordings of earthquake magnitude began in 1899. The energy released in the Sumatra earthquake was the equivalent of detonating 190 million tonnes of TNT.

The two tectonic plates that slipped past each other were the Australian-Indian Plate and the Eurasian Plate. Generally the plates that make up the Earth's crust are moving imperceptibly slowly, at speeds around 5cm per year, the speed at which fingernails grow. The Australian-Indian Plate moves northwards at about that speed in relation to the Eurasian Plate, and the line separating the two runs north-south just west of Sumatra. But the movement is not smooth. The great slabs of rock are jammed against one another by friction for decades at a time, the pressure building and building until at last they jump past one another. In the Boxing Day earthquake, the pressure had been building up over the past 100 years. The focus of the big earthquake was on the same plate boundary as the big Toba eruption of

75,000 years earlier, and only 160km from the huge forgotten crater left by the ancient eruption. Banda Aceh and the other coastal towns wrecked in the Boxing Day disaster were arranged in a ring round the edge of the Toba crater. This book began with an epoch-making, world-changing, literally world-shaking event in northern Sumatra; now it ends with another in the same place.

Slabs of rock 2km long were shaken loose from ridges on the seabed and swept up to 10km in a series of underwater landslides triggered by the earthquake. Photographs taken by a British survey ship show what observers described as an 'alien landscape'. Some chunks of rock as big as St Mary's in the Scilly Isles were swept down ridges and across plains on the seabed at 150km per hour.

After the earthquake, Sumatra was in a different place; it had moved 40m to the south-west, along with the chain of islands along its west coast. The plates on each side of the plate boundary had moved 20m vertically in relation to each other.

The earthquake was in itself a major event. It lasted ten minutes, when most earthquakes last only a few seconds. There were many aftershocks, with epicentres scattered along the plate boundary from Sumatra northwards, and some of the aftershocks were over seven on the Richter Scale, big events in their own right. The deadliest earthquake in history is thought to have taken place in China over 400 years ago, the Shansi earthquake of 1556, which killed 830,000 people.

But surprisingly it was not this gigantic Sumatran earthquake that caused death and destruction round the Indian Ocean basin on Boxing Day 2004 – it was the tsunami that it triggered. The submarine disaster created chaos on the ocean floor, and during the earthquake one of the plates was jerked up 20m underwater in a few seconds, pushing a huge volume of water up and then outwards at the surface; this is what unleashed the tsunami.

The earthquake happened just before one in the morning, and just eight minutes later it was picked up by seismographic instruments in Australia. Australian seismologists immediately alerted the Pacific Tsunami Warning Centre in Hawaii about the earthquake, because of the possible danger of a tsunami. Just seven minutes after that the Warning Centre in Hawaii sent a bulletin alerting all the member states participating in the Tsunami Warning System in the Pacific. Unfortunately the system did not extend to the Indian Ocean. India, Sri Lanka, Thailand and the Maldives were not member states, so they were, extraordinarily, not informed of the impending tsunami. At 3.30 am the Warning Centre heard about the Indian Ocean tsunami, not from their scientific instruments, but through the Internet, where the first news of casualties from Sri Lanka was breaking. By then, tens of thousands of people had already been drowned – by the tsunami that the scientists had known would be generated by the seabed earthquake. The lack of a formal warning system has been offered as an explanation, but the lack of an informal warning has still not been satisfactorily explained.

The people on the island of Simeulue, which was very close to the epicentre, felt the force of the big earthquake and headed for the hills, expecting that a tsunami would follow. They were right, and they were safe. But no-one else round the Indian Ocean basin had any warning or took any precautionary measures at all. The victims were all taken by surprise – except on one beach on Phuket. There a ten year old British girl, Tilly Smith, applied what she had learnt in a geography lesson at school. She had been taught that just before a tsunami the sea draws back a long way. Tilly saw the sea receding and knew what it meant. She and her family managed to persuade everyone on the beach to head for higher ground and they were all safely evacuated by the time the tsunami arrived. But on many other beaches, people were intrigued by the sea drawing back 2km or more, and went out onto the seabed to have a look and catch stranded fish; few of those who did so lived. If only more people lived their lives like Tilly Smith. She saw the knowledge she had acquired in school as connected to what she was seeing happening in front of her, understood and was ready to put it to immediate practical use. She saw and made use of the connection.

The tsunami travelled outwards from the epicentre in a series of huge concentric oval ripples. They travelled at enormous speed in open water, around 800km per hour, but as very broad low waves – too low to be noticeable. Satellites that happened to be passing overhead measured them as being only half a metre high. As the waves approached the coasts, they slowed down and the water piled up into towering 30m waves, though still moving at a dangerous 50–60 km per hour. The waves that hit Aceh (pronounced arch-ay), the province of northern Sumatra nearest to the epicentre, smashed into coastal towns and villages with unimaginable force, huge volumes of water sweeping inland, pushing a maelstrom of debris along with them. People who were caught by the tsunami were dashed against buildings and trees and in many cases killed by floating debris hurtling along in the water.

First Aceh in Sumatra, then Thailand and Myanmar (Burma), then Sri Lanka and India were hit by the tsunami. The waves spread ever-wider, eventually reaching the Maldives, Somalia, Kenya and Tanzania. Even though the tsunami struck at different times in different places, no-one had any warning. Even in the Maldives, beyond Sri Lanka and India, there was no warning.

The worst affected area was the province of Aceh in northern Sumatra. The town of Banda Aceh at the northern tip of Sumatra was flattened, and so were the towns of Meulaboh and Calaya on the west coast. Inevitably, the greatest death toll was in the country closest to the earthquake epicentre, the source of the tsunami, and in Indonesia 126,000 people died; the next highest was Sri Lanka, where 30,000 died. Along the African coast, where the waves were much lower, the danger was much reduced; only one person is thought to have died in Kenya. The most distant death to be caused by the tsunami was at Port Elizabeth in South Africa, 8,000km away from the epicentre and 16 hours after the earthquake – ample time, one would have thought, for the warning to stay off the beaches to have reached everywhere along the coastline of the Indian Ocean. The tsunami spread across the Pacific Ocean, and was even detected in Chile and Mexico, where there were waves 2m higher than normal.

Many bodies were buried under the debris swept along and deposited by the tsunamis. Bodies were still being dug out of the debris at a rate of 500 a day in February 2005. The task of finding and identifying the often mutilated and decomposed bodies was overwhelming. Many bodies were swept out to sea when the force of the great waves was spent and the huge volumes of water drained back into the sea; they will never be found. It will never be known for certain how many people died altogether, but it is thought to be in the region of 250,000. A quarter of a million people wiped out in one morning, on 26 December 2004. One-third of those who died were children. This is partly because many of the countries affected were poor countries where the birth rate is still high. Of the children who survived, many were in a traumatized state. Oxfam pointed out that four times as many women died in the disaster as men, probably because they were waiting on beaches for the fishermen to return from the open sea, or were in their coastal huts looking after their children; in other words they were in the most vulnerable location.

Little that was positive came out of the Boxing Day tsunami disaster. At Mahabalipuram, just to the south of Madras, the tsunami scoured the sand off the seabed, exposing a long-forgotten city 800m out from the shore. It was the lost City of the Seven Pagodas, dating from the Pallava dynasty of Hindu kings 1,500 years ago.

The response to this terrible disaster from the rest of the world was immediate and unstinting. Huge amounts of money were given in donations by private individuals, overshadowing the government aid that was offered. This response was partly prompted by the fact that the disaster was entirely natural, and partly by the fact that so many already poverty-stricken communities were affected. But 9,000 foreign tourists also died. The British film producer Lord Attenborough lost three members of his family. The hardest hit European country was Sweden, but people from all over the world were swallowed up by the tsunami. The Boxing Day tsunami disaster was felt, perhaps uniquely in human history, as a global natural disaster, an event that brought the world together.